D0139587

Freedom Seekers

In this fascinating book, Damian Alan Pargas introduces a new conceptualization of "spaces of freedom" for fugitive slaves in North America between 1800 and 1860, and answers the questions: How and why did enslaved people flee to – and navigate – different destinations throughout the continent, and to what extent did they succeed in evading recapture and reenslavement? Taking a continental approach, this study highlights the diversity of slave flight by conceptually dividing the continent into three distinct – and continuously evolving – spaces of freedom. Namely, spaces of *informal freedom* in the US South, where enslaved people attempted to flee by passing as free blacks; spaces of *semi-formal freedom* in the US North, where slavery was abolished but the precise status of fugitive slaves was contested; and spaces of *formal freedom* in Canada and Mexico, where slavery was abolished and runaways were considered legally free and safe from reenslavement.

Damian Alan Pargas is Professor of North American History and Culture at Leiden University and Director of the Roosevelt Institute for American Studies in Middelburg, the Netherlands. He is the author of two books, *The Quarters and the Fields* (2010) and *Forced Migration in the Antebellum South* (2014).

CAMBRIDGE STUDIES ON THE AMERICAN SOUTH

Series Editors:

Mark M. Smith, *University of South Carolina, Columbia*
Peter Coclanis, *University of North Carolina at Chapel Hill*

Editor Emeritus:

David Moltke-Hansen

Interdisciplinary in its scope and intent, this series builds upon and extends Cambridge University Press's longstanding commitment to studies on the American South. The series offers the best new work on the South's distinctive institutional, social, economic, and cultural history and also features works in a national, comparative, and transnational perspective.

Titles in the Series

Freedom Seekers

Fugitive Slaves in North America, 1800–1860

DAMIAN ALAN PARGAS

Leiden University

CAMBRIDGE
UNIVERSITY PRESS

CAMBRIDGE
UNIVERSITY PRESS

University Printing House, Cambridge CB2 8BS, United Kingdom

One Liberty Plaza, 20th Floor, New York, NY 10006, USA

477 Williamstown Road, Port Melbourne, VIC 3207, Australia

314–321, 3rd Floor, Plot 3, Splendor Forum, Jasola District Centre,
New Delhi – 110025, India

103 Penang Road, #05–06/07, Visioncrest Commercial, Singapore 238467

Cambridge University Press is part of the University of Cambridge.

It furthers the University's mission by disseminating knowledge in the pursuit of
education, learning, and research at the highest international levels of excellence.

www.cambridge.org
Information on this title: www.cambridge.org/9781107179554
DOI: 10.1017/9781316832264

© Damian Alan Pargas 2022

This publication is in copyright. Subject to statutory exception
and to the provisions of relevant collective licensing agreements,
no reproduction of any part may take place without the written
permission of Cambridge University Press.

First published 2022

A catalogue record for this publication is available from the British Library.

Library of Congress Cataloging-in-Publication Data
NAMES: Pargas, Damian Alan, author.
TITLE: Freedom seekers : fugitive slaves in North America, 1800–1860 / Damian Alan Pargas.
DESCRIPTION: Cambridge ; New York, NY : Cambridge University Press, 2022. |
SERIES: Cambridge studies on the American South | Includes bibliographical references and index.
IDENTIFIERS: LCCN 2021026780 (print) | LCCN 2021026781 (ebook) |
ISBN 9781107179554 (hardback) | ISBN 9781316832264 (epub)
SUBJECTS: LCSH: Fugitive slaves–United States–History–19th century. | Fugitive slave
communities–United States–History–19th century. | Maroons–United States–History–19th
century. | Slaves–Emancipation–North America–History–19th century. | BISAC: HISTORY /
African American & Black
CLASSIFICATION: LCC E450 .P234 2022 (print) | LCC E450 (ebook) | DDC 973.7/115–dc23
LC record available at https://lccn.loc.gov/2021026780
LC ebook record available at https://lccn.loc.gov/2021026781

ISBN 978-1-107-17955-4 Hardback
ISBN 978-1-316-63135-5 Paperback

Cambridge University Press has no responsibility for the persistence or accuracy
of URLs for external or third-party internet websites referred to in this publication
and does not guarantee that any content on such websites is, or will remain,
accurate or appropriate.

Contents

Figures

Acknowledgments

This book is the result of a generous five-year "Vidi" research grant awarded by the Dutch Scientific Council (NWO) for the project "Beacons of Freedom: Slave Refugees in North America, 1800–1860." I am infinitely grateful to the Vidi Committee at NWO for funding this study and providing me with the opportunity to more fully explore this topic. I am also extremely grateful to the three researchers who worked so diligently on this project and shared their sources and findings with me: Viola Müller, Thomas Mareite, and Oran Kennedy. Viola, Thomas, and Oran have each written their own books on the case studies laid out in the present study, and I recommend anyone who is interested in the topic of freedom seekers in nineteenth-century North America to consult their expertise.

During the past five years I have tested my ideas and shared my research at numerous conferences and with expert scholars around the world. I express my sincere gratitude to Stanley Harrold, Randall Miller, the *Journal of Early American History*, and the University Press of Florida for publishing earlier results of this research project. I also thank Graham Russel Gao Hodges, Gordon Barker, Roy Finkebine, Matthew Pinsker, Sylviane Diouf, Kyle Ainsworth, Mekala Audain, James David Nichols, Jeffrey Kerr-Ritchie, Bertrand van Ruymbeke, Mariana Dantas, Paul Lovejoy, Jane Landers, Rebekka von Mallinckrodt, Trevor Burnard, Stephan Conermann, and Jeannine Bisschoff, as well as my esteemed colleagues at Leiden University, the Roosevelt Institute for American Studies, the Rothermere American Institute at Oxford University, and the Bonn Center for Dependency and Slavery Studies, for all of their helpful feedback and advice.

Finally, I am particularly grateful to Mark M. Smith, Peter Coclanis, Victoria Inci Phillips, Cecelia Cancellaro, Shaheer Anwarali, and the entire team at Cambridge University Press for their patience and efficiency. It is a pleasure to work with such a fine press.

Introduction

On the weekend of June 8–9, 1844, the slaveholding class of southern Louisiana found itself absorbed by the excitement of the upcoming presidential and congressional elections. Just a week earlier in Baltimore, the Democratic National Convention had nominated former Tennessee Governor James Polk for president, a compromise candidate who nevertheless unabashedly embraced westward expansion and the immediate annexation of the neighboring Republic of Texas. The news – just now trickling into the southwestern states – raised serious concerns about a looming war with Mexico but also sparked renewed enthusiasm for the expansion of the slave South all the way to the Rio Grande and beyond.[1]

As their masters reveled in visions of a vast slaveholding empire and furiously debated the merits and wisdom of a possible war with Mexico, dozens of enslaved people from the region were attempting to liberate themselves from the suffocating institution of slavery once and for all. *The Daily Picayune* – one of over a dozen newspapers published in New Orleans at the time – advertised no less than eleven runaway slaves on its two-page print that weekend. One freedom seeker, a twenty-year-old named John ("calls himself JOHN HUNTER") who had "some marks of

---

[1] *The Planters' Gazette*, June 8, 1844 (quote); *The Daily Picayune*, June 8, 1844, June 9, 1844; William Dusinberre, *Slavemaster President: The Double Career of James Polk* (New York: Oxford University Press, 2003); Steven E. Woodworth, *Manifest Destinies: America's Westward Expansion and the Road to Civil War* (New York: Knopf, 2003); Andrew J. Torget, *Seeds of Empire: Cotton, Slavery, and the Transformation of the Texas Borderlands, 1800–1850* (Chapel Hill: University of North Carolina Press, 2018), ch. 6; Matthew Karp, *This Vast Southern Empire: Slaveholders at the Helm of American Foreign Policy* (Cambridge, MA: Harvard University Press, 2016).

the whip on the back of his neck" and was considered "very likely and intelligent," was presumed to have false papers and be hiding within the city of New Orleans itself. John's owner had "no doubt" that he was being "harbored by some one," and that he had "a pass in his possession that enables him to keep out, as there was one taken from him a short time before he left with the signature of Cuyler Jauncey to it, and he may have another." The slaveholder warned residents of the city that "all passes or papers, if he should have any in his possession, are unauthorized by me." Another runaway named "Catherine or *Cassey*," aged forty to forty-five and known as a "*Marchandé*" in the city, left fewer clues as to her whereabouts, but her owner clearly worried that she intended to smuggle herself onboard one of the northbound steamers that crowded the city's harbor in a bid to make it to a free state. He issued an explicit warning to "captains of steamboats," whom he "cautioned not to harbor said slave, under penalty of being prosecuted according to law." Meanwhile, a group of "EIGHT NEGRO SLAVES," all of them river pilots owned by the Louisiana Pilot's Association, were advertised as having stolen the vessel upon which they worked, the *Lafayette*, and headed out from the South West Pass into the Gulf of Mexico, "with the wind from the South-Eastward." Their intention was to flee the United States altogether, as their owners "presumed that they will make for the coast of ... Mexico."[2]

The presumed destinations of the runaways were remarkably diverse. They included places where slavery was unequivocally the law of the land but where sizeable free black populations made it possible for runaways to navigate city streets anonymously and undetected, or even "pass for free" (New Orleans); places within the United States where slavery had been abolished but where fugitive slave laws called for rendition and criminalized assistance to runaways, including by unknowing steamboat captains (the Northern United States); and places beyond the borders of

---

[2] *The Daily Picayune*, June 9, 1844 (quotes). For recent scholarship on escapes to and from New Orleans, see for example S. Charles Bolton, *Fugitivism: Escaping Slavery in the Lower Mississippi Valley, 1820–1860* (Fayetteville: University of Arkansas Press, 2019), esp. 97–148; Viola Müller, "Cities of Refuge: Slave Flight and Illegal Freedom in the American Urban South, 1800–1860" (PhD diss., Leiden University, Leiden, the Netherlands, 2020); Rashauna Johnson, *Slavery's Metropolis: Unfree Labor in New Orleans during the Age of Revolutions* (New York: Cambridge University Press, 2016), 24–54; Thomas Mareite, "Conditional Freedom: Free Soil and Fugitive Slaves from the US South to Mexico's Northeast, 1803–1861" (PhD diss., Leiden University, Leiden, the Netherlands, 2020), 69–71.

the United States where slavery had been abolished but where no fugitive slave laws or extradition treaties applied (Mexico).

The runaway slave ads published in the *Daily Picayune* on that single weekend in 1844 illuminate the complicated geography of slavery and freedom that existed in North America in the decades preceding the US Civil War. For enslaved people seeking to flee bondage in the antebellum South, freedom from slavery could be found in virtually every direction and in a wide variety of geographical, political, and social settings. Freedom could be forged by crossing state or international borders, or by remaining within the slaveholding states; it could be attained by disguising one's true identity or by openly claiming asylum with a friendly government. Reaching and navigating different destinations required different strategies of absconding and entailed different types of risks and obstacles, and no destination constituted an ideal sanctuary for runaways by any stretch of the imagination. Yet, however imperfect, North America provided enslaved people with various *spaces of freedom* to which they could flee to try to escape slavery in the half-century before emancipation in the United States. Sustained slave flight in turn contributed to the further development and defense of these spaces as potential beacons of freedom for those still trapped in bondage.

How was slave flight in North America characterized? How and why did enslaved people flee to – and navigate – different destinations throughout the continent, and to what extent did they succeed in evading recapture and reenslavement? *Freedom Seekers* examines the experiences of permanent runaways from southern slavery – those who had no intention of returning to their owners – between the end of the American Revolution and the outbreak of the Civil War. Taking a broad and continental approach, this study highlights the diversity of slave flight in North America by conceptually dividing the continent into three distinct (and continuously evolving) spaces of freedom for runaway slaves. First, it explores the prevalence of slave flight to spaces of *informal freedom*. These were places within the slaveholding states where enslaved people attempted to flee slavery by trying to disguise their identities and pass for free, especially in urban areas with relatively substantial free black communities such as Baltimore, the District of Columbia, Richmond, Charleston, and New Orleans, but also in a myriad of smaller towns scattered all across the South. In spaces of informal freedom, runaways had no legal claim to freedom or protection from reenslavement. Their successful navigation of freedom and evasion of recapture was based almost exclusively on their ability to hide their true identities, often by employing strategies aimed at achieving anonymity, integrating into free black communities, and procuring false documents (especially passes and freedom certificates).[3]

Second, this book explores the phenomenon of slave flight to spaces of *semi-formal freedom*, or places where slavery was abolished according to free soil principles, but where the precise status of fugitive slaves, as well as the conditions for their potential reenslavement, was contested by different legal authorities representing overlapping jurisdictions. In spaces of semi-formal freedom, slavery either did not exist or was on the path to destruction, but asylum for refugees from slavery was not guaranteed. The concept refers specifically to the northern states in the antebellum period, where slavery was abolished (either gradually or immediately) but where overarching federal fugitive slave laws, enshrined in Article IV of the US Constitution as well as the Fugitive Slave Act of 1793 and its amended version of 1850, theoretically allowed for the rendition of runaway slaves to their owners in the southern states. Conflicting interpretations of federal fugitive slave laws and constitutional protections of due process, as well as state anti-kidnapping and personal liberty laws, however, often resulted in serious challenges to fugitive slave renditions, including legal disputes and mass civil disobedience. Refugees from slavery in the antebellum Northern United States enjoyed more protections from reenslavement than their counterparts passing for free in southern towns and cities, but their freedom nevertheless remained precarious, highly dependent on the compliance of sympathetic members of the community (including local authorities), and subject to conflicting interpretations of the law.[4]

---

[3] For slave flight within the urban South, see for example: Müller, "Cities of Refuge"; Damian Alan Pargas, "Seeking Freedom in the Midst of Slavery: Fugitive Slaves in the Antebellum South," in Damian Alan Pargas, ed., *Fugitive Slaves and Spaces of Freedom in North America* (Gainesville: University Press of Florida, 2018), 116–136; Viola Franziska Müller, "Illegal but Tolerated: Slave Refugees in Richmond, Virginia, 1800–1860," in Pargas, ed., *Fugitive Slaves and Spaces of Freedom*, 137–167; Bolton, *Fugitivism*, 117–148; John Hope Franklin and Loren Schweninger, *Runaway Slaves: Rebels on the Plantation* (New York: Oxford University Press, 1999), 124–148; Amani Marshall, "'They Will Endeavor to Pass for Free': Enslaved Runaways' Performances of Freedom in Antebellum South Carolina," *Slavery & Abolition* 31, no. 2 (2010): 161–180.

[4] The literature on slave flight to the Northern United States is vast. For more on the conflicts regarding fugitive slaves in particular, see for example: Andrew Delbanco, *The War before the War: Fugitive Slaves and the Struggle for America's Soul from the Revolution to the Civil War* (New York: Penguin Press, 2018), 2–3 (first quotes); Thomas D. Morris, *Free Men All: The Personal Liberty Laws of the North, 1780–1861* (Baltimore: The John Hopkins University Press, 1999), ix (second quote); Richard

Third, this study examines the increasing popularity of slave flight to spaces of *formal freedom* beyond the borders of the United States in the late antebellum period, especially from the 1830s through the 1850s. Spaces of formal freedom were places where slavery was abolished according to free soil principles but where *no* extradition or rendition agreements with southern slaveholders existed that might theoretically make refugees from slavery vulnerable to rendition and reenslavement. In spaces of formal freedom, asylum for runaway slaves from the United States was unconditional and guaranteed, at least on paper. In the Age of Revolution various spaces of formal freedom developed in the immediate vicinity of the United States and within reach of the most determined of runaway slaves, most notably after abolition policies were enacted in British Canada (between 1793 and 1833) and the Republic of Mexico (1829), but also throughout the Caribbean (such as Haiti in 1804; the British Empire – including Bahamas – in 1833; and the French colonies in 1848). This book focuses in particular on refugees from slavery in British Canada and Mexico, the two most popular and easily reached free soil territories on the mainland to which southern freedom seekers fled in the antebellum period.[5]

The development of each of these three spaces of freedom was inextricably linked with the broader structural changes in the geography of

---

M. Blackett, *The Captive's Quest for Freedom: Fugitive Slaves, the 1850 Fugitive Slave Law, and the Politics of Slavery* (New York: Cambridge University Press, 2018); John L. Brooke, *"There Is a North": Fugitive Slaves, Political Crisis, and Cultural Transformation in the Coming of the Civil War* (Amherst: University of Massachusetts Press, 2019); Robert H. Churchill, *The Underground Railroad and the Geography of Violence* (New York: Cambridge University Press, 2020); Oran Kennedy, "Northward Bound: Slave Refugees and the Pursuit of Freedom in the Northern US and Canada, 1775–1861" (PhD diss., Leiden University, Leiden, the Netherlands, 2021), 67–129.

[5] Franklin and Schweninger briefly touch upon Canada and Mexico as destinations for runaways, but do not delve into the legal regimes of freedom in either. See Franklin and Schweninger, *Runaway Slaves*, 116–123. Jeffrey Kerr-Ritchie examined slave flight to various destinations in North America, including Canada and Mexico, in his seminal article, "Fugitive Slaves across North America," in Leon Fink, ed., *Workers across the Americas: The Transnational Turn in Labor History* (New York: Oxford University Press, 2011). Kerr-Ritchie's other work deals more specifically with spaces of freedom in the British Caribbean. See for example: Jeffrey Kerr-Ritchie, "The US Coastal Passage and Caribbean Spaces of Freedom," in Pargas, ed., *Fugitive Slaves and Spaces of Freedom*; Jeffrey Kerr-Ritchie, *Rebellious Passage: The Creole Revolt and America's Coastal Slave Trade* (New York: Cambridge University Press, 2019). Matthew Clavin similarly examines the post-emancipation circum-Caribbean as a broad destination for runaway slaves from the United States. See Matthew J. Clavin, *Aiming for Pensacola: Fugitive Slaves on the Atlantic and Southern Frontiers* (Cambridge, MA: Harvard University Press, 2015).

slavery and freedom that shook the Atlantic world in the Age of Revolution. Put simply, the last quarter of the eighteenth century and first half of the nineteenth century paradoxically witnessed both an unprecedented expansion of black freedom and an unprecedented expansion of slavery. For millions of African Americans, this was an age of emancipation. Whereas prior to the American Revolution slavery was legally sanctioned and rarely challenged throughout the Western Hemisphere, during the second half of the eighteenth century bondage came under increasing attack by prominent thinkers in Europe and America who condemned the institution as immoral, sinful, inefficient, socially undesirable, and politically untenable. Transatlantic discourses and social and political movements had a profound effect upon public opinion and the very status of slavery throughout the Atlantic world. This period witnessed the legal abolition of slavery in various parts of the Americas – starting with revolutionary Vermont in 1777 – and of the transatlantic slave trade. It also witnessed a significant spike in manumissions and self-purchase schemes by slaveholders who for whatever reason – whether ideological, religious, or financial – wished to free some or all of their bondspeople, resulting in the emergence or bolstering of free black communities even *within* slaveholding territories, especially in urban areas.[6]

Even as significant numbers of enslaved people exited slavery during this period, however, millions more found themselves increasingly trapped in what Dale Tomich has dubbed the "second slavery," a period of intensification and expansion of slavery in regions such as the US

[6] Steven Hahn, "Forging Freedom," in Trevor Burnard and Gad Heuman, eds., *The Routledge History of Slavery* (New York: Routledge, 2010), 298–299; Christopher Brown, *Moral Capital: The Foundations of British Abolitionism* (Chapel Hill: University of North Carolina Press, 2006); Seymour Drescher, "Civil Society and Paths to Abolition," *Journal of Global Slavery* 1, no. 1 (April 2016): 44–71; David Brion Davis, *The Problem of Slavery in the Age of Revolution, 1770–1823* (New York: Oxford University Press, 1975); David Brion Davis, *The Problem of Slavery in the Age of Emancipation* (New York: Knopf, 2014); Robin Blackburn, *The American Crucible: Slavery, Emancipation and Human Rights* (New York: Verso, 2011), 162–169; Manisha Sinha, *The Slave's Cause: A History of Abolition* (New Haven, CT: Yale University Press, 2017), 34–193; Ada Ferrer, *Freedom's Mirror: Cuba and Haiti in the Age of Revolution* (New York: Cambridge University Press, 2014). For the prevalence of manumissions in revolutionary North America, see Peter Kolchin, *American Slavery, 1619–1877* (New York: Hill & Wang, 2003), 80–85; Ira Berlin, *Generations of Captivity: A History of African-American Slaves* (Cambridge, MA: Harvard University Press, 2003), 119–123, 135–150; and Rosemary Brana-Shute and Randy J. Sparks, eds., *Paths to Freedom: Manumission in the Atlantic World* (Columbia: University of South Carolina Press, 2009).

South, Brazil, and Cuba, largely as a result of the successful adoption and rapid expansion of American short-staple cotton, Brazilian coffee, and Cuban sugarcane production around the turn of the nineteenth century. Indeed, the entrenchment of slavery in certain regions, even as antislavery scored its first victories in others, constituted one of the great paradoxes of the Atlantic world. While some parts of the Americas (such as the Northern United States) saw their free black populations considerably augmented, others devolved into "freedom's mirror," as Ada Ferrer recently argued.[7]

The geography of slavery and freedom that emerged in North America in the half-century following the American Revolution was messy and exceedingly complicated. The Northern United States, British Canada, and the Republic of Mexico all abolished slavery within their borders between 1777 and 1833. The first strikes were enacted in the Northern United States, where state-level abolition was achieved through a maze of gradual emancipation acts, state constitutional clauses, and court verdicts between 1777 and 1804. By 1804, all of the states and territories north of the Mason–Dixon line and Ohio River had either prohibited slavery or put it on the path to destruction with gradual emancipation policies. Yet, unlike other parts of the continent or hemisphere, northern free soil was severely compromised by its union with the southern slaveholding states. As stated above, overarching federal fugitive slave laws upheld the rights of slaveholders to recover runaways in other states, extending the principle of "extraterritoriality" (whereby state laws that allowed slavery were extended into the jurisdictions of other states) to the North and rendering northern "free soil" theoretically inapplicable to escaped slaves from the South. And although northern representatives to the federal government specifically supported these statutes, ordinary citizens and local authorities increasingly came to view them as breaches of state sovereignty, as they forced northern communities to accept slavery in

---

[7] Dale W. Tomich, "The 'Second Slavery': Bonded Labor and the Transformations of the Nineteenth-Century World Economy," in Francisco O. Ramírez, ed., *Rethinking the Nineteenth Century: Contradictions and Movement* (New York: Greenwood Press, 1988), 103–117; Dale W. Tomich and Michael Zeuske, eds., "The Second Slavery: Mass Slavery, World Economy, and Comparative Microhistories, Part I" [special issue], *Review: A Journal of the Fernand Braudel Center* 31, no. 2 (2008): 91–247; Anthony E. Kaye, "The Second Slavery: Modernity in the Nineteenth-Century South and the Atlantic World," *Journal of Southern History* 75, no. 3 (August 2009): 627–650; Javier Lavina and Michael Zeuske, eds., *The Second Slavery: Mass Slaveries and Modernity in the Americas and in the Atlantic Basin* (Berlin: Lit Verlag, 2014); Ferrer, *Freedom's Mirror*.

their midst. Massive pushback against federal fugitive slave laws – through state-level legislation, legal challenges, and widespread civil disobedience – caused the northern states to essentially develop into a battleground over the meanings of free soil and abolition in the United States.[8]

British Canada and Mexico achieved – eventually – less ambiguous and less heavily contested versions of free soil within their jurisdictions, although even their transitions from slavery to freedom were painfully long and complicated affairs. Like the Northern United States, abolition in Canada began at the local level, beginning with a gradual emancipation act adopted by the legislature of Upper Canada in 1793. Additional legislation was subsequently passed to hasten and fulfill legal emancipation in the province, while in the maritime provinces a series of court verdicts in the early nineteenth century rendered slavery all but inoperable in those parts of the dominion as well. By the time the British definitively abolished slavery throughout the empire in 1833, slavery in Canada had already virtually disappeared. Mexico's path to abolition was far more tumultuous and less linear. Ideological opposition to slavery in Mexico emerged as early as 1810, during the advent of the nation's independence movement, but upon achieving independence in 1821 the new republic experienced constant power struggles between different factions that either supported or rejected abolition, resulting in a confusing series of often contradictory decrees concerning the legality of slavery at both the state and federal levels. Only in 1829 did the federal government bring order to the wide spectrum of slavery and freedom throughout the republic by declaring national abolition, a declaration that was heavily contested by American settlers in Texas and that would ultimately lead to Texan secession from Mexico in 1836. The loss of Texas only made the Mexican government more committed to free soil, however. By the mid-

---

[8] Berlin, *Generations of Captivity*, 119–123, 135–150, 159–244; Kolchin, *American Slavery*, 80–85; David Brion Davis, *Inhuman Bondage: The Rise and Fall of Slavery in the New World* (New York: Oxford University Press, 2006), 141–156; Sue Peabody and Keila Grinberg, "Free Soil: The Generation and Circulation of an Atlantic Legal Principle," *Slavery & Abolition* 32, no. 3 (2011): 331–339; Eric Foner, *Gateway to Freedom: The Hidden History of the Underground Railroad* (New York: W. W. Norton, 2015), 38–39; Sinha, *The Slave's Cause*, 65–96; Arthur Zilversmit, *The First Emancipation: The Abolition of Slavery in the North* (Chicago: University of Chicago Press, 1967); Steven Hahn, *The Political Worlds of Slavery and Freedom* (Cambridge, MA: Harvard University Press, 2009).

1830s both Canada and Mexico had developed into uncontested free soil territories that offered asylum to runaway slaves from the United States.[9]

As vast swaths of the continent embraced abolition and a commitment to free soil in the late eighteenth and early nineteenth centuries, the Southern United States rejected abolition but briefly opened the doors to black freedom by facilitating individual manumission and self-purchase arrangements in the immediate aftermath of the American Revolution. As a result, free black communities, especially in the Upper South, grew significantly between 1790 and 1810. Indeed, by 1810 more than 10 percent of the African-American population of the Upper South was classified as free. Even in the Lower South the proportion of free blacks of the total black population increased from 1.6 percent in 1790 to 3.9 percent in 1810. Cities such as Baltimore, Washington, Richmond, Charleston, and countless smaller towns across the southern states saw their free black populations considerably augmented at the turn of the nineteenth century. By 1810, however, the revolutionary fervor had largely died out; the pendulum began to swing in the opposite direction and manumission became more circumscribed. The swift reversal of legal opportunities for black freedom in the South coincided with – and was strongly influenced by – renewed economic prospects for slavery as a result of the cotton revolution in the southern interior. As the South entered its age of second slavery, southern bondage expanded significantly across the newly acquired territories of the Deep South, fueled by a massive domestic slave trade and a fanatical ideological commitment to retaining and protecting slavery at all costs.[10]

---

[9] Gordon S. Barker, "Revisiting 'British Principle Talk': Antebellum Black Expectations and Racism in Early Ontario," in Pargas, ed., *Fugitive Slaves and Spaces of Freedom*, 34–69; Afua Cooper, "Acts of Resistance: Black Men and Women Engage Slavery in Upper Canada, 1793–1803," *Ontario History* 99, no. 1 (2007): 5–17; D. G. Bell, J. Barry Cahill, and Harvey Amani Whitfield, "Slavery and Slave Law in the Maritimes," in Barrington Walker, ed., *The African Canadian Legal Odyssey: Historical Essays* (Toronto: University of Toronto Press, 2012), 363–420; Sean Kelley, "'Mexico in His Head': Slavery and the Texas-Mexico Border, 1810–1860," *Journal of Social History* 37 (Spring 2004): 711–715; Mareite, "Conditional Freedom," 130–131; Manuel Ferrer Muñoz, *La Cuestión de la Esclavitud en el México Decimonónico: Sus Repercusiones en las Etnias Indígenas* (México, DF: Instituto de Estudios Constitucionales Carlos Restrepo Piedrahita, 1998), 13–15; Jaime Olveda Legaspi, "La abolición de la esclavitud en México, 1810–1917," *Signos históricos* 29 (2013): 8–34.

[10] Sinha, *The Slave's Cause*, 91–92; Kolchin, *American Slavery*, 80–85; Berlin, *Generations of Captivity*, 119–244; Müller, "Cities of Refuge," 23–50; Walter Johnson, *River of Dark Dreams: Slavery and Empire in the Cotton Kingdom* (Cambridge, MA: Harvard University Press, 2013); Walter Johnson, *Soul by Soul: Life Inside the Antebellum Slave*

The changing geography of slavery and freedom not only provided enslaved people trapped in the second slavery with a renewed sense of urgency to flee bondage but also new opportunities to actually do so. Prior to the American Revolution, the possibilities to escape slavery were largely limited to strategies of wilderness marronage; passing for free in port towns that had very small free black populations; and fleeing to the enemies of their masters in specific geopolitical conflicts. None of these options were very reliable or sustainable in the long term, and relatively few enslaved people succeeded in attaining freedom by such means. The expansion of black freedom in the revolutionary era, however – both in free soil territories and in urban areas within slaveholding territories – greatly enhanced enslaved people's possibilities to successfully flee slavery. It disrupted the link between blackness and slavery that had hitherto prevailed (and been taken for granted) throughout the hemisphere. By the early nineteenth century, various parts of North America constituted spaces where African Americans were not – or at least not automatically – marked as enslaved, and where runaways could realistically attempt to live as free people. In spaces of informal freedom throughout the urban South, for example, enslaved people could navigate public spaces in broad daylight, pretending to be members of burgeoning free black communities. In spaces of semi-formal freedom in the northern states, African Americans were presumed free and treated as such unless proven otherwise, and even then the conditions for their rendition were often disputed. And in spaces of formal freedom beyond the borders of the United States, all African Americans were legally free from enslavement, including reenslavement by means of extradition back to the United States. The spaces of freedom that developed in the period between the American Revolution and the Civil War indeed provided enslaved people trapped in the second slavery with *options*. A runaway from the Virginia countryside in the 1840s could attempt to escape slavery in Baltimore, Pennsylvania, or Upper Canada – and, as this book will argue, there were good reasons for individual runaways to prefer certain destinations over others, depending on their circumstances.[11]

Market (Cambridge, MA: Harvard University Press, 1999); Damian Alan Pargas, *Slavery and Forced Migration in the Antebellum South* (New York: Cambridge University Press, 2014), 17–55.

[11] Slave flight in the colonial period will be discussed in more depth in Chapter 1 of the present volume. For overviews of the three strategies of slave flight before the American Revolution, see for example: Sylviane A. Diouf, *Slavery's Exiles: The Story of the American Maroons* (New York: New York University Press, 2014), 3; Nathaniel

Freedom Seekers contributes to an ever-growing body of scholarship on fugitive slaves in North America. The pathbreaking publication of John Hope Franklin and Loren Schweninger's seminal work *Runaway Slaves* in 1999 sparked renewed interest in the experiences of runaway slaves throughout the continent, and recent years have witnessed a surge in acclaimed academic studies on slave flight in particular contexts. Much of the focus has been on northbound runways to the free states and Canada in the age of the second slavery, with a particular emphasis on themes such as the active role that African Americans played in liberating themselves and others, and the political consequences of the fugitive slave issue in an era of rising sectional tensions in the antebellum United States. Sydney Nathan's *To Free a Family* (2012), Richard Blackett's *Making Freedom* (2013), Eric Foner's *Gateway to Freedom* (2015), Andrew Delbanco's *The War Before the War* (2018), and Robert Churchill's *The Underground Railroad and the Geography of Violence* (2020) stand out as perhaps the most well-known works of the last few years.[12]

Scholars are also intensifying their research on southbound runaways who fled to Mexico and other destinations in the Caribbean, revealing not only on the nature of slave flight itself but also the domestic and geopolitical repercussions for the region. Alice Baumgartner's recent work *South to Freedom* (2020), James David Nichols' *The Limits of Liberty* (2018), as well as studies by Sarah Cornell, Mekala Audain, and Thomas Mareite, among others, are pioneering new perspectives on the fugitive slave issue in the Texas-Mexican borderlands, while Matthew Clavin's

Millett, "Defining Freedom in the Atlantic Borderlands of the Revolutionary Southeast," *Early American Studies* 5 (Fall 2007): 367–394; Leslie M. Harris, *In the Shadow of Slavery: African Americans in New York City, 1626–1863* (Chicago: University of Chicago Press, 2003), 21–22, 29, 36–39; Graham Hodges, *Pretends to Be Free: Runaway Slave Advertisements from Colonial and Revolutionary New York and New Jersey* (New York: Routledge, 1994); Jane Landers, "'Giving Liberty to All': Spanish Florida as a Black Sanctuary, 1673–1790," in Viviana Díaz Balsera and Rachel A. May, eds., *La Florida: Five Hundred Years of Hispanic Presence* (Gainesville: University Press of Florida, 2014), 117–140.

[12] Franklin and Schweninger, *Runaway Slaves*; Sydney Nathans, *To Free a Family: The Journey of Mary Walker* (Cambridge, MA: Harvard University Press, 2012); Richard Blackett, *Making Freedom: The Underground Railroad and Politics of Freedom* (Chapel Hill: University of North Carolina Press, 2013); Foner, *Gateway to Freedom*; Delbanco, *The War before the War*; Churchill, *The Underground Railroad and the Geography of Violence*. See also Graham Russel Gao Hodges, *David Ruggles: A Radical Black Abolitionist and the Underground Railroad in New York City* (Chapel Hill: University of North Carolina Press, 2012); Steven Lubet, *Fugitive Justice: Runaways, Rescuers, and Slavery on Trial* (New York: Cambridge University Press, 2010).

work *Aiming for Pensacola* (2015) and Jeffrey Kerr-Ritchie's *Rebellious Passage* (2019) have expanded our understanding of escapes from slavery in the circum-Caribbean.[13]

Slave flight within the US South, by contrast, remains a relatively understudied phenomenon. Scholars such as Franklin and Schweninger, as well as Stephanie Camp, explored various aspects of *truancy*, the act of absconding temporarily to borderland wilderness areas or nearby towns, often as kneejerk reactions to (the threat of) punishment, but with no intention of remaining at large permanently. Only very recently have scholars begun to examine internal runaways as potential permanent freedom seekers. Sylviane Diouf, for example, has argued that many "borderland maroons" who escaped to the woodland areas in the immediate vicinity of their farms and plantations in fact intended to stay there permanently, while other scholars, including Charles Bolton, Viola Müller, Amani Marshall, and myself, have in recent years begun to examine attempts by freedom seekers to pass for free in towns and cities across the South. The ongoing collection and digitization of runaway slave ads in the widely publicized *Freedom on the Move* database, meanwhile, is making clear just how prevalent slave flight to urban areas was, and encourages scholars to look more closely at cities as important destinations for freedom seekers in the antebellum South.[14]

Taken collectively, these pioneering works and projects underscore that slave flight in the period between the American Revolution and the

---

[13] Alice L. Baumgartner, *South to Freedom: Runaway Slaves to Mexico and the Road to Civil War* (New York: Basic Books, 2020); James David Nichols, *The Limits of Liberty: Mobility and the Making of the Eastern US-Mexico Border* (Lincoln: University of Nebraska Press, 2018); James David Nichols, "Freedom Interrupted: Runaway Slaves and Insecure Borders in the Mexican Northeast," in Pargas, ed., *Fugitive Slaves and Spaces of Freedom in North America*, 251–274; Sarah E. Cornell, "Citizens of Nowhere: Fugitive Slaves and Free African Americans in Mexico, 1833–1857," *Journal of American History* 100, no. 2 (2013): 351–374; Mekala Audain, "Mexican Canaan: Fugitive Slaves and Free Blacks on the American Frontier, 1804–1867" (PhD diss., Rutgers University, 2014); Thomas Mareite, *Conditional Freedom: Free Soil and Fugitive Slaves from the US South to Mexico's Northeast, 1803–1861* (Boston: Brill, forthcoming 2022).

[14] Franklin and Schweninger, *Runaway Slaves*, 124–148; Stephanie M. H. Camp, *Closer to Freedom: Enslaved Women and Everyday Resistance in the Antebellum South* (Chapel Hill: University of North Carolina Press, 2004), 35–59; Diouf, *Slavery's Exiles*; Müller, "Cities of Refuge"; Müller, "Illegal but Tolerated"; Bolton, *Fugitivism*, 117–148; Marshall, "'They Will Endeavor to Pass for Free'"; Damian Alan Pargas, "Urban Refugees: Fugitive Slaves and Spaces of Informal Freedom in the American South, 1800–1860," *Journal of Early American History* 7, no. 3 (2017): 262–284. The *Freedom on the Move* database can be accessed at freedomonthemove.org.

Civil War was a truly continental phenomenon. As various spaces of freedom developed throughout North America, enslaved people undertook daring attempts to permanently break the chains of bondage by fleeing in every possible direction and employing every possible strategy. The destinations of runaways differed by degrees and evolved over time. Indeed, time and space were intrinsically linked with successive flows of slave flight. Towns and cities in the antebellum South drew increasing numbers of runaways as their free black populations grew larger and as the domestic slave trade wrought even more havoc on local slave communities; northern border states received disproportionate numbers of refugees from neighboring slave states as they completed their transition from slavery to freedom in the early nineteenth century; and British Canada and Mexico became even more attractive destinations for runaway slaves after the controversial Fugitive Slave Law of 1850 was passed. The meanings of freedom in all of these different destinations continuously evolved over time as well. As the status of fugitive slaves in the Northern United States became more precarious over time, for example, that of exiles beyond the borders evolved in the opposite direction, as British Canada and Mexico steadfastly refused to extradite fugitive slaves back to the United States.

This book aims to "reroute" and reconceptualize the geography of slavery in freedom in North America. Two methodological elements in particular stand out. First, this is the first study on runaway slaves to make a conceptual distinction between spaces of informal, semi-formal, and formal freedom. This typology does not pretend to be static but rather encourages scholars to consider how various legal regimes affected the strategies and experiences of runaways from slavery. Drawing from a wide variety of source material – including newspapers, court records, legislative petitions, slave narratives, and vigilance committee records, among others – it examines both the migration and settlement processes of runaways in various spaces of freedom, revealing the similarities and differences in their intentions, experiences and vulnerability. It explores enslaved people's motivations for fleeing to certain destinations; the networks that facilitated their escape; their status and the ways they navigated different destinations; and the interconnectedness of different spaces of freedom. Second, this is the first book to provide a continental perspective on runaway slaves in North America. It does *not* constitute a fully comprehensive history of runaways in every corner of the continent, nor does it pretend to. (Notably absent are case studies on runaways among Native American communities, for example.) Rather, the intention of this study is to zoom out and move away from national and regional paradigms of analysis, thereby broadening our understanding of how runaways viewed and utilized the continuously evolving landscape of freedom to their advantage as they sought to permanently escape slavery.[15]

Freedom Seekers is divided into four thematic chapters. Chapter 1 examines the changing landscape of slavery and freedom that developed in North America in the revolutionary era. It explores how and why opportunities for enslaved people to permanently escape bondage expanded significantly between the colonial era and the early nineteenth century. Chapter 2 delves into slave flight to spaces of informal freedom in the urban South, the most immediate and easily reached destinations for runaways trapped in the second slavery. It considers why enslaved people chose to go to the trouble of fleeing bondage yet remaining within the slaveholding states; the networks that helped them do so; the strategies they employed to hide their identities, sustain themselves, and remain at large indefinitely; and the risk they ran of recapture. Chapter 3 explores slave flight to spaces of semi-formal freedom in the antebellum North. It analyzes why freedom seekers sought to risk their lives to escape the South rather than flee to nearby spaces of informal freedom; how they did so; their settlement processes; and how they fared in the legal quagmire of rendition and reenslavement. Finally, Chapter 4 examines slave flight to spaces of formal freedom beyond the borders of the United States, to British Canada and Mexico from the 1830s through the 1850s. These two destinations for refugees from American slavery shared important similarities but also differed by degrees. The chapter will explore why some enslaved people sought to flee the United States altogether; how they settled into new communities; and the risk of both extradition and illegal recapture by slave catchers and agents from the antebellum South.

---

[15] Rachel Adams called upon scholars to "reroute" the geography of freedom in North America by taking a continental approach to research on fugitive slaves. See Rachel Adams, *Continental Divides: Remapping the Cultures of North America* (Chicago: University of Chicago Press, 2009), 61–100.

I

The Changing Geography of Slavery and Freedom

Although the extent to which it definitively abolished slavery in Massachusetts is a matter of debate, few scholars would disagree that the final judgment in *Commonwealth* v. *Jennison* (also known as the Quock Walker case), which came before the state's highest court in April 1783, hastened the legal emancipation of African Americans held in bondage throughout the state. Walker, a twenty-eight-year-old man who had been born a slave, was promised his freedom at age twenty-five by his master. When his master died, however, Walker was reenslaved and severely beaten by his mistress's new husband; he subsequently brought suit against his captor for assault and battery on the grounds that he was a free man and had therefore been wrongly abused. In what became a series of three trials between 1781 and 1783, Walker's freedom was consistently upheld by the courts – including the Massachusetts Supreme Judicial Court – and in the end his would-be enslaver was fined 40 shillings for the assault. The final opinion written by Chief Justice William Cushing, however, proved to be a watershed for the fate of other African Americans held as slaves throughout the Commonwealth. Cushing declared that the Declaration of Rights embedded in the Massachusetts Constitution of 1780 was reason enough to confirm Walker's freedom, arguing that the constitution's affirmation that "all men are born free and equal" rendered irrelevant whether or not Walker had been promised his freedom by his former master. The chief justice went so far as to argue that in both spirit and wording the document was "totally repugnant to the idea of being born slaves." Whatever had theretofore been the common practice, Cushing opined, "a different idea has taken place with the people of America, more favorable to the natural

rights of mankind, [and] innate desire of Liberty, with which Heaven
(without regard to color, complexion, or shape of noses) has inspired
all the human race." Announcing that "slavery is inconsistent with our
own conduct and Constitution" and that "there can be no such thing
as perpetual servitude of a rational creature," he essentially destroyed
the legal basis for slavery in Massachusetts, and the state legislature subsequently found it unnecessary to enact any formal abolition. Slaveholders
reluctantly acquiesced and the institution quickly eroded. The federal census
of 1790 recorded no slaves living anywhere in the Commonwealth – by
then all African-American residents of Massachusetts were considered
legally free.[1]

The actions of the Massachusetts courts reflected a broader trend in
North America. Whereas prior to the American Revolution slavery had
been ubiquitous and gone largely unchallenged throughout the continent,
in the revolutionary era the very legitimacy of human bondage seemed
under attack, not only in Massachusetts but indeed almost everywhere. In
the wake of the ideological fervor that rocked the Atlantic world in the
late eighteenth and early nineteenth centuries, local and national legislatures and courts grappled with, debated, and tested the boundaries
between slavery and freedom in profound ways.[2] In some places the
institution was abolished, in others it was abolished for some but not
for others, and in yet other places manumission was temporarily facilitated even as the institution itself remained intact. Nowhere was the strike
against slavery perfectly linear and everywhere it was riddled with

---

[1] "*Commonwealth* v. *Jennison*," April 20, 1783, *Proceedings of the Massachusetts
Historical Society (1873–1875)*, vol. XIII (1875): 292–294, 294 (quotes); George
H. Moore, *Notes on the History of Slavery in Massachusetts* (New York: Appleton &
Co., 1866), 247. The Quock Walker case built upon an earlier case in which an enslaved
woman, "Mum Bett" (later known as Elizabeth Freeman), successfully sued for her
freedom in 1781 on the grounds that the preamble of the Massachusetts Constitution
entitled her to the same rights as white residents of the Commonwealth. See Gary B. Nash,
*The Unknown American Revolution: The Unruly Birth of Democracy and the Struggle to
Create America* (New York: Penguin, 2005), 408–409; Douglas R. Egerton, *Death or
Liberty: African Americans and Revolutionary America* (New York: Oxford University
Press, 2009), 93–121.

[2] The literature on the increasing attacks on slavery in the Age of Revolutions is vast. For
relatively brief overviews, see, for example, Seymour Drescher, "Civil Society and Paths to
Abolition," *Journal of Global Slavery* 1, no. 1 (April 2016): 44–71; David Brion Davis,
The Problem of Slavery in the Age of Revolution, 1770–1823 (New York: Oxford
University Press, 1975); Sylvia R. Frey, *Water from the Rock: Black Resistance in a
Revolutionary Age* (Princeton, NJ: Princeton University Press, 1991), 45–80; Manisha
Sinha, *The Slave's Cause: A History of Abolition* (New Haven, CT: Yale University Press,
2017), 34–193.

exceptions and inconsistencies, but whatever the precise legal actions taken, black people throughout North America exited slavery in record numbers in the half-century following the American Revolution. The subsequent emergence of free soil territories and significant growth of free black communities across the continent created potential sites of refuge for runaway slaves, stimulating new waves of freedom-based migration among enslaved people who found themselves still trapped in bondage.

How was the geography of slavery and freedom transformed in the Age of Revolution? And how did this changing landscape affect opportunities to run away from slavery? This chapter provides the foundation for understanding southern enslaved people's escape attempts in the era of the second slavery by examining the evolution of various spaces of freedom in North America in the late eighteenth and early nineteenth centuries.

SANCTUARY SPACES IN THE COLONIAL PERIOD

Running away from slavery was of course nothing new in the early nineteenth century. The endemic slave flight that characterized black resistance in the age of the second slavery was, indeed, built upon strategies of absconding that were originally established in the colonial period. Long before the first states moved to facilitate manumission or abolish slavery, enslaved people in North America tried to escape bondage whenever they were presented with opportunities to do so. Sites of formal freedom were absent – as slavery was legally sanctioned everywhere – but sanctuary spaces and places did exist where daring refugees from slavery could (and did) attempt to carve out lives of informal and even semi-formal freedom for themselves. Three strategies in particular were employed, all of which were extremely risky and only seldom successful on a long-term basis. First, they practiced wilderness marronage – hiding out in forests, swamps, and other sparsely settled areas that constituted sites of informal freedom. Second, they concealed themselves in towns or attempted to pass for free in places that already had free black populations, again clandestinely navigating sites of informal freedom. And third, they took advantage of temporary wartime situations and geopolitical conflicts to flee to their masters' enemies. Whether they crossed political borders, escaped behind military lines, or fled to local Native American communities, the official status of slave refugees in these latter sites of semi-formal freedom was usually conditional, ambiguous, and unclear, but runaways nevertheless pressed for – and were often granted – protection from rendition and reenslavement. All three strategies established a culture of seeking, creating, and even forcing sanctuary spaces that would later more widely be employed – in a changed landscape of slavery and freedom – in the nineteenth century.

Wilderness areas constituted important sites of informal freedom for fugitive slaves in the colonial era. These were spaces legally claimed by governments that sanctioned slavery but where *in practice* the authority of the state did not penetrate or was ineffective in actually enforcing bondage. Marronage in colonial America was in fact far more common than is often assumed. Until recently most historians of slavery argued that North America was notable for its *lack* of maroon communities, especially compared to other slave societies in the Caribbean and South America. Whereas the maroons of Jamaica, Surinam, and Brazil have warranted numerous academic studies, for example, runaway slaves who fled into the North American wilderness have either largely eluded the attention of scholars or been dismissed as barely worthy of the title "maroon." Their small numbers and perceived lack of self-sufficient and sustainable community formation, as well as the absence of major revolts or extensive guerilla activity against colonial authorities or their enslavers – both of which characterized maroon communities in colonial Surinam and Jamaica – have caused many historians to categorize such runaways as temporary rather than permanent refugees from slavery. Even in the age of slavery itself North Americans usually reserved the term "maroon" for wilderness runaways in the Caribbean, calling such fugitives in their own midst simply "runaways" or "outliers."[3]

---

[3] Herbert Aptheker was a notable exception, having argued in the 1930s that at least fifty maroon settlements existed within the borders of the current United States. See Herbert Aptheker, "Maroons within the Present Limits of the United States," *Journal of Negro History* 24 (April 1939): 167–184; Richard Price, *Maroon Societies: Rebel Slave Communities in the Americas* (Baltimore: Johns Hopkins University Press, 1973); Eugene D. Genovese, *From Rebellion to Revolution: Afro-American Slave Revolts in the Making of the Modern World* (Baton Rouge: Louisiana State University Press, 1979), 51–81; Gad Heuman, ed., *Out of the House of Bondage: Runaways, Resistance and Marronage in Africa and the New World* (London: Frank Cass, 1986); Jerome S. Handler, "Escaping Slavery in a Caribbean Plantation Society: Marronage in Barbados, 1650s–1830s," *New West Indian Guide* 71, no. 3–4 (1997): 183–225; John Hope Franklin and Loren Schweninger, *Runaway Slaves: Rebels on the Plantation* (New York: Oxford University Press, 1999), 98–103; Timothy James Lockley, *Maroon Communities in South Carolina: A Documentary Record* (Columbia: University of South Carolina Press, 2009); Sylviane A. Diouf, *Slavery's Exiles: The Story of the American Maroons* (New York: New York University Press, 2014), 3; Nathaniel Millett,

This view has begun to change, however. Recent studies of marronage in North America have argued that maroon communities throughout the continent not only were more extensive than previously believed but also bore striking similarities to those found elsewhere in the Atlantic world. The Dismal Swamp that straddles the border between Virginia and North Carolina alone harbored hundreds of permanent runaways from slavery – some estimates put the number at more than 1,000 – who could safely be categorized as maroons. Numerous sightings and encounters were reported by surveyors and travelers who visited the wild and desolate region, and advertisements such as the following from 1768 were a common sight in local newspapers: "RUN away from the subscriber, a Negro man named HARRY ... a very sensible and artful fellow ... he is supposed to be about the Dismal Swamp." In 1770 "three negro fellows, imported this last summer from Africa" likewise absconded to the nearby wilderness of the Chicahominy and were presumed to be "lurking about the skirts of that swamp."[4]

Many such runaways did more than simply "lurk about." Throughout Virginia maroon communities were rebellious and lawless enough that colonial authorities offered rewards and mobilized militias for their recapture. Other colonial societies along the eastern seaboard and beyond were confronted with similar challenges. Georgia's House of Assembly enacted a legislation in the mid-eighteenth century to regulate the distribution of rewards to residents who succeeded in capturing "fugitive slaves belonging to the inhabitants of this province [who] have assembled themselves together in the River Swamp on the North Side of the River Savannah[,] from whence they have of late frequently come into the plantations on the South side ... and Committed several robberies and depredations." The law even specified rewards for women and children, suggesting that the maroon community living in the swamp consisted of entire families. White residents of colonial South Carolina were also harassed by armed maroons who regularly robbed and plundered local plantations. Indeed, rumors of an all-out war between maroons and

"Defining Freedom in the Atlantic Borderlands of the Revolutionary Southeast," *Early American Studies* 5 (Fall 2007): 367–394.

[4] Ted Maris-Wolf, "Hidden in Plain Sight: Maroon Life and Labor in Virginia's Dismal Swamp," *Slavery & Abolition* 34, no. 3 (2013): 446–464; Daniel O. Sayers, *A Desolate Place for a Defiant People: The Archaeology of Maroons, Indigenous Americans, and Enslaved Laborers in the Great Dismal Swamp* (Gainesville: University Press of Florida, 2016); Lockley, *Maroon Communities in South Carolina*, xvi–xvii; *Virginia Gazette*, October 6, 1768 (first quote); Ibid., December 13, 1770 (second quote).

colonial authorities in Colleton County during the Christmas holidays of 1765 sufficiently "alarmed the minds of the people" that the House of Assembly "judged very necessary to hunt out the Recesses where the runaway negroes harbor," even soliciting the assistance of "a party of the Catawba Indians to go upon that service." In Louisiana a widely feared maroon community living deep in the swamps and cypress forests of the Gaillardeland successfully evaded French and Spanish colonial authorities for years, raiding plantations, ambushing militias sent to hunt them down, and illegally trading in weapons and ammunition with local residents. Such conflicts echoed the experiences of other Atlantic slave societies where marronage was considered a major threat to colonial authority.[5]

Scholars' recent attempts to redefine and reconceptualize marronage have led to an even greater appreciation of its prevalence in colonial North America. Historians have traditionally made conceptual distinctions between *petit marrons* (defined as temporary runaways, also frequently referred to as "absentees," "truants," or "outliers," who often depended on aid from local slave communities to sustain themselves) and *grand marrons* (defined as permanent runaways who lived detached from plantation society), but recently there has been a push for a broader, more inclusive definition of marronage that transcends such narrow concepts and allows for a fuller understanding of how runaway slaves made use of the landscape to escape bondage. Sylviane Diouf, for one, dismisses scholars' tendency to define *grand marrons* as runaways who lived completely detached from plantation society, as even in the Caribbean maroons maintained contact with slave communities and regularly emerged from the wilds to plunder local plantations for supplies and recruits. Diouf also includes what she calls "borderland maroons" in her analysis of the North American maroon landscape: runaway slaves who lived in the wilds that bordered plantations (in most cases remaining within their master's property lines) or otherwise within shouting distance of larger slave communities. Borderland maroons were abundant in

---

[5] Lockley, *Maroon Communities in South Carolina*, 17–18 (first quote); Samuel Wyley Esq. to Col. Jackson, December 30, 1765, reprinted in ibid., 25 (second quote); Thor Ritz, "Marronage Unbound: Colonial Governance and Maroon Resistance to Enslavement in the French Caribbean" (PhD diss., City University of New York, 2016), 73–84; Hugo Prosper Leaming, "Hidden Americans: Maroons of Virginia and the Carolinas" (PhD diss., University of Illinois at Chicago, 1979), 5; Gwendolyn Midlo Hall, *Africans in Colonial Louisiana: The Development of Afro-Creole Culture in the Eighteenth Century* (Baton Rouge: Louisiana State University Press, 1992), 98–118.

colonial America. They could even be found on the outskirts of urban areas, including the northern colonies. One study found that the destinations of runaway slaves in colonial New York and New Jersey included the woods on northern Manhattan Island as well as the swamps and forests that bordered the farming districts of New Jersey. Hiding out but maintaining regular contact with local slave communities – a vital lifeline for the procurement of supplies and victuals – borderland maroons throughout the continent were often able to remain undetected for extensive periods of time.[6]

Enslaved people in colonial America also fled to towns in attempts to either hide out with friends and family or disguise themselves as free blacks, even before the wave of manumissions and abolition acts of the revolutionary era. Ad hoc manumissions were certainly not unknown in the colonial period, and the tiny core of a permanent free black population – constituting less than 5 percent of the total black population when the American Revolution broke out – was established early on. Even in the southern colonies, where manumissions were legally most circumscribed, a small free black population existed from the outset. In the Chesapeake, some African Americans from what Ira Berlin has dubbed the "charter generations" were able to secure freedom prior to the plantation revolution that began around 1660, and when slavery took off in earnest the class of free blacks that already existed was not eliminated, although colonial authorities undertook strict measures to check its growth. As early as 1691, the Virginia General Assembly forbade masters from freeing their slaves unless they paid for the latter's transportation out of the colony, for example, and in 1723 manumissions were prohibited barring the approval of the governor, who could only grant freedom for "meritous services." Similar measures were proposed elsewhere, though sometimes only implemented well into the eighteenth century. Manumissions in Maryland were not restricted until 1753, for example, but by then a small free black population was already well established there.[7]

[6] Diouf, *Slavery's Exiles*, 4–9; Graham Russell Gao Hodges, *Root and Branch: African Americans in New York and East Jersey, 1613–1863* (Chapel Hill: University of North Carolina Press, 1999), 131.

[7] Donald R. Wright, *African Americans in the Early Republic, 1789–1831* (Arlington Heights, IL: Harlan Davidson, 1993), 126; Ira Berlin, *Generations of Captivity: A History of African-American Slaves* (Cambridge, MA: Harvard University Press, 2003), 21–49; Ariela Gross and Alejandro de la Fuente, "Slaves, Free Blacks, and Race in the Legal Regimes of Cuba, Louisiana, and Virginia: A Comparison," *North Carolina*

Despite their small numbers, the very existence of a class of free blacks in the southern colonies accustomed white townspeople to the notion of black freedom, a notion that provided runaway slaves with opportunities to escape slavery by passing themselves off as free. Many at least made the attempt. In 1751 one Stepney, a runaway from King Williams County, Virginia, was presumed to be living in Williamsburg and "pretend[ing] to be a free Negroe." Pompy, a cooper by trade who "speaks good English," ran away from his master in South Carolina in 1756 and was "supposed to be harboured about Charles Town." Another Virginia slave crossed the Potomac River in 1768 with the intention of fleeing to Annapolis and attempting to "pass for a free Man." And Caesar, a "Yellow negro fellow," ran away from his master in 1774, supposedly "pass[ing] himself for a free Man" in the harbor district of Norfolk. A perusal of runaway slave ads from colonial southern newspapers suggests that these were not isolated cases. Betty Wood has calculated that of 453 runaway slave ads published between 1763 and 1775 in the *Georgia Gazette*, colonial Georgia's only newspaper, some 36 were specifically suspected of being in, near, or heading for Savannah.[8]

In northern towns, despite the widespread existence of slavery there as well, free blacks were a common enough sight that runaway slaves routinely attempted to pass for free in places such as New York and Philadelphia. New York City and its hinterlands, such as Brooklyn, served as magnets for fugitive slaves in the colonial period, especially for those escaping from the immediate vicinity and surrounding regions, including New Jersey and Long Island. Philadelphia held a similar attraction for runaway slaves from both the northern and the southern colonies. Providing illegal refuge for runaways in Philadelphia was apparently so

Law Review 91 (2013): 1727–1730; Edmund Morgan, *American Slavery, American Freedom: The Ordeal of Colonial Virginia* (New York: W. W. Norton, 1975), 154–155, 337; General Assembly of Virginia, "An Act for Suppressing Outlying Slaves (1691)," reprinted in William Waller Hening, ed., *The Statutes at Large: Being a Collection of All Laws of Virginia, from the First Session of the Legislature, in the Year 1619* (Philadelphia: R. & W. & G. Bartow, 1823), vol. 3, 86–88; Mariana L. R. Dantas, *Black Townsmen: Urban Slavery and Freedom in the Eighteenth-Century Americas* (New York: Palgrave Macmillan, 2008), 97–99.

[8] *Virginia Gazette*, August 8, 1751 (first quote); *South Carolina Gazette*, October 6, 1756 (second quote); *Maryland Gazette*, October 27, 1768 (third quote); *Norfolk Intelligencer*, June 9, 1774 (fourth quote); Betty Wood, "Some Aspects of Female Resistance to Chattel Slavery in Low Country Georgia, 1763–1815," *The Historical Journal* 30, no. 3 (September 1987): 612–613. See also Gerald Mullin, *Flight and Rebellion: Slave Resistance in Eighteenth-Century Virginia* (New York: Oxford University Press, 1972).

common that as early as 1725, colonial authorities passed a law threatening any free black who endeavored to "harbor or entertain" a fugitive slave with a fine of 5 shillings for the first hour and 1 shilling for each subsequent hour – an exorbitant penalty at the time. Still, freedom seekers continued to trickle in, sometimes traversing considerable distances to escape bondage. One North Carolina slave who "pretends to be free" was suspected of having made his way to family and friends in Philadelphia in 1769.[9]

Finally, enslaved people wishing to flee bondage in colonial America took advantage of wartime situations and geopolitical conflicts to flee to their masters' enemies. The intention of these refugees was not only to put distance between themselves and their masters but also to find protection with (and fight for) various groups who, for whatever reason, were hostile to their masters and unlikely to return valuable property to them. Acting upon the conviction that "my master's enemy is my friend," enslaved people most glaringly employed this strategy when they sought asylum in Spanish Florida, with local Native American communities, and ultimately – to place one foot in the revolutionary era itself – behind British lines during the American Revolution. The status of slave refugees in all three cases was often conditional, ambiguous, and uncertain.[10]

Spanish Florida serves as an interesting case in point. The colony was itself a society with slaves during the first century of its existence, but in its struggle to protect its northern borderlands from English settlement, it developed into a refuge for runaway slaves from neighboring colonies.

---

[9] Leslie M. Harris, *In the Shadow of Slavery: African Americans in New York City, 1626–1863* (Chicago: University of Chicago Press, 2003), 21–22, 29, 36–39; Graham Russell Gao Hodges, *Pretends to Be Free: Runaway Slave Advertisements from Colonial and Revolutionary New York and New Jersey* (New York: Routledge, 1994); Hodges, *Root and Branch*, 130–131; Eric Foner, *Gateway to Freedom: The Hidden History of the Underground Railroad* (New York: W. W. Norton, 2015), 30–32; Anne-Claire Faucquez, "De la Nouvelle-Néerlande à New York: la naissance d'une société esclavagiste, 1624–1712" (PhD diss., Université Paris VIII, 2011), ch. 7; General Assembly of Pennsylvania, *An Act for the Better Regulating of Negroes in This Province*, section V, passed March 5, 1725; *Cape Fear Mercury*, November 24, 1769 (second quote). A recent study of runaway advertisements in colonial New York City newspapers reveals that up to 42 percent were suspected of hiding out with loved ones. See Richard E. Bond, "Ebb and Flow: Free Blacks and Urban Slavery in Eighteen-Century New York" (PhD diss., Johns Hopkins University, 2005), 242–245.

[10] This strategy of absconding has global precedents. David Brion Davis has argued that in all slave societies, from the Roman Empire to Muslim societies and beyond, wartime weakened masters' authority and stimulated both flight and enlistment of runaway slaves by armies. See David Brion Davis, *Inhuman Bondage: The Rise and Fall of Slavery in the New World* (New York: Oxford University Press, 2006), 143.

As early as 1687, in the wake of a series of raids and skirmishes between Spanish Florida and South Carolina, a group of eight slaves from Carolina made their way in a canoe to St. Augustine and requested baptism into the Catholic church, apparently having heard rumors that conversion could serve as a vehicle to freedom in the Spanish colonies. Their official status was unclear – Spanish authorities had received no orders to grant asylum to fugitive slaves – but as the colony was chronically undermanned, the runaways were nevertheless received, baptized, and immediately put to work. The following year an agent from South Carolina arrived to reclaim the runaway slaves, but the Spanish governor refused, citing their conversion to Catholicism as his reason. Instead, he offered to pay the slaveholders by way of compensation. This single incident gave rise to a regular stream of enslaved asylum-seekers, who began to trickle into St. Augustine either singly or in small groups. When colonial authorities requested guidance from Spain about how to handle the refugee situation, King Carlos II issued a royal proclamation authorizing colonial authorities to give "liberty to all" runaway slaves from the British colonies who sought conversion and baptism, effecting what Jane Landers has described as "a major policy revision ... that would shape the geopolitics of the Southeast and the Caribbean for years to come." Although the king emphasized humanitarian and religious concerns to justify his decision, political and military motives were clearly his main focus, as Florida's governors desperately needed the labor and military service of runaway slaves to protect their contested frontier from their English rivals. The fugitives, for their part, were more than willing to provide such services in return for a life of freedom.[11]

Despite the royal proclamation, however, Florida fell short of developing into a space of formal freedom, not least because the Spaniards continued to employ slave labor themselves (there was no abolition policy, nor even talk of one) but also because the precise status of fugitive slaves from the British colonies remained unclear to colonial authorities in various periods. In 1725 Governor Antonio de Benavides famously sold a group of newly arrived fugitive slaves at a public auction because South

[11] Jane Landers, "'Giving Liberty to All': Spanish Florida as a Black Sanctuary, 1673–1790," in Viviana Díaz Balsera and Rachel A. May, eds., *La Florida: Five Hundred Years of Hispanic Presence* (Gainesville: University Press of Florida, 2014), 125–126 (quote); Peter Wood, *Black Majority: Negroes in Colonial South Carolina* (New York: Knopf, 1974), 239; Millett, "Defining Freedom in the Atlantic Borderlands," 367–394; Larry Eugene Rivers, *Slavery in Florida: Territorial Days to Emancipation* (Gainesville: University Press of Florida, 2000), 4–5.

Carolina slaveholders were threatening to come and reclaim them by force, and when he wrote to Spain to inquire if the slaves were entitled to sanctuary, he received no reply. In 1733 the Spanish Crown reiterated its decree to grant asylum to runaway slaves who sought conversion, but due to local uncertainty about how to interpret the initial proclamation, some refugees who were already living in the colony were still considered slaves. Others were betrayed and sold upon arrival. At best Spanish Florida thus constituted a space of semi-formal freedom, where runaway slaves were usually safeguarded from extradition but where their status remained ambiguous and vulnerable to conflicting interpretations of royal policy.[12]

Enslaved people who sought refuge with Native American communities were often confronted with similar uncertainties. Betting on a presumed unwillingness by Native Americans to return runaway slaves to English colonists, bondspeople throughout the colonies fled to local indigenous settlements to escape slavery. Indeed, a number of runaways who eventually found asylum in Spanish Florida were Carolina slaves who had first fled to the Yamasee and fought with them against the English. Other South Carolina slaves fled westward into enemy Indian country in 1735 and were "sheltered and protected by the Tuskerora Indians," a situation that so infuriated the colonial assembly that it offered a bounty to freemen or slaves who killed or captured any members of that nation. In colonial Georgia, twenty runaway slaves advertised between 1763 and 1775 were headed for indigenous

---

[12] In 1738 the first free black community in North America was founded by slave refugees at Gracia Real de Santa Teresa de Mose, just 2 miles north of St. Augustine, a settlement they fiercely defended against a series of English invasions. The most famous mass escape attempt took place in September 1739, when the Stono Rebellion erupted 20 miles outside of Charleston. Motivated by Spanish offers of freedom, a group of slaves and maroons that eventually amassed between 60 and 100 members raided a store for guns and ammunition (decapitating the store's owner and displaying it prominently on the front steps) and marched southward in almost military style, killing whites and destroying property as they went. Landers, "'Giving Liberty to All,'" 127, 131–132; Jane Landers, *Black Society in Spanish Florida* (Urbana: University of Illinois Press, 1999), 28–39; Larry Eugene Rivers, *Rebels and Runaways: Slave Resistance in Nineteenth-Century Florida* (Gainesville: University Press of Florida, 2013), 3; Wood, *Black Majority*, 308–326; Kevin Mulroy, *Freedom on the Border: The Seminole Maroons in Florida, the Indian Territory, Coahuila, and Texas* (Lubbock: Texas Tech University Press, 1993), 8–9; Lockley, *Maroon Communities in South Carolina*, 12–13; Mark M. Smith, ed., *Stono: Documenting and Interpreting a Southern Slave Revolt* (Columbia: University of South Carolina Press, 2005); David A. Copeland, ed., *Debating the Issues in Colonial Newspapers: Primary Documents on Events of the Period* (Westport, CT: Greenwood, 2000), 81–93.

communities in the backcountry. Protection for fugitives was not always forthcoming, however, and many Native American communities were known to return runaway slaves to the English or even kill them. The Creek signed a treaty with the governor of South Carolina in 1721 in which they promised to apprehend and return "any Negro or other Slave which shall run away from any English Settlements to our Nation." In North Carolina slaveholders believed that marronage would have been more extensive "were [the slaves] not so much afraid of the Indians, who have such a natural aversion to the Blacks, that they commonly shoot them when ever they find them in the Woods or solitary parts of the country." It is unclear to what extent runaway slaves who ended up finding protection with Native American communities were simply maroons who happened upon indigenous settlements by chance, or whether they were actually fleeing *to* indigenous communities. It appears that some certainly absconded with the intention of seeking asylum. In 1759 a group of enslaved men from New York stole a number of guns and hatchets from their owners and attempted to flee to a local Native American village with which one of the men had had previous contact. They were captured, but their attempt was not uncommon for New York and speaks volumes to slaves' hopes of being granted freedom and protection by specific Native American communities.[13]

Perhaps the most daring attempts by enslaved people to attain freedom by fleeing to and fighting for their masters' enemies occurred during the chaos of the American Revolution. The war ushered in what amounted to the first major fugitive slave crisis in North American history. Even before the war started in earnest, enslaved people were defecting to the British Army in the mistaken belief that British views of slavery were different from those of the colonists. Their confusion was understandable; the English courts had recently (in 1772) declared Britain free soil for slaves brought there by their masters. This decision in no way affected the status of slavery in the colonies, but many enslaved people in North America believed that the British would declare them free if they fled to loyalist lines. Realizing the potential of enlisting the services of slave refugees, Virginia's governor John Murray, Earl of Dunmore, reached out to the enslaved population as potential allies against the rebels in November

---

[13] Landers, *Black Society in Spanish Florida*, 27; Wood, *Black Majority*, 260 (first quote), 261 (second quote); Wood, "Some Aspects of Female Resistance," 613; Lockley, *Maroon Communities in South Carolina*, 132 (third quote); Bond, "Ebb and Flow," 242–243; Foner, *Gateway to Freedom*, 30–32.

1775, when he issued a proclamation offering freedom to all slaves who would bear arms for the king's cause. Even under such promising circumstances, however, freedom was never *guaranteed* to all those who sought it and British lines never became unconditional spaces of formal freedom. As Sylvia Frey has argued, the British were never genuinely committed to any structural liberation for slaves – theirs was at best a selective offer of freedom that was designed to meet specific manpower needs and help suppress the rebellion.[14]

The proclamation nevertheless turned the British Army into a powerful magnet for enslaved people all along the Atlantic seaboard who wished to escape bondage. Dunmore's Ethiopian Regiment donned uniforms with sashes bearing the inscription LIBERTY TO SLAVES and fought "with the intrepidity of lions," according to one observer. Fearing a massive insurrection, patriot slaveholders made public spectacles of punishing (usually executing) bondspeople who were caught fleeing, but slaves continued to flock to British lines throughout the Chesapeake and beyond. Prominent leaders of the revolution in Virginia, including Thomas Jefferson and James Madison, lost dozens of slaves due to defections during the conflict. Runaway slave ads indicate that ordinary slaveholders throughout the region suffered regular losses. In 1781, for example, one Thomas Cabeen of Crosscreek, North Carolina, who had been taken prisoner by the British, came home to discover that "the greater part of his negroes had gone off with them." Caesar, owned by a slaveholder from Southampton County, Virginia, "absconded with the British and has not been heard of since." In the Lower South, the British occupation of Charleston and Savannah provided opportunities for vast numbers of enslaved people to escape; when the British evacuated both cities at the end of the war some 10,000 slave refugees left with them. "Nearly the whole of the slaves" of one slaveholder in Charleston District "absconded and went off with the British Army." In the span of only a few years as much as 5 percent of all southern slaves – literally tens of thousands – are thought to have fled to the British during the war, and thousands more were evacuated from New York. Not all of those evacuated were granted freedom – some were reenslaved in the British West Indies, a testament to

[14] Peter Kolchin, *American Slavery, 1619–1877* (New York: Hill & Wang, 1993), 70–73; Sylvia R. Frey, "Between Slavery and Freedom: Virginia Blacks in the American Revolution," *Journal of Southern History* 49 (August 1983): 375–398; Benjamin Quarles, *The Negro in the American Revolution* (Chapel Hill: University of North Carolina Press, 1961); Frey, *Water from the Rock*, 172–205; Egerton, *Death or Liberty*; Nash, *The Unknown American Revolution*, 157–166.

Britain's real motives behind recruiting American slaves for the war effort. Still, the revolution linked freedom with the British in the minds of an entire generation of enslaved people.[15]

THE FIRST EMANCIPATION AND ITS LIMITS: THE NORTHERN UNITED STATES

Strategies of running away were firmly established long before any legislatures in North America moved to strike at slavery in a fundamental way. What changed in the Age of Revolution was the emergence of more permanent and structural spaces of freedom for enslaved people who wished to flee bondage. It began with the partial, gradual, or wholesale abolition of slavery, most notably in the northern states of the newly formed American republic, British Canada, and independent Mexico, a process that was largely complete by the mid-1830s. The "free soil" territories of the northern Atlantic by that time also included Haiti and the British West Indies, as well as Western Europe.[16]

The first meaningful actions against slavery were undertaken in the wake of the first political revolution of the western hemisphere, in the United States. State-level abolition in the Northern United States – what scholars have dubbed the "First Emancipation" – was achieved in the revolutionary era through a complicated maze of constitutional clauses, court verdicts, and gradual emancipation acts. Most northern states abolished slavery in a protracted manner, and most had to eventually pass subsequent legislation to definitively end the institution. The northern commitment to free soil, which began in 1777, was virtually set in

---

[15] Aline Helg and Lara Vergnaud, *Slave No More: Self-Liberation before Abolitionism in the Americas* (Chapel Hill: University of North Carolina Press, 2019), 118–122; Robin Blackburn, *American Crucible: Slavery, Emancipation, and Human Rights* (New York: Verso, 2011), 124; Kolchin, *American Slavery*, 70–73; Frey, "Between Slavery and Freedom," 375–398; Frey, *Water from the Rock*; Davis, *Inhuman Bondage*, 150–151; Nash, *The Unknown American Revolution*, 157–166; Petition of Thomas Cabeen to the Honourable the General Assembly of the State of North Carolina, June 8, 1781, Race and Slavery Petitions Project (hereafter RSPP), Series 1, Legislative Petitions, Accession #11278101; Petition of William Massenburg to the worshipful Court of Southampton County in Chancery, VA, March 1788, RSPP, Series 2: County Court Petitions, Accession #21678801; Petition of William Simmons et al. to the Honorable the Judges of the Court of Equity for South Carolina, 1817, RSPP, Series 2: County Court Petitions, Part D (NC/SC), Accession #21381715.

[16] Davis, *Inhuman Bondage*, 142; Sue Peabody and Keila Grinberg, "Free Soil: The Generation and Circulation of an Atlantic Legal Principle," *Slavery & Abolition* 32, no. 3 (2011): 331–339.

stone by 1804, however, when all states and territories north of the Mason–Dixon line and Ohio River – including the federal Northwest Territory – had either prohibited slavery or enacted gradual abolition acts. By the opening decade of the nineteenth century the national division between a slave South and a free North was clearly visible.[17]

Calls for the eradication of slavery in the Northern United States built upon public debates and discussions that emerged on both sides of the Atlantic on the eve of the Revolution itself. Although racial slavery provided the material, social and ideological *basis* for many white Americans' commitment to revolutionary ideals, especially in the southern colonies – as Manisha Sinha recently highlighted, "no 'contagion of liberty' flowed inexorably according to its own logic to slaves" – the revolutionary era also witnessed the first sustained ideological challenges to the institution. As early as the mid-eighteenth century the wisdom and morality of holding slaves had for many Americans become a contested issue. By the time of the Revolution, as David Brion Davis put it, "New forms of religious revivalism, and Anglo-American popular culture, typified in countless poems, essays and editorials, and even plays, had helped to push slavery in many Anglo-American minds beyond the boundaries of accepted exploitation."[18]

Religious arguments against slavery proved especially influential. In the wake of the revivals of the First Great Awakening, notable ministers and theologians in New England and Pennsylvania began to construct a Christian antislavery narrative predicated on the belief that slavery and the slave trade were sinful, inhumane, and undermined the equality of all men before God. Their arguments included a wider critique of materialism and the accumulation of wealth – many saw slavery as symptomatic of a corrupt and greedy society that had strayed from its spiritual roots and in the process become blind to human suffering. An epistle written in 1754 by French-born teacher and abolitionist Anthony Benezet for the

---

[17] Nash, *The Unknown American Revolution*, 157–165, 223–231, 320–338, 407–416; Berlin, *Generations of Captivity*, 119–123, 135–150, 159–244; Kolchin, *American Slavery*, 80–85; Sinha, *The Slave's Cause*, 65–96; Arthur Zilversmit, *The First Emancipation: The Abolition of Slavery in the North* (Chicago: University of Chicago Press, 1967); Steven Hahn, *The Political Worlds of Slavery and Freedom* (Cambridge, MA: Harvard University Press, 2009), 4.

[18] Sinha, *The Slave's Cause*, 35 (first quote); Davis, *Inhuman Bondage*, 144 (second quote); Kolchin, *American Slavery*, ch. 3; Frey, *Water from the Rock*, 45–80; Ira Berlin, *The Long Emancipation: The Demise of Slavery in the United States* (Cambridge, MA: Harvard University Press, 2015), ch. 1.

annual meeting of the Quaker Society of Friends is illustrative. In it, Benezet forcefully made the case that "to live in ease and plenty by the toil of those whom violence and cruelty have put in our power, is neither consistent with Christianity nor common justice." New ideas about the spiritual morality of keeping slaves enflamed public opinion and spurred some pious Americans to call for the abolition of slavery. In the decades prior to the war numerous antislavery pamphlets were published by religious abolitionists, especially Quakers such as Benezet, Ralph Sandiford, Benjamin Lay, and John Woolman. Taking the lead in condemning slavery and calling for its extinction, Quakers explicitly forbade their congregations from keeping slaves, and by 1775 Pennsylvania Quakers had established a Society for the Relief of Free Negroes Unlawfully Held in Bondage, an organization that later morphed into The Pennsylvania Society for Promoting the Abolition of Slavery.[19]

Religious critiques of slavery dovetailed with economic indictments of forced labor as inefficient, and even more importantly with political ideals of liberty, equality, and natural rights in the 1760s and 1770s. As colonists formulated their grievances against Great Britain in terms of freedom versus slavery – by loudly proclaiming that they would not be the "slaves" of the mother country – more than a few acknowledged the irony of also keeping slaves themselves. Some argued that slavery, which seemed increasingly archaic and unenlightened to many thinkers (even in Virginia, the largest slaveholding colony), was incompatible with social justice and political stability. Thomas Jefferson made no secret of his opinion that slavery was wrong for both moral and practical reasons (an opinion he would later reverse in the nineteenth century). Thomas Paine, another Virginian, considered slavery an affront to "Justice and Humanity." Other respected and influential voices in revolutionary America expressed pragmatic concerns that their demands would not be taken seriously in London if they continued to hold slaves. Benjamin Rush, for one, confided to a friend that Americans' complaints were

---

[19] Sinha, *The Slave's Cause*, 35; Davis, *Inhuman Bondage*, 144 (quote); Matthew Mason, *Slavery and Politics in the Early American Republic* (Chapel Hill: University of North Carolina Press, 2006), 12–13; Richard Newman, "The Pennsylvania Abolition Society and the Struggle for Racial Justice," in Richard Newman and James Mueller, eds., *Antislavery and Abolition in Philadelphia: Emancipation and the Long Struggle for Racial Justice in the City of Brotherly Love* (Baton Rouge: Louisiana State University Press, 2011), 120. Anthony Benezet, *Epistle of Caution and Advice Concerning the Buying and Keeping of Slaves* (Philadelphia: James Chattin, 1754). For Benezet see also Nash, *The Unknown American Revolution*, 42.

"useless" as long as they "continue to keep our fellow creatures in slavery just because their color is different from ours." His concerns were hardly unfounded; British critics indeed regularly mocked slaveholding colonists who demanded more rights and liberty. In a scathing and oft-quoted rebuttal of Americans' refusal to accept taxation by Parliament, Tory author and political theorist Samuel Johnson famously asked, "How is it that we hear the loudest *yelps* for liberty among the drivers of negroes?"[20]

Despite the antislavery sentiments expressed by many leaders of the Revolution and founders of the republic, however, few proactively introduced practical measures to abolish the institution until they felt overwhelming pressure to do so. The actions of African Americans themselves were in fact crucial in effecting real change in the northern states. African Americans helped sway public opinion in the North by demonstrating their commitment to revolutionary ideals, most notably by enlisting in the Patriot cause and fighting in the Continental Army (the northern colonies permitted black enlistment in integrated units), but also by stoking fear in the hearts and minds of many Patriot leaders by responding in even greater numbers to British promises of freedom and fleeing to the redcoats. Rumors of a massive slave rebellion during the chaos of the war helped fan the flames even further. Even more importantly, African Americans gave voice to their ideas and desires in forums of revolutionary discourse by engaging in civic debates and employing legal tactics to push for freedom, demanding that the glaring inconsistencies between revolutionary ideals and practice be rectified. Antislavery committees consisting of slaves and free blacks who dubbed themselves the "Sons of Africa" were organized in New England even before the Quakers organized their first abolition society in Philadelphia. As early as the 1770s black activists published political pamphlets and presented colonial courts with freedom petitions for themselves and their communities, employing revolutionary language and using it against their enslavers by declaring that they had "a naturel right to be free." Many such petitions specifically called for New England colonial assemblies to enact universal emancipation within

---

[20] Alan Taylor, *American Revolutions: A Continental History, 1750–1804* (New York: W. W. Norton, 2016), 116–117; Nash, *The Unknown American Revolution*, 114–128; Kolchin, *American Slavery*, 77; Thomas Paine, quoted in Sinha, *The Slave's Cause*, 36 (first quote); Benjamin Rush, quoted in Davis, *Inhuman Bondage*, 145 (second quote); Samuel Johnson, *Taxation No Tyranny: An Answer to the Resolutions and Address of the American Congress* (London: T. Cadell, 1775), 89 (third quote).

their jurisdictions. Their actions forced legislators and courts to confront the issue for the first time.[21]

The First Emancipation was therefore in a very real sense initiated and enforced through the efforts of African Americans themselves, their activism fusing with the efforts of a number of increasingly influential white antislavery societies and lawyers. Without such activism it is difficult to imagine that emancipation would have been enacted at all. Although the northern states were not classic slave societies and slavery was not central to the economic order there, economic arguments on their own were not a strong enough reason to abolish the institution. Rather, abolitionist mobilization and black efforts to attain freedom were the dominant forces behind revolutionary emancipation, as Manisha Sinha has forcefully argued. Even in Vermont, where the African-American population was miniscule and where slavery was abolished outright through its constitution of 1777 – it was condemned as a violation of "unalienable rights" – a series of court cases brought by African Americans unjustly held as slaves between 1779 and 1806 were necessary to ensure that freedom on paper would translate into freedom in practice. In Massachusetts, the only other northern state to enact immediate abolition, freedom came about as a result of lawsuits brought by African Americans such as Elizabeth Freeman and Quock Walker, as discussed in the Introduction.[22]

All of the other northern states embraced gradualism and ultimately – under sustained pressure from black activists and sympathetic white abolitionist lawyers and lawmakers – enacted emancipation schemes that proved painfully slow. Most legislators aimed to strangle slavery within their borders in ways that would prevent major disruptions to the economy and private property, and allow for a proper transition period to

---

[21] Graham Russell Gao Hodges, "Black Self-Emancipation, Gradual Emancipation, and the Underground Railroad in the Northern Colonies and States, 1763–1804," in Damian Alan Pargas, ed., *Fugitive Slaves and Spaces of Freedom in North America* (Gainesville: University Press of Florida, 2018), 21–33; Sinha, *The Slave's Cause*, 42–43, 48–50; Davis, *Inhuman Bondage*, 152; Taylor, *American Revolutions*, 116–117; Nash, *The Unknown American Revolution*, 407–417.

[22] Edie L. Wong, *Neither Fugitive nor Free: Atlantic Slavery, Freedom Suits, and the Legal Culture of Travel* (New York: New York University Press, 2009); Sinha, *The Slave's Cause*, 65–96; Berlin, *Generations of Captivity*, ch. 3; David, *Inhuman Bondage*, 152–153; Hodges, "Black Self-Emancipation"; Joanne Pope Melish, *Disowning Slavery: Gradual Emancipation and "Race" in New England, 1780–1860* (Ithaca, NY: Cornell University Press, 1998); Taylor, *American Revolutions*, 465–470; Emily Planck, *Tyrannicide: Forging an American Law of Slavery in Revolutionary South Carolina and Massachusetts* (Athens: University of Georgia Press, 2014), 118–127.

prepare the slave population for freedom. The emancipation statutes of the northern states employed grandiose and self-congratulatory language, and were full of revolutionary rhetoric and allusions to the advancement of civilization and natural rights, but they freed no slaves immediately. Instead, they freed the children of slaves upon reaching a certain age (usually adulthood). Pennsylvania's Act for the Gradual Abolition of Slavery (1780), the first gradual emancipation law enacted in the United States, serves as an illustrative case in point. Referencing the tyranny of life under British rule and the horrors of war, as well as the "manifold Blessings which we have undeservedly received from the hand of that Being from whom every good and perfect Gift cometh," the General Assembly decided that "it is our duty, and we rejoice that it is in our Power, to extend a Portion of that freedom to others, which hath been extended to us," namely its enslaved population, despite their "difference in Feature and Complexion." The act only freed those born after passage of the act, however, and even they were to be considered indentured servants under the employ of their masters until the age of twenty-eight.[23]

Other states passed similar legislation, causing slavery in the northeast to peter out in the span of decades. Only through the unrelenting activism of African Americans and abolitionist societies was additional legislation eventually passed that declared slavery officially dead, sometimes well into the antebellum period (in Connecticut and New Hampshire the official death blows did not come until 1848 and 1857, respectively). Yet in practice all of the northern states were considered free territory by the 1820s and the remaining slave population was limited to only a handful of unlucky souls. At the federal level northern politicians had by then also secured the prohibition of slavery in the new midwestern states and territories that lie north of the Ohio River, a policy that was initiated with the Northwest Ordinance of 1787 but finalized when last-ditch efforts to reinstate slavery in Indiana and Illinois failed (in 1810 and 1824, respectively), and when the prohibition of slavery was extended

[23] Taylor, *American Revolutions*, 465–470; Steven Hahn, "Forging Freedom," in Gad Heuman and Trevor Burnard, eds., *The Routledge History of Slavery* (New York: Routledge, 2010), 300; Planck, *Tyrannicide*, 118–127; General Assembly of the Commonwealth of Pennsylvania, *An Act for the Gradual Abolition of Slavery* (March 1, 1780); Gary Nash and Jean R. Soderlund, *Freedom by Degrees: Emancipation in Pennsylvania and Its Aftermath* (New York: Oxford University Press, 1991); Gary Nash, *Forging Freedom: The Formation of Philadelphia's Black Community, 1720–1840* (Cambridge, MA: Harvard University Press, 1991), 66–99.

to the rest of the continent north of the 36°30′ parallel in the Missouri Compromise of 1820.[24]

News that the northern states had abolished slavery – or begun the process of phasing it out – traveled through slave communities in the South like wildfire. From the perspective of enslaved people, the North came to symbolize freedom in a way that it had not in the colonial period. All of a sudden, free spaces were opening up that were dedicated to free soil and the eradication of human bondage. Surely such places would offer asylum to those unfortunate enough to find themselves on the wrong side of the border. The ink on the various legal parchments and abolition acts had barely dried before slaves started planning their escape from the South. In runaway slave advertisements, the North suddenly appeared as a major destination for freedom seekers. From as far away as Pasquotank County, North Carolina, plans were discovered "by a number of Negro slaves" in 1792 to steal a boat and make their way up the coast "to the Northern States." Even Martha Washington's favorite chambermaid Oney Judge, in an embarrassing and much publicized act of defiance, "absconded from the household of the President" and fled to Philadelphia in 1796, later moving further north to New Hampshire, where she lived out the rest of her life.[25]

Asylum was never as easy as crossing state lines, however, and the question of whether slaves became free when they crossed into "free soil" territory was heavily contested from the start. It is indeed important to note just how new and confusing the concept of "free soil" was in the late eighteenth century. The pathbreaking *Somerset* v. *Stewart* case in Great

---

[24] Hahn, "Forging Freedom," 300; Taylor, *American Revolutions*, 465–470; Sinha, *The Slave's Cause*, 66–99; George William Van Cleve, "Founding a Slaveholders' Union, 1770–1797," in John Craig Hammond and Matthew Mason, eds., *Contesting Slavery: The Politics of Bondage and Freedom in the New American Nation* (Charlottesville: University of Virginia Press, 2011), 117–137; George William Van Cleve, *A Slaveholders' Union: Slavery, Politics, and the Constitution in the Early Republic* (Chicago: University of Chicago Press, 2010), 64–90; Joseph A. Ranney, *Wisconsin and the Shaping of American Law* (Madison: University of Wisconsin Press, 2017), 53; Paul Finkelman, "Slavery and the Northwest Ordinance: A Study in Ambiguity," *Journal of the Early Republic* 6, no. 4 (1986): 343–370.

[25] Petition to the Worshipful the County Court of Quarter Sessions for the County of Pasquotank Sitting, December 6, 1792, RSPP, Series 2: County Court Petitions, Accession #21279202; *Pennsylvania Gazette & Universal Daily Advertiser*, May 24, 1796 (first quote); Rev. T. H. Adams, "Washington's Runaway Slave, and How Portsmouth Freed Her," *The Granite Freeman* (Concord, NH), May 22, 1845; John W. Blassingame, ed., *Slave Testimony, Two Centuries of Letters, Speeches, Interviews, and Autobiographies* (Baton Rouge: Louisiana State University Press, 1977), 248–250.

Britain, which established free soil as a legal concept, had only just been decided on the eve of the American Revolution, in 1772 – and it concerned a so-called sojourn controversy rather than a fugitive slave controversy. The question in *Somerset* was whether a slaveholder's property rights still applied if he traveled with his slave to a place where slavery did not exist. The case revolved around an American slave whose master had brought him to England, where slavery was prohibited. In what was widely perceived as a landmark victory for critics of slavery, the courts granted the enslaved man freedom on the grounds that he could not be kept in bondage in a country where slavery was prohibited. *Somerset* was what had sparked the initial defections to British lines during the American Revolution, and it stoked fear in the minds of slaveholders throughout the colonies.[26]

When the first northern states began to abolish slavery in the 1770s and 1780s, therefore, slaveholders in the South were terrified that their slaves (whether runaways or on sojourns with their masters) would be granted freedom there based on *Somerset* principles, and they demanded legal guarantees that their property rights be respected in any union with the "free" states. Their demands resulted in the enactment of safeguards at both the local and federal level. At the state level temporary sojourns with slaves were permitted throughout the North during the first decades of the republic. Northern representatives to the federal government furthermore acquiesced to a series of federal fugitive slave laws – embedded in Article IV of the US Constitution (1787) and later reaffirmed in the Fugitive Slave Acts of 1793 and 1850 – that upheld the rights of slaveholders to recover runaway slaves who had fled to other states, theoretically curtailing northern legislation against slavery. In other words, even as the northern states transitioned out of slavery, enslaved people who crossed into the "free" states and territories had no constitutional right to freedom or asylum, at least in theory.[27]

---

[26] Eric Foner argued that *Somerset* gave rise to the "freedom principle." See Foner, *Gateway to Freedom*, 38; Taylor, *American Revolutions*, 118–119, 381; Gordon S. Barker, "Revisiting 'British Principle Talk': Antebellum Black Expectations and Racism in Early Ontario," in Damian Alan Pargas, ed., *Fugitive Slaves and Spaces of Freedom in North America* (Gainesville: University Press of Florida, 2018), 36–40.

[27] Andrew Delbanco, *The War before the War: Fugitive Slaves and the Struggle for America's Soul from the Revolution to the Civil War* (New York: Penguin Press, 2018), 65–106; Van Cleve, "Founding a Slaveholders' Union," 117–137; Ranney, *Wisconsin and the Shaping of American Law*, 54; Sean Wilentz, *No Property in Man: Slavery and Antislavery at the Nation's Founding* (Cambridge, MA: Harvard University Press, 2018), 115–151; Matthew Pinsker, "After 1850: Reassessing the Impact of the Fugitive Slave

In practice, however, the enforcement of federal fugitive slave laws in the free states proved to be a legal quandary that would pit state and federal officials against each other right up through the Civil War, not infrequently to the advantage of runaway slaves. Ordinary citizens and local authorities in the North were often unclear about the precise status of fugitive slaves in their midst and especially the legal procedures required to send them back into slavery. The matter of rendition lay at the heart of the confusion. The framers of the constitution carefully avoided the words "slavery" and "slave" in the nation's founding document, as did the legislators who drafted the 1793 Fugitive Slave Act (which was actually titled "An Act Respecting Fugitives from Justice, and Persons Escaping from the Service of Their Masters") and its amended, more draconian version of 1850. The laws merely referred to "fugitives from labor," "persons escaping from the service of their masters," and "Person(s) held to Service or Labour in one State." As historian Matthew Pinsker has recently argued, the intentional omission of the word "slave" in all of these documents was significant because it made the law ambiguous: the law explicitly referred to "persons," but federal law also allowed slaveholders to legally treat African-American slaves as property (nonpersons). *Habeas corpus* principles were called into question – "persons" have a constitutional right to due process, whereas property does not. Since the constitution failed to require any specific judicial procedure in the recovery of fugitive slaves, slaveholders initially felt well within their right to simply seize runaways as their property and return them directly to slavery without going through any hearing. This made northern free blacks especially vulnerable to potential kidnapping and enslavement without a hearing, however – and as "persons" they had an indisputable right to due process. To many northerners, therefore, it stood to reason that runaway slaves in their states should be presumed free and accorded the same constitutional rights as "persons" until proven to be slaves, and should therefore be remitted back into slavery only after a proper hearing and judicial review.[28]

Law," in Damian Alan Pargas, ed., *Fugitive Slaves and Spaces of Freedom in North America* (Gainesville: University Press of Florida, 2018), 95–98.

[28] Pinsker, "After 1850," 95–98; David Walstreicher, *Slavery's Constitution: From Revolution to Ratification* (New York: Hill & Wang, 2009); Thomas D. Morris, *Free Men All: The Personal Liberty Laws of the North, 1780–1861* (Baltimore: Johns Hopkins University Press, 1974); Don E. Fehrenbacher and Ward M. McAfee, *The Slaveholding Republic: An Account of the United States Government's Relations to*

As the constitution was silent on the issue, northerners concluded that it was up to the states to determine the judicial procedures for rendition, and they interpreted the fugitive slave clause accordingly. Nothing in the constitution prevented them from protecting their free black populations from kidnapping or presuming runaways free until proven otherwise. Pennsylvania, for example, went to great lengths to enact legal mechanisms designed to prevent the kidnapping of free blacks within its borders. The Pennsylvania legislature passed laws in 1788 and 1790 that threatened fines and punishments for unlawful "man-stealing" of African Americans and prohibited their removal from the state. Massachusetts already had a *habeas corpus* statute on the books from 1785 that made no distinction between white and black, which it subsequently applied to African Americans threatened with forced removal after the US Constitution was ratified. Other northern states applied similar *habeas corpus* laws in cases of rendition of fugitive slaves. Runaways who fled to the North found a significant degree of safety in these state laws, as they resulted in their being presumed free unless proven otherwise in a court of law. This allowed them considerable leeway to "pass for free" north of the Mason–Dixon line and Ohio River.[29]

Southern slaveholders almost immediately became frustrated with the inefficiency of the fugitive slave clause during the first few years of its existence. The Fugitive Slave Act of 1793 was indeed enacted as a knee-jerk response to the spike in refugee migration – especially to Pennsylvania – that followed in the wake of the first northern emancipation laws. This included slaves who escaped while on sojourns in the North with their masters. The 1793 act permitted slaveholders (or their agents) to seize alleged fugitive slaves in the free states but also required them to bring their captives before a federal judge, who had to give his permission before the runaway was sent back into slavery. The only evidence necessary to prove that the suspect was a fugitive slave was oral testimony or an affidavit provided by a white man, making the legal basis for such seizures extremely dubious. The act also stipulated a maximum

Slavery (New York: Oxford University Press, 2001), 102; Willentz, *No Property in Man*, 165–166, 172–179, 226–228.

[29] Pinsker, "After 1850," 95–98; Walstreicher, *Slavery's Constitution*; Morris, *Free Men All*; Fehrenbacher and McAfee, *Slaveholding Republic*, 102; Willentz, *No Property in Man*, 165–166, 172–179, 226–228; Richard S. Newman, "'Lucky to Be Born in Pennsylvania': Free Soil, Fugitive Slaves, and the Making of the Pennsylvania Anti-Slavery Borderland," *Slavery & Abolition* 32, no. 3 (2011): 414.

penalty of $500 civil fine or one year in jail for knowingly harboring or liberating runaway slaves. Washington's abovementioned fugitive slave Oney Judge was therefore far from safe when she sought freedom in the North in 1796; indeed, sometime after her arrival in New Hampshire she was pursued by an agent of the president "with orders to take her by force" back to slavery in Virginia. Kept hidden by friends on a nearby farm until the agent gave up, she was able to remain free, but such incidents scared African Americans throughout the northern states.[30]

Although the 1793 act proved unpopular in the northern states from its initial passage, by the 1820s two developments had made it even more controversial and problematic. First, the northern free black population increased dramatically as gradual abolition ran its course. And second, the demand for slave labor and the volume of the domestic slave trade exploded due to the spectacular success of cotton (and sugar) in the Deep South. The scant evidence required by the 1793 act to prove the identity and ownership of runaway slaves clearly made northern free blacks vulnerable to unlawful abductions, but now the threat of such abductions seemed greater than ever. Any agent of a slaveholder could simply snatch any African American in any northern town, drag him before a judge, testify that he was a runaway slave, and sell him or her for huge profits in the South. Professional slave-catching and kidnapping expanded significantly, and by the 1820s northern state legislatures (beginning with Pennsylvania, New York, and New Jersey) had grown sufficiently alarmed that they enacted "personal liberty laws" that reaffirmed the right to *habeas corpus*, gave captured fugitives a right to a hearing and even a jury trial upon appeal, provided defendants with attorneys, forbade their detention in local and state jails, and required more critical review of evidence provided by slave catchers. In 1838 Maine became the first state to enact a "prohibitory" personal liberty law that forbade state and local officials from even assisting in the capture and return of fugitive slaves. The era also witnessed the emergence of a fiery antislavery

---

[30] Second Congress of the United States, "An Act Respecting Fugitives from Justice, and Persons Escaping from the Service of Their Masters," *Proceedings and Debates of the House of Representatives of the United States at the Second Session of the Second Congress, Begun at the City of Philadelphia, November 5, 1792* (November 5, 1792 to March 2, 1793), 1414–1415; Delbanco, *The War before the War*, 85–106; Pinsker, "After 1850," 95–98; Walstreicher, *Slavery's Constitution*; Morris, *Free Men All*; Fehrenbacher and McAfee, *Slaveholding Republic*, 102; Willentz, *No Property in Man*, 165–166, 172–179, 226–228; Rev. Benjamin Chase, "Interview with Oney Judge Staines," *The Liberator*, January 1, 1847 (quote).

movement and northern "vigilance committees" – consisting of concerned citizens dedicated to protecting free blacks from kidnapping and
fugitive slaves from recapture – that paved the way for some of the most
daring and celebrated fugitive slave rescues of the antebellum period, as
will be elaborated upon in Chapter 3.[31]

Well into the antebellum period the difficulties of retrieving fugitive
slaves in the North continued to provoke lawsuits and political conflicts.
In 1836 Massachusetts became the first state to go so far as to reject
traditional sojourn laws, the state supreme court declaring that slaves
would henceforth be considered free the instant their master brought
them across the state border. By the late 1830s the status of fugitive slaves
in the northern states was commanding national attention, and antislavery lawyers were repeatedly and openly beginning to challenge the
1793 Fugitive Slave Act as unconstitutional. They failed, but even when
Pennsylvania's personal liberty laws were invalidated by the Supreme
Court in the case of *Prigg v. Pennsylvania* (1842), the Court simultaneously upheld the constitutionality of "prohibitory" laws by conceding
that the rendition of fugitive slaves was a federal responsibility, so local
and state officials were under no obligation to cooperate in the recapture
of fugitive slaves with their own police forces or judicial apparatuses.
Northern legislatures wasted no time in passing a flurry of new prohibitory laws as a result – Massachusetts' 1843 "Latimer Law" prohibited
state officials from assisting in the detention of fugitive slaves, for
example, and other states instructed their officials to refuse to recognize
fugitive slave claims. To their credit, northerners proved relentless and
northern state legislatures essentially became committed to a strategy of
nullification in fugitive slave cases (Figure 1.1).[32]

---

[31] Pinsker, "After 1850," 93–115; Delbanco, *The War before the War*, 164–186; Stanley
W. Campbell, *The Slave Catchers: Enforcement of the Fugitive Slave Law 1850–1860*
(Chapel Hill: University of North Carolina Press, 1970), 184–185; Robert H. Churchill,
The Underground Railroad and the Geography of Violence in Antebellum America (New
York: Cambridge University Press, 2020); Walstreicher, *Slavery's Constitution*; Morris,
Free Men All; Fehrenbacher and McAfee, *Slaveholding Republic*; Willentz, *No Property
in Man*, 165–166, 172–179, 226–228; Ranney, *Wisconsin and the Shaping of American
Law*, 54.

[32] Delbanco, *The War Before the War*, 164–186; Pinsker, "After 1850," 93–115; Morris,
Free Men All; Ranney, *Wisconsin and the Shaping of American Law*, 55; Wong, *Neither
Fugitive nor Free*; Prigg v. Pennsylvania, 41 U.S. (16 Pet.) 539 (1842); Gordon S. Barker,
Fugitive Slaves and the Unfinished American Revolution: Eight Cases, 1848–1856
(Jefferson, NC: McFarland, 2013).

It is a dark spot on the face of the nation; such a state of things cannot always exist.—La Fayette.

FIGURE 1.1 Julius Rubens Ames, moral map of the USA, 1847.
Source: Cornell University Library, P. J. Mode Collection of Persuasive Cartography.

So effective were local efforts to prevent the recapture of fugitive slaves that only the widely unpopular Fugitive Slave Law of 1850 seemed to really make clear that fugitive slaves were not safe from reenslavement on northern soil. The law constituted an amendment to the 1793 act, specifying harsh penalties for aiding or harboring fugitive slaves, and outlining an ambitious plan to employ a network of specially designated US commissioners to oversee a more efficient national rendition system. Most controversially, the 1850 law penalized local and state officials for non-compliance – slaveholders (or their agents) had only to provide sworn testimony that a suspect was in fact their runaway slave, and law enforcement officials were required to arrest the suspect or be fined $1,000. The law essentially made northern officials unwilling agents of the slaveholders. Frederick Douglass famously declared that the result of the 1850 law was that "slavery has been nationalized in its most horrible and revolting form .... The power to hold, hunt, and sell men, women, and children as slaves remains *no longer a mere state institution* but is now an institution of the whole United States." As his statement makes clear, he and many other northerners felt that up until that point it was up to the states to decide whether or not to comply with (or how to interpret) federal fugitive slave laws. Now that power seemed to lie squarely with the federal government.[33]

Even then, however, resistance to the law was fierce enough to render it largely ineffective in actually getting fugitive slaves sent back to the South. Wisconsin formally nullified the 1850 law altogether (a move that was overturned by the Supreme Court in 1859); Vermont passed a "Habeas Corpus Law" that required law enforcement to assist fugitive slaves; several northern states passed yet another wave of personal liberty laws in the late 1850s, some of which specifically prohibited state officials from complying with the 1850 act; and northern juries de facto nullified the act by routinely acquitting law enforcement officials who had been arrested for noncompliance. After the *Dred Scott* v. *Sanders* case (1857) – whereupon a Missouri slave who had been brought to Wisconsin on a sojourn by his master unsuccessfully sued for his freedom – established that African Americans were not US citizens, had no claims to freedom and indeed "no rights which the white man was bound to respect," including due process, northern abolitionists became even more committed to openly flouting federal law, harboring fugitive slaves, and helping refugees reach sites of formal freedom in Canada. By 1860 the fugitive slave issue was so unpopular that Pennsylvania's Anti-Slavery Society openly

---

[33] Churchill, *The Underground Railroad and the Geography of Violence*, 139–224; Stanley Harrold, *Border War: Fighting over Slavery before the Civil War* (Chapel Hill: University of North Carolina Press, 2010), ch. 7; Pinsker, "After 1850," 93–115; Morris, *Free Men All*; Campbell, *The Slave Catchers*; R. J. M. Blackett, *Making Freedom: The Underground Railroad and the Politics of Slavery* (Athens: Ohio University Press, 2007); Frederick Douglass, "What to the Slave Is the Fourth of July?" in John W. Blassingame, ed., *The Frederick Douglass Papers, Series 1: Speeches, Debates, and Interviews, vol. 2: 1847–1854* (New Haven, CT: Yale University Press, 1982), 359–387 (italics mine).

refused to endorse any political candidate who vowed to uphold the US Constitution, including Lincoln.[34]

These actions certainly helped to protect many runaway slaves from reenslavement, but they were still a far cry from full legal immunity from rendition to the South. Sites of freedom for fugitive slaves in the northern states remained *semi-formal*: refugees found themselves theoretically on free soil where slavery had been abolished, but their hopes of attaining freedom and asylum remained precarious and contested between state and federal authorities. As Andrew Delbanco recently argued, the union came to resemble "two countries where the law of the land pretended there was only one."[35]

FAILED ABOLITION AND THE SECOND SLAVERY:
THE SOUTHERN UNITED STATES

The revolutionary climate that transformed black life in the northern states also had important repercussions in the southern states, leading to the significant growth of free black communities across the region and the emergence of informal spaces of freedom for runaway slaves. Historians have long underscored that in the revolutionary South the relationship between slavery and ideals of republican liberty was complex and often contradictory. In Virginia, especially, slavery and racism formed the ideological basis for white citizens' revolutionary claims to freedom and equality, as argued by prominent historians such as David Brion Davis,

---

[34] Andrew K. Diemer, "'Agitation, Tumult, Violence Will Not Cease': Black Politics and the Compromise of 1850," in Van Gosse and David Waldstreicher, eds., *Emancipations, Reconstructions, and Revolutions: African American Politics and U.S. History from the First to the Second Civil War* (Philadelphia: University of Pennsylvania Press, 2020); Churchill, *The Underground Railroad and the Geography of Violence*, 139–224; Harrold, *Border War*, ch. 7; Foner, *Gateway to Freedom*; H. Robert Baker, *The Rescue of Joshua Glover: A Fugitive Slave, the Constitution, and the Coming of the Civil War* (Cambridge, MA: Harvard University Press, 2010); Barker, *Fugitive Slaves and the Unfinished American Revolution*; "Pennsylvania A.S. Society," *The Liberator*, November 9, 1860.

[35] Second Congress of the United States, "An Act Respecting Fugitives from Justice and Persons Escaping from the Service of Their Masters"; Thirty-First Congress of the United States, Session I, *An Act to Amend, and Supplementary to, the Act Entitled "An Act Respecting Fugitives from Justice and Persons Escaping from the Service of Their Masters"* (September 18, 1850), 462–465; Hodges, *Root and Branch*, 161–165; Shane White, *Somewhat More Independent: The End of Slavery in New York, 1770–1810* (Athens: University of Georgia Press, 1991), 141–147; Delbanco, *The War before the War*, 106 (quote).

among others. The paradox of a revolution that was cloaked in rhetoric that appeared to delegitimize slavery on the one hand (and that was interpreted as such in the northern states), but that left slavery intact and even strengthened in the South on the other, is obvious. Yet during the tumult of war and revolution slavery was also challenged – albeit with less vigor – in the southern states, especially in the Upper South, where many Quaker and Methodist abolitionists and antislavery societies were active. Attempts to abolish slavery there failed, but it is deeply significant that abolition was actually proposed and debated in the Chesapeake. The era also witnessed a brief but significant relaxation of manumission laws, again particularly in the Upper South, as well as a spike in manumissions and self-purchase arrangements throughout the slave states. Such policies facilitated the creation of informal spaces of freedom in the postrevolutionary era.[36]

The experience of Virginia is illuminating. As discussed above, several prominent Virginians of the revolutionary generation openly expressed their doubts about the legitimacy and desirability of slavery in the new republic, even before many of the northern states moved to abolish the institution. By the time the Quock Walker case came before Chief Justice Cushing in Massachusetts, the General Assembly of Virginia had already enacted a law aimed at greatly facilitating and stimulating the manumission of slaves held in that state. While it did *not* abolish slavery itself, the Act to Authorize the Manumission of Slaves of 1782 simplified the freeing of bondspeople under the age of forty-five held by slaveholders of the revolutionary generation who – for whatever reason – struggled with the idea of their slaves living out the rest of their lives in perpetual servitude. The act specified that "it shall hereafter be lawful for any person, by his or her last will and testament, or by any other instrument in writing ... to emancipate and set free, his or her slaves, or any of them, who shall thereupon be entirely and fully discharged from the performance of any contract entered into during servitude, and enjoy as full freedom as if they had been particularly named and freed by this act." Considering that Virginia was the largest slave state the act certainly seemed like a change

---

[36] Davis, *Inhuman Bondage*, 145; Sinha, *The Slave's Cause*, 86–96; Kolchin, *American Slavery*, ch. 3; A. Glenn Crothers, *Quakers Living in the Lion's Mouth: The Society of Friends in Northern Virginia, 1730–1865* (Gainesville: University Press of Florida, 2012); Eva Sheppard Wolf, *Race and Liberty in the New Nation: Emancipation in Virginia from the Revolution to Nat Turner's Rebellion* (Baton Rouge: Louisiana State University Press, 2006), chs. 1–3; Bruce Dain, *A Hideous Monster of the Mind: American Race Theory in the Early Republic* (Cambridge, MA: Harvard University Press, 2002), 26–39.

in course, and Virginia slaveholders indeed made good use of it in the decades subsequent to its passage, including some of the wealthiest and most respected gentlemen in the Commonwealth. George Washington famously employed the act to arrange for the manumission of his slaves in his will (he died in 1799). Robert Carter III – the largest slaveholder in Virginia – moved to release 452 slaves from bondage between 1791 and his death in 1804. The example of these icons of the slaveholding class was followed by countless smaller slaveholders in every corner of the state. Whereas before 1782 less than 1 percent of Virginia's African-American population was free, by 1790 free blacks accounted for 4.2 percent of the total and by 1810 they had reached 7.2 percent, surging in absolute numbers from 1,800 to 30,570 in less than thirty years. Towns throughout the region saw their free black populations grow considerably. Manumissions in northern Virginia even led to the growth of the free black population in the newly created District of Columbia. The free black population of the small port town of Alexandria, officially ceded to DC in 1801 (it was retroceded back to Virginia in 1846), was established almost entirely as a result of the manumission arrangements of nearby grandees in Fairfax and Loudoun Counties (including George Washington), growing from fifty-two souls in 1790 to 1,168 in 1820.[37]

Manumissions spiked throughout the Chesapeake in the revolutionary era, not just in Virginia but even more so in neighboring states. Maryland reversed its colonial restrictions on individual manumissions in 1796, and by 1810 almost a quarter of its African-American population was free. In Delaware 78 percent of the black population was free by the end of the first decade of the nineteenth century. One visitor to the region noted as early as 1792 that "the little state of Delaware" appeared to be "followi[ing] the example of Pennsylvania. It is peopled mostly by quakers – instances of giving freedom are therefore numerous." In the Upper South as a whole more than 10 percent of the African-American

---

[37] General Assembly of Virginia, "An Act to Authorize the Manumission of Slaves (May 1782)." Reprinted in William Waller Hening, ed., *The Statutes at Large; Being a Collection of All the Laws of Virginia from the First Session of Legislature, in the Year 1619* (Richmond, VA: George Cochran, 1823), vol. 11, 39 (quote); St. George Tucker, *A Dissertation on Slavery: With a Proposal for the Gradual Abolition of It in the State of Virginia* (Philadelphia: Mathew Carey, 1796); *The Constitution of the Virginia Society, for Promoting the Abolition of Slavery and the Relief of Negroes, etc.*, reprinted in the *Virginia Gazette & Petersburg Intelligencer*, July 8, 1790; Kolchin, *American Slavery*, 81; United States Population Census, 1790 and 1820, NARA; Wolf, *Race and Liberty in the New Nation*, 110–111.

population had legally exited slavery by 1810, and by the eve of the Civil War parts of the Upper South had come to virtually resemble free states. In 1860 more than 90 percent of the black population of Delaware and 49 percent of that of Maryland was free. In absolute numbers, Maryland contained the largest free black population in the entire country between 1830 and 1860. Cities such as Baltimore and Washington had free black populations that outnumbered their slave populations, often by substantial margins, as manumitted slaves from rural areas gravitated toward urban centers. Even further south in North Carolina, some 10 percent of the African-American population was free by 1860, with established free black communities in towns such as Wilmington and Raleigh.[38]

Although manumissions rose sharply among Chesapeake slaveholders in the revolutionary era, attempts to enact gradual abolition throughout the region were unsuccessful and spaces of formal or semi-formal freedom for runaway slaves therefore failed to emerge. Many prominent thinkers and statesmen in revolutionary Virginia, Maryland, and Delaware fully expected slavery to ultimately be abolished in their part of the country – a conviction predicated more on the collapse of the tobacco economy and the transition to wheat and grains (crops that did not necessitate slave labor to produce) than on revolutionary ideals. With a naturally growing slave population and a surfeit of slave labor, combined with declining profits and soil depletion, most elites and lawmakers quickly calculated that the institution of slavery was untenable in the long term. Yet support for abolition schemes consistently failed to reach a critical mass in each of these states, despite the presumed impending doom of the slave economy.

---

[38] Nash, *The Unknown American Revolution*, 157–165, 223–231, 320–338, 407–416; Berlin, *Generations of Captivity*, 119–123, 135–150, 159–244; Kolchin, *American Slavery*, 80–85; "On the Laws of the Different American States for the Manumission of Slaves; From M. Brissot de Warville's Travels in the United States," *The Universal Asylum and Columbian Magazine* (Philadelphia) (November 1792): 311 (quote); Sean Condon, "The Slave Owner's Family and Manumission in the Post-Revolutionary Chesapeake Tidewater: Evidence from Anne Arundel County Wills, 1790–1820," in Rosemary Brana-Shute and Randy J. Sparks, eds., *Paths to Freedom: Manumission in the Atlantic World* (Columbia: University of South Carolina Press, 2009), 339–362; Ellen Eslinger, "Liberation in a Rural Context: The Valley of Virginia, 1800–1860," in Brana-Shute and Sparks, eds., *Paths to Freedom*, 663–680; Christopher Phillips, *Freedom's Port: The African American Community of Baltimore, 1790–1860* (Urbana: University of Illinois Press, 1997); Ira Berlin, *Slaves without Masters: The Free Negro in the Antebellum South* (New York: Pantheon, 1981), 174; T. Stephen Whitman, *The Price of Freedom: Slavery and Manumission in Baltimore and Early National Maryland* (Lexington: University Press of Kentucky, 1997).

Thomas Jefferson drafted several bills of abolition for the legislature of his native Virginia, for example, but complained in 1786 that while there were "men enough of virtue and talent in the General Assembly to sponsor" his legislation, "they saw that the moment for doing it with success was not yet arrived." Lawmakers in Virginia feared that abolition in their state would be too complicated and chaotic to carry out in practice. With its relatively large (and steadily growing) slave population, it was feared that abolition in Virginia would lead to major disruptions to the social order. For one thing, Virginia's elites were afraid that freeing the black population in its entirety would spark widespread crime and poverty – even the abolition schemes that were proposed therefore entailed resettlement outside of the state. Virginians also feared that abolition would cripple an already weak economy, and that compensation schemes would prove too costly. As one French visitor to Virginia explained:

The Virginians are persuaded of the impossibility of cultivating tobacco without slavery; they fear, that if the blacks become free, they will cause trouble; on rendering them free, they know not what rank to assign them in society; whether they shall establish them in a separate district, or send them out of the country. These are objections which you will hear repeated every where against the idea of freeing them.

Instead, most Virginians advocated simply opening the doors to manumission and self-purchase schemes, and letting slaveholders release surplus bondspeople at their own pace. Similar sentiments were expressed throughout the Chesapeake, especially Maryland and Delaware. In both of those states abolition societies were established in the revolutionary era, but in both states their activities failed to convince a majority of lawmakers to eradicate slavery. In Delaware they came close – with citizens arguing in legislative petitions that slavery was "totally repugnant to the Spirit of the American Revolution" – but an attempt to abolish slavery in the state constitution of 1792 there failed, and subsequent gradual emancipation bills in 1796, 1797, and 1803 were all voted down. The 1803 abolition bill even received 50 percent support among delegates but the Speaker of the House killed it with a tiebreaking vote.[39]

---

[39] Sinha, *The Slave's Cause*, 91–92; Thomas Jefferson quoted in Gary B. Nash, *Race and Revolution* (Lanham: Rowman & Littlefield, 1990), 15 (first quote); "On the Laws of the Different American States for the Manumission of Slaves," 311 (second quote); Petition of Nicholas Way et al. to the General Assembly of Delaware, January 1791, RSPP, Series 1, Legislative Petitions, Accession #10379107 (third quote); William H. Williams, *Slavery*

At the federal level prominent politicians from the Upper South ironically supported (and sometimes even proposed) legislation that appeared antislavery, such as the Northwest Ordinance of 1787, which prohibited the introduction of slaves into the territories north of the Ohio River. In 1784 Thomas Jefferson himself proposed a federal bill to exclude the introduction of slavery in all of the territories west of the Appalachians, a piece of legislation that came within one vote of passing. Upper South representatives also supported the abolition of the Atlantic slave trade in 1808, a trade they had no use for since they had far more slaves than they could use on their struggling tobacco and wheat farms. But at the state level, all discussions regarding the abolition of slavery had ground to a halt by the beginning of the nineteenth century. As late as the 1820s a handful of manumission societies and "concerned residents" in Virginia, Maryland, Delaware, North Carolina, and even as far south as Tennessee were still petitioning their state legislatures to enact a gradual abolition of slavery, but by then such schemes had virtually no chance of passing – not even in Delaware, where a majority of the black population was already free. Slavery clung stubbornly to life. As the northern slave population was gradually *replaced* by free blacks, therefore, in the Upper South the new free black population grew *alongside* a growing slave population. Sharp divisions between free and slave never really emerged in the Upper South, as black communities throughout the region saw some family members freed while others remained in bondage. In the Upper South, as Ira Berlin has argued, "the fate of free and slave blacks was entwined" more profoundly than in any other part of the United States.[40]

In the Lower South the revolutionary doctrine of natural rights led to far fewer manumissions and virtually no earnest talk of eradicating or restricting slavery. Unlike the Upper South, the future of the plantation economy in the eighteenth-century Lower South seemed secure. Planters

and Freedom in Delaware, 1639–1865 (Wilmington, DE: Scholarly Resources, 1996), 171; Anne E. Siemer, "Henry Laurens and Robert Carter III: The Failure of Abolition in the Federal Era" (PhD diss., Drew University, 2010).

[40] Davis, *Inhuman Bondage*, 154; Berlin, *Generations of Captivity*, 123 (quote); Siemer, "Henry Laurens and Robert Carter III"; Peter S. Onuf, "'To Declare Them a Free and Independent People': Race, Slavery, and National Identity in Jefferson's Thought," *Journal of the Early Republic* 18 (Spring 1998): 1–46; Dain, *A Hideous Monster of the Mind*, 26–39. For antislavery petitions from outside the Chesapeake, see for example: Petition of Richard Mendenhall to the General Assembly of North Carolina, November 1824, RSPP, Series 1, Legislative Petitions, Accession #11282405; Petition of Isaac Lenning et al. to the Senate and House of Representatives of Tennessee, 1819, RSPP, Series 1, Legislative Petitions, Accession #11481918.

in South Carolina and Georgia emerged from the Revolutionary War not with a surfeit but rather an acute shortage of slave labor. Georgia lost some two-thirds of its slave population (to death, flight, or evacuation by the British) during the war; South Carolina lost one-third. What these states wanted – needed – was more slaves, not less. State militias were mobilized to hunt down maroons in the swamplands; on plantations captured runaways and slaves who evoked the rhetoric of natural rights to demand their freedom were punished with extreme violence. Indeed, not only was abolition never seriously considered in the Carolinas and Georgia, but at the federal level representatives from South Carolina and Georgia to the nation's First Congress in 1790 responded with fiery threats of war and disunion to a petition from the Pennsylvania Abolition Society that called for the federal government to grant liberty to slaves. They also succeeded in significantly delaying the abolition of the Atlantic slave trade – and as the trade neared its legal end date South Carolina gorged on Africans, importing some 38,000 slaves in just five years.[41]

At the state level, manumission laws in the Lower South were not relaxed in a meaningful way, and the number of manumissions therefore remained far more limited than in the Upper South in the revolutionary era. Nevertheless, the proportion of free blacks in the Lower South doubled from 1.6 percent of the black population in 1790 to a 3.9 percent in 1810 – still nowhere near the 10 percent achieved in the Upper South, but not insignificant either. In the lowcountry, the colonial practice of manumitting favorite slaves (not unfrequently the mulatto offspring of slaveholders) and setting them up in urban trades continued after the Revolution. One Charleston District slaveholder, for example, obtained special permission from the state senate to emancipate a slave family for "faithful services, and meritorious character." Such practices augmented the number of "free persons of color," often tied through patronage to the planter class, laying the groundwork for the region's antebellum free black population, especially in major cities such as Charleston (where a third of the free black population of South Carolina lived), Savannah and later Atlanta, as well as countless smaller towns. Charleston's free black population grew from 950 in 1790 to almost 4000 by 1850, increasing by

---

[41] Davis, *Inhuman Bondage*, 155; Sinha, *The Slave's Cause*, 93–94; Kolchin, *American Slavery*, 81; Berlin, *Generations of Captivity*, 127–128; Siemer, Henry Laurens and Robert Carter III," ch. 6; Paul Finkelman, *Slavery and the Founders: Race and Liberty in the Age of Jefferson* (New York: Routledge, 2014), 133–192.

50 percent in the 1810s alone. The largest free black population in the revolutionary Lower South, however, lived in Louisiana, beyond the borders of the United States at that time. Between 1769 and 1803 Spanish laws in the territory facilitated self-purchase arrangements, and as a result the free black population in port towns all along the Gulf coast "spiraled upwards," as Ira Berlin put it. This was especially the case in New Orleans, the territorial capital. In the 1790s the city's free black population was further augmented by the migration of "free people of color" from Saint-Domingue. By the time the United States took control in 1803, over 37 percent of the black population in New Orleans was free.[42]

Even as manumissions spiked across the South in the revolutionary period, however – significantly in the Upper South and more modestly in the Lower South – white southerners grew increasingly anxious about the growth of the free black population in their own midst. This was especially so in the wake of the insurrection on Saint-Domingue, where free blacks and slaves joined forces to oust or gruesomely eradicate the white slaveholding class, a terrifying prospect made even more terrifying by rumors of insurrection within the South itself. In particular the infamous plot of Gabriel Prosser, a manumitted blacksmith in Virginia who attempted to organize a major slave rebellion in the Richmond area in the summer of 1800, convinced many white southerners that free blacks formed a potential threat to their society. The fading of the revolutionary era and the transition to the antebellum period witnessed a conservative backlash throughout the southern states, characterized by renewed attempts to crack down on the free black population, check its growth,

---

[42] Petition of Claude Rame to the Legislature of South Carolina, n.d. 1824, RSPP, Series 1, Legislative Petitions, Accession #11300002 (quote); Davis, *Inhuman Bondage*, 155; Sinha, *The Slave's Cause*, 93–94; Kolchin, *American Slavery*, 81; Berlin, *Slaves without Masters*, 174; Berlin, *Generations of Captivity*, 127–128, 137, 142; Robert Olwell, "Becoming Free: Manumission and the Genesis of a Free Black Community in South Carolina, 1740–1790," in Jane G. Landers, ed., *Against the Odds: Free Blacks in the Slave Societies of the Americas* (New York: Routledge, 1996), 1–19; Laurence J. Kotlikoff and Anton Rupert, "The Manumission of Slaves in New Orleans, 1827–1846," *Southern Studies* 19, no. 2 (1980): 173–174; T. Stephen Whitman, "Diverse Good Causes: Manumission and the Transformation of Urban Slavery," *Social Science History* 19, no. 3 (1995): 333–370; Shawn Cole, "Capitalism and Freedom: Manumissions and the Slave Market in Louisiana, 1725–1820," *Journal of Economic History* 65, no. 4 (2005): 1021–1023.

prevent the entry of free blacks from other states, and close the doors to manumission.[43]

In both South Carolina and Virginia, the most important slave states of the South, the backlash commenced even before the turn of the new century. In 1797 almost a hundred residents of Charleston, concerned about the "dangerous designs and machinations of certain french West India Negroes," collectively petitioned the state legislature to tighten restrictions on the arrival of "free French people of color" and demanded that those who were already in South Carolina be deported. By 1800 South Carolina had passed an antimanumission law that required slaveholders to secure approval from the courts before freeing any slaves; by 1820 manumission could only be granted by the General Assembly, and by 1841 manumissions were barred altogether. In Virginia, the legislature prohibited the entry of free blacks from other states in 1793, and in 1806 it passed its own antimanumission law that required all freed slaves to leave the state – a virtually unenforceable requirement that few actually followed and that thus resulted in the proliferation of a free black population living in a curious legal situation whereby they were free but illegal residents. Despite the widespread assault on free blacks and manumission in the early nineteenth century, however, nowhere were free black communities eradicated. By 1806 the free black population of Virginia was already well established, and once established, it continued to grow naturally in subsequent decades. Indeed, as free blacks painstakingly scrimped and saved to buy family members still enslaved – in Virginia often holding them officially as "slaves" in order to circumvent the law that required their removal from the state – the southern free black population grew even larger than it would have through natural increase alone. For this reason, as Peter Kolchin has argued, the wave of manumissions at the turn of the nineteenth century "provided the basis for the South's free black population in the antebellum period."[44]

---

[43] James Sidbury, *Ploughshares into Swords: Race, Rebellion, and Identity in Gabriel's Virginia, 1730–1810* (New York: Cambridge University Press, 1997); Sinha, *The Slave's Cause*, 92–95; Kolchin, *American Slavery*, ch. 3; Viola Fraanziska Müller, "Cities of Refuge: Slave Flight and Illegal Freedom in the American Urban South, 1800–1860" (PhD diss., Leiden University, 2020), 26–27.

[44] Petition to the Honorable the Speaker, and other members of the House of Representatives of South Carolina, December 1797, Race and Slavery Petitions Project, Series 1, Legislative Petitions, Accession #11379706 (first quote); "An ACT to Amend the Several Laws Concerning Slaves" (1806), in *The Statutes at Large of Virginia, from October Session 1792, to December Session 1806*, comp. Samuel Shepherd (Richmond: n.p., 1836), 252; Sinha, *The Slave's Cause*, 86, 94; Bernard E. Powers, *Black*

The tightening commitment of the southern states to slavery at the turn of the nineteenth century was not only a kneejerk response to the insurrection on Saint-Domingue and the fear of similar plots within the South. It was also a rational and calculated response to improved economic conditions for slavery in the expanding southern frontier. Just as the doors to manumission were being slammed shut for enslaved people living in the South, southern slavery became revitalized as the "second slavery" came into its own, especially with the adoption of cotton plantation agriculture around the turn of the nineteenth century. Slavery in the US South not only failed to die out, as many revolutionary leaders from the Upper South initially believed it would, but it continued to grow at a feverish pace between the American Revolution and the Civil War, following the expansion of cotton into the southern interior and generating a lucrative domestic slave trade that washed almost a million American-born slaves from the Upper South and eastern seaboard to the Deep South.[45]

It would be impossible to underestimate the importance of cotton to revitalizing the institution of slavery in the new republic. As early as the late eighteenth century there arose an explosive demand for American cotton in Great Britain, a demand that could never fully be met by the geographically limited production of long-staple ("sea-island") cotton that was cultivated as a secondary crop in the rice lands of the South Carolina and Georgia lowcountry. American planters along the eastern seaboard were keenly aware of the potentially lucrative production of the short-staple variety, but experience had shown this to be ultimately too

Charlestonians: A Social History, 1822–1885 (Fayetteville: University of Arkansas Press, 1994); Siemer, "Henry Laurens and Robert Carter III," chs. 6–7; Kolchin, *American Slavery*, 81 (second quote).

[45] Ada Ferrer, *Freedom's Mirror: Cuba and Haiti in the Age of Revolution* (New York: Cambridge University Press, 2014). For more on "second slavery" in the Atlantic world, see: Dale W. Tomich, "The 'Second Slavery': Bonded Labor and the Transformations of the Nineteenth-Century World Economy," in Francisco O. Ramírez, ed., *Rethinking the Nineteenth Century: Contradictions and Movement* (New York: Greenwood Press, 1988), 103–117; Dale W. Tomich, *Through the Prism of Slavery: Labor, Capital, and World Economy* (Lanham, MD: Rowman and Littlefield, 2004); Dale W. Tomich and Michael Zeuske, eds., "The Second Slavery: Mass Slavery, World Economy, and Comparative Microhistories, Part I" [special issue], *Review: A Journal of the Fernand Braudel Center* 31, no. 2 (2008): 91–247; Anthony E. Kaye, "The Second Slavery: Modernity in the Nineteenth-Century South and the Atlantic World," *Journal of Southern History* 75, no. 3 (August 2009): 627–650; Javier Lavina and Michael Zeuske, eds., *The Second Slavery: Mass Slaveries and Modernity in the Americas and in the Atlantic Basin* (Berlin: Lit Verlag, 2014).

expensive because of the difficulties in separating its seeds. The invention of the cotton gin in 1793, and subsequent improvements thereof, however, solved this problem, increasing productivity exponentially and paving the way for the "cotton fever" that gripped the American South in the antebellum period.[46]

Due to climatic conditions, the short-staple variety was best cultivated in the vast and as yet sparsely settled lands of the interior rather than the coastal plains where most planters and slaves lived at the time of the Revolution. Gradually moving inland, the piedmont regions of South Carolina and Georgia were the first to be cleared and converted to cotton at the turn of the nineteenth century, but the westward expansion quickly spilled into the new territories of the Deep South. To contemporaries, opportunities to convert new frontiers into profitable cotton plantations seemed limitless because the land itself seemed limitless. The close of the Revolutionary War had resulted in the acquisition of most of the lands east of the Mississippi, and the subsequent purchase of the Louisiana Territory in 1803 increased the territory in which cotton could potentially be cultivated by millions of acres – southern Louisiana even proving lucrative to sugar production, another boom crop. Settlers from the eastern seaboard rushed to establish themselves in a beckoning "cotton kingdom" that ultimately stretched from South Carolina through the Gulf states. Southern cotton production soared, becoming the nation's primary export product, generating unfathomable wealth, and sustaining an almost insatiable demand for slave labor in the new states of the Deep South. The domestic slave trade from the Upper South to the cotton and sugar regions radically transformed the profitability of slavery in states such as Virginia and Maryland. Slavery proved so difficult to abolish in the Chesapeake at the turn of the nineteenth century precisely because the value of slaves from Virginia and Maryland skyrocketed due to the explosive demand for slave labor in the expanding Deep South, especially after the Atlantic slave trade was abolished in 1808. Chesapeake slaveholders, who at the time of the Revolution assumed that slavery would

---

[46] Robert William Fogel, *Without Consent or Contract: The Rise and Fall of American Slavery* (New York: W. W. Norton, 1989), 64–65; Kolchin, *American Slavery*, 94–95; Steven Deyle, *Carry Me Back: The Domestic Slave Trade in American Life* (New York: Oxford University Press, 2006), 20–22; Lewis C. Gray, *History of Agriculture in the Southern United States to 1860* (Washington, DC: Carnegie Institution, 1933), vol. 2, 678–695; Joyce E. Chaplin, "Creating a Cotton South in Georgia and South Carolina, 1760–1815," *Journal of Southern History* 57 (May 1991): 171–200; Sven Beckert, *Empire of Cotton: A Global History* (New York: Vintage, 2015).

eventually die out in their region, now renewed their commitment to the institution, earning a tidy profit selling slaves to the southern interior. By the late antebellum period the new center of gravity for American slavery had shifted from the eastern seaboard to the lower Mississippi Valley, and southerners had become so obsessed with "niggers and cotton–cotton and niggers" that they spoke of little else, according to traveler James Stirling, who visited the region in 1857.[47]

Upper South slaves in particular found themselves confronted with not only rapidly closing avenues to manumission and legal freedom but also increased prospects of being forcibly removed to distant cotton plantations in Georgia, Alabama, Mississippi, and Louisiana. After a brief period of relaxation in the wake of the Revolution, slavery now seemed to be getting worse. Its grip seemed to be tightening. Its expansion seemed limitless. Enslaved people who were dispatched to the lower Mississippi Valley found themselves torn from family and community, and performing backbreaking labor under difficult circumstances. The chances of being manumitted in many parts of the Deep South were virtually nonexistent: By 1860 the US census counted less than a thousand free blacks in all of Mississippi, for example. For those caught in the storm of the second slavery, fleeing to urban areas and passing for free seemed like a legitimate way to escape an ever-worsening system of bondage. Free black communities in urban areas increasingly became beacons of informal freedom for enslaved people living in the surrounding hinterlands. In major towns and cities of the South where free blacks constituted a significant part of the population, runaways found that they could easily get lost in the crowd and were often presumed free by white passersby. Even in the smaller provincial towns of the South, free black communities

---

[47] Walter Johnson, *Soul by Soul: Life Inside the Antebellum Slave Market* (Cambridge, MA: Harvard University Press, 1999), 5–6; Fogel, *Without Consent or Contract*, 30, 64–65; Kolchin, *American Slavery*, 94–96; Deyle, *Carry Me Back*, 20–21; Gray, *History of Agriculture*, vol. 2, 678–695; Anthony Gene Carey, *Sold Down the River: Slavery in the Lower Chattahoochee Valley of Alabama and Georgia* (Tuscaloosa: University of Alabama Press, 2011), 14–70; Adam Rothman, *Slave Country: American Expansion and the Origins of the Deep South* (Cambridge, MA: Harvard University Press, 2005), 37–72. See also Daniel S. Dupre, *Transforming the Cotton Frontier: Madison County, Alabama, 1800–1840* (Baton Rouge: Louisiana State University Press, 1997); Henry A. Tayloe to B. O. Tayloe, January 5, 1835, Tayloe Family Papers, Records of Ante-Bellum Southern Plantations (hereafter RASP), Series E., Part 1 (microfilm), JFK Institute, Freie Universität, Berlin; John Knight to Wm. M. Beall, September 10, 1835, John Knight Papers, RASP, Series F, Part 1 (microfilm), JFK Institute, Freie Universität, Berlin; James Stirling, *Letters from the Slave States* (1857; New York: Negro Universities Press, 1969), 179 (quote).

became potential sites of refuge for those who found themselves still trapped in bondage.[48]

The revolutionary transformations of the late eighteenth and early nineteenth centuries were Atlantic in scope and therefore not limited to the United States. Beyond the borders of the newly established republic lawmakers similarly opened the doors to freedom for enslaved African Americans. And crucially, those regions were not bound to constitutional compromises with US slaveholders over the rendition of runaways. By the mid-1830s the United States indeed found itself virtually surrounded by territories that had not only fully abolished bondage but also developed into spaces of formal freedom for fugitive slaves.[49]

The British dominion of Canada – with its relatively small slave population, never numbering more than a couple thousand souls – followed roughly the same trajectory of gradually abolishing slavery and transitioning into free soil as the Northern United States. Unlike the Northern United States, however, Canada eventually developed into an uncontested space of formal freedom for slave refugees from the United States. By the time Great Britain delivered the final death blow to slavery throughout its empire in 1833, Upper Canada (present-day Ontario) in particular had already long been pursuing a policy of granting formal asylum to runaway slaves and stoutly denying extradition requests from American slaveholders. By the eve of the US Civil War communities of slave refugees were scattered throughout the border region and the province was widely known as a "Refuge for the Oppressed" among African Americans, according to abolitionist Benjamin Drew.[50]

---

[48] US Population Census of 1860: Slave Schedules (NARA); Berlin, *Generations of Captivity*, ch. 4; Franklin and Schweninger, *Runaway Slaves*, 124–148; Damian Alan Pargas, "Urban Refugees: Fugitive Slaves and Spaces of Informal Freedom in the American South, 1800–1860," *Journal of Early American History* 7, no. 3 (December 2017): 262–284; Viola Franziska Müller, "Illegal but Tolerated: Slave Refugees in Richmond, Virginia, 1800–1860," in Pargas, ed., *Fugitive Slaves and Spaces of Freedom in North America*, 137–168.

[49] Franklin and Schweninger briefly refer to free soil parts of North America, including the Northern United States, Canada, and Mexico, as "promised lands." See Franklin and Schweninger, *Runaway Slaves*, 115–120.

[50] Gordon S. Barker, "Revisiting 'British Principle Talk': Antebellum Black Expectations and Racism in Early Ontario," in Pargas, ed., *Fugitive Slaves and Spaces of Freedom in*

That reputation took decades to earn, however, and in practice the development of Canada into a space of formal freedom was a protracted affair that followed slowly in the wake of the First Emancipation in the neighboring states of the Northern United States. Initial policies regarding slavery in fact looked disheartening – as late as 1790 British authorities granted American slaveholders official permission to bring their slaves with them to Canada in an effort to encourage Loyalist immigration after the American Revolution. Only three years later, however – but *ten years* after the abolition of slavery in Massachusetts – the tide began to turn. The legislature of Upper Canada took the first steps toward enacting gradual abolition in 1793, when it passed An Act to Prevent the further Introduction of Slaves and to limit the Term of Contracts for Servitude within this Province. Lieutenant Governor John Graves Simcoe – a friend of the prominent British abolitionist William Wilberforce – pressured lawmakers to pass the act in reaction to a widely reported incident by which an enslaved woman from Niagara named Chloe Cooley violently and publicly resisted her master as he attempted to transport her to the United States to be sold. Nobly declaring it "unjust that a people who enjoy Freedom by Law should encourage the introduction of Slaves" and "highly expedient to abolish Slavery in this Province, so far as the same may gradually be done without violating private property," Simcoe's plan was a compromise at best. It had to be, since at least six members of the colonial legislature and three members of the Executive Council owned slaves. The act decreed that no new slaves could be imported or brought into the province and that children born to slave mothers would be freed by age twenty-five, but it also complicated manumission by forcing slave owners to provide a security for any slaves they freed and guaranteed that slaves already living in the province would remain enslaved for life. Despite its shortcomings, however, Simcoe's legislation paved the way for the gradual emancipation of more than 1,000 slaves living in the province and is widely seen as the catalyst for the demise of slavery in the entire British dominion. By the early 1800s the courts in neighboring

North America, 34–69; Oran Patrick Kennedy, "Northward Bound: Slave Refugees and the Pursuit of Freedom in the Northern US and Canada, 1775–1861" (PhD diss., Leiden University, 2021), 49–51; Robin W. Winks, *The Blacks in Canada: A History* (Montreal: McGill-Queen's University Press, 1971), 96–98; Robin W. Winks, "'A Sacred Animosity': Abolitionism in Canada," in Martin B. Duberman, ed., *The Antislavery Vanguard: New Essays on the Abolitionists* (Princeton, NJ: Princeton University Press, 1991), 301–342; Benjamin Drew, *A North-Side View of Slavery: The Refugee; or the Narratives of Fugitive Slaves in Canada* (Boston: John P. Jewett & Co., 1856), 17.

Lower Canada, New Brunswick, and Nova Scotia had put slavery on the road to destruction there as well. Although several serious attempts at the turn of the nineteenth century to formally abolish bondage in those provinces failed, sympathetic judges set in motion the slow strangulation of the institution by consistently liberating local runaway slaves on minor technicalities or insufficient proof of ownership by their masters. By 1810 it was clear that slavery had no future in Canada, and that the courts were more likely to side with slaves than their masters in a wide variety of disputes.[51]

The gradual demise of slavery in Canada did not necessarily translate into free soil or formal asylum for runaway slaves from the United States, at least not at first. Indeed, there are even documented cases of Canadian slaves – including some from Upper Canada who were *not* emancipated by Simcoe's act – fleeing to the US side of the border, apparently under the impression that the emancipation policies in the northern states would set them free. Yet by the first decade of the nineteenth century most of the slave refugee migration was clearly trickling in the opposite direction. As historian Gordon Barker has argued, colonial authorities in the province took particular pains to strengthen Canada's status as a safe haven for enslaved people from south of the border. During the War of 1812, for example, thousands of American slaves fled or were evacuated to Canada in what amounted to a virtual repeat of the American Revolution. Canadian authorities subsequently refused to extradite these fugitive slaves after the war was over, despite persistent demands from the American government. A few years later, in 1819, Canadian officials responded to President James Monroe's demand for an extradition treaty by declaring that the *Somerset* case of 1772 applied to Canadian soil as

---

[51] "An Act to Prevent the further Introduction of Slaves and to limit the Term of Contracts for Servitude within this Province" (July 9, 1793), in *A Collection of the Acts Passed in the Parliament of Great Britain, Particularly Applying to the Province of Upper-Canada, and of Such Ordinances of the Late Province of Quebec, as Have Force of Law Therein* (York: R. C. Horne, 1818), 30–32, 30 (quotes); Sigrid Nicole Gallant, "Perspectives on the Motives for the Migration of African Americans to and from Ontario, Canada: From the Abolition of Slavery in Canada to the Abolition of Slavery in the United States," *Journal of Negro History* 86 (Summer 2001): 392–393; Barker, "Revisiting 'British Principle Talk,'" 35; Winks, *The Blacks in Canada*, 97, 102; Afua Cooper, "Acts of Resistance: Black Men and Women Engage Slavery in Upper Canada, 1793–1803," *Ontario History* 99, no. 1 (2007): 5–17; D. G. Bell, J. Barry Cahill, and Harvey Amani Whitfield, "Slavery and Slave Law in the Maritimes," in Barrington Walker, ed., *The African Canadian Legal Odyssey: Historical Essays* (Toronto: University of Toronto Press, 2012), 363–420.

well – a revisionist interpretation at best, since *Somerset* did not mention the status of slavery in the colonies. The Canadian Chief Justice John Robinson nevertheless argued that the "Law of England" applied "in all questions relative to property and civil rights, and [personal] freedom" in Canada, and that "whatever may have been the condition of these Negroes in the Country to which they formerly belonged, here they are free." The province even authorized land grants to black veterans of the War of 1812 who had fought for the British.[52]

The American government continued to press for an extradition treaty well into the 1820s, but was consistently frustrated in its efforts to formalize any agreement with Canadian officials, even in cases of run-away slaves who had been accused of crimes. Indeed, as the British abolition movement gained traction and plans to abolish slavery through-out the empire appeared within reach, authorities in both London and Canada became even more steadfast in their commitment to protecting runaway slaves who sought asylum. London dispatched a response to Washington in 1828, for example, that stated that parliament "gave freedom to every slave who effected his landing upon British ground," including Canada, again referencing the *Somerset* decision. By the early 1830s the Americans were clearly fighting a losing battle against an empire that was making earnest attempts to reprofile itself as slavery's foe: *Somerset* had been revised to the extent of applying to both sides of the Atlantic, British abolitionists were clamoring for immediate abolition in the colonies, and Britain had not only signed treaties with European powers to end the transatlantic slave trade but its navy was also aggres-sively pursuing violators on the high seas. Britain's reputation as a world power committed to freedom for slaves seemed all but sealed. For enslaved people living in the United States – whose experiences during the American Revolution and War of 1812 had already convinced them that the British were allies rather than enemies – the Imperial

---

[52] For cases of slaves in Canada fleeing to the United States, see for example *Upper Canada Gazette*, July 4, 1793; Kennedy, "Northward Bound," 48–49; Afua Cooper, "The Secret of Slavery in Canada," in Margaret Hobbs and Carla Rice, eds., *Gender and Women's Studies in Canada: Critical Terrain* (Toronto: Women's Press, 2013), 254–266; Gregory Wigmore, "Before the Railroad: From Slavery to Freedom in the Canadian-American Borderland," *Journal of American History* 98, no. 2 (2011): 437–445; Barker, "Revisiting 'British Principle Talk,'" 35–36 (quotes); Daniel G. Hill, *The Freedom-Seekers: Blacks in Early Canada* (Toronto: Stoddart, 1992), 18–19; Alan Taylor, *The Internal Enemy: Slavery and War in Virginia, 1772–1832* (New York: W. W. Norton, 2013), 1–4.

Emancipation that went into effect in 1834 merely finalized Canada's transition into a space of formal freedom, an attractive alternative to the Northern United States, where freedom for runaway slaves was becoming increasingly contested by that time. Indeed, as Matthew Clavin recently demonstrated, it even opened up new potential sites of formal freedom in the circum-Caribbean, including the Bahamas. Whether they looked north or south, enslaved people who wished to flee the slave states increasingly understood that British soil was unequivocally free soil, especially by the mid-1830s.[53]

The development of Mexico into a site of formal freedom for runaway slaves in the early nineteenth century, meanwhile, was a far more complicated process, made even more complicated by two factors: first, the confusing patchwork of Spanish asylum policies for runaway slaves from rival empires that long predated Mexican independence (1821); and second, the shifting boundaries between slavery and freedom that both precipitated and resulted in Texan independence (1836) and subsequent annexation by the United States (1845).

Mexico certainly did not start out as a site of freedom for runaway slaves, not even during most of its colonial period when it was part of the viceroyalty of New Spain – to which Spanish Florida, which *did* serve as a beacon of freedom for slaves in colonial South Carolina and Georgia, incidentally also belonged. Spanish sanctuary policies for runaway slaves from rival empires mostly developed in very localized settings, usually in direct response to the arrival of freedom seekers from across the border who sought protection from rendition and reenslavement. These policies often applied to only specific parts of the empire or specific groups of slaves, but not to others. Freedom for runaway slaves in early Spanish Florida, for example, did not automatically translate into freedom for runaway slaves in other parts of New Spain.[54]

---

[53] Barker, "Revisiting 'British Principle Talk,'" 35–36; Winks, *The Blacks in Canada*, 102 (quote); Matthew J. Clavin, *Aiming for Pensacola: Fugitive Slaves on the Atlantic and Southern Frontiers* (Cambridge, MA: Harvard University Press, 2015); George Hendrick and Willene Hendrick, *Black Refugees in Canada: Accounts of Escape During the Era of Slavery* (Jefferson, NC: McFarland, 2010), 11; Matthew Karp, *This Vast Southern Empire: Slaveholders at the Helm of American Foreign Policy* (Cambridge, MA: Harvard University Press, 2016), 12; Edward B. Rugemer, "The Southern Response to British Abolitionism: The Maturation of Proslavery Apologetics," *Journal of Southern History* 70, no. 2 (2004): 221–248.

[54] Thomas Mareite, "Conditional Freedom: Free Soil and Fugitive Slaves from the US South to Mexico's Northeast" (PhD diss., Leiden University, 2020), 115–135; Landers, "'Giving Liberty to All,'" 117–140.

At least seven separate royal decrees were issued in the seventeenth and eighteenth centuries that dealt with fugitive slaves in the Spanish circum-Caribbean, beginning with Trinidad in 1680 and Florida in 1693, both of which granted foreign runaway slaves conditional freedom upon conversion to Catholicism. A more comprehensive royal decree was finally issued in 1750, which directed all Spanish colonies throughout the empire to grant asylum to runaway slaves from Protestant territories as long as they converted to the Catholic faith. Yet even this decree was limited, as it was mainly directed at slaves from the British and Dutch colonies, and stipulated religious conversion as a condition for freedom. Only in 1789 did yet another royal decree grant unconditional freedom to all foreign runaway slaves who reached Spanish soil – but it had virtually no impact because it was revoked indefinitely only a few months after it was issued (as a response to widespread fears of the spread of radicalism during the French Revolution, as well as sustained British and American pressure on the Spanish to end their sanctuary policy in Florida). During all of this time, it should be remembered, slavery was still perfectly legal and uncontested within the Spanish empire. Asylum policies – where applicable – only applied to runaways from outside the Spanish territories.[55]

With the exception of the 1750 decree, local authorities in the part of New Spain that would later develop into an independent Mexico (including Texas) never received any specific instructions regarding fugitive slaves, and for most of the eighteenth century they failed to enact or enforce any consistent policy of protecting runaways from abroad. The 1750 decree that provided for conditional freedom upon conversion to Catholicism did not apply to runaway slaves from the French colonies because they were already Catholic, moreover, and since most runaway slaves into northeastern New Spain (especially Texas) were from the neighboring territory of French Louisiana, they were routinely caught and sent back to their masters. The 1789 decree that provided for unconditional freedom to runaway slaves was revoked soon after it was issued,

---

[55] Thomas Mareite, "Conditional Freedom: Free Soil and Fugitive Slaves from the US South to Mexico's Northeast" (PhD diss., Leiden University, 2020), 115–135; Landers, "'Giving Liberty to All,'" 117–140.

Lucena Salmoral, *Regulación de la Esclavitud en las Colonias de América Española (1503–1886): Documentos para su Estudio* (Alcalá de Henares: Universidad de Alcalá, 2005); Mareite, "Conditional Freedom," 115–135; Landers, *Black Society in Spanish Florida*, 24–45, 75–83.

as stated above, but it would have hardly mattered even if it had endured, because between 1769 and 1803 Louisiana was incorporated into the Spanish empire, so runaway slaves from Louisiana who fled west to Texas were considered "internal" runaways and denied any protections or freedom. In sum, the northeastern Mexican borderlands failed to develop into a refuge for runaway slaves prior to 1803 – when Louisiana was retroceded to France and subsequently sold to the United States – despite royal decrees that granted asylum in other parts of the empire.[56]

The US acquisition of the Louisiana Territory changed everything, however. By the early nineteenth century the United States was already expanding at an alarming rate due to the success of the cotton revolution in the Deep South. When New Spain officials found their viceroyalty sharing a – poorly defined – border with a rival and expanding US empire that threatened to engulf its northern territories, they started to revise their stance on fugitive slaves in the Texas-Louisiana borderlands. Indeed, simply delineating where the border exactly was proved to be a contested issue in many areas, and authorities in New Spain used the fugitive slave issue as a weapon against potential US incursions into what they claimed to be Spanish territory. In August 1805, for example, they issued a warning to the Americans that any acts of hostility or illegal incursions into Texas would result in an open proclamation of freedom to runaway slaves from the United States. One year after that, in 1806, the contested borderlands between Texas and Louisiana were temporarily declared "neutral ground" after authorities failed to agree where to delineate the border – in other words, both parties agreed that neither would have jurisdiction in parts of the borderland in order to prevent rising tensions from erupting into a military conflict. The compromise proved advantageous to runaway slaves running west from Louisiana, who upon reaching the easternmost fringes of Texas found themselves in a juridical

---

[56] Mareite, "Conditional Freedom," ch. 3; James Harrison, "The Failure of Spain in East Texas: The Occupation and Abandonment of Nacogdoches, 1779–1821" (PhD diss., University of Nebraska, 1980), 207; H. Sophie Burton and F. Todd Smith, *Colonial Natchitoches: A Creole Community on the Louisiana-Texas Frontier* (College Station: Texas A&M University Press, 2008), 71; Hall, *Africans in Colonial Louisiana*, 98–118, 202–236; Rosalie Schwartz, *Across the Rio to Freedom: US Negroes in Mexico* (El Paso: Texas Western University Press, 1975), 5–6; Eric Herschthal, "Slaves, Spaniards and Subversion in Early Louisiana: The Persistent Fears of Black Revolt and Spanish Collusion in Territorial Louisiana, 1803–1812," *Journal of the Early Republic* 36 (Summer 2016): 283–311.

no-man's-land where their masters could not legally come and claim them. Spanish officials, for their part, generally proved willing to protect runaway slaves from rendition, even those who had fled further into the viceroyalty and away from the neutral border zone.[57]

Such policies and protections echoed earlier Spanish decrees that ambiguously granted refuge to runaway slaves from rival empires, even while maintaining the institution of slavery within the Spanish territories themselves. The emergence of an independence movement in early-nine-teenth-century Mexico, however, placed the country more firmly on the path to becoming a free soil territory. As in other parts of the hemisphere, Mexican calls for republican independence were issued in an atmosphere that was largely critical of slavery. The movement's founding document – Father Hidalgo's *Grito de Dolores* (1810) – explicitly called for the eradication of slavery throughout New Spain, and prominent revolution-aries forcefully demanded the abolition of social hierarchies in general, including slavery, peonage, and other forms of debt bondage. Such ideas resonated with large segments of Mexican society, but were contested and opposed by elites and other proslavery groups. The issue of slavery therefore constituted a political battle zone during the long struggle for independence and well into the first decade of the republic.[58]

When Mexico finally did achieve independence from Spain in 1821, political rivalries and tumultuous shifts in power between various pro- and antislavery factions resulted in a series of confusing and often contra-dictory decrees regarding the legality of the institution, at least at the

---

[57] Nancy Blythe, "Fugitives from Servitude: American Deserters and Runaway Slaves in Spanish Nacogdoches, 1803–1808," *East Texas Historical Journal* 38, no. 2 (2000): 1–14; Jeremy Adelman and Stephen Aron, "From Borderlands to Borders: Empires, Nation-States, and the People in between in North American History," *The American Historical Review* 104, no. 3 (1999): 814–841; Julia Kathryn Garrett, "Dr. John Sibley and the Louisiana Texas Frontier, 1803–1814," *Southwestern Historical Quarterly* 49 (January 1946): 403–404; Bram Hoonhout and Thomas Mareite, "Freedom at the Fringes? Slave Flight and Empire-Building in the Early Modern Spanish Borderlands of Essequibo-Venezuela and Louisiana-Texas," *Slavery & Abolition* 40, no. 1 (2019): 61–86.

[58] Sean Kelley, "'Mexico in His Head': Slavery and the Texas-Mexico Border, 1810–1860," *Journal of Social History* 37 (Spring 2004): 711–715; Andrew Jonathan Torget, "Cotton Empire: Slavery and the Texas Borderlands, 1820–1837" (PhD diss., University of Virginia, 2009), 210–211; Mareite, "Conditional Freedom," 130–131; Manuel Ferrer Muñoz, *La Cuestión de la Esclavitud en el México Decimonónico: Sus Repercusiones en las Etnias Indígenas* (México, DF: Instituto de Estudios Constitucionales Carlos Restrepo Piedrahita, 1998), 13–15; Jaime Olveda Legaspi, "La abolición de la esclavitud en México, 1810–1917," *Signos históricos* 29 (2013): 8–34.

central level. The strangulation of slavery in Mexico came in fits and starts, with sometimes wild pendulum swings back and forth between gradual abolition policies and exemptions for certain groups from those same policies. As in the Northern United States and British Canada, most abolition laws in Mexico were passed by the individual states, not by the central government in Mexico City. The federalist constitution of 1824 indeed relegated the issue of slavery to the states. The central government nevertheless weighed in at certain key moments with sweeping decrees that superseded local legislation. It ordered unequivocally in 1823 that all slave children under the age of fourteen be emancipated, for example, and on September 15, 1829 President Vicente Guerrero formally abolished slavery outright, announcing in the simplest and most unambiguous terms possible: *"Queda abolida la esclavitud en la República"* ("Slavery in the Republic is abolished"), and *"Son consiguiente libres los que hasta hoy se habian considerado como esclavos"* ("Those who until today were considered slaves are hereafter free"). Even then, however, fierce resistance to the decree among proslavery US settlers living in Texas (which was incorporated into the Mexican state of Coahuila y Tejas), resulted in an exemption for Texas being issued that same year, adding even more confusion to an already dizzying and erratic series of laws regarding the legality of slavery.[59]

The Mexican independence struggle and subsequent calls for the abolition of slavery alarmed and incensed proslavery Anglo-Texans – who had initially been invited to settle the northern borderlands – as well as slaveholders in the American Deep South, who feared sharing yet another border with a "free soil" part of the continent. The idea of annexing Texas and turning it into a slaveholding state or republic arose early, even before Mexico gained its independence. Attempts by American mercenaries and revolutionaries to seize Texas by force and declare it independent from New Spain – usually with the implicit and sometimes explicit support of US officials – were numerous. Texas was indeed invaded by bands of American fighters at least six times between 1813 and 1816 alone. By the time Mexico finally did achieve independence in 1821, the

---

[59] Kelley, "'Mexico in His Head,'" 710–715; Torget, "Cotton Empire," 210–211; Mareite, "Conditional Freedom," 135–145; "Decreto del gobierno – Abolición de la esclavitud" (September 15, 1829), in Manuel Dublán et al., *Legislación mexicana; o colección completa de disposiciones legislativas expedidas desde la independencia de la República* (México: Imprenta de Comercio, 1876), vol. 2, 163 (quotes).

Texas-Louisiana borderlands had witnessed a decade of armed skirmishes.[60]

By the mid-1820s most districts in central and eastern Texas had developed into virtual American enclaves and southern-style slave societies, complete with cotton plantations and proslavery political fervor. Under the leadership of Stephen Austin a majority of Anglo-Texan settlers roundly refused to entertain the prospect of any government meddling with their human property. Austin tirelessly agitated for exemptions from the abolition proposals that were being discussed at both the state and federal levels. When Texan slaveholders were granted an exemption from the 1829 abolition decree, however, runaway slaves from within Texas itself as well as from neighboring US states undermined the compromise policy by seeking asylum in nearby non-Anglo communities, which they presumed to fall outside of the exemption. Confusion ensued about the status of such refugees – Anglo-Texans demanded their slaves' return while Mexican authorities often declared that those jurisdictions were bound by the national abolition decree. The US government, meanwhile, made repeated attempts to secure a fugitive slave treaty with Mexico between 1825 and 1833, but without success, as Mexican officials consistently upheld asylum policies for American runaway slaves, especially after the abolition of slavery in 1829.[61]

To many US settlers in Texas, the future of slavery seemed untenable under Mexican sovereignty, despite their exemption from the 1829 decree. Slavery and the fugitive slave issue indeed significantly contributed to the outbreak of the Texan Revolution and subsequent secession from Mexico in 1835–1836. By the mid-1830s the slave population in the river plantation districts of Mexican Texas had grown more concentrated; American settlers were increasingly committed to maintaining slavery and evading the issue of abolition altogether. They also increasingly found themselves in conflict with Mexican authorities, as attempts to forcefully retrieve runaway slaves there often provoked local conflicts

---

[60] Mareite, "Conditional Freedom," 135–162; David Head, *Privateers of the Americas: Spanish American Privateering from the United States in the Early Republic* (Athens: University of Georgia Press, 2015), 98; Kelley, "'Mexico in His Head,'" 713.

[61] Head, *Privateers of the Americas*, 98; Kelley, "'Mexico in His Head,'" 713; Mareite, "Conditional Freedom," ch. 3; Randolph B. Campbell, *An Empire for Slavery: The Peculiar Institution in Texas, 1821–1865* (Baton Rouge: Louisiana State University Press, 1991), 10–34; Andrew J. Torget, *Seeds of Empire: Cotton, Slavery, and the Transformation of the Texas Borderlands, 1800–1850* (Chapel Hill: University of North Carolina Press, 2015), chs. 2–3.

and led to confusing legal situations. Mexico, meanwhile, became increasingly committed to preventing Texas from veering into the US economic orbit and frustrated with Anglo-Texans' incursions into neighboring communities to catch runaway slaves, as well as their evasion of the entire slavery issue. Starting in 1830 Mexico banned further immigration from the United States, infuriating American settlers and galvanizing armed conflicts against the Mexican state. As confrontations between Texas and Mexico descended into warfare in 1835, enslaved people residing in the new plantation districts of Texas increasingly fled to non-Anglo communities or to the Mexican Army. Mexican authorities and military officials were often confused about the exact status of these refugees – many afforded them protection, while others allowed their masters to reclaim them. But whatever the exact policies regarding freedom for Texan slaves and exemptions for Texan slaveholders from abolition, what is important is that enslaved people associated Mexico with freedom throughout the conflict, "invest[ing] the border with liberationist significance," as Sean Kelley has argued.[62]

The liberationist significance of the border between Texas and the rest of Mexico became even more important when Anglo-Texans succeeded in ultimately expelling the Mexican Army. The victors of the Texan Revolution wasted no time in establishing a slaveholding republic in 1836, adopting a constitution with several proslavery clauses and legally securing the future of bondage throughout the territory. Ironically, however, Texan independence erased any confusion regarding the status of runaway slaves who fled into Mexico. The vague exemptions that had previously applied to Texan slaveholders were now stricken from the books – all Mexican soil was now free soil. Enslaved people living in Texas, therefore, now even more firmly associated the Mexican border with freedom and refuge, and flight attempts increasingly led southward. When Texas was annexed by the United States in 1845 and admitted to the Union as a southern slave state, moreover, enslaved people in other

---

[62] Paul D. Lack, *The Texas Revolutionary Experience: A Political and Social History, 1835–1836* (College Station: Texas A&M University Press, 1992), 243–244; Paul D. Lack, "Slavery and the Texas Revolution," *Southwestern Historical Quarterly* 89 (October 1985): 188–191; James David Nichols, *The Limits of Liberty: Mobility and the Making of the Eastern US-Mexico Border* (Lincoln: University of Nebraska Press, 2018), 67–70; Mareite, "Conditional Freedom," 159–162; Torget, *Seeds of Empire*, chs. 2–3; Kelley, "'Mexico in His Head,'" 709 (quote), 713–718.

parts of the Deep South began to eye the Rio Grande as a borderline of freedom as well.[63]

The Age of Revolution radically transformed the landscape of slavery and freedom throughout North America and beyond. Henry Stanton, a prominent Massachusetts politician, observed on the floor of the state House of Representatives in 1837 that "every free state is now an asylum for runaway slaves, as are the West Indies, Mexico, our Western forests, and the monarchies of Europe." By the mid-1830s, enslaved people who found themselves trapped in the second slavery of the American South indeed saw spaces of freedom in every direction: an informal variant within urban areas in the South itself; a contested variant in the Northern United States; and formal variants beyond the borders of the United States.[64]

---

[63] Sean Kelley, "'Mexico in His Head,'" 716–717; Sean M. Kelley, *Los Brazos de Dios: A Plantation Society in the Texas Borderlands, 1821–1865* (Baton Rouge: Louisiana State University Press, 2010), 100; Mareite, "Conditional Freedom," ch. 4; Campbell, *An Empire for Slavery*, 50–67; Alwyn Barr, "Freedom and Slavery in the Republic: African American Experiences in the Republic of Texas," in Kenneth W. Howell and Charles Swanlund, eds., *Single Star of the West: The Republic of Texas, 1836–1845* (Denton: University of North Texas Press, 2017), 423–436.

[64] Henry B. Stanton, *Remarks of Henry B. Stanton, in the Representatives' Hall, on the 23nd (sic) and 24ᵗʰ of February, before the Committee of the House of Representatives, of Massachusetts, to Whom Was Referred Sundry Memorials on the Subject of Slavery* (Boston: I. Knapp, 1837), 62 (quote).

2

"Lurking amongst the Free Negroes"

Spaces of Informal Freedom in the Urban South *

Moses Hutcherson, a "likely black fellow about twenty-three years old, five feet four or five inches high, neck somewhat long, and rather a prominent nose for a negro," decided in the spring of 1825 to make a bid for freedom. Surveying the possibilities to escape bondage from his farm on the Potomac River in southern Maryland, he concluded that his best bet would be to flee to Pennsylvania, where slavery had been abolished. It was an option fraught with peril, of course. Despite the close proximity of the neighboring free state, flight attempts across the Mason–Dixon line were risky. Moses would have to traverse dozens of miles of slaveholding borderland undetected by heavily armed patrols and professional slave catchers. In order to reduce the risk of capture he took the logical precautions – procuring forged free papers under the false name of John Henry before starting off, in case he was stopped by anyone – and slipped away from his master's residence on April 1. His hopes of reaching Pennsylvania were dashed when he was caught near Baltimore and thrown into jail, however. His master recovered him and dragged him back to the shores of the Potomac. Undaunted, Moses escaped again a month later. This time, however, he fled not to the "free" North but to the nearby slaveholding District of Columbia, where he changed his name

---

* Excerpts from this chapter were previously published in adapted form in: Damian Alan Pargas, "Urban Refugees: Fugitive Slaves and Spaces of Informal Freedom in the American South, 1800–1860," *Journal of Early American History* 7, no. 3 (December 2017): 262–284; Damian Alan Pargas, "Seeking Freedom in the Midst of Slavery: Fugitive Slaves in the Antebellum South," in Damian Alan Pargas, ed., *Fugitive Slaves and Spaces of Freedom in North America* (Gainesville: University Press of Florida, 2018), 116–136.

again and passed himself off as a free black. Having been hired out in Washington before, Moses engaged the help of his contacts within the free black community to conceal his true identity and assist him in finding accommodation and employment. In the months that followed, he "served in many of the Taverns and Boarding Houses in [the] District," and remained harbored by "free negroes in [that] place," with whom he had come to have "considerable intercourse."[1]

Unlike thousands of his fellow bondsmen who escaped slavery by crossing state or international borders to parts of the continent where the institution had been abolished, Moses Hutcherson attempted to craft a life of freedom for himself by simply disguising his slave status and passing himself off as a free black in a city *within* the slaveholding South. His story – and there are innumerable such cases in the history of the antebellum South – complicates our understanding of the geography of slavery and freedom in North America.

Southern towns and cities have not featured prominently in the historical scholarship as sites of freedom for runaway slaves. And to be sure, they were not the only southern sites of freedom available to enslaved people in the antebellum period. Many bondspeople caught in the storm of the second slavery continued to employ "traditional" strategies of absconding within the South, such as marronage. A perusal of runaway slave ads, court documents, and local legislation reveals that cases of enslaved people running into the wilderness in the decades preceding the Civil War were not uncommon. Joshua, a Tennessee slave, "took to the woods" in 1843 "& absented & secreted himself entirely ... from the possession & control of any one." Mary Smith, a Virginia slave of "verry bad character" took her two children and remained "almost constantly in the woods so as to run away" in 1847. Demos, another slave from Virginia, "without any ostensible cause ranaway and remained secreted in the Dismal Swamp" in 1852. Susan and her son Jim absconded from their masters in South Carolina and "for a long space of time absented themselves in the woods." And John and Tom, enslaved in Jackson County, Florida, were claimed to "have been in the woods for about two months" in 1858, when their mistress finally petitioned the county court for permission to formally sell them in their absence. Cases of

[1] *Daily National Intelligencer* (Washington, DC), July 4, 1825 (quotes); Richard S. Newman, "'Lucky to Be Born in Pennsylvania': Free Soil, Fugitive Slaves, and the Making of Pennsylvania's Anti-Slavery Borderland," *Slavery & Abolition* 32, no. 3 (September 2011): 413–430.

runaway slaves "lurking in swamps, woods and other obscure places, killing hogs and committing other injuries to the inhabitants of the Territory" of antebellum Florida were common enough that in 1828 a law was enacted to regulate their recapture by ordinary white civilians. Bands of runaways in the lowcountry swamps of South Carolina in the 1820s caused such "alarm and danger" to local plantation owners that they petitioned the state legislature for military assistance, convinced that the maroons were preparing to launch an insurrection.[2]

Life in the wilderness was certainly not for everyone, however, and the continual growth of urban free black populations in the postrevolutionary period provided fugitive slaves with an attractive alternative to marronage: flight to urban sites of informal freedom, where runaways could attempt to cloak themselves in anonymity and pass themselves off as free. The antebellum South's largest cities, which also contained its largest urban African-American populations – especially Baltimore, the District of Columbia, Richmond, Charleston, and New Orleans – developed into major beacons of freedom to enslaved people living in their respective regional hinterlands. By 1860 Baltimore's black population numbered a staggering 28,000 (25,680 free); the District of Columbia was home to more than 14,000 African Americans (11,131 free); Richmond's African-American population numbered over 14,400 (2,576 free); Charleston's black population reached 17,100 (more than 3,200 free); and New

---

[2] Sylviane Diouf, *Slavery's Exiles: The Story of the American Maroons* (New York: New York University Press, 2014); Ted Maris-Wolf, "Hidden in Plain Sight: Maroon Life and Labor in Virginia's Dismal Swamp," *Slavery & Abolition* 34, no. 3 (2013): 446–464; Petition of Samuel W. Gentry to the Honl Lumsford M. Bramlette, Chancellor of the Middle Chancery Division, Maury County, TN, September 21, 1843, Race and Slavery Petitions Project (hereafter RSPP), Series 2: County Court Petitions, Accession #21484335; Petition of William A. Jones to the worshipful County Court of Southampton in Chancery, VA, February 1847, RSPP, Series 2: County Court Petitions, Accession #21684706; Petition of James Clayton to the worshipful County Court of Southampton County in Chancery, VA, August 1852, in RSPP, Series 2: County Court Petitions, Accession #21684706; Petition of Thomas Limehouse to the Honorable the Chancellors of South Carolina, January 4, 1836, RSPP, Series 2: County Court Petitions, Part D (NC/SC); Petition of Harriet R. Long to the Honorable Robert S. Dickson, Judge of Probate of Jackson County, FL, February 27, 1858, RSPP, Series 2, County Court Petitions, Accession #20585801; "An Act Related to Crimes and Misdemeanors Committed by Slaves, Free Negroes and Mulattoes," in *Acts of the Legislative Council of the Territory of Florida, Passed at Their Seventh Session* (Tallahassee, FL: William Wilson, 1828), 174–190; Petition of Inhabitants of Clarendon, Claremont, St. James, St. Stephens, and Richland districts to the Senate of South Carolina, ca. 1824, transcribed in John Hope Franklin and Loren Schweninger, *Runaway Slaves: Rebels on the Plantation* (New York: Oxford University Press, 1999), 303–306.

Orleans counted 25,400 black residents (10,700 of whom were registered as free). Anonymity certainly seemed feasible in these cities, especially Baltimore and DC, where a majority of the black population was free. But even in smaller towns with fewer free blacks, runaway slaves could attempt to pass for free because by the early decades of the nineteenth century white southerners had grown accustomed to the notion of urban black freedom. They knew that at least *some* black residents in their towns were (or could be) free. This facilitated a degree of limited anonymity for runaway slaves in mid-sized towns as well – places such as Natchez, Mississippi (with 800 free blacks in 1860); Augusta, Georgia (almost 500 free blacks in 1860); Lexington, Kentucky (roughly 500 free blacks in 1860); and Fredericksburg, Virginia (roughly 350 free blacks in 1860). In Maryland, where by the eve of the Civil War half of the black population was already free, runaway slaves lurked about in virtually every county seat and even the most modest of crossroads.[3]

Scholars have often characterized runaways who made for southern towns and cities as "truants," "absentees," or "transients" rather than permanent freedom seekers. Franklin and Schweninger, for example, underscored the importance of urban areas as destinations for fugitive slaves, described most such runaways as "temporary sojourners" who were either just passing through (on their way to sites of formal freedom) or who went to towns to enjoy a "brief respite from bondage" – at best a "break ... of longer duration" – before either returning of their own accord or being caught and sent back to their masters. Only occasionally a very few "shrewd runaways remained at large for years." Matthew Clavin's work on fugitive slaves in antebellum Pensacola, as well as Christopher Phillips' study of antebellum Baltimore, both similarly underscore the transience of runaways in those port towns, many of whom fled there with the intention of securing onward passage to the northern states or circum-Caribbean.[4]

---

[3] US Population Census, 1860 (microfilm), National Archives and Records Administration, Washington, DC; Viola Franziska Müller, "Cities of Refuge: Slave Flight and Illegal Freedom in the American Urban South, 1800–1860" (PhD diss., Leiden University, Leiden, the Netherlands, 2020), 36–44, 89–105; Ira Berlin, *Slaves without Masters: The Free Negro in the Antebellum South* (New York: Pantheon, 1974), 46, 136; Leonard P. Curry, "Free Blacks in the Urban South, 1800–1850," *Southern Quarterly* 43, no. 2 (2006): 35–51; Leonard P. Curry, *Free Blacks in Urban America, 1800–1850: The Shadow of the Dream* (Chicago: University of Chicago Press, 1981).

[4] Franklin and Schweninger, *Runaway Slaves*, 126–134, 112 and 126 (quotes); S. Charles Bolton, *Fugitivism: Escaping Slavery in the Lower Mississippi Valley, 1820–1860*

Runaway slave advertisements, court records, and southern jail registers, however, suggest that many fugitive slaves who concealed themselves in southern towns and cities navigated urban spaces as actual sites of freedom in their own right, and not merely as gateways to freedom in other parts of the hemisphere or sites of temporary respite from rural bondage. In other words, many runaway slaves to urban areas within the South were *permanent* freedom seekers – at least by intent, and often by outcome. Seeking freedom in the midst of slavery, they daringly made illegal attempts to rebuild their lives in informal freedom rather than bolt for geographic spaces where slavery had been abolished. Understanding why and how they did so is crucial for rethinking how enslaved people viewed the landscape of slavery and freedom in the antebellum period.[5]

Taking a broad scope, this chapter examines fugitive slaves who remained in the antebellum South as permanent refugees from slavery. It touches upon themes such as the motivations that led enslaved people to flee within the South rather than other parts of the continent; the cooperation between free and enslaved blacks that enabled and facilitated their escape attempts and settlement processes; and the ways in which runaways attempted to evade recapture and reenslavement. Its overarching aim is to insert freedom seekers in the urban South into a broader narrative of freedom seekers in antebellum North America by

(Fayetteville: University of Arkansas Press, 2019), 117–148; Stephanie M. H. Camp, *Closer to Freedom: Enslaved Women and Everyday Resistance in the Plantation South* (Chapel Hill: University of North Carolina Press, 2003). Matthew Clavin's recent work views Pensacola as a conduit for fugitive slaves fleeing southward into the Caribbean (especially the British Caribbean). Matthew J. Clavin, *Aiming for Pensacola: Fugitive Slaves on the Atlantic and Southern Frontiers* (Cambridge, MA: Harvard University Press, 2015); Christopher Phillips, *Freedom's Port: The African American Community of Baltimore, 1790–1860* (Urbana: University of Illinois Press, 1997).

[5] For brief treatment of truancy within the South, especially in urban areas, see for example Camp, *Closer to Freedom*, 35–59; and Franklin and Schweninger, *Runaway Slaves*, 97–103, 124–148. Franklin and Schweninger argued that "few absconders [within the South] remained permanently at large." See John Hope Franklin and Loren Schweninger, "The Quest for Freedom: Runaway Slaves and the Plantation South," in Ira Berlin, Scott Hancock, and G. S. Boritt, eds., *Slavery, Resistance, Freedom* (New York: Oxford University Press, 2007), 21–39, 25 (quote). For southern runaways as permanent freedom seekers, see Clavin, *Aiming for Pensacola*; Amani Marshall, "'They Will Endeavor to Pass for Free': Enslaved Runaways' Performances of Freedom in Antebellum South Carolina," *Slavery & Abolition* 31 (May 2010): 161–180; and Diouf, *Slavery's Exiles*; Alan Taylor, *The Internal Enemy: Slavery and War in Virginia, 1771–1832* (New York: W. W. Norton, 2014). Rachel Adams calls for a broader understanding of the geography of slavery and freedom in North America. See Rachel Adams, *Continental Divides: Remapping the Cultures of North America* (Chicago: University of Chicago Press, 2009), 61–100.

illuminating how fugitive slaves like Moses Hutcherson fled to – and navigated – sites of informal freedom.

THE ROADS TO TOWN

Two factors in particular motivated freedom seekers to make for nearby towns and cities within the slaveholding states, rather than spaces of formal freedom beyond the South. First, enslaved people's social and occupational networks often lured and led them to urban areas. Runaway slave advertisements in southern newspapers as well as ante-bellum court records reveal that runaways within the South usually had free black contacts in urban areas to whom they directed their course and who could provide them with vital assistance and information. Whether family, friends, friends of friends, or acquaintances made during a hiring stint or while running an errand for the master in town, established networks between rural and urban black communities blazed well-worn paths that runaway slaves utilized to escape their masters.[6]

Second, and just as important, was the fact that flight to southern towns and cities provided freedom seekers with opportunities to flee slavery *without severing all ties with loved ones.* Fleeing beyond the borders of the antebellum South might have provided runaways with a safer and more legitimate claim to freedom, but, like crossing the Berlin Wall, it also had the major disadvantage of separating refugees from their homes and families – potentially forever. For many freedom seekers, even those who lived within relatively easy reach of free soil, state and inter-national borders seemed like a door of no return that they were unwilling to pass through if they could avoid it. Crafting lives of informal freedom within the urban South, by contrast, allowed them to "live free" without permanently separating them from loved ones and having to live as castaways in some distant and unknown part of the continent.[7]

---

[6] Franklin and Schweninger, *Runaway Slaves,* 126–127, 130–145; Müller, "Cities of Refuge," 32–36; Curry, "Free Blacks in the Urban South," 36; Anthony E. Kaye, "Neighborhoods and Solidarity in the Natchez District of Mississippi: Rethinking the Antebellum Slave Community," *Slavery & Abolition* 23, no. 1 (2002): 1–24.

[7] On the importance of not severing ties with family and loved ones, even if it meant remaining within the slave South, see for example: Calvin Schermerhorn, *Money over Mastery, Family over Freedom: Slavery in the American Upper South* (Baltimore: Johns Hopkins University Press, 2011); Ted Maris-Wolf, *Family Bonds: Free Blacks and Re-enslavement Law in Antebellum Virginia* (Chapel Hill: University of North Carolina Press, 2015).

Indeed, the importance of family as a factor in informing runaways' strategies of escape can hardly be overemphasized. Enslaved people ran away for all kinds of reasons – some desperately sought to escape harsh punishments or physical abuse, while others felt compelled to leave because of a burning desire to self-emancipate and become masters of their own destinies. Most probably fled because of a combination of several factors. The threat or reality of forced separation from loved ones, however, constituted one of the most important catalysts for slave flight within the South. Unlike in the colonial period, *all* antebellum slave flight occurred against the haunting backdrop of massive waves of internal forced migration. In the era of the second slavery, when the Atlantic slave trade had been abolished and the domestic slave trade in the southern states flourished, forced separations wrought havoc on slave families. Ira Berlin famously dubbed this generation of enslaved people "the migration generations." Almost a million enslaved African Americans were forcibly displaced across state lines via the domestic slave trade between the American Revolution and the outbreak of the Civil War. Local sales and the westward migration of slaveholders from the eastern seaboard to the southern interior, moreover, severed cross-plantation marriages and extended family bonds in countless slave communities across the South.[8]

Within this context of constant and excruciating separations, flight within the South became an important vehicle by which victims of forced migration attempted to either prevent separations or reunite bonds torn

---

[8] Franklin and Schweninger explain various motivations for running away in general, with a particular focus on the threat of family separations. See Franklin and Schweninger, *Runaway Slaves*, chs. 2–3. There is a rich literature on the domestic slave trade and the extent to which sales, estate divisions, and long-term hiring forcibly separated slave families in the antebellum period. See for example: Michael Tadman, *Speculators and Slaves: Masters, Traders, and Slaves in the Old South* (Madison: University of Wisconsin Press, 1989); Walter Johnson, *Soul by Soul: Life Inside the Antebellum Slave Market* (Cambridge, MA: Harvard University Press, 1999); Steven Deyle, *Carry Me Back: The Domestic Slave Trade in American Life* (New York: Oxford University Press, 2005); Robert H. Gudmestad, *A Troublesome Commerce: The Transformation of the Interstate Slave Trade* (Baton Rouge: Louisiana State University Press, 2003); Damian Alan Pargas, *Slavery and Forced Migration in the Antebellum South* (New York: Cambridge University Press, 2014); Ira Berlin, *Generations of Captivity: A History of African-American Slaves* (Cambridge, MA: Harvard University Press, 2003), ch. 3. For an interesting contemporary account of the domestic slave trade and its effects on slave families, see Ethan Allen Andrews, *Slavery and the Domestic Slave Trade, in a Series of Letters Addressed to the Executive Committee of the American Union for the Relief and Improvement of the Colored Race* (1836; Freeport, NY: Libraries Press, 1971).

asunder. Prevention, especially, underlay innumerable escape attempts. Estate divisions and financial setbacks of slaveholders prompted enslaved people throughout the southern states to flee before their number was called, often even before any news of potential sale was issued. This occurred everywhere, but was especially prevalent in the supply regions of the domestic slave trade such as Virginia and Maryland, which incidentally also contained the South's largest free black populations and most expansive urban spaces of informal freedom to which enslaved people could run. Southern newspapers and county court records are replete with references to fugitive slaves who belonged to the "estate" of a slaveholder, meaning runaways who fled while negotiations over a possible sale were pending. Estate records from Baltimore County and Anne Arundel County, Maryland, where anonymity for runaway slaves could easily be found in nearby Baltimore, are illustrative. When Maryland slaveholder William Hayes passed away in 1807, three of his slaves wasted no time in taking advantage of a protracted lawsuit between the heirs to slip away, presumably to Baltimore. Court records reveal that "while this Business [between the heirs] was pending," the three bondsmen "absconded & Have never been Heard of Since." Another Maryland enslaved man named Sandy was caught trying to flee twice during an estate division in 1818 – the administrators requested permission from the courts to expedite Sandy's sale in order to avoid him fleeing again and inflicting "great injury to the Estate." Administrators for the Richard Wells estate in Anne Arundel County in 1819 complained to the courts that "there is now in Baltimore a Negro man belonging to the Estate," and that they were "apprehensive" that any attempt to track him down and apprehend him would cause him to "run off and be a total loss."[9]

When initial fears turned into concrete plans, enslaved people fled with even more frequency. Runaway slave ads and city jail records provide an abundance of illuminating examples. Fifty dollars reward was offered in North Carolina in 1822 for the apprehension of Jack, a "common mulatto, about 40 years of age," who took with him "his Wife and two Children." Running to prevent a possible separation, the family was suspected of "lurking in Fayetteville, Newbern, or Washington, amongst

[9] Petition of Elizabeth Hayes to the Orphans Court of Baltimore County, November 18, 1807, RSPP, Series 2: County Court Petitions, Accession #20980715; Petition of Osborn Belt Jr. to the Orphans Court of Anne Arundel County, September 15, 1818, RSPP, Series 2: County Court Petitions, Accession #20981823; Petition of Thomas S. Bowie and James Shaw to the Orphans Court of Anne Arundel County, April 22, 1819, RSPP, Series 2: County Court Petitions; Müller, "Cities of Refuge," 32–36.

the free negroes." In 1835 a forty-five-year-old slave woman named Mary, from the South Carolina lowcountry, disappeared among the free black population of Charleston (where she had a husband) when she was confronted with the prospect of moving over a 100 miles to the state capital. A runaway slave advertisement in the *Charleston Courier* admitted that "the cause of her running away was her dislike to be brought to Columbia." And Joe, a forty-five-year-old Maryland slave from Charles County, "ran off immediately after the appraisement" of his master's estate, "knowing that he was to be sold in a few weeks." Joe was suspected of "lurking about the neighborhood of Bryan Town" and passing for free. Some fugitives who absconded within the South were enslaved people who had recently arrived at urban marketplaces to be disposed of, who fled in last-ditch attempts to avoid removal. "Lucy M Downman['ls man [N]at absconded" upon arrival in Richmond in March 1834, for example, suspected of having disappeared among the city's large black population. Nat's owner "had Sent him to Richmond for Sale." Likewise, a "Slave Traders man Henry Jackson" disappeared in Richmond in 1834 to avoid being shipped south in the domestic slave trade.[10]

For those who were unable to *prevent* forced removal, fleeing served as a vehicle to reconnect with loved ones lost through forced migration. Many runaway slaves lurking about the southern states were themselves forced migrants who had already been sold away from their home communities, and who were running in order to see their families again. Rather than flee to destinations where they could be legally free, they more often fled "home," or to urban areas in the general vicinity of home. Enslaved people who had been sold or removed locally (within the same state or region) were often in the best position to do so. Maria Hamilton, for example, a twenty-four-year-old enslaved woman from Alexandria, DC, who was sold into the Virginia countryside in 1826, was suspected of having run either back to Alexandria, where she had a husband, or across the river to Washington City, where her (free) sister and brother-in-law lived: "She may in all probability have gone there." The runaway Osborn,

---

[10] *Raleigh Register and North Carolina Gazette*, April 26, 1822 (first quote); *Charleston Courier*, September 3, 1835 (second quote); Daybook of the Richmond, Virginia Police Guard, October 9, 1834 (third quote); Daybook of the Richmond, Virginia Police Guard, March 12, 1834, in "Daybook of the Richmond, Virginia Police Guard, 1834–1844," trans. by Leni Ashmore Sorensen, "Absconded: Fugitive Slaves in the Daybook of the Richmond Police Guard" (PhD diss., College of William & Mary, 2005), appendix A (fourth quote); Ibid., July 22, 1834 (fifth quote); Müller, "Cities of Refuge," 32–36.

newly purchased by one William Davison of Winchester, Virginia, had "expressed a desire to visit his relations" down the Potomac River in his home village of Nanjemoy, Maryland, and was suspected of hiding out there. The newspaper advertisement that announced the escape of Charles, who in 1848 absconded from his new plantation in St. John Baptist Parish, Louisiana, stated that he had been recently purchased from Natchez, "where he has a wife and children" and where he would presumably bend his course. A South Carolina slave family consisting of a man named Simon, who "appears much alarmed, and has a wild look," along with his wife Daphne and son Charles were sold away from their home community in the lowcountry to a planter living upcountry near Santee in the spring of 1822. They escaped, their master lamenting that they "were brought from the low country, and it is supposed they will endeavor to return."[11]

Remarkably, some fugitive slaves traversed (or attempted to traverse) truly vast distances in order to be reunited with families forcibly left behind. Southern newspapers and county court records from receiving societies of the domestic slave trade are full of references to forced migrants making ambitious attempts to return to far-off home communities. When Mathy, "a griff aged about 38 years," and his wife Litty, "black, aged about 35 years," ran away from a Louisiana plantation in the summer of 1845, they boarded a flatboat "on their way to South Alabama, where they were lately owned." William, who fled his new plantation near Lexington, South Carolina, in 1830, was presumed to be "mak[ing] his way for North Carolina, as he was purchased ... and brought from there." A Virginia enslaved woman named Patsey absconded from a Georgia plantation and was suspected to have "endeavored to get back to Virginia," where she had relations. Interstate migrant Nicholas similarly left his South Carolina plantation in an attempt "to make his way to Maryland," where he was originally from. Sally, originally owned by the estate of George Mason in northern Virginia but purchased by an Alabama slaveholder, ran away "a few days" after arriving in the Deep South, suspected of making her way back home. Six enslaved people between the ages of twenty-five and thirty – including one married couple – disappeared from a Georgia plantation in

---

[11] *Alexandria Gazette*, August 7, 1826 (first quote); *Alexandria Advertiser and Commercial Intelligencer*, July 9, 1803 (second quote); *Daily Picayune*, January 26, 1848 (third quote); *Charleston Courier*, May 25, 1822 (fourth quote); Müller, "Cities of Refuge," 32–36.

1849 and were suspected of "endeavoring to reach North Carolina, as they were brought from the latter State."[12]

The trajectories of some of these runaways speak volumes to how enslaved people viewed the landscape of freedom in the antebellum period. Free soil was tantalizingly close to some documented victims of forced migration, for example, and yet in their flight attempts they pointed their compasses home rather than to nearby spaces of more formal freedom. Family, in other words, appears to have been more important to them than legal freedom. Isaac, a Louisiana slave who was sold upriver to St. Louis in 1851, ran hundreds of miles back *south* in an attempt to reach Alexandria, Louisiana, despite the fact that the city of St. Louis bordered the free state of Illinois. Others amazingly even crossed *into* free states in order to return *south* to their home regions. "Five Negro Men" from Maryland who were sold to western Kentucky all absconded together in 1809, suspected of having "endeavor[ed] to get to Cincinnati" (in the free state of Ohio) and "from thence to Baltimore." The story of Tom, originally enslaved in Middleburg, in Virginia's Shenandoah Valley, similarly appears to defy all logic. As an adolescent Tom was sold to an interstate slave trader operating out of Richmond, who subsequently shipped him to New Orleans, where he lived for twenty years. Eventually Tom managed to escape the South altogether on board a vessel to Boston. His arrival in a free state – not just any free state but Massachusetts, the beating heart of abolitionist activity in antebellum North America – did little to assuage his homesickness, however. In an endeavor to get back to his home community in Virginia Tom reportedly "follow[ed] the water" back south until his luck ran out and he was finally apprehended in Norfolk, Virginia, in 1849, where he was thrown into jail. His Louisiana master was called upon to arrange for his transport back to the Deep South. In some cases enslaved people even ran to *follow* a loved one sold out of state. Dick, a thirty-seven-year-old slave from Kentucky, a border state, ran south all the way to New Orleans, where he attempted to pass for free in order to be with his wife, who was "living in that city" after being sold there. North Carolina bondsman Drew, traveling under the alias "Jerry," was arrested in 1839 after making a desperate attempt to get to his wife, "who had been taken to

---

[12] *The Times Picayune*, July 10, 1845 (first quote); *Charleston Courier*, March 7, 1835 (second quote); *Charleston Courier*, October 29, 1830 (third quote); *Huntsville Democrat*, June 16, 1838 (fourth quote); *Georgia Journal & Messenger*, December 19, 1849 (fifth quote).

Tennessee." Such flight attempts within the South may appear foolhardy on their surface, but serve as a remarkable testament to enslaved people's commitment to family reunification – even above formal freedom – amid the onslaught of forced migration.[13]

Whatever the distances they covered to avoid severing all ties to loved ones, fugitive slaves who remained within the South often tapped into networks that – eventually – led them to towns and cities. Some headed straight to their final destinations, running in the dead of the night, smuggling themselves onto riverboats or other vessels that called at busy ports all over the South, or, by the 1840s, even hopping onto the new railroad cars. An enslaved man named Aaron slipped away from his master in North Carolina in 1827 and was presumed to be traveling along the overland roads in an "endeavor to make his way to Virginia, whence he was originally brought." Aaron was trying to reach the city of Petersburg, where he was expected to "lurk about." An enslaved boy named Charles, only thirteen years old, escaped from a New Orleans boat captain in 1854 and was suspected of fleeing over water to southern Alabama, presumably by smuggling himself on board another vessel that plied the waters of the Gulf coast. His master was convinced that Charles would "endeavor to get to Mobile, where he has a sister living." Another Louisiana enslaved man named Charles Roger, who ran away to New Orleans from his native St. Charles Parish in the summer of 1849, simply "came to the city ... in the cars." Finding suitable towns and cities to run to was as simple as following the established roads, waterways, and train tracks that connected urban nodes throughout the southern states.[14]

Others, however, followed a more winding path. Many runaways arrived in urban areas indirectly, having fled first to family members in the countryside, who provided them with the means to sustain themselves for short periods of time. Runaways hiding out in the southern countryside were indeed usually suspected of being "harbored" by friends and family, within slave households or in the forests that bordered the

---

[13] *New Orleans Daily Picayune*, January 15, 1851 (first quote); *The Reporter* (Lexington, KY), December 2, 1809 (second quote); *New Orleans Daily Picayune*, March 13, 1849 (third quote); *Lexington Intelligencer*, July 7, 1838 (fourth quote); Petition of George Ruth to Chancery Court of Bedford County, TN, June 3, 1839, RSPP, Series 2, County Court Petitions, Accession #21483901 (fifth quote).

[14] *Raleigh Register and North Carolina Weekly Advertiser*, April 3, 1827 (first quote); *Daily Picayune*, June 15, 1854 (second quote); *New Orleans Picayune*, July 1, 1849 (third quote); Müller, "Cities of Refuge," 68–78; Franklin and Schweninger, *Runaway Slaves*, 109–111.

plantations or farms where they were originally from, effectively becoming what Sylviane Diouf has called "borderland maroons." Southern newspapers are full of ads for runaway slaves who were suspected of hiding out on or near plantations where they had intimate connections. In February 1850, for example, $100 reward was offered for "the arrest and conviction of the person who has harbored a slave contrary to law named MARGARET," who had been sold away from her native Lake Providence and was now "supposed to be at or near Lake Providence" again, hiding out near her old community. The master of Gilbo, a North Carolina runaway who absconded in 1828, suspected that he may "possibly be lurking" around the residence of his wife, who lived on another plantation. Another runaway from North Carolina named Frank Burr, described as "lazy [and] very talkative," had a father living at one "Mr. Pollock's farm," and was suspected of "lurking about the plantations of Mr. Pollock ... where he has connexions." Ramsay, enslaved in Hanover County, Virginia, ran away from his master in 1854 and was presumed to be hiding out somewhere in the vicinity of his "wife at Mr. Abram W. Skinner's ... near Suffolk."[15]

Such arrangements were desperate and often ad hoc by nature, and they were seldom intended to be permanent, even when they lasted months. Although in most cases they did *not* constitute truancy (these fugitives appear to have had no intentions of ever returning to slavery), they failed to provide sustainable long-lasting solutions to refugees' predicament. Fugitives who were harbored by loved ones in the countryside can more accurately be perceived as runaways in transit. Out of necessity most eventually felt compelled to move on, often to urban areas within a few days' radius of their home communities. In some cases fleeing to loved ones in the countryside and subsequently moving on to urban areas appears to have indeed been part of the plan in the first place. In 1849 a twenty-year-old enslaved man named Asa, originally from Georgia but sold to Chambers County, Alabama, fled his new owner and was

---

[15] *Daily Picayune*, February 21, 1850 (first quote); *North Carolina Sentinel*, August 9, 1828 (second quote); *Carolina Centinel*, March 1, 1820 (third quote); *Democratic Pioneer*, August 29, 1854 (fourth quote). See also Müller, "Cities of Refuge," 68–78; Rebecca Ginsburg, "Escaping through a Black Landscape," in Clifton Ellis and Rebecca Ginsburg, eds., *Cabin, Quarter, Plantation: Architecture and Landscapes of North American Slavery* (New Haven, CT: Yale University Press, 2010), 51–66; Anthony E. Kaye, *Joining Places: Slave Neighborhoods in the Old South* (Chapel Hill: University of North Carolina Press, 2009), 129–135. For a detailed analysis of long-term or even semi-permanent maroon communities in the American South, see Diouf, *Slavery's Exiles*.

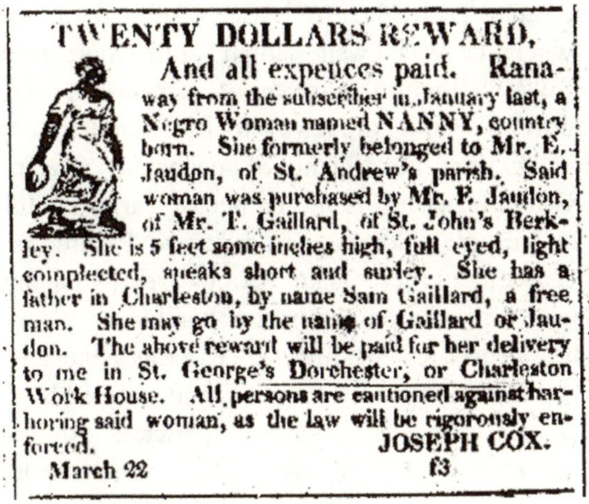

TWENTY DOLLARS REWARD,
And all expences paid. Rana-
way from the subscriber in January last, a
Negro Woman named NANNY, country
born. She formerly belonged to Mr. E.
Jaudon, of St. Andrew's parish. Said
woman was purchased by Mr. F. Jaudon,
of Mr. T. Gaillard, of St. John's Berk-
ley. She is 5 feet some inches high, full eyed, light
complected, speaks short and surley. She has a
father in Charleston, by name Sam Gaillard, a free
man. She may go by the name of Gaillard or Jaudon. The above reward will be paid for her delivery
to me in St. George's Dorchester, or Charleston
Work House. All persons are cautioned against harboring said woman, as the law will be rigorously enforced.   JOSEPH COX.
    March 22   f3

FIGURE 2.1 Runaway slave ad for Nanny, 1822.
Source: Charleston Courier, 3 April 1822.

suspected of having made his way back to Georgia. In the runaway slave ad that announced his escape, Asa's master warned that the fugitive was trying to get back to the "old plantation of George Whitfield" in Houston County, where he had connections, but that his ultimate plan was to "endeavor to get into Monroe," a town near Atlanta with cotton mills. In other words, Asa aimed to get to a town in Georgia *via* his home community in Houston County, which entailed a significant detour. Six years prior Asa had made a similar escape attempt and ended up passing for free in the town of Macon, even closer to Houston County, but had been caught and sent back to Alabama. This time he was going to try his luck further north in Monroe.[16]

Who Asa's contacts were in Monroe or Macon is a matter of conjecture, but freedom seekers who ended up in towns and cities within the South – whether directly or indirectly – rarely pointed their compasses to places where they had no contacts at all. In most cases they had relations, acquaintances, or connections further down in their social webs who already lived there and upon whom they could call for assistance (Figure 2.1). In certain parts of the South, especially in the immediate hinterlands of towns and cities, rural slave communities were well connected to urban African-American communities. Bob, a North Carolina

---

[16] *Georgia Journal and Messenger*, December 19, 1849 (quote). See also Müller, "Cities of Refuge," 68–78; Ginsburg, "Escaping through a Black Landscape," 51–66.

enslaved man, ran off in 1840 and was suspected of having run to
Stantonburg, where he was "well known" and where he had "a free
woman for a wife." Tarlton, a twenty-four-year-old carpenter from
Powhatan County, Virginia, ran away to Richmond in 1834 and was
suspected of hiding out at the residence of one Stephen Green, "a free man
who lives in Richmond [who] is the Father of Tarlton." Julia Johnson,
from Staunton, Virginia, likewise ran away to Richmond, the police
noting that her acquaintance "Isaac Adams free [was] Susp[ecte]d of
decoying hir [sic] off" and arranging for her hiding place in the city.
Molly, who disappeared in Alexandria, DC, was believed to be "connected with some evil disposed free negroes, and secreted by them." Rose,
who absconded her master in Beaufort District, South Carolina, was
"well known about Savannah, where it is supposed she is harbored."
Adam, from St. Andrews Parish in South Carolina, ran away to
Charleston in 1822 and was described as "well known in town." James
Lamar, who fled to New Orleans in 1845, was "harbored near the lower
vegetable market, by a free black woman" who sold "victuals and coffee
in said market." And Alexis, of Iberville Parish, Louisiana, ran away to
New Orleans in 1834 and lived with a free woman of color named Marie
Rose Hudson for four years before he was discovered and apprehended.[17]

Sometimes these contacts were family members, spouses, or lovers. But
enslaved people also established professional networks with urban black
communities as a result of hiring practices, during which they lived and
worked in towns and cities for months or even years at a time. The Upper
South in particular made extensive use of slave hiring in the antebellum
period, allowing enslaved people from the countryside to make contacts
and develop friendships with African Americans who would later be in a
position to assist them as runaways. A Virginia enslaved woman who
went missing in the District of Columbia in 1825 "had been hired in
Alexandria for some months past," her owner lamenting that "she is well
known" there and would no doubt be aided in her flight. In 1858 a
Maryland runaway named Sophie George was "believed to be among
associates formed in Washington where she has been often hired."

---

[17] *Tarboro Press*, February 1, 1840 (first quote); Daybook of the Richmond, Virginia Police
Guard, March 14, 1834 (second quote); Ibid., September 28, 1834 (third quote);
Alexandria Advertiser and Commercial Intelligencer, December 8, 1803 (fourth quote);
Georgia Gazette, February 20, 1800 (fifth quote); *Charleston Courier*, June 8, 1822
(sixth quote); *Daily Picayune*, November 2, 1845 (seventh quote); Petition of Auguste
Christin to the First District Court of Louisiana, April 28, 1838, RSPP, Series 2, County
Court Records, Accession #20883814.

Another runaway suspected of hiding out in Richmond in 1839 had "acquaintances working at almost every Tobacco factory in the place" due to previous hiring stints. Little did antebellum slaveholders know that by hiring out surplus enslaved people to towns and cities across the South, they provided them with opportunities to sow the seeds for future bids to self-emancipate.[18]

SETTLING IN AS BLACK TOWNSPEOPLE

Runaways' social networks not only informed their paths *to* town but also showed them the way upon arrival *in* town. Most gravitated to streets, neighborhoods, and houses where their free black contacts lived. Although free blacks by no means lived strictly segregated from white residents in most urban areas during the antebellum period, larger cities did have neighborhoods with relatively high concentrations of African Americans where runaways could more easily get lost in the crowd and where they were therefore more likely to end up. In Baltimore fugitives made for the harbor and Fell's Point in the early decades of the nineteenth century; after the 1830s they followed free blacks out to the "cheap tenement housing" in the "maze of alleyways and court-yards" in the Western Precincts, as historian Christopher Phillips described it, where the poor laboring classes lived. In the District of Columbia free black neighborhoods were dispersed throughout Washington City and the federal territory, including across the river in Alexandria, where the earliest pockets arose in areas known as The Bottoms, Hayti, Uptown, and Fishtown. In Richmond African Americans crowded together in industrial and low-lying neighborhoods such as Shockoe Creek, Bacon Bottom, and Jackson Ward, but also in shanties just beyond the city limits where night watchmen rarely ventured. In Charleston free blacks lived concentrated in several streets around town, but almost two-thirds lived in shacks in the upper wards on the Neck, an overcrowded area that was described by a grand jury in 1856 in unflattering terms:

---

[18] *Daily National Intelligencer*, February 20, 1826 (first quote); *National Intelligencer*, November 16, 1858 (second quote); Viola Franziska Müller, "Illegal but Tolerated: Slave Refugees in Richmond, Virginia, 1800–1860," in Damian Alan Pargas, ed., *Fugitive Slaves and Spaces of Freedom in North America* (Gainesville: University Press of Florida, 2018), 147 (second quote); Franklin and Schweninger, *Runaway Slaves*, 134–148.

In these negro rows as many as fifty to one hundred negroes, or free persons of color, are sometimes residing, shut out from the public street by a gate, all the buildings having but one common yard, and not a single white person on the premises.

The ramshackle tenements were considered a violation of the city's prohibition of black assembly. In New Orleans free blacks lived dispersed throughout the city, but most lived concentrated in specific neighborhoods, especially the 5th, 6th, and 7th Wards, pockets of which constituted "the safest hiding places for runaway slaves," according to one incensed local slaveholder, writing in the *Daily Picayune* in 1859. Even smaller towns and cities had free black "streets" or "neighborhoods" – Springfield in Augusta, Georgia; Pitt and Charles Streets in Fredericksburg, Virginia. Neighborhoods such as these became prime destinations for runaways seeking cover and assistance.[19]

Free African Americans throughout the South received, assisted, and harbored fugitive slaves at great risk to their own bodies, lives, and freedom. All southern cities and states repeatedly passed and renewed legislation that threatened free black residents with heavy penalties for hiding or in any way helping to hide runaways, and court records reveal plenty of examples of offenders being taken up and dragged in front of a magistrate. North Carolina defined "harboring or maintaining a runaway slave" as "secretly aiding him *by any means* to continue absent from his master, knowing at the time of rendering such aid, that he was a runaway." The North Carolina courts routinely convicted free blacks for "secretly, clandestinely and fraudulently harboring and maintaining a runaway slave ... in open disregard of the rights of the owner." The General Assembly of Virginia specified that any free person "concerned in the escape of any slave" would receive a prison sentence of five to ten years and a public whipping, a penalty that was certainly enforced on occasion. One free black man in Richmond was whipped in 1853 for

---

[19] Phillips, *Freedom's Port*, 104–105 (first quote); Müller, "Illegal but Tolerated," 149; Elsa Barkley Brown and Gregg Kimball, "Mapping the Terrain of Black Richmond," *Journal of Urban History* 21, no. 3 (1995): 302; Midori Takagi, *"Rearing Wolves to Our Own Destruction": Slavery in Richmond, Virginia, 1782–1865* (Charlottesville: University of Virginia Press, 1999); Bernard E. Powers, *Black Charlestonians: A Social History, 1822–1885* (Fayetteville: University of Arkansas Press, 1994), 25 (second quote); Müller, "Cities of Refuge," 98–105; *Daily Picayune*, October 22, 1859 (third quote); Ruth C. Fitzgerald, *A Different Story: A Black History of Fredericksburg, Stafford, and Spotsylvania* (Fredericksburg, VA: Unicorn, 1979); Richard C. Wade, *Slavery in the Cities: The South, 1820–1860* (New York: Oxford University Press, 1964), 150–151.

allowing a fugitive slave to live in his cellar; a year later another Petersburg resident was brought before the mayor's court for harboring several runaways at his residence. In many southern jurisdictions harboring a fugitive slave was not only a crime in and of itself but was also considered a form of grand theft. The District of Columbia threatened any free person who assisted a runaway slave with theft of the same, and subject to compensation for the full value of the runaway and/or one year in prison. The General Assembly of Mississippi, following the examples set by southern states with larger free black populations and exasperated by the assistance provided to runaway slaves by free blacks in Natchez and Jackson, passed a similar law in 1839 stating that any free black who helped a slave "to escape from his or her master or owner" would be found guilty of "feloniously stealing [said] slave or slaves." The fines slapped on free blacks who defied such laws were often exorbitant indeed. Celeste Bertrand, a "free woman of color" living in New Orleans who was charged with feloniously hiding a runaway slave in her home for seven months in 1847, was ordered to pay a fine of $403 for theft, plus $35 for advertising fees related to the runaway and another $50 for the reward offered to the person who ultimately discovered and apprehended the runaway.[20]

The laws and penalties for harboring runaway slaves were similarly harsh throughout the southern states, but they did not always serve as effective deterrents to free African Americans determined to provide assistance and protection to runaways in need. The most logical explanation for the assistance provided by free blacks to runaway slaves in most urban areas was their social proximity to – and interconnectedness with – enslaved people. Due to the ad hoc and often clumsy execution of manumissions in the postrevolutionary period, most southern free blacks were closely related to, and remained in close contact with, enslaved people, as explained above. But solidarity among free and enslaved

---

[20] *The State v. John Hathaway*, June 1838, North Carolina Supreme Court, Raleigh, NC (Slavery, Abolition, and Social Justice Database, Leiden University) (first quote, italics mine); William A. Link, *Roots of Secession: Slavery and Politics in Antebellum Virginia* (Chapel Hill: University of North Carolina Press, 2005), 104–105 (second quote); Worthington G. Snethen, *The Black Code of the District of Columbia, in Force September 1ˢᵗ, 1848* (New York: A.&F., W. Harned, 1848), 19; T. J. Fox Alden and J. A. van Hoesen, *Digest of the Laws of Mississippi, Comprising All the Laws of a General Nature, Including the Acts of Session of 1839* (New York: Alexander Gould, 1839), 763 (third quote); Petition of Adelaide Detilly Vinot, Orleans Parish, May 17, 1848, RSPP, Accession #20884862. See also Maris-Wolf, *Family Bonds*; Franklin and Schweninger, *Runaway Slaves*, 109–110.

African Americans may also have been strongly influenced by shared experiences and a common plight. As Ira Berlin argued in his seminal work *Slaves without Masters*, free blacks and enslaved people in most southern towns and cities had much more in common than their different legal statuses would suggest. Barred from certain occupations, denied political and civil rights, subjected to the harshest executions of justice (including reenslavement) without being allowed to testify in court on their own behalf, harassed by night watchmen and patrols for violating curfews and prohibitions of assembly, and generally relegated to abject poverty, free African Americans were only a few short steps removed from their enslaved brothers and sisters. Black Codes in all southern states became increasingly harsh in the Jacksonian years and nowhere were free blacks afforded the rights and privileges that free whites enjoyed. By 1835 most southern legislatures had indeed barred free blacks from other states from entering or residing in their states without special permission; required manumitted slaves to leave the state; dictated that free blacks who could not prove themselves to be "industrious" enough could be forcibly hired out; and flatly denied that free blacks were citizens at all. The Arkansas courts bluntly declared in 1846 that free blacks held "a kind of quasi citizenship," and Georgia passed a unanimous resolution in 1842 that denied free blacks US citizenship and declared them in a state of "pupilage." Both Louisiana and Florida passed laws that encouraged free blacks to seek out white guardians for their own protection. These restraints and restrictions on their freedom were not always enforced, but their threat was always present and may have made free blacks identify more strongly with the enslaved population – and show more empathy with the plight of runaways – than their legal status would suggest.[21]

Indeed, the black populations of most southern towns and cities consisted of such a wide and blurry spectrum of legal statuses that it is difficult to neatly split them into "free" and "slave," and it is likely that they themselves did not see as much difference between each other as one might assume. Among the legally unfree were of course runaways and

---

[21] Rogers M. Smith, *Civic Ideals: Conflicting Visions of Citizenship in U.S. History* (New Haven, CT: Yale University Press, 1997), 253–258; Berlin, *Slaves without Masters*; Seth Rockman, *Scraping By: Wage Labor, Slavery, and Survival in Early Baltimore* (Baltimore: Johns Hopkins University Press, 2009), 16–44; Kaye, "Neighborhoods and Solidarity in the Natchez District," 1–24; Müller, "Cities of Refuge," 98–117; Michael P. Johnson, "Runaway Slaves and Slave Communities in South Carolina, 1799–1830," *William & Mary Quarterly* 38, no. 3 (1981): 418–441.

urban slaves, but there were also in-between categories such as urban hirelings, who were legally enslaved but many of whom lived apart from their masters, much like free blacks. Though widely condemned and even illegal, "living out" was not uncommon for hirelings throughout the urban South. In Richmond, tobacco factories and ironworks gave hirelings a dollar per week to rent their own rooms in town. Tom and West, two enslaved men from Prince Edward County, Virginia, were sent by their master to Richmond to hire themselves out and find their own lodgings – they were arrested by Richmond authorities. Frederick Law Olmsted, the famous journalist for the *New York Daily Times*, visited a Virginia coal-mining town in 1853 where the miners – the majority of whom were hired slaves – were given a certain amount to find their own boarding arrangements. In Charleston a full 15 percent of the slave population in 1860 consisted of hirelings who lived apart from their owners, and who saw them only once a week to collect their earnings. Hirelings who "lived out" often acted and appeared free to casual observers – indeed, they themselves often claimed as much in postbellum interviews and memoirs. Isaac Throgmorton, a Kentucky slave who was allowed to hire his own time in Louisville, arranged to live with free blacks, boasting in an interview that "it was just as though I was free." Other "slaves" in southern towns fell into yet another curious category of the unfree: those owned by free black family members who were unable to – or declined to – manumit them due to the increased restrictions on manumission in the antebellum period. Although legally enslaved, these people also lived like (and with) free blacks. And then there were the various categories of the free, which included free blacks who for one reason or another resided illegally in town – who were denied permits, for example, or who had somehow lost their free papers. The most secure urban free blacks were those who resided legally and who were in possession of their free papers, but even they were subject to discrimination and regular harassment by city authorities and white residents.[22]

---

[22] Jonathan D. Martin, *Divided Mastery: Slave Hiring in the American South* (Cambridge, MA: Harvard University Press, 2004), 164–168; Wade, *Slavery in the Cities*, 62–75; Takagi, *"Rearing Wolves to Our Own Destruction,"* 37–40; Schermerhorn, *Money over Mastery, Family over Freedom*, 135–140; Nancy C. Frantel, comp., *Richmond, Virginia Uncovered: The Records of Slaves and Free Blacks Listed in the City Sergeant Jail Register, 1841–1846* (Richmond, VA: Heritage Books, 2010), 30; Frederick Law Olmsted, *A Journey in the Seaboard Slave States; with Remarks on Their Economy* (New York: Dix and Edwards, 1856), 47; Isaac Throgmorton, in John W. Blassingame, ed., *Slave Testimony: Two Centuries of Letters, Speeches, Interviews, and*

Not only were various categories of free and unfree African Americans
in southern towns and cities often virtually indistinguishable in public
spaces, but they intermingled to such an extent that they often formed a
single polyglot urban community. They worked together, lived together,
frequented the same taverns and grog shops, established families across
legal lines, and worshipped together. Free black churches in particular
formed the center of urban black social life – of all legal categories – and
proved a vital lifeline to runaway slaves who wished to live in freedom
and integrate with free African Americans. Most southern cities contained
at least one free black church, often of a Baptist or Methodist denomin-
ation, which served both the enslaved and free black communities. The
District of Columbia had the well-known Alfred Street Baptist Church
(originally called the First African Baptist Church, established in 1803) in
the Bottoms neighborhood of Alexandria, for example; Richmond established a First African Baptist Church in 1841; Charleston had an African
Methodist Episcopal (AME) Church until 1822, when city authorities
destroyed it in the wake of the Denmark Vesey insurrection plot;
Savannah had a First and Second African Baptist Church by the 1850s;
Baltimore had at least eight established free black churches, both Baptist
and AME; and New Orleans was home to at least four black Methodist
churches before the Civil War. Born out of a desire for racial segregation
in the spiritual sphere, white townspeople spawned independent free
black churches by kicking out free black worshippers from their own
churches, but then ironically often complained about the existence of free
black churches in their midst, precisely because they perceived them to be
harborers of runaways and agitators of freedom. Concerned residents in
Charleston in 1820 objected to plans to establish another free black
church in their city, considering it "highly impolitic & dangerous" to
allow an institution that might attract African Americans "bond and
free" to flock to their city.[23]

Autobiographies (Baton Rouge: Louisiana State University Press, 1977), 432–433
(quote); Müller, "Cities of Refuge," 98–117.

[23] Albert J. Raboteau, *Slave Religion: The "Invisible Institution" in the Antebellum South*
(New York: Oxford University Press, 2004), 85; Berlin, *Generations of Captivity*; Müller,
"Illegal but Tolerated," 150–151; Jason Poole, "On Borrowed Ground: Free African-
American Life in Charleston, South Carolina, 1810–61," *Essays in History* 36 (1994):
1–33; Rashauna Johnson, *Slavery's Metropolis: Unfree Labor in New Orleans during the
Age of Revolutions* (New York: Cambridge University Press, 2016); Whittington
B. Johnson, *Black Savannah, 1788–1864* (Fayetteville: University of Arkansas Press,
1999), 113; Christopher Phillips, "'Negroes and Other Slaves': The African American
Community of Baltimore, 1790–1860" (PhD diss., University of Georgia, 1992), 7;

Black life in southern towns and cities, in short, tended to connect and integrate African Americans from a wide variety of legal categories. The city of Richmond – home to a sizeable black population with a dizzying variety of legal categories, of which documented free people always formed a minority – serves as an illuminating case study. Virginia experienced a significant wave of manumissions after the American Revolution, but, as noted in Chapter 1, the doors to manumission closed again in 1806. In that year the Virginia General Assembly not only made it far more difficult for slaves to be manumitted, but it also required all manumitted slaves to leave the state within twelve months (a precedent later taken up by other southern states as well). Most did not, either because they refused to leave their loved ones still in slavery, or because they lacked the means to emigrate. This left the state with a large population of free blacks who had free papers, but who were residing illegally in the state. Many of these illegal residents – according to one estimate literally thousands – gravitated to urban centers such as Richmond.[24]

Virginia's deportation requirement was difficult to enforce and largely ignored, but when it was enforced it often resulted in confusing legal quandaries and confronted free African Americans with an excruciating choice: either leave their loved ones behind and retain their freedom, or submit to reenslavement. Research by Ted Maris-Wolf shows that between 1854 and 1864 more than 100 free African Americans who were threatened with deportation actually volunteered to be reenslaved in order to prevent separations with loved ones. Other illegal residents were denied a choice at all and forcibly reenslaved. Lucy Wright and Lucy Claiborne, for example, were manumitted by their master in 1813, but neither one of them had "the means to emigrate," and so they both made their way to Richmond and illegally took up residence there. In 1821 they were picked up by the overseers of the poor and, unable to provide a good reason for why they were still in the state of Virginia, declared slaves again. By then they each had two children, however, whom the Richmond city courts – apparently confused about their own state laws – declared

Petition of William C. Meggett et al. to the General Assembly of South Carolina, 1820, RSPP, Series 1, Legislative Petitions, Accession #11382008.

[24] General Assembly of Virginia, "An ACT to Amend the Several Laws Concerning Slaves" (1806); Müller, "Illegal but Tolerated," 142; A. Leon Higginbotham, *In the Matter of Color: Race and the American Legal Process. The Colonial Period* (New York: Oxford University Press, 1978), 206; Müller, "Cities of Refuge," 42–49; Kolchin, *American Slavery*, 82–84; Martha S. Jones, *Birthright Citizens: A History of Race and Rights in Antebellum America* (New York: Cambridge University Press, 2018), 4–5, 19, 24.

free-born, despite having been born after the twelve-month deportation deadline whereby their mothers were legally considered reenslaved. William, another Virginia slave who was emancipated in 1819, illegally resided in Richmond for almost twenty years before finally being arrested in 1838. For violating the deportation order he was also forcibly reenslaved and sold at public auction, but managed to escape and fled to New York. Though rare, such cases sent shock waves throughout Richmond's African-American community.[25]

Ironically, because manumission became so difficult after 1806, the heirs of some Virginia slaveholders who specified in their wills that certain slaves should be "freed" simply let their bondspeople loose, providing little more than an oral guarantee that they were free but without bothering to obtain the proper papers (which in most cases would have been denied). Many of these freedpeople gravitated to Richmond as well, further complicating the already confusing spectrum of black legal statuses in that city. On top of that, the city teemed with a wide spectrum of unfree African Americans: hirelings who "lived out," urban slaves, "slaves" owned by free black family members, and runaways. In short, Richmond's black population was far too varied and confusing to fall into the neat legal categories established by the US census enumerators. By 1850 Richmond was *officially* home to more than 10,000 enslaved people (roughly half of them hirelings) and 2,400 free blacks. But the actual black population was much higher – so much so that indeed the city authorities themselves did not know how many black people resided in their city or what their exact legal status was. Any African American on the streets of antebellum Richmond could be a free black, a free black residing illegally in the state, an enslaved person, a hired slave who lived independently of his or her master, or a runaway slave who was pretending to be free. African Americans from various legal categories lived in the same neighborhoods and boarded in the same boarding houses, worked together at the same job sites, socialized together, and attended the same First African Baptist Church. Indeed, the minute book of the church, which contained a separate column to note the legal status of members, reveals just how interconnected Richmond's black population was by the

---

[25] Petition of Lucy Wright and Lucy Claiborne to the Senate and House of Delegates of Virginia, December 1821, RSPP, Series 1, Legislative Petitions, Accession #11682109; Petition of Richard S. Rice to the General Assembly of Virginia, January 5, 1840, RSPP, Series 1, Legislative Petitions, Accession #11684004; Müller, "Illegal but Tolerated," 142–149; Müller, "Cities of Refuge," 42–49; Maris-Wolf, *Family Bonds*, esp. 207. Maris-Wolf found that the expulsion requirement was rarely enforced in Virginia.

1840s and 1850s. Church officials conducted marriages between free and unfree African Americans, for example, as well as baptisms and funerals for members whose legal status was either unknown or in question. Next to some members' names, for example, the legal status column was left blank; next to others church officials wrote "free?" Such blurred lines between legal categories in a major city such as Richmond worked in runaways' favor, as it increased anonymity and a sense of solidarity and identification among African Americans of all legal categories.[26]

An inherent solidarity between free African Americans and runaway slaves could never be *assumed*, however, and in some southern cities free blacks very publicly disassociated themselves from "lesser" enslaved people in an attempt to mitigate white persecution and discrimination. Charleston and New Orleans, where hierarchies of skin color and class divided urban black populations, provide the clearest examples. In Charleston free blacks indeed defined themselves in opposition to slavery, going so far as to establish elitist mutual aid societies – the Brown Fellowship Society (established by and for free mulattoes in 1790), and the Free Dark Men of Color (established by and for the black elite in 1791) – with the intention of closing ranks and improving the lives of their members to the exclusion of other African Americans. New Orleans' mixed-race *gens de couleur libres* famously constituted an exclusive and elitist racial class that routinely rubbed shoulders with the city's white elite. That is not to say that runaway slaves were not harbored by free blacks in these cities – clearly they were. But such divisions underscore the importance of *personal contacts* for freedom seekers in the urban South. Runaways could not simply knock on the door of an anonymous free African American and assume protection or assistance. Those who gravitated to urban areas usually had specific personal contacts upon whom they depended to keep their true identities hidden and help them navigate city life.[27]

---

[26] Müller, "Illegal but Tolerated," 141–142, 150–151; Maris-Wolf, *Family Bonds*, 207; Frantel, *Richmond, Virginia Uncovered*; Gregg D. Kimball, *American City, Southern Place: A Cultural History of Antebellum Richmond* (Athens: University of Georgia Press, 2000); Raboteau, *Slave Religion*, 197. For examples of unclear status of black members of the FABC, see for example First African Baptist Church (Richmond, VA) Minute Books, 1841–1930, July 2, 1848 and May 12, 1849 (Library of Virginia, Richmond, VA).

[27] Poole, "On Borrowed Ground," 33; Junius P. Rodriguez, "Ripe for Revolt: Louisiana and the Tradition of Slave Insurrection, 1803–1865" (PhD diss., Auburn University, 1992), 47–48; Kimberly S. Hanger, *Bounded Lives, Bounded Places: Free Black Society in Colonial New Orleans, 1769–1803* (Durham, NC: Duke University Press, 1999);

"Lurking about" and navigating public spaces in southern towns and cities did not entail remaining physically invisible to the hustle and bustle, of course. Few runaways went into permanent hiding in the cellars, attics, or backyard kitchens of free blacks' homes, the way Harriet Jacobs famously did in Edenton, North Carolina, for example. Quite the opposite was true. In urban areas refugees from slavery entered spaces where they could walk down the street in broad daylight, and where they could realistically attempt to establish a *permanent* base for themselves in informal freedom – a freedom that did not exist on paper but that de facto allowed them to escape bondage. Anonymity was the key to their doing so successfully. The social transformations of the revolutionary era, as Ira Berlin put it, "broke the coincidence between blackness and slavery" in urban areas. "No longer could every black person be presumed a slave." Presumptions of freedom allowed runaways to get lost in the crowd and largely conceal their true identities and slave status. Their most important strategies for successfully doing so entailed changing or adapting their appearances. As Amani Marshall has argued, successful procurement of informal freedom in southern cities required runaway slaves to assume "free identities," which they did by engaging in "intricate performances in which they exploited colour, dress, language, and employment skills to transcend lines of race and class." For slave refugees, passing for free meant *looking* and *acting* free. Visibility was everything – erasing all markers of their slave identity was the key to navigating urban spaces.[28]

For some runaways, exploiting presumptions of freedom related to skin color facilitated their ability to navigate public urban spaces. Intriguingly, there are cases of light-skinned runaways who attempted – sometimes successfully – to pass for *white*. Granderson, a twenty-three-year-old carpenter from North Carolina who ran away to Washington, was "remarkably white for a slave, and might be readily taken for a white man … His eyes are blue, his hair very straight … His purpose is doubtless to pass as a free man." Louisa, a mulatto slave woman from

---

Johnson, *Slavery's Metropolis*, 85–124. Anthony Kaye has similarly underscored the importance of personal contacts for fugitive slaves in Natchez, and the hesitation of many free blacks in that city to harbor "strangers." See Kaye, "Neighborhoods and Solidarity in the Natchez District," 1–24.

[28] Ira Berlin, *The Making of African America: The Four Great Migrations* (New York: Penguin, 2010), 90 (quote); Amani Marshall, "'They Will Endeavor to Pass for Free': Enslaved Runaways' Performances of Freedom in Antebellum South Carolina," *Slavery & Abolition* 31, no. 2 (June 2010): 161–180, 161 (second quote).

Louisiana, was discovered to be living in New Orleans "where she was living as Joseph Tisdale's concubine and passing for a white free person" in 1848. Dick Frazier, a runaway originally from Columbia, South Carolina, was "lately known to be working about the Railroad in Alabama, near Moore's Turn Out, and passed as a white man by the name of *Jesse Teams*."[29]

Such cases were exceptions to the rule, but in some southern cities – again, most notably New Orleans and Charleston – most free blacks were light-skinned African Americans, providing mixed-race runaway slaves with clear advantages for disguising their true identities and evading detection. Antebellum newspapers from New Orleans are replete with runaway slave ads for light-skinned fugitives attempting to pass for free. In 1854 one runaway slave woman named Mildred who was presumed to be passing for free in the city was described as "griffe color" and "has straight hair." Valentin, a twenty-year-old "mulatto boy" from a plantation in Lafourche Interior, ran away to New Orleans in 1846 and expected "to try to pass for free." Philander, a "bright mulatto" with "straight hair" from East Feliciana Parish, ran away to New Orleans in 1845 and had been heard to be working there as a free carpenter. In Charleston, fully 73 percent of the "free people of color" in 1860 were mulattoes, similarly facilitating the escape attempts of light-skinned enslaved people who fled to that city from its hinterlands. Merriman, a "Mulatto Fellow" from the vicinity of Statesburg, South Carolina, who was often sent to Charleston to run errands for his master, disappeared after one such errand in 1822 and was presumed to be living as a free man in the neighborhood where his free wife also lived. Clarinda, a runaway with a "yellow complexion" also ran away to Charleston, where she was "well known" and had "many relatives."[30]

In other parts of the South, however – certainly in the Upper South – the link between light skin and freedom was far less important. For the vast majority of refugees in southern cities, looking and acting like free

---

[29] *Daily National Intelligencer*, July 4, 1825 (first quote); Petition of Mary Amelia Wilson Tisdale to the Fifth District Court of Louisiana, November 9, 1848, RSPP, Series 2, County Court Petitions, Accession #20884846 (second quote); *Daily Picayune*, August 14, 1846 (third quote).

[30] *Daily Picayune*, December 1, 1854 (first quote); *Daily Picayune*, September 17, 1854 (second quote); *Daily Picayune*, June 24, 1825 (third quote); *Charleston Courier*, March 27, 1822 (fourth quote); Ibid., April 13, 1822 (fifth quote). For more on the importance of complexion in facilitating escape to southern cities such as Charleston and New Orleans, see Müller, "Cities of Refuge," 80–81.

blacks entailed more theater than anything else, whether they were light-skinned or not. Indeed, upon arrival in urban areas, or even during the flight attempt itself, runaways' first order of business was often to procure the more fanciful clothing of the free black population to replace the ragged clothes that gave them away as country slaves. Sam, "an artful fellow" from eastern Maryland who had been sold to Kentucky, was presumed to have made his way all the way back to his native town "and will probably exchange his dress" to disguise his slave status. One runaway slave who was suspected of lurking about Livingston, Alabama, was seen wearing "a black cashmere over-coat ... and a silver huntsman's watch," no garb for a slave. Louisa, a "Mulatto Girl" from South Carolina who ran away to Charleston in 1822, was supposed to have "taken more than one dress with her, [and] it is likely she will change often." A young enslaved man named "JIM or ARMSTEAD, aged about 22 years," who had been sold away from his home in Tennessee to New Orleans and subsequently to Alabama, ran away in 1838 and was presumed to have gone to Nashville, where his mother – a free black woman – lived. The runaway sported "a fur cap, brown cloth frock coat, boots, &c.; had with him a variety of clothing, description not recollected, and will most likely dress very well and in newest fashion." He even ran off in style on the back of "a large bay horse ... with a Spanish saddle quilted cover." It is unlikely any resident of Nashville would have taken the runaway for a slave from an Alabama plantation when he strode into the city.[31]

The physical appearance of legal freedom was crucial not only for navigating public spaces anonymously but also for finding employment and making a living. Southern towns and cities were attractive destinations for permanent freedom seekers in part because they provided them with opportunities to perform various occupations and earn money to sustain themselves indefinitely. This they did by hiring out their services as if they were free – which meant looking and acting free – to the great consternation of slaveholders throughout the South, who often explicitly warned white urban residents against employing their escaped slaves in the mistaken belief that they were free blacks. Runaway slave

---

[31] *Frankfort Argus*, May 28, 1814 (first quote); *Mississippi and State Gazette*, September 5, 1851 (second quote); *Charleston Courier*, May 25, 1822 (third quote); *Tennessee Republican Banner*, December 26, 1838, (fourth quotes); see also appendix 1 in Franklin and Schweninger, *Runaway Slaves*, 298; Shane White and Graham White, "Slave Clothing and African-American Culture in the Eighteenth and Nineteenth Centuries," *Past & Present* 148, no. 1 (1995): 166.

advertisements regularly included cautionary warnings. When an enslaved man named Cyrus absconded from his master's residence in Louisiana in 1853, for example, the runaway slave ad that announced his disappearance suggested that he had gone to New Orleans and "may probably be at work on the Levee .... Masters of steamboats are warned against employing said boy." The master of Sidney, who was "lurking about the town" of New Bern, North Carolina, in 1838, similarly cautioned the town's residents against "harboring [or] employing" the runaway, "as the law will be rigorously enforced against anyone so offending." The owner of George, a South Carolina enslaved man who ran away to Charleston in 1825 and was "well known in this city as a Tailor," warned the city's residents "against employing ... the said Fellow, as the law will be rigidly enforced against them." Such phrasing was common.[32]

Skilled enslaved men were often in the best position to hire themselves as if they were free, as their services were in high demand in urban centers and their occupations were often associated with economic activities usually performed by free blacks. Indeed, both the confidence felt by skilled slaves and their expansive professional networks made them more prone to run away to southern towns and cities in the first place. Runaway slave ads from throughout the southern states confirm that skilled men – from carpenters to river pilots to cigar makers – tended to flee to urban areas within the South with remarkable frequency. In the summer of 1849, for example, $500 reward was offered for the apprehension of four bondsmen from a plantation in Rowland's Springs, Georgia, all of them skilled men endeavoring to get to Charleston: Two "first rate carpenters," a "first rate blacksmith," and a "tinner by trade" named Hercules who had been sold to Georgia from the South Carolina low-country and who therefore had an added incentive to flee to Charleston. Similarly, in 1813 a twenty-two-year-old mulatto slave named Joseph, who had been trained as a tailor, ran away from his master in Ascension Parish, Louisiana, and made for New Orleans, where he was able to sustain himself for over a year until he was discovered to be a runaway slave and thrown into jail. Edmund, a Louisiana runaway who escaped to

---

[32] Louisiana Runaway Slave Advertisements, 1836–1865, Louisiana Digital Library, Baton Rouge, LA, RSA00001178 (first quote); *Newbern Spectator and Literary Journal*, June 15, 1838 (second quote); *Charleston Courier*, January 8, 1825 (third quote); Judith Kelleher Schafer, "New Orleans Slavery in 1850 as Seen in Advertisements," *Journal of Southern History* 47, no. 1 (1981): 33–56.

New Orleans in 1854 and was suspected of lurking about the Second District, was described as "a cook, and will endeavor to get employment in that capacity." Henry Wilson, from a cotton plantation in Iberville Parish, Louisiana, likewise ran away to New Orleans and was known to be "working in this city" and "attempt[ing] to pass himself off for a free man." Henry was described as "a good brick layer, plasterer, and mattress maker, can read and write well, and has some pretensions to preaching." Dick, also suspected of hiding out in New Orleans, was advertised as "a good butcher, horse-breaker, house painter, cook, and whitewasher, and a fair shoemaker." Such descriptions are common in antebellum southern newspapers.[33]

Yet it is important not to overemphasize opportunities for enslaved men to actually *perform* highly specialized occupations upon arrival in southern towns and cities, even those who were skilled in a particular trade. Practicing a skilled profession may have seemed like an obvious and lucrative way to sustain oneself, but it also made runaways more easily identifiable and vulnerable to recapture. Recent research on urban runaways by Viola Müller reveals that in some southern cities fugitives felt a particular imperative to seek employment in "low profile jobs" so as to avoid detection, whatever their previous training on the plantation – at least upon arrival, when they were still afraid of recapture and attempting to get settled. Much depended on the skill, city, and amount of risk a runaway was willing to take to earn some money. A black tailor in a black neighborhood of a large city such as New Orleans, or a lowcountry river pilot plying into and out of a bustling port such as Charleston (where virtually all river pilots were black), may not have aroused much suspicion, for example. But for most male runaways, ordinary day labor – on

---

[33] Müller, "Cities of Refugees," 51–88, 119–159; *Greenville Mountaineer*, August 17, 1849 (first quote); Petition of Antoine Bayon to the Second District Court of Louisiana, April 26, 1814, RSPP, Series 2, County Court Petitions, Accession #20881457; *Daily Picayune*, April 20, 1854 (third quote); *Daily Picayune*, January 13, 1846 (fourth quote); *Daily Picayune*, August 14, 1846 (fifth quote). Scholarship has consistently shown that skilled enslaved men were often overrepresented in antebellum runaway slave ads. Franklin and Schweninger, *Runaway Slaves*, 135. Larry Rivers recently argued in his study of slave resistance in antebellum Florida that an exceptionally high proportion of male runaways in that state were skilled, especially carpenters, blacksmiths, and river pilots. See Larry Eugene Rivers, *Rebels and Runaways: Slave Resistance in Nineteenth-Century Florida* (Urbana: University of Illinois Press, 2012), 66–67. A study of runaway slave profiles in North Carolina comes to the same conclusion, with blacksmiths, carpenters, coopers, and shoemakers heavily overrepresented in runaways from that state. See Freddie L. Parker, "Runaway Slaves in North Carolina, 1775 to 1835" (PhD diss., University of North Carolina, 1987), 197–199.

construction sites, as stevedores loading and unloading vessels in the wharves of port towns, laying railroad track, peddling produce in market halls, working in tobacco factories and flour mills – not only provided regular opportunities to earn a dollar, but were also the safest options. The prevalence of black laborers and high turnover rates in such "low profile" sectors made it difficult for employers or the authorities to keep track of who was employed at any given time, much less figure out their legal status. In Richmond (and its vicinity) runaways easily found work at tobacco factories, in coal pits, and with construction companies. In other cities runaways gravitated to crowded harbors and busy market halls. Ben Elliott, a twenty-five-year-old runaway originally from Charleston but sold to Augusta in 1833, had been missing for five months before his new master placed an advertisement in the *Charleston Courier* for his recapture. Ben was presumed to be hiding out with his mother in Charleston, a free woman "named Pheobe Elliott, who sells fruit in the market," and he was heard to be passing himself off as a free black and "working about the wharves, and on board vessels, as a Stevedore or an Assistant." Peter Youngblood fled his new Charleston residence for the town of Beaufort, "as he has a wife on Mrs. Hamilton's Plantation, in that neighborhood." He, too, was suspected of working about the waterfront and being "employed in fishing in the neighborhood of that city." Wilson, a Louisiana runaway who crafted a life of informal freedom for himself at New Orleans, was "seen many times" working "on board steamboats" and as a "marchand at the market house of the First Municipality."[34]

Opportunities for runaways to find either skilled or unskilled labor in any sector were always more readily available for men than women, which may explain why young men in their twenties and thirties ran away to southern towns and cities with more frequency than women. Historians have consistently argued that enslaved men were more likely to run away – to any destination – than enslaved women, partly because enslaved women were less mobile due to childcare responsibilities but also because they had less opportunities to leave the vicinity of their home farms and plantations and develop the geographical knowledge and social

[34] *Charleston Courier*, March 7, 1835 (first quote); Ibid., September 28, 1830 (second quote); *Daily Picayune*, April 11, 1844 (third quote); Müller, "Illegal but Tolerated," 152–153; Müller, "Cities of Refuge," 119–159; Michael D. Thompson, *Working on the Dock of the Bay: Labor and Emancipation in an Antebellum Southern Port* (Columbia: University of South Carolina Press, 2015), 30.

networks necessary to make a successful bid for freedom. In the case of runaways to southern towns and cities, a perusal of the jail registers for some of the major destinations – such as the District of Columbia and Richmond, for example – indicates just how prevalent men were among the runaway slave population. In the District of Columbia some two-thirds (67.5 percent) of runaways arrested between 1848 and 1860 were men. In Richmond fully 90 percent of the runaways who were arrested in the period 1841–1846 were men.[35]

Such statistics may simply indicate that male runaways were more likely to be taken up than women, but African-American women in southern cities almost certainly had fewer avenues open to them to earn a living. Most worked as seamstresses, laundresses, and domestic servants in white households, their employers assuming that they were free blacks. Mildred Jackson, a twenty-six-year-old enslaved woman hiding out in New Orleans in 1854, was "supposed to be harbored in the Fourth District by her husband," and was described as "a good seamstress, and she may be employed by some one not knowing she has run away." "Fifty Dollars Reward" was offered "for the apprehension of TENAH, a female servant, who ran away from Barnwell Court House" in South Carolina in 1830. Tenah had been separated from her loved ones when she was sold from a plantation near Charleston to Barnwell. The runaway slave ad that announced her flight stated that she was undoubtedly "harbored in Charleston by a free person," her husband being "a free man by the name of William Lewy, who lives in Goose Creek, and has been seen in her company at the person's house in which she is harbored." Tenah was suspected of illegally passing herself off as a free black woman in order to gain employment, as her master "understood that she has been (perhaps unknowingly) employed by a white person as a washerwoman." In North Carolina a runaway named Milly was described as a "good seamstress and knitter," and suspected of similarly "trying to pass as a free woman" in Fayetteville. For good measure, Milly had also somehow managed to

[35] Franklin and Schweninger, *Runaway Slaves*, 210–213. Statistics for Washington tabulated based on the Washington DC, Department of Corrections, Runaway Slave Book, 1848–1863 (microfilm), Smithsonian Library, Washington, DC. Statistics for Richmond were tabulated based on the City Sergeant Jail Records, 1841–1846, compiled and transcribed in Frantel, *Richmond, Virginia Uncovered*. See also Müller, "Illegal but Tolerated," 158–160.

steal a small trunk with $700 from her master, an exorbitant nest egg for a newcomer in town.[36]

A significant portion of the enslaved population in any southern town or city consisted of hirelings, and hirelings in turn constituted an important category of runaway slaves in urban areas. As argued above, self-hire arrangements, whereby a slave was sent by his or her master to the city to hire his- or herself, were common enough that some runaway slaves in the cities even attempted to disguise their identities by passing for hired slaves rather than free blacks. John Lewis, a Kentucky slave, ran away to Lexington with the intention of pretending "he has hired his own time," for example. Others were legitimate hirelings – both men and women – who really had been sent to the city to hire their own time, but who took advantage of the situation to break ties with their masters and attempt to keep their earnings for themselves. Dinah, an enslaved woman who was sent to Charleston in 1822 with an "unlimited ticket, to look for a master," disappeared within the city, "having a great many free relations" there who were suspected of harboring her while she worked for herself. Henry, a runaway in New Orleans who had been "hired in this city as a drayman," broke ties with his master and found work for himself "in the shipping and about the levee," keeping his earnings for himself. Indeed, hired slaves' absence from their masters, relative lack of supervision and freedom of movement, as well as their first-hand experience with urban labor markets, placed them in an advantageous position to navigate southern cities disguised as free blacks. They knew the ropes, worked with and rubbed shoulders with free black populations, and were keen to trade in their "quasi-freedom" (as Jonathan Martin dubbed it) for freedom, albeit informal freedom. For these runaways, the determination to live in freedom and the conviction that they deserved to keep the fruits of their own labor were important motivations to flee bondage.[37]

Despite opportunities for employment, however, the nature of urban economies in the antebellum South relegated runaways and free blacks alike – even those who were skilled – to the very bottom of the economic ladder. Informal freedom may have been preferable to slavery, but it was a far cry from the good life. Most runaways eked out a living at best, lived

[36] *Daily Picayune*, December 1, 1854 (first quote); *Charleston Courier*, January 4, 1830 (second quote); *Fayetteville Observer*, January 15, 1840 (third quote).

[37] Martin, *Divided Mastery*, 161–187; Franklin and Schweninger, *Runaway Slaves*, 134–145; *The Reporter* (Lexington, KY), April 1, 1812 (first quote); *Charleston Courier*, March 26, 1822 (second quote); *Daily Picayune*, February 19, 1850 (third quote).

under difficult circumstances, and resorted to theft and other illegal activities when the going got tough. The city of Charleston, South Carolina, again provides illuminating examples. Runaway slaves in Charleston were routinely accused of using "forged permits" and collaborating with free blacks to steal cotton bales stored at city wharves and sell them to "unscrupulous store owners" or even ship them out of the state. Local businessmen estimated that as many as 500 bales were stolen each year. Skilled black bricklayers and carpenters in the same city were charged by white practitioners of their trade with unfair competition due to theft of building materials, white artisans complaining that blacks "undervalue Work, by undertaking it for very little more than Materials would cost, by which it is evident the Stuff they work with cannot honestly be acquired." The white coopers of Charleston also charged blacks with stealing materials and then charging unreasonably low rates, making it impossible for white artisans to compete. By 1828 "sundry mechanics" were joining forces and submitting collective petitions to the state legislature, crying out that "almost all the Trades, but especially those of Carpenters, Bricklayers, Plasterers, Wheelwrights, House-painters, Shoe-makers, &c. are beginning to be engrossed by Black & Colored workmen," who were "swarming" the city and selling their services wages so low that their materials were almost certainly procured through dishonest means. Similar complaints were filed throughout the South. In Virginia, outraged residents of Richmond demanded a free black quarry worker on the James River Canal named John King be forced to leave the state after he was caught enticing runaway slaves to commit a robbery and receive stolen goods. North Carolina residents repeatedly submitted complaints to their state legislature in the 1850s in which they accused free and unfree blacks – described in one such petition as naturally "indolent lazy & thievish" – of coordinating schemes to steal and resell stolen goods in public marketplaces. Such cases suggest that African Americans in the urban South, including runaway slaves, were often forced to desperation in order to make a living.[38]

---

[38] Petition of James Adger et al. to the Senate of the State of South Carolina, n.d., RSPP, Series 1, Legislative Petitions, Accession #11300005 (first quote); Petition of Daniel Cannon et al. to the House of Representatives of the State of South Carolina, February 1783, RSPP, Series 1, Legislative Petitions, Accession #11378304 (second quote); Petition of McCulley Righton et al. to the House of Representatives of the State of South Carolina, December 1793, RSPP, Series 1, Legislative Petitions, Accession #11379309; Petition to the President and Members of the Senate of South Carolina, circa 1828, RSPP #11382813; Petition of Oliver H. Rand et al. to the Legislature of Virginia, March

EVADING THE AUTHORITIES

Participating in such illegal schemes was dangerous, of course, as they made fugitive slaves vulnerable to potential exposure and recapture. White southerners needed little pretext for demanding harsh crackdowns on runaways and the free blacks who harbored and assisted them. The near constant reminders that fugitive slaves were passing themselves off as free and living illegally in their midst – for which they needed only to glance at the front page of a newspaper on any given day – not only produced great anxiety among slaveholders and concerned white citizens but also stimulated loud and frenzied calls for states and municipalities to hunt down runaway slaves and more severely punish complicit urban free blacks.

Fears of theft, violent robberies, and illegal economic activities in particular led to flurries of petitions to southern legislatures calling for immediate action to limit opportunities for association between free blacks and enslaved people, and tighten restrictions and police supervision of African Americans' movement and economic activities in public spaces. Some were submitted by white mechanics' or merchants' organizations who cried foul and unfair competition, as discussed above. Others were issued by ordinary citizens anxious of threats to the public order by perceived bands of runaways lurking about waiting to commit a robbery or engage in some other fraudulent activity. White Virginians submitted a petition to their state assembly in 1817 complaining of the "evils" committed by "slaves & free persons of colour," which they claimed resulted in "great annoyance, & disturbance of the peace & tranquility of society," and which threatened the safety of "the persons, [and] the property, of the Citizens." They suggested significantly increasing the "penalty on free persons for harbouring runaway slaves" to "be rendered as severe as would comport with the genious [*sic*] & principles of the Government," specifically by making it a capital offence – a remedy they admitted was "very severe" but that they deemed absolutely necessary. South Carolina planters from the lowcountry whose plantations

1852, RSPP, Series 1, Legislative Petitions, Accession #11685204; Petition of Onslow County to the General Assembly of North Carolina, December 3, 1858, RSPP, Series 1, Legislative Petitions, Accession #11285802. Viola Müller has argued that runaways who fled to southern cities were aware of "limited economic opportunities and ... economic shortcomings but preferred a life in poverty over a life in bondage." See Müller, "Cities of Refuge," 152.

were connected to Charleston "by navigable water," complained in 1829 about the increasing number of runaways in their parish, many of whom committed "depredations upon our property, crops and cattle" on their way to the city. They called for a reversal of an 1821 law that imposed harsh penalties for killing another man's slave, as they claimed this law only prevented white citizens from effectively capturing runaways and combatting local crime, emboldened runaways to become "reckless of consequences," and encouraged other slaves who wished to run away "to follow the same course." Other petitions were less extreme. In New Bern, North Carolina, residents petitioned the state legislature to crack down on free blacks engaged in the fishing business without a license, because they "corrupt the slaves of your Petitioners, and induce them to run away, and when runaway employ them, in dragging skimming nets for the purpose of catching fish," a habit that not only "much injured" white fishermen but also slaveholders in the surrounding region, who suffered regular defections from their plantations. In many such petitions an inextricable link was made between crime, runaway slaves, and free blacks.[39]

The most extreme petitions were usually shelved, but city councils and state legislatures throughout the South explicitly complied with calls to restrict African Americans' economic activities, more severely punish free blacks who harbored or hired runaway slaves, and limit the association between enslaved people and free blacks, at least on paper. From the Upper South to the Lower South, practices such as hiring African Americans who lacked proper documentation, or trading with African Americans who had no written permission to do so (or who claimed to be free) was illegal. The Slavery Code of the District of Columbia stated that "no person whatsoever, shall trade, barter, commerce, or any way deal" with any African American who could not produce "leave or license." In Alabama towns such as Montgomery and Mobile, any person caught illegally trading with any African American who turned out to be a slave could be subject to a fine amounting to four times the amount of the commodity being bought or sold. Even the small city of Little Rock passed "an ordinance, concerning Slaves, and free Negroes and

---

[39] Petition to the General Assembly of the State of North Carolina, December 19, 1831, RSPP, Series 1, Legislative Petitions, Accession #11283107; Petition of John Jonah Murrel, Joseph Maybank, et al., to the South Carolina House of Representatives, 1829, reprinted in Franklin and Schweninger, *Runaway Slaves*, 307–309; Petition of Josiah Halleman, et al., to the General Assembly of Virginia, December 12, 1817, reprinted in Franklin and Schweninger, *Runaway Slaves*, 301–302.

Mulattos" in 1836 that declared among other things that "no person shall buy or receive from any slave any commodity whatever in this City, unless the said slave shall produce a written permit from his or her master, mistress or overseer." Among other things, such ordinances were intended to force white employers and customers to ask black job seekers and hucksters for papers before hiring or purchasing any wares from them, in order to make sure they were not fugitive slaves living illegally in the city.[40]

In practice such laws were often poorly enforced, however, by the authorities as well as by white employers and customers. As the black populations of the South's major cities continued to grow, local authorities proved both unable and unwilling to effectively monitor the movement and activities of suspected runaway slaves. By 1858 the formal ban on self-hire for African Americans who lacked proper documentation in the city of Charleston was so poorly enforced that frustrated white members of the South Carolina Mechanics Association declared it a "dead letter." In New Orleans the pass system that was supposed to regulate black mobility and economic activities had by 1854 deteriorated to such an extent that the local newspaper *Daily Picayune* complained that black people had "the run of the city." Indeed, one study shows that in the period from 1852 to 1855 the only illegal economic activities that enslaved people were arrested for in that city were selling liquor (amounting to 4.1 percent of slave arrests) and gambling (1.7 percent) – authorities appear to have been uninterested in enforcing other illegal practices such as peddling "innocent" wares or undocumented self-hire.[41]

Despite loud cries to crack down on undocumented labor and trade by African Americans in southern towns and cities, urban white southerners

---

[40] *The Slavery Code of the District of Columbia* (Washington, DC: L. Towers & Co., 1862), sec. 43 (first quote); John G. Aikin, comp., *A Digest of the Laws of the State of Alabama...etc.* (Philadelphia: Alexander Towar, 1833), 393; *Arkansas Gazette*, January 12, 1836 (quote); Kimball, *American City, Southern Place*, 124–158; Rockman, *Scraping By*, 52–53; James M. Campbell, *Slavery on Trial: Race, Class, and Criminal Justice in Antebellum Richmond* (Gainesville: University Press of Florida, 2007), 146–185; Thomas C. Buchanan, "Rascals on the Antebellum Mississippi: African American Steamboat Workers and the St. Louis Hanging of 1841," *Journal of Social History* 34 (Summer 2001): 797–817.

[41] Franklin and Schweninger, *Runaway Slaves*, 129; Petition of S. Daggett et al. to General Assembly of South Carolina, November 1858, RSPP, Series 1, Legislative Petitions, Accession #11385801; Stacy K. McGoldrick, "The Policing of Slavery in New Orleans, 1852–1860," *Journal of Historical Sociology* 14, no. 4 (December 2001): 405–406, 406 (quote).

found it either impractical and economically unwise to fully eradicate such activities. And except for during certain frenzied periods of increased raids and crackdowns – such as after the Nat Turner uprising – not a single southern town or city even tried. Southern industries and shipping were dependent on cheap black labor; urban grocers and shopkeepers were dependent on black customers; genteel urban households were dependent on cheap handymen and domestic servants. The simple nature of supply and demand in antebellum southern towns and cities encouraged white townspeople not to ask questions – to basically pursue a "don't ask, don't tell" policy with regard to black employment, black customers, and black hucksters. Activities that constituted "vices," such as selling liquor, gambling, and prostitution, were the only sectors that seemed to be on the radar of city police and patrolmen – presumably because they were often linked to violence and therefore threatened the public order. And even then there were calls for lenience by whites who had an economic stake in such activities. In Charleston in 1827 a group of white grocers sought the repeal of an 1815 city ordinance that prohibited the sale of liquor to any "Negro or person of Color," arguing that the loss of clientele was causing substantial hardship on their businesses.[42]

Indeed, even as concerned white citizens and white professional associations petitioned their city and state representatives to impose harsher restrictions on illegal economic activities by African Americans of all categories, white employers who had an economic stake in a reliable supply of cheap black labor petitioned lawmakers to *do away* with certain restrictions that they feared might scare away their workforce. In Virginia towns and cities, for example, some business owners openly expressed their desire to have the deportation requirement for manumitted slaves reversed. Over the years the law had done little more than produce a large population of urban free blacks who lacked the proper documentation to reside in the state and hire themselves out legally; as a result, white employers feared that some potential laborers preferred to work in the shadows rather than formally hire themselves out at legitimate establishments. As late as 1852 a group of prominent Virginians petitioned the state assembly to pass a law allowing free people of color to remain

---

[42] Petition of George Jacobs et al. to the Senate of South Carolina, 1827, RSPP, Series 1, Legislative Petitions, Accession #11382707. For a thorough discussion of why the economies of southern cities such as Baltimore, Richmond, Charleston, and New Orleans favored a relatively "tolerant" attitude toward employing "illegal" black labor, see Müller, "Cities of Refuge," 161–196.

within the state under the condition that free men under the age of forty-five be required to hire themselves out – or, if they were unable to find employment, to submit to forced hiring by county commissioners. Although never passed, such a measure would have not only benefited the state's captains of industry but it would have also benefited runaway slaves, as it would have further blurred the lines between the undocumented free and the undocumented unfree in cities such as Richmond, Petersburg, and Alexandria.[43]

Southern states and municipalities passed strict legislation aimed at unblurring those lines and enhancing the visibility of free blacks and slaves, such as requiring slaves to carry passes, hired slaves to carry badges, and free blacks to carry free certificates of freedom at all times. In the end, however, their attempts to distinguish between free blacks and runaway slaves in public spaces largely failed, mainly because runaways devised cunning strategies to circumvent the laws by procuring false documentation. Fugitive slaves who remained in the South knew that their precarious existence was primarily based on the fact that they lacked formal papers to prove that they either had permission to reside in the city or that they were free. As illegals and noncitizens, the very public spaces that often provided them with anonymity could also produce dangerous encounters with whites that might reveal their true identities. Authorities and vigilant residents were constantly warned to be on the lookout for African Americans who roamed the streets with "neither ticket nor badge, as required by the City Ordinance," as one woman was described in Charleston in 1859. Documentation – false documentation – was a great advantage for those who could procure it, and many runaways appear to have known how to do so.[44]

Enslaved people who could read and write were in a position to forge their own passes or free papers, and many did. Frederick, a Georgia slave who was suspected of having run to Augusta in 1825, was presumed to be carrying "a forged pass with him, as he can read and write." Ben, a Virginia slave who ran away with his three daughters to Washington, could "write a pretty good hand, and no doubt has copied the papers of some free man," his master even having "reason to believe he stole the

---

[43] Petition of John S. Robins et al. to the General Assembly of Virginia, February 1852, RSPP, Series 1, Legislative Petitions, Accession #11685202; Müller, "Cities of Refuge," 161–196; Rockman, *Scraping By*, 4; Fields, *Slavery on the Middle Ground*, 67; Takagi, "*Rearing Wolves to Our Own Destruction*," 32–33.

[44] Müller, "Cities of Refuge," 82–87; Franklin and Schweninger, *Runaway Slaves*, 131–136; *Charleston Courier*, January 1, 1859 (quote).

Stafford County seal and attached the impression of it to his papers."
Gilbert, a runaway from Louisiana who was suspected of having fled to
New Orleans in 1851, was described as "a very good looking boy, and
can read and write." Jacob and his wife Judy both ran away from their
master in Edgecomb County, North Carolina, and were suspected of
"lurking about in Edenton." Both were advertised as being able to read
and write "a little," and "have with them a free pass, which they will
impose upon most people from the plausible manner in which it is made
out." Such tricks infuriated slaveholders and white residents throughout
the South. In 1828 residents of Charleston demanded stricter enforcement
of the law prohibiting slaves from learning how to read and write,
because it allowed them to forge passes, permits, and free papers.[45]

A vast majority of enslaved people could not read or write, however,
and therefore depended on free blacks to provide them with the false
documentation necessary to evade detection. Perhaps unsurprisingly, a
black market in forged passes and facsimiles of free papers for runaway
slaves – the antebellum equivalent of a fake passport for undocumented
immigrants – flourished in urban areas, despite strict legislation against it.
In the District of Columbia, where the buying and selling of free papers
for runaway slaves was considered completely out of control, the law
threatened "any free negro or mulatto" caught selling "such certificate to
any slave, by which such slave may be enabled to abscond" with legal
prosecution and a fine "not exceeding the sum of three hundred dollars" –
and if the offender was unable to pay he or she would be "sold" into
forced labor for a period of up to seven years by way of recompense. In
Mississippi, where runaways usually made for Natchez, Jackson, or New
Orleans, the general assembly explicitly threatened "any free negro or
mulatto who shall deliver or transfer to any slave the copy of the register
of his or her freedom ... with the intent to enable such slave to escape
from his or her master" with a felony. Every other southern state had
similar legislation on the books – by the eve of the Civil War even the
sparsely settled southwestern territory of New Mexico threatened that
"any person furnishing slaves free papers is liable to an imprisonment of

---

[45] *Augusta Chronicle*, October 8, 1825 (first quote); *Daily National Intelligencer*, July 4,
1825 (second quote); *New Orleans Picayune*, July 15, 1851 (third quote); *Edenton
Gazette and North Carolina General Advertiser*, January 25, 1820 (fourth quote);
Petition of Joseph Johnson to the House of Representatives of South Carolina, 1828,
RSPP, Series 1, Legislative Petitions, Accession #11382808; Müller, "Cities of Refuge,"
82–87.

not less than six months nor more than five years, and a fine of not less than $100 nor more than $1000."[46]

Yet runaway slave ads, court records, and even planters' records reveal that forged papers procured from free blacks were common anyway. One North Carolina slaveholder sent a friend to Suffolk, Virginia, to track down some runaways who were rumored to be working in a cotton factory and employed about construction jobs in that city in the summer of 1848. The friend reported back that "from the best information I can gather" the runaways had used forged passes to obtain work at a construction site: "there [sic] papers were examined by Mr. E. D. B. Howell – Mr. Everitt & others they were closely questioned, [and] finding there [sic] answers to correspond with there [sic] papers, the papers having the County seal, these persons come to the conclusion that they were actually free." Runaway slave ads are full of references to forged passes. Nancy, a "bright mulatto, aged about 25 years" and originally from the Natchez area of Mississippi, absconded from her new master in Plaquemines Parish, Louisiana, but had "lately been heard of in the neighborhood of Natchez with a forged pass." Kitty, a Virginia slave suspected of having run to Washington, was advertised as "uncommonly artful, and no doubt will have free papers." Amanda, from Monroe County, Georgia, fled to Augusta with "a pass given her" so that she could "attempt to pass as a free person." Will, a Virginia runaway, "probably has a pass or counterfeit papers of freedom." Bill, an Alabama enslaved man from Alabama was "making his way to Macon, Ga., and very probably he has a free pass." Some runaways who were unable to purchase or otherwise procure counterfeit documents resorted to stealing them from free blacks, placing both themselves and their victims in legal jeopardy. Allen Floyd, for example, a free black from North Carolina, was robbed of his free papers by a runaway slave in 1859. When the runaway was arrested in Wilmington and turned out to be passing himself off as Floyd, the real Floyd was threatened with arrest on suspicion of having illegally sold his papers to the runaway slave. Indeed, because illegally acquiring false papers in southern towns and cities was so rampant, some cities such as Charleston required certain categories of black residents to carry badges or medallions instead, presumably because these were more difficult to

---

[46] Snethen, *Black Code of the District of Columbia*, 28–29 (first quote); Alden and van Hoesen, *Digest of the Laws of Mississippi*, 763 (second quote); *Bangor (ME) Whig and Courier*, March 17, 1859 (third quote); Müller, "Cities of Refuge," 82–87; Franklin and Schweninger, *Runaway Slaves*, 135; Berlin, *Slaves without Masters*, 93–94.

duplicate. Even that did not stop many runaways from trying (or stealing them), however. One runaway slave ad for a young woman suspected of lurking about Charleston, where she had "many relations," specifically mentioned that she "has a badge, No. 176."[47]

To make matters even more confusing to city authorities and slave catchers, fugitive slaves not only often secured false documentation, but false documentation under one or more aliases, as runaway slave ads from throughout the South make abundantly clear. One runaway to New Orleans who was suspected of lurking about with false papers, for example, was "familiar with the names Hildreth, Brown and Walker." In 1824 a lowcountry runaway named Mary was heard to have changed her name to Jane and to be living "with a forged pass" in Charleston, where she worked in a "house of ill fame" owned by a white woman. Another runaway with the immediately recognizable name "Americus" changed his name to William and was presumed to be "lurking about Nashville" in the fall of 1840. The master of a Georgia runaway named Ruben who disappeared to Mobile, Alabama, claimed that "his intention is doubtless to pass as a free man, as he carried off papers with him to that effect, and will probably pass by the name of GEORGE WALKER or JOHN McDONAL."[48]

Because assuming a false identity and a false legal status was so crucial to fugitives' lives in urban areas, those who failed to procure documents ran high risks of discovery and recapture. City authorities tended not to simply believe an African American when he or she claimed to be a free

---

[47] A. Riddick to William Glover, July 22, 1848, reprinted in appendix 6, Franklin and Schweninger, *Runaway Slaves*, 326–327 (first quotes); *The Times Picayune*, July 30, 1845 (second quote); *Alexandria Gazette*, January 1, 1822 (third quote); *Augusta Chronicle*, July 13, 1827 (fourth quote); *Daily National Intelligencer*, January 8, 1820 (fifth quote); *Georgia Journal & Messenger*, December 17, 1851 (sixth quote); Petition of Allen Floyd to Randolph County Superior Court, August 20, 1859, Randolph County, NC, RSPP, Series 2, County Court Petitions, Accession #21285913; *Charleston Courier*, April 13, 1822 (seventh quote). For more on cooperation between urban free blacks and slaves within the realm of resistance, see: Kimball, *American City, Southern Place*, 124–158; Rockman, *Scraping By*, 52–53; Campbell, *Slavery on Trial*, 146–185; Buchanan, "Rascals on the Antebellum Mississippi," 797–817. William Link has found that the policing of documentation for free blacks and slaves in urban environments in Virginia was at best "sloppily maintained." See Link, *Roots of Secession*, 106. Viola Müller's recent sampling of 200 runaway slave advertisements from North Carolina in the 1820s revealed more than forty-eight specific mentions to "passing for free" with false documents. See Müller, "Cities of Refuge," 82.

[48] *Daily Picayune*, March 3, 1850 (first quote); *Charleston Courier*, November 8, 1824 (second quote); *Nashville Union*, November 12, 1840 (third quote); *Charleston Mercury*, March 30, 1836 (fourth quote).

black. William Green, a Virginia runaway passing for free in Richmond, for example, was arrested in 1841 "for want of his free papers," having told the authorities that he was free when they stopped him. They quickly discovered, however, that "he was a runaway" and delivered him back to his master. In the best cases recapture entailed reenslavement and whatever punishment their owners saw fit to inflict for insubordination. In the worst cases it also entailed abysmal confinement in dark and disgusting jails, brutal forced labor for the city or state (sometimes in "work houses"), and/or sale. Henry Meredith, a slave from Georgia, ran away from his master in February 1843, his owner claiming that he had "never heard of him since." It later turned out that Henry was arrested and jailed while attempting to pass for free in North Carolina in 1845, and when nobody came to claim him, he was simply sold at auction to a new master. Lucy, picked up in Richmond for "want of her free papers" and going around "at Large ... contrary to law," was thrown into jail on August 9, 1841. Still unable to prove her freedom by January 28, she was sold. St. Louis authorities arrested a runaway slave named William Anderson in 1843 and kept him incarcerated for an exceptionally long period of time – 478 days – before finally selling him at auction. In Charleston, runaways were confined to the city work-house and put to heavy labor. Runaway slave ads in local newspapers even specifically called for vigilant citizens to forcibly take them up and deliver them there. The owner of Hannah, who ran away in 1822 and was suspected of being harbored in the city, promised twenty dollars "on lodging said wench Hannah in the work-house." In Savannah, runaways were similarly processed in the widely feared Savannah Workhouse and Gaol, where fugitives who were not reclaimed (or refused to identify themselves) were interned, advertised, and sold at public auction. The city of New Orleans, where according to one study runaways constituted 39 percent of slave arrests in the 1850s, even had a "Runaway Slave Depot" where unclaimed fugitives were held in horrendous conditions and put to forced labor in chain gangs about the city, especially on the levees.[49]

---

[49] The case of William Green is registered in the Richmond jail records; see Frantel, *Richmond, Virginia Uncovered*, 10 (first quote). The case of Henry Meredith is described in: Petition of Nicholas Wylie to the Worshipful Justices of the Court, April 10, 1845, Caswell County, NC, RSPP, Series 2, County Court Petitions, Accession #21284510. Lucy's case is registered in the Richmond jail records; see Frantel, *Richmond, Virginia Uncovered*, 10 (second quotes). The case of William Anderson is found in: Petition to the General Assembly of Missouri, St. Louis County, ca. 1846, RSPP, Series 1: Legislative Petitions, Accession #11184604, http://library.uncg.edu/slavery/petitions/details.aspx?

Refusing to fully give up, some fugitive slaves stoically attempted to negotiate for some improvement to their lives even after they were apprehended by city authorities, hoping to prevent a worst-case outcome. Many tried to influence to whom they were "returned" by confusing their captors about their true owners. The story of Valentin, an enslaved man originally owned by grandee sugar planter Valcour Aime in St. James Parish, Louisiana, provides an interesting example. Valentin was sold away from his home plantation, eventually ending up in the hands of a planter named Valentin Michel in St. Charles Parish. He fled his new master, resurfacing again in New Orleans in 1824 and passing for free under the pseudonym Louis. Upon arrest Valentin told the jailor that "he belonged to Valcour Aime," apparently in an attempt to be sent back "home" to his original master. Only after "several questions [were] put to him" was it "discovered that he once belonged to Mr. Valcour Aime, who sold him to Mr. Armstrong, who afterwards sold him to said Valentin Michel" in St. Charles Parish. Some runaways who fled to urban areas and were apprehended by city authorities – particularly those who had fled especially abusive masters – actually *preferred* to be sold rather than be returned to their owners, apparently in the belief that they were better off taking their chances with anybody else. When an enslaved man named Simon from Tennessee, for example, was apprehended while attempting to pass for free in Nashville without proper documentation in 1843, he refused to tell the authorities to whom he belonged. Indeed, he deceived them, telling them that his master was "some one living & resident in Williamson County" named Peter. In reality his master's name was John Woods, from Bedford County. Unable to locate Simon's owner, the Nashville authorities kept Simon in a filthy jail for twelve months and ultimately sold him to another master in the city. It appears that Simon deliberately concealed his master's true identity in order to prevent being sent back to Bedford County, knowing full well that he would be sold if he was left unclaimed. In a similar case, "Jno alias Bob" was arrested as a runaway slave in Richmond, Virginia, but refused to tell the authorities to whom he belonged. The jailor recorded simply that Jno was owned by

pid=604; *Charleston Courier*, March 25, 1822 (third quote); Betty Wood, "Some Aspects of Female Resistance to Chattel Slavery in Low Country Georgia, 1763–1815," *The Historical Journal* 30, no. 3 (September 1987), 619–620; McGoldrick, "The Policing of Slavery in New Orleans," 404.

"some person unknon." Six days later his master found him, however, and Jno was sent home.[50]

Recapture was a regular occurrence in most of the urban South. The jail registers for some southern cities provide an interesting glimpse into the likelihood of arrest and the profiles of African Americans who became entangled in the nets of slave catchers and city authorities. It appears that in certain cities at certain times, the likelihood of arrest was higher than in others, with the largest cities seeing the lowest arrest rates. In the six-year period between April 1809 and May 1815, for example, some 737 runaways were locked up in the Savannah Workhouse and Gaol, evenly spread out over the entire period. This was a city with a total population in 1810 of 5,215, including 578 free African Americans and 2,195 enslaved people. It was also an unusual period, which included a more than doubling of the city's free black population (making it increasingly attractive to runaway slaves) and heightened vigilance due to the War of 1812. Nevertheless, calculations based on the surviving jail register for those six years reveal that around ten African Americans were picked up every month by city authorities and accused of being runaways, or about one every three days.[51]

In Richmond, Virginia, the arrest rates were even lower. The City Sergeant Jail Record for Richmond lists only 218 runaway slaves arrested in the five-year period 1841–1846. Among those caught some 196 (90 percent) were men and only 22 (10 percent) women, an overwhelming majority from nearby central Virginia counties such as Chesterfield, Hanover, and King William. Another ninety-seven (apparently legitimate) free blacks were picked up and thrown into jail for failing to produce free papers when questioned, but were later released. According to census data Richmond had a total population of roughly 27,700 in 1840, including an "official" black population of 12,400 – around 10,000 slaves and 2,400 free blacks, although in practice the black population was considerably augmented by the influx of runaway slaves and other

---

[50] *Couirier de la Louisiane*, November 16, 1824 (first quote); Petition of John Woods to the Chancery Court of Davidson County, TN, May 26, 1845, RSPP, Series 2, County Court Petitions, Accession #21484524; Jno's case is registered in the Richmond jail records; see Frantel, *Richmond, Virginia Uncovered*, 9.

[51] Wood, "Some Aspects of Female Resistance," 621; Johnson, *Black Savannah*, 108; Michele Gillespie, *Free Labor in an Unfree World: White Artisans in Slaveholding Georgia, 1789–1860* (Athens: University of Georgia Press, 2004), 27. See also Jerry M. Hynson, comp., *Absconders, Runaways and Other Fugitives in the Baltimore City and County Jail* (Westminster, MD: Willow Bend Books, 2004).

illegal black residents, as discussed earlier. The jail register shows that in this large and bustling city during this five-year period, roughly 3.6 runaway slaves got caught up in the nets of the authorities every month, or about one every nine to ten days.[52]

The Department of Corrections for the District of Columbia likewise kept a "Runaway Slave Book" from 1848 through the Civil War. In the twelve-year period from April 6, 1848 through April 6, 1860, a total of 1,176 runaway slaves were committed to jail, roughly two-thirds (67.5 percent) of whom were men and one-third (32.5 percent) women. (This number does not include 524 slaves who were committed to jail "for safekeeping" during estate divisions or pending sale in this period. Nor does it include eighty-nine free blacks who were arrested but released upon proving their freedom.) This amounted to an average of ninety-eight runaway slave arrests per year – just more than eight per month, or about one every four days – in a city of between 50,000 and 75,000 inhabitants in the 1850s, including a black population of about 14,000, of whom about 11,000 were free. The vast majority were reclaimed by their masters (including prominent figures such as Col. Robert E. Lee) or agents of their masters, although three died in custody and a significant number were delivered to notorious slave traders such as Benjamin O. Sheckells, Joseph Bruin, and Price, Birch & Co., who operated from across the river in Alexandria, Virginia. Sheckells alone came to reclaim forty runaway slaves in the DC jail during this period.[53]

The mention of legitimate free blacks getting caught up in the nets of the authorities in both cities – ninety-seven in Richmond and eighty-nine in Washington, respectively – speaks volumes to the confusing legal spectrum attached to race in the antebellum urban South. The presence of free blacks in urban spaces provided runaway slaves with opportunities to disguise their status and pass for free, but inversely, the presence of runaway slaves in those same spaces often served to degrade free blacks into suspected fugitive slaves until proven free. A perusal of habeas corpus petitions from the Circuit Court of the District of Columbia provides

---

[52] Calculated from Richmond Virginia City Sergeant Jail Records, 1841–1846; see Frantel, *Richmond, Virginia Uncovered*; Müller, "Illegal but Tolerated," 141.

[53] Statistics based on: *District of Columbia Department of Corrections, Runaway Slave Book, 1848–1863*, transcribed by Jerry M. Hynson (Westminster, MD: Willow Bend Books, 1999). For DC population data, see US Population Census, 1850 (NARA). In 1850 DC counted 51,687 inhabitants, including 13,746 blacks (of whom 10,059 were free). In 1860 DC had grown to 75,080 inhabitants, including 14,316 blacks (11,131 were free).

chilling examples of unlucky free blacks who were seized and unlawfully detained upon suspicion of being runaway slaves. In 1820, one John McHenry "humbly sheweth that is in Jail and wants to get out – that he is free and ought to get out – that he had free papers and sufficient evidence of his freedom and never ought to have been put there...." William Sammon was detained in 1822 "as a runaway" but ordered discharged from the city jail, "having produced satisfactory evidence of his freedom." John Lee, confined to jail on the charge of being a runaway slave in 1842, sought a writ of habeas corpus, claiming that he had been manumitted by the last will and testament of his former master (a request that was apparently never formally registered, as was common).[54]

The inability to effectively distinguish between free blacks and run-away slaves with false papers in urban spaces led to such confusion and frustration that some exasperated southerners declared black freedom and black slavery intrinsically incompatible. Extreme measures to nip the problem in the bud and just get rid of free blacks altogether were proposed by citizens throughout the South, including forced deportation and reenslavement. While such measures were almost universally con-sidered too extreme by lawmakers – not only for their potential economic repercussions but also because of logistical impracticalities and the risk of rebellion – it is significant that the internal fugitive slave issue caused white southerners to redirect their dissatisfaction onto the very existence of black freedom, which made defections within the South possible in the first place. White residents of Wilmington, Delaware, who were con-cerned about the expanding black population, petitioned their state legis-lature in 1827 for "the removal of these people" to the "coast of Africa." A group of frustrated citizens of South Carolina petitioned the state legislature in 1858 to force free blacks out of the state or reduce them to slavery, due to the problems that arose from the "association of slaves and free Negroes." In the northern Virginia counties that bordered the District of Columbia white residents became so fed up with the free black population that a group of them petitioned the state legislature in 1847 to "rid the State of this growing fungus," either by deporting them to Africa or remanding them to slavery. Fifty-one residents of North Carolina

---

[54] Petition of John McHenry, October 31, 1820, Habeas Corpus Case Records, US Circuit Court for the District of Columbia, 1820–1863, Reel #1, NARA (first quote); Petition of Wm Sammon, April 21, 1822, Habeas Corpus Case Records, US Circuit Court for the District of Columbia, Reel #1, NARA (second quote); Petition of John Lee, August 3, 1842, District of Columbia, RSPP, Series 1: Legislative Petitions, Accession #20484203.

complained to their state legislature that free blacks were a "perfect Nuisance, to civilized Society," and that their "communications with the slave population" rendered the latter "disobedient and turbulent." They recommended the government "compel [free blacks] to emigrate," either to Africa or to "a location for them in the far West."[55]

The urban South thus simultaneously constituted both an attractive and a hostile environment for fugitive slaves and for African Americans in general. Not all fugitive slaves lurking about in southern towns and cities, including those who acquired the means to pass for free, decided to remain in the danger zone permanently. Scholars such as Stephen Hahn and Matthew Clavin have correctly argued some southern cities served as "gateways to freedom" for runaways who wished to seek freedom outside of the South. Clavin's case study of Pensacola as a jumping-off point for those looking to flee to the British Caribbean is a prime example, but black towns and neighborhoods throughout the antebellum South constituted key depots on runaway routes to both the Caribbean and the northern United States. New Orleans served as a site of informal freedom in its own right, but also as a maritime gateway to both the North and the circum-Caribbean, for example. To cite just one illustrative case, an enslaved man named Ned escaped from his Louisiana master and went to New Orleans in 1814; two weeks later he was "detained on board" the US schooner *Caroline*, having smuggled himself on board in an attempt to flee the South altogether. Chesapeake ports such as Richmond and Norfolk likewise offered opportunities for slaves to escape to free soil in the North and beyond the United States. In the winter of 1855, a "young, strong and hearty negro" from Lancaster County, Virginia, attempted to attain his freedom while hired out in Richmond, where he escaped his employer and illegally "pretended he was a free man," with the intention

[55] Petition of the Wilmington Union Colonization Society to the State of Delaware, January 11, 1827, RSPP, Series 1: Legislative Petitions, Accession #10382701; Petition of Philip McElveen et al. to the General Assembly of South Carolina, 1858, RSPP, Series 1, Legislative Petitions, Accession #11385913; Petition of James Rose et al. to the Senate of South Carolina, 1860, RSPP, Series 1, Legislative Petitions, Accession #11386004; Petition of Loudoun County residents to General Assembly of Virginia, December 10, 1847, RSPP, Series 1: Legislative Petitions, Accession #11684708; Petition of Sampson County residents to the General Assembly of North Carolina, November 22, 1852, RSPP, Series 1: Legislative Petitions, Accession #11285206; Franklin and Schweninger, *Runaway Slaves*, 110.

to save his money and bide his time till spring, and to "go to the north as soon as navigation opened."[56]

Many slaves who ultimately passed through such gateways (or attempted to do so), however, were in fact runaways who had initially attempted to create lives for themselves in informal freedom in towns and cities across the South, but felt compelled to take flight again when they were detected. No destination for fugitive slaves was completely permanent, and when the threat of recapture seemed imminent, they often fled again, sometimes to geographic spaces of formal freedom, a risky venture that was wrought with hazards. One slave couple named George and Jane, from Henrico County, Virginia, was recaptured in an escape attempt that illustrates the volatile existence of runaways in gateway cities. Having each fled the employers to which they were respectively hired in 1833, the two fugitives came together and made their way to nearby Richmond. Upon arrival "George passed himself off as a freeman & hired himself as a cook on bord [sic] the schooner John Bendil," docked in the James River. When the captain of the ship eventually asked for George's free papers before departure, he "found that he was in fact a slave & not a freeman having a right to hire himself." Panicking, George fled, concealing himself on board a schooner bound for New York, where he was later discovered and arrested. Jane was also arrested, "making similar efforts to leave the state" and join her husband in the North.[57]

The experiences of freedom seekers who, like George and Jane, attempted to escape slavery by reaching free soil will be delved into in Chapter 3. A thorough understanding of the geography of slavery and freedom on the North American continent in the antebellum period must include closer analysis of fugitive slaves who sought freedom by remaining within the slaveholding states, however. The actions of these runaways went far beyond mere truancy, as is often suggested in the literature. Many fugitives to urban areas clearly attempted to live their

---

[56] Clavin, *Aiming for Pensacola*; Steven Hahn, *The Political Worlds of Slavery and Freedom* (Cambridge, MA: Harvard University Press, 2009), 41–43; Cheryl Janifer LaRoche, *Free Black Communities and the Underground Railroad: The Geography of Resistance* (Urbana: University of Illinois Press, 2013); Petition of Jeremiah Spiller to the First District Court of Louisiana, December 5, 1814, RSPP, Series 2, County Court Petitions, Accession #20881437; Petition of Thomas Oldham to Lancaster County Court, February 19, 1855, RSPP, Series 2, County Court Petitions, Lancaster County, VA, Accession #21685504.

[57] "Thomas Cowles to the County Court, Henrico County, Virginia, 1833," in Loren Schweninger, ed., *The Southern Debate over Slavery, volume 2: Petitions to Southern County Courts, 1775–1867* (Urbana: University of Illinois Press, 2008), 163 (quotes).

lives there indefinitely. Distinguishing between sites of formal freedom (where fugitives could be legally free) and informal freedom (where fugitives attempted to live free illegally) as permanent destinations for runaway slaves is also crucial in understanding how slaves understood freedom (i.e., not always in legal terms) and what their prime motivations for fleeing bondage were. Indeed, many of those who sought informal freedom appear to have placed maintaining contact with loved ones still in bondage – even if it meant living illegally within the slave states – above the procurement of legal rights, which supports recent scholarship by historians such as Calvin Schermerhorn, who argued that those enslaved in the antebellum South often preferred "family over freedom" – at least *formal* freedom.[58]

---

[58] Schermerhorn, *Money over Mastery, Family over Freedom.*

3

"As If Their Own Liberty Were at Stake"

Spaces of Semi-Formal Freedom in the Northern United States

On May 20, 1836, a light-skinned enslaved woman from Missouri named Matilda undertook a daring action that would expose to the entire nation the legal ambiguities regarding fugitive slaves in the northern states. She escaped from her master – one Larkin Lawrence, who was also her father – during an out-of-state trip up the Ohio River. This wide and slow-moving waterway, which for almost all of its meandering 980 miles not only constituted the border between the free North and the slave South but also served as a busy transportation route for the domestic slave trade (the vessels of which frequently docked on the free side of the river), confronted many enslaved people who found themselves plying its waters with an overwhelming urge to flee slavery. For Matilda the temptation was simply too great to be contained. She had already pleaded with Lawrence earlier in the trip to manumit her, and when he refused, she seized the opportunity to liberate herself while the vessel that carried her and her master was docked on the free side of the river at Cincinnati. Managing to secretly disembark and disappear into the city, she found safety with a black barber in Church Alley and remained hidden until she received notice that Lawrence had finally gone back to Missouri. With the danger of immediate recapture seemingly behind her, Matilda emerged from her hiding place and quickly went about settling into her new life as a free woman. Her new friends helped her gain employment as a nurse in the household of James Birney, a renowned abolitionist who later claimed he had no idea she was a runaway slave because she had hidden her true identity from him.[1]

---

[1] Salmon P. Chase, *Speech of Salmon P. Chase in the Case of the Colored Woman, Matilda, Who Was Brought before the Court of Common Pleas of Hamilton County, Ohio, by*

Matilda's master was not going to let her get away that easily. Ten months later she was rumored to still be "concealed or lurking" about in Cincinnati, and an agent for Lawrence arrived in town with orders to secure her recapture. When he discovered that she was working at the Birney residence, the agent filed an affidavit and a request for assistance with the Hamilton County (Ohio) court, and the local sheriff was commanded to "pursue after the said Matilda ... and take her and safely keep her" so that she could be "further dealt with according to law." Matilda was arrested on March 10, 1837. Her ordeal did not end there, however, because the Birney family mobilized into action, securing the counsel of antislavery lawyer Salmon P. Chase, who formally contested Matilda's arrest and petitioned the Court of Common Pleas for a writ of habeas corpus, arguing that his client had been "confined and detained ... without lawful authority." The case went to trial – one closely followed in Cincinnati, a border city and major destination for runaway slaves from the southern states. Indeed, as Chase emphasized in his opening statements to the court, it was clear that "the questions, involved in this case, are regarded with deep interest by the community. Many seem to feel something of a personal interest in its event: some, as if their own liberty were at stake ..."[2]

A skilled lawyer, Chase purposefully abstained from resorting to any appeals to emotion and refused to discuss the moral merits or demerits of slavery during the trial. Instead, and quite remarkably, he argued process, confining himself solely "to the legal and constitutional aspects of the case before the Court." The question at hand, Chase insisted, was whether "Matilda, is, or is not now unlawfully restrained of her liberty" in the free state of Ohio, "by whose fundamental law slavery is positively and forever interdicted." The heart of Chase's argument, as he laid out in great detail, was that even if one were to admit that Matilda was once a slave in Missouri, it "still by no means follows that she is now a slave, or now legally constrained. On the contrary," he argued, she was "now legally free" because Ohio recognized no property rights in man. As such she could only be arrested and detained with the same rights as a free

---

Writ of Habeas Corpus, March 11th, 1837 (Cincinnati, OH: Pugh & Dodd, 1837); Stephen Middleton, *The Black Laws: Race and the Legal Process in Early Ohio* (Athens: Ohio University Press, 2005), 112–113. See also Matthew Salafia, "Searching for Slavery: Fugitive Slaves in the Ohio River Valley Borderland," *Ohio Valley History* 8, no. 4 (2008): 28–63.

[2] Chase, *Speech of Salmon P. Chase*; Middleton, *The Black Laws*, 112–113; Salafia, "Searching for Slavery," 38–63.

person. According to Chase, that had not happened. The warrant that had been issued for Matilda's detainment had in effect violated her right to due process, since it did not describe the crime for which she was being arrested and was indeed designed for the detainment of a slave, not the arrest and formal indictment of a legal person with rights. And if the constitutional rights of the defendant were violated upon arrest, Chase underscored, the law required the defendant to be "discharged from custody." He furthermore argued that the sheriff had had no authority to arrest Matilda in the first place, since federal fugitive slave law did not call for or even allow state or municipal officers to do so. The entire process, in short, was according to Chase "illegal and void." For good measure, he concluded by providing lengthy arguments to the court about why the federal Fugitive Slave Act of 1793 was unconstitutional "and directly repugnant to some of its plainest provisions," including the Article I right to habeas corpus, the Fourth Amendment right to protection from unreasonable search and seizure, and the Fifth Amendment right to protection from being deprived of liberty without due process of law.[3]

The eloquent arguments made by Chase were not enough to convince the conservative judge overhearing the case, who ultimately decided in favor of Lawrence and ordered that Matilda be transported out of state and remanded to slavery. Floated across the river to slaveholding territory in Covington, Kentucky, she was incarcerated and subsequently shipped off, never to be heard from again. Despite losing her claim to freedom as a refugee in the northern states, however, Matilda unknowingly spurred renewed legal and civic activism in the fugitive slave issue. Her case commanded national attention, and the powerful arguments delivered by Chase – published and distributed throughout the northern states – inspired the passage of new personal liberty laws and encouraged fugitive slaves to increasingly contest their rendition and apply for writs of habeas corpus upon recapture, forcing the courts and the nation to confront what appeared to be clear violations of their constitutional rights to due process in free soil territory. Not all such cases ended in favor of the runaways, as even in the North many judges remained swayed by the power of slavery and southern interpretations of federal law. But some did. The Matilda case laid bare the conflicts between state and constitutional laws as they applied to fugitive slaves in the antebellum North, and it stimulated

[3] Chase, *Speech of Salmon P. Chase*; Middleton, *The Black Laws*, 112–113; Salafia, "Searching for Slavery," 38–63.

renewed legal challenges regarding the precise status of African-American refugees in the free states, sometimes to the advantage of the runaways. It also encouraged northerners to commit acts of civil disobedience to obstruct the execution of federal fugitive slave laws in their own communities. Matilda's fate ironically helped protect thousands of other runaways living as refugees in the northern states.[4]

As a "gateway to freedom" and destination for fugitive slaves from the southern states in the period between the Revolution and the Civil War, the Northern United States has received more attention from scholars than any other part of the continent. And understandably so. Even if most runaways never made it out of the South, estimates of those who reached free soil in the North run upward of 100,000 in the antebellum period, a "mass exit" by any definition. Most of the historical scholarship on northbound runaways has broadly centered around two main themes. Perhaps unsurprisingly, slave flight itself – in particular the Underground Railroad (UGRR) and its related networks and activists – has long featured prominently in the literature. Early histories heavily emphasized the role of mainly white abolitionist "conductors" in aiding and even rescuing runaway slaves from the South, while post-civil-rights era studies – beginning with Larry Gara's seminal work *The Liberty Line* (1961) – have shifted the focus to the actions of slave refugees and African-American communities in the northern states. More recent works, such as Eric Foner's *Gateway to Freedom* (2016), have depicted runaways and African Americans as the primary actors in northbound slave flight, while others emphasize the importance of overlapping and interracial networks in facilitating slave escapes from the southern states.[5]

---

[4] William E. Baringer, "The Politics of Abolition: Salmon P. Chase in Cincinnati," *Cincinnati Historical Society Bulletin* 29, no. 2 (1971): 86–87; Randy E. Barnett, "From Antislavery Lawyer to Chief Justice: The Remarkable but Forgotten Career of Salmon P . Chase," *Case Western Reserve Law Review* 63, no. 3 (2013): 658–663.

[5] For more on "mass exits" and desertions in the early modern world, see Marcel van der Linden, "Mass Exits: Who, Why, How?" in Matthias van Rossum and Jeannette Kamp, eds., *Desertion in the Early Modern World: A Comparative History* (London: Bloomsbury, 2016), 31–45. Statistics on northbound slave flight can be found in Eric Foner, *Gateway to Freedom: The History of the Underground Railroad* (New York: W. W. Norton, 2016), 45. The Underground Railroad (and northbound slave flight) has an extensive literature. The following constitutes a sampling of the most well-known works: William Still, *The Underground Railroad: A Record of Facts, Authentic Narratives, Letters, etc.* (Philadelphia: Porter & Coates, 1872); William H. Siebert, *The Underground Railroad from Slavery to Freedom* (New York: Macmillan, 1898); Larry Gara, *The Liberty Line: The Legend of the Underground Railroad* (Lexington: University of Kentucky Press, 1961); John Hope Franklin and Loren Schweninger, *Runaway Slaves:*

A second overarching theme in the historical literature is the extent to which the free soil states extended protections from slavery to African-American refugees from the southern states, and the heated sectional tensions that disputes over the status and legal rights of fugitive slaves unleashed, which ultimately led to civil war. As Andrew Delbanco has forcefully argued, the fugitive slave conflict between the northern and southern states "exposed the idea of the 'united' states as a lie." Slave refugees who fled north confronted Americans in the free states with the glaring contradiction "between the myth that slavery was a benign institution and the reality that a nation putatively based on the principle of human equality was actually a prison house in which millions of Americans had virtually no rights at all." By fleeing north of the Mason–Dixon line and Ohio River, they forced antebellum northern authorities and ordinary citizens to take sides in the ever-deepening crisis over the meanings of freedom from slavery in the free soil states and territories. The fugitive slave issue pressured northern states to enact "complete programs for the elimination of slavery and then [experiment] with ways to protect people in danger of being seized as slaves and removed to the South," in the words of Thomas Morris. Indeed, the most recent studies on fugitive slaves in the Northern United States have even underscored the regional differences *within* the North in their efforts to protect fugitive slaves and thereby secure free soil status within state borders. Robert Churchill subdivides the northern states into three geographical regions, with the border states constituting the least safe destinations for runaway slaves, followed by the "contested" middle states, with only the northeastern states truly constituting free soil. Oran Kennedy has similarly highlighted the differences in legal regimes and sentiments toward fugitive slaves in the Mason–Dixon borderland, the northeast, and the Ohio River and Mississippi River borderlands.[6]

Rebels on the Plantation (New York: Oxford University Press, 1999); Keith Griffler, *Front Line of Freedom: African Americans and the Forging of the Underground Railroad in the Ohio Valley* (Lexington: University of Kentucky Press, 2004); Fergus Bordewich, *Bound for Canaan: The Epic Story of the Underground Railroad, America's First Civil Rights Movement* (New York: HarperCollins, 2005); Richard M. Blackett, *Making Freedom: The Underground Railroad and the Politics of Slavery* (Chapel Hill: University of North Carolina Press, 2013); Cheryl Janifer LaRoche, *Free Black Communities and the Underground Railroad: The Geography of Resistance* (Urbana: University of Illinois Press, 2014); Foner, *Gateway to Freedom*.

[6] Andrew Delbanco, *The War before the War: Fugitive Slaves and the Struggle for America's Soul from the Revolution to the Civil War* (New York: Penguin Press, 2018), 2–3 (first quotes); Thomas D. Morris, *Free Men All: The Personal Liberty Laws of the*

How and why did runaway slaves from the southern states flee to the free states of the North, and how did they navigate spaces of semi-formal freedom there? This chapter will build upon the voluminous existing scholarship on fugitive slaves in the northern states by illuminating their experiences as refugees in a part of the continent where their status and freedom was highly contested between state and federal authorities. It will consider both of the abovementioned historiographical themes, and will place the fugitive slave issue in a wider context by juxtaposing the experiences of northbound runaways with their counterparts who remained within the slaveholding South, exploring the similarities and differences in their attempts to secure freedom from slavery. It will highlight the unique nature of slave flight to the northern states by considering the motivations and paths that lured freedom seekers northward, the settlement processes of refugees in the free soil territories, and the consequences of the legal battles waged as a result of the fugitive slave issue for the safety of runaways who sought asylum there.

ESCAPING THE SLAVE SOUTH

The paths that led north for freedom seekers from the southern states were not always as clear and straight as is often assumed. While many northbound escapes were premeditated affairs that involved years of careful planning and even a string of aborted or unsuccessful previous attempts, others appeared to be based more on spur-of-the-moment decisions. In the case of Matilda, for example, a daring disembarkation from a vessel docked on the free soil side of the Ohio River removed her valuable body from the grips of a slaveholder to the "free" North. Such escapes of opportunity were not uncommon. Rebecca Ginsburg has argued in her study of the landscape of North American slavery that "journeys of circumstance" undertaken by fugitive slaves who relied "more on luck and opportunity than on prearranged plans [or] networks

North, 1780–1861 (Baltimore: The John Hopkins University Press, 1999), ix (second quote); Richard M. Blackett, *The Captive's Quest for Freedom: Fugitive Slaves, the 1850 Fugitive Slave Law, and the Politics of Slavery* (New York: Cambridge University Press, 2018); John L. Brooke, *"There Is a North": Fugitive Slaves, Political Crisis, and Cultural Transformation in the Coming of the Civil War* (Amherst: University of Massachusetts Press, 2019); Robert H. Churchill, *The Underground Railroad and the Geography of Violence* (New York: Cambridge University Press, 2020); Oran Kennedy, "Northward Bound: Slave Refugees and the Pursuit of Freedom in the Northern US and Canada, 1775–1861" (PhD diss., Leiden University, 2021), 67–129.

of conductors" were probably more common than organized escapes that depended on the safe houses and routes that would ultimately be immortalized as the Underground Railroad. Just because their journeys appeared to be strongly influenced by ad hoc opportunities and triggers, however, does not mean that northbound runaways were inherently indifferent to their ultimate destinations or that they had not given thorough consideration to what they were doing when they made their escapes. Whether they ran in split-second opportunistic decisions or as part of elaborate plans, slaves who sought refuge in the northern states appear to have had clear ideas about where they wanted to go and what they expected to find there.[7]

Why some enslaved people chose to run north rather than to spaces of informal freedom in the South is a question that deserves more serious scholarly attention. The decision to escape at all was not made easily, let alone across heavily patrolled state borders into free soil territory that effectively served as portals of no return. What, then, motivated some runaways to risk everything – including their very lives – to reach free soil, rather than simply try to pass for free in the urban South? The question is not easily answered, as no single factor ever constituted *the* reason. Rather, several interwoven considerations usually conspired to push runaways to make for the northern states rather than a nearby southern city, including obvious factors of circumstance such as the enticing proximity of free soil itself. Franklin and Schweninger have referred to this as "the accident of location." A vast majority of runaways to the northern states were indeed from the Upper South, where distances to free soil were relatively short. The runaways registered in the records of the Vigilance Committee of Philadelphia (VCP), for example, were nearly all from Maryland and Virginia. All of the 119 fugitive slaves recorded in Chester County, Pennsylvania, between the years 1820 and 1839, were from neighboring Maryland, Virginia, and Delaware. Most runaways in Ohio were similarly from across the river in Kentucky. Some runaways had even *visited* neighboring free states prior to their flight attempts. One Kentucky slaveholder complained in a letter to a family member in 1824 that one of his slaves had disappeared and was presumed to be in Ohio; he admitted that the young enslaved man had "travelled with me

---

[7] Van der Linden, "Mass Exits," 34–35; Rebecca Ginsburg, "Escaping through a Black Landscape," in Clifton Ellis and Rebecca Ginsburg, eds., *Cabin, Quarter, Plantation: Architecture and Landscapes of North American Slavery* (New Haven, CT: Yale University Press, 2010), 53 (quote); Franklin and Schweninger, *Runaway Slaves*, 97–123.

frequently, and consequently would be able to make his way, better than common negroes." Another enslaved man from western Virginia who fled north told an interviewer that he had "been to Cincinnati to sell produce" before fleeing.[8]

Throughout the borderlands, northbound runaways tended to make for nearby and in rare cases familiar patches of free soil, yet this fact alone is clearly insufficient to explain the decision to run north, since most runaways who chose lives of informal freedom in places such as Baltimore, District of Columbia, and Richmond were also from the Upper South. Northbound runaways indeed often had to *pass through* these sites of informal freedom in order to reach the Pennsylvania border. Even northbound refugees from the Lower South often fled by smuggling themselves on board vessels bound for the North from port cities such as Charleston, Natchez, and New Orleans – cities that also served as sites of informal freedom in their own right. The proximity of free soil or the availability of opportunities to flee there from certain port cities is not enough to explain northbound slave flight, at least not on their own.

A second factor of circumstance that was clearly important in many northbound runaway cases was the nature of the runaways' social networks – the existence of friends or family who had fled north before them, or a lack of family or acquaintances in nearby urban areas that they deemed suitable to a successful flight attempt within the South. This factor will be more fully explored below. Again, however, retaining ties to extended family and community still in slavery often served as a powerful motivator to flee *within* the South, as explained in the previous chapter.

Perhaps just as important as the proximity of free soil and the social networks of freedom seekers were the different *expectations* that northbound runaways had of freedom itself. This factor deserves closer analysis. A *desire to be free* – to live on free soil – was an important motivating

---

[8] Franklin and Schweninger, *Runaway Slaves*, 25 (first quote), se also ch. 5, esp. 116–124; Still, *The Underground Railroad*; Chester County, PA, Fugitive Slave Records, 1820–1839 (www.chesco.org/1722/Fugitive-Slave-Records-1820-1839); William Buckner to Thomas Buckner, April 29, 1824, quoted in Kennedy, "Northward Bound," 107 (second quote); Thomas Johnson, in Benjamin Drew, *A North-Side View of Slavery: The Refugee, or the Narratives of Fugitive Slaves in Canada* (Cleveland, OH: John P. Jewett & Co., 1856), 379–381 (third quote). See also Kennedy, "Northward Bound," 62, 67–129; Matthew Salafia, *Slavery's Borderland: Freedom and Bondage along the Ohio River* (Philadelphia: University of Pennsylvania Press, 2011), 129; S. Charles Bolton, *Fugitivism: Escaping Slavery in the Lower Mississippi Valley, 1820–1860* (Fayetteville: University of Arkansas Press, 2019), 97–116.

factor behind decisions to flee to the northern states. Indeed, the northern states were often alluded to as a "promised land," a label never used to describe Baltimore or New Orleans or other spaces of informal freedom in the urban South. Freedom seekers who fled the South altogether experienced what Oran Kennedy has called a "tipping point" – a point at which they perceived life in the slave South as so stifling and so dangerous for black people that it was no longer worth living, such that even informal freedom in urban areas within the slaveholding states seemed too unsatisfactory to be worth the risks involved. William Still, the famous African-American abolitionist and "conductor" of runaways in Philadelphia, hinted at this mentality when he claimed in 1872 that in his experience, runaways in the northern states were "intellectually above the average order of slaves. They were determined to have liberty even at the cost of life." Many northbound runaways indeed exhibited a conscious desire to seize their "right" to live in freedom. In other words, escape attempts to the Northern United States were often permeated with not only a desire to *escape slavery*, or escape their masters, but also to *be free*, to live in a free society where their humanity was recognized and where slavery did not exist. It was positive freedom that they sought, rather than simply their extrication from slavery. As S. Charles Bolton recently argued, "The pull of self-actualization and anticipated happiness was often more important to the decision [to flee the South] than the push of exploitation." Even if many actual escape attempts were ad hoc and spur-of-the-moment, northbound runaways' clear desire to leave the entire institution of slavery behind them and live the rest of their lives on free soil was deeply rooted and had often been simmering for years before they actually fled.[9]

This inner rejection of southern slavery and desire to live in a slave-free society can be gleaned from a wide variety of source material, including court cases and runaway slave ads in which the owners of northbound freedom seekers claimed that their runaways appeared to have fled for no specific reason. Northbound runaways were indeed often described as unusually angry, unruly, or possessed by a bad disposition, which might be interpreted as evidence of a profound dissatisfaction with slavery and a burning commitment to break all ties with slaveholding society. William

[9] Kennedy, "Northward Bound," 57–64; Still, *The Underground Railroad*, 2 (first quote); Bolton, *Fugitivism*, 8 (second quote); Foner, *Gateway to Freedom*, 12. Franklin and Schweninger examine the unwavering commitment to living in freedom in their discussion of "habitual runaways." They also refer to the northern states as "promised lands" and discuss the "dream of freedom" in free soil states, a dream that went unfulfilled for most runaways. See Franklin and Schweninger, *Runaway Slaves*, 37–42, 116.

Henry Thomas, a Maryland slave only sixteen years old, for example, was arrested in 1856 while "making his way to a free state." His owner sought permission from the courts to sell him out of state, confessing that William was completely unmanageable and that he refused to live in slavery. The slaveholder did "not [know] what other disposition to make of him." Another Maryland slave was reported by his owner to have "been well fed & Clothed since your petitioner owned him." Despite such decent treatment, however, the enslaved man openly declared that he would not remain in servitude and subsequently ran away. Caleb, a Delaware slave who ran north and was recaptured eighteen months later, was described by his master as a dangerous man with a violent disposition, "unfit to live in the State" and unlikely to remain subjugated to any master. The slaveholder requested permission to sell him out of state. The owner of a Virginia slave similarly petitioned for a permit to sell his bondsman out of state, claiming that he had "become unmanageable," that he "refused to work," despite being a "young, strong and hearty negro." The slaveholder feared that his bondsman would soon make "an effort to get into a free state." Alfred, an enslaved man in South Carolina, was described by his owner in 1856 as "very difficult to manage, & while hired out, has made several attempts to escape into a free state." Sam, a "likely boy about forty-five years of age" from Tennessee, was described by his master in 1854 as "wild" and "ungovernable," adding that during a recent escape attempt Sam had come "very near making it to a Free State." Fearing he would lose his investment, he petitioned the Maury County court to sell Sam and use the proceeds to purchase "some other better and more tractable slave."[10]

Many northbound runaways appeared to have held the conviction that they had some legitimate *claim* to freedom. Sometimes these claims arose not from any specific incident of abuse but rather a close identification with free society or an unrealized promise of freedom by their master.

---

[10] Petition of Henry A. Inloes to the Baltimore City Orphans Court, MD, August 26, 1856, Race and Slavery Petitions Project (hereafter RSPP), Series 2: County Court Petitions, Accession #20985631 (first quote); Petition of James S. Wilson to Orphans Court of Anne Arundel County, MD, September 15, 1859, RSPP, Series 2: County Court Petitions, Accession #20985958 (second quote); Petition of Burton Conner to Kent County Court, DE, May 4, 1829, RSPP, Series 2, Accession #20382901 (third quote); Petition of Thomas Oldham to Lancaster County Court, VA, February 19, 1855, RSPP, Series 2, Accession #21085504 (fourth quote); Petition of Thomas J. Davis to Edgefield County Court, SC, April 9, 1856, RSPP, Series 2, Accession #21385606 (fifth quote); Petition of David F. Wilson et al., to Maury County Court, TN, October 30, 1854, RSPP, Series 2, Accession #21485411 (sixth quote).

Light-skinned slaves, including those who were themselves fathered by slaveholders, for example, show up frequently in the historical records of northbound runaways, perhaps at least in part because of their frustration at being kept enslaved in a racialized society where they appeared to look more like the master class than like their fellow slaves. The abovementioned Matilda, for one, was the daughter of her own master, a fact referred to frequently during her trial, suggesting that she felt she had some right to freedom because her father was free and because she was so light-skinned. It is likely that she expected at some point to be manumitted – the fact that she openly attempted to negotiate her own manumission with her father before she fled speaks volumes to how she thought about her own right to freedom. Similar examples can be interpreted from other court records. In 1853, the owner of one Virginia bondsman named Cary explained to a Petersburg city court that his slave had a "very bad character" and was in the habit of undertaking flight attempts to the North. Interestingly, the slaveholder complained that Cary "is almost white and has made attempts to run away & indeed at one time got far from home before he was arrested," implying that Cary was light-skinned enough to virtually pass for free, a factor that doubtless influenced his conviction that he should therefore *be* free. Margaret Mason, the owner of an enslaved man from Tennessee named Green, similarly sought permission from a Giles County court in 1857 to sell her bondsman out of state, fearing that he would successfully flee to free soil. Green was described as "white & could easily pass himself for a white man anywhere." Mason added that she "has good reason to believe that said slave is restless & dissatisfied with the condition of slavery, and contemplates an escape," an undertaking that would probably succeed "both from his color and general appearance as from his intelligence & shrewdness."[11]

Unfulfilled promises of manumission spurred many bondspeople to claim their "right" to freedom. Elijah Turner, a Virginia slave who was sold away from his family several times and ultimately ended up in Alabama, claimed in a narrative published after his successful flight (he eventually ended up in Canada) that he developed the conviction that he had a right to freedom after a combination of living a life of relative material luxury during slavery followed by broken promises of eventual

[11] Petition of Edward Hugh Caperton and Robert Dunn to Petersburg City Court, January 1853, RSPP, Series 2, Accession #21685309 (first quote); Petition of Margaret J. Mason to Giles County Court, August 31, 1857, RSPP, Series 2, Accession #21485723 (second quote). See also Franklin and Schweninger, *Runaway Slaves*, 37–42.

manumission. By the time Turner was sixteen years old he had become his master's favorite personal servant and enjoyed many privileges: he had enough to eat and few material complaints, earned tips which he spent on his own "vanity," and was even afforded opportunities to travel with his master and meet new people. Yet the more comfortable his life became, the more his "longing for freedom increased," precisely because he was exposed to just enough comfort and free society to understand what he was missing. Despite his life of relative luxury, "still there was this consciousness that I was but a 'slave,'" Turner wrote, "a piece of property controlled, and owned by another..." A few years later, Turner's master admitted on his deathbed that he had wanted to manumit him in his will, but that he feared his wife would need his services, and so chose to keep him in bondage. It was at that point – the final closing of the door to legal freedom by a young enslaved man who felt that he had a right to be free – that Elijah Turner decided to "strike for liberty or death." Citing these revolutionary ideals, he fled the South.[12]

Stories like these were not uncommon. Indeed, term slaves from the Upper South – those who had been promised their freedom after a certain number of years – are heavily represented in county court cases and other records that deal with northbound runaways. In such cases the runaways' claims to freedom were rooted in the fact that their masters had already designated them for manumission, and they either did not want to wait until that day came or did not trust their owners to follow through on their promise. Jacob Younker, a mulatto slave from Maryland, was owned by a woman named Eleanor Brosins "for and during her natural life," but when Brosins died in 1857 her will stipulated that Younker should "belong to the children" until October 12, 1869, after which he should be manumitted. Whether out of impatience or a distrust of Brosin's heirs, Younker had no intention of waiting another twelve years for his freedom. Instead, he fled to Pennsylvania on October 10, 1857 (he was ultimately caught and sent back to Maryland). An almost identical case occurred just a few months later in the same county when an enslaved woman named Annetta, whose late master had stipulated in his will that she serve his son "until she arrived at the age of thirty-six," ran away to Pennsylvania but was caught and sent back to her owner. In 1858 one Henry Oberne, an enslaved man from Seaport, Maryland,

[12] Henry Goings, *Rambles of a Runaway from Southern Slavery*, edited by Calvina Schermerhorn, Michael Plunkett, and Edward Gaynor (Charlottesville: University of Virginia Press, 2012), 31, 37, 39.

successfully escaped to Philadelphia, claiming to agents of the local Vigilance Committee that he was twenty-one years old and was set to be freed at age twenty-eight, but he preferred his freedom now, "especially as he was not certain that 28 would ever come." Another Virginia woman named Julia was promised her freedom upon the death of her mistress, but when her mistress died the heirs decided to sell her instead. She fled north together with her husband in 1854. A young enslaved man named Jacob, from Maryland, arrived with his wife at the doors of the New York Committee of Vigilance in 1855, telling agent Sydney Howard Gay that he had been promised his freedom at age twenty-one, but when his mistress died before that time he was held by the heirs as a slave. When his wife was subsequently threatened with sale the couple decided that they had had enough, and resolved to seek freedom in free soil territory.[13]

Hirelings – especially those who were permitted by their masters to hire their own time – also appear with frequency in the records on runaway slaves. Indeed, hirelings were already heavily represented among runaways who ran away to southern cities, but also among northbound freedom seekers, as many developed the conviction that they deserved to be legally free because they had already learned to sustain themselves and live like free blacks. Court cases and northern abolitionist records often make specific reference to runaways who had been hirelings before taking flight. Appollo and Hannah, an enslaved couple from Davidson County, Tennessee, for example, ran away to a free state in 1847, but Appollo was arrested along the way and thrown into jail. In the court records relating to the case it is mentioned that Appollo had been "allowed to hire his own time" and that Hannah "lived almost as a free person." Both had apparently long "entertained" the idea of fleeing to the North. A Missouri Supreme Court case relating to an enslaved man who absconded from St. Louis to Illinois in 1849 similarly made reference to the fact that the fugitive had unlawfully been "allowed by plaintiff to go at large on the hiring of his own time," a practice that was thought to have encouraged the slave to run north. Jack Scott, a runaway from Richmond, Virginia, who was entered into the records of the Vigilance

---

[13] Petition of Daniel Brosins et al., to the Orphans Court of Washington County, MD, November 13, 1857, RSPP, Series 2: County Court Petitions, Accession #20985717 (first quote); Petition of Andrew Hogmire to the Orphans Court of Washington County, MD, May 4, 1858, RSPP, Series 2: County Court Petitions, Accession #20985812 (second quote); Still, *The Underground Railroad*, 105 (third quote); Ibid., 142; Sydney Howard Gay, "Record of Fugitives," December 5, 1855, Sydney Howard Gay Papers, accessed via https://exhibitions.library.columbia.edu/exhibits/show/fugitives/record_fugitives.

Committee of Philadelphia as a refugee in 1859, claimed that he had been hired out year after year by his owner, and that he had decided to flee because he was tired of working for "white people for nothing."[14]

In rare cases, northbound refugees claimed to actually have a natural-born legal right to freedom. John Merry, who ran away from a New Orleans slaveholder in 1826 and got as far as the Illinois border before being caught and thrown into a St. Louis jail, argued that he had been born in Illinois after the passage of the Northwest Ordinance and was therefore "free according to the laws of the land," but had been deprived of that freedom and eventually sold to New Orleans. William Anderson was born to a free black woman in Virginia but illegally sold as a slave when he was a child, eventually ending up on a Mississippi plantation. He ran away to Indiana in 1836, reclaiming a free status that he had been robbed of by his enslavers. In his 1857 memoir Anderson claimed that there came a point when he "made up my mind to run away, let the consequences be what they would. Patrick Henry's words became my motto, via: 'Give me liberty or give me death.'" The free backgrounds of Merry and Anderson were clearly exceptional among northbound runaways, but they connect to a pattern of runaways to the free states who felt that they had a claim to freedom because they were somehow more deserving of freedom than other enslaved people.[15]

Other refugees from slavery developed the conviction that they deserved freedom because they subscribed to the quintessentially revolutionary principle that "all men are created equal," a phrase that was virtually impossible to keep secret from enslaved people of the postrevolutionary era. This creed led some runaways to reject the authority of the slaveholding class and seize their right to live as free people. One extremely light-skinned and literate slave from Charleston named William Cooper, for example, successfully fled to Syracuse in 1858, claiming that he had been owned by an elderly lady who had never

---

[14] Petition of George W. Martin to Davidson County Court of Chancery, October 4, 1847, RSPP, Series 2, Accession #21484717 (first quote); Petition of Fleming Calvert and Mary Ann Calvert, Supreme Court of Missouri, August 28, 1851, RSPP, Series 2, Accession #21185105 (second quote); Still, *The Underground Railroad*, 104 (third quote). Franklin and Schweninger discuss the dissatisfaction of hired slaves and their prevalence in runaway slave ads. See Franklin and Schweninger, *Runaway Slaves*, 33–37.

[15] Petition of John Murray to the Circuit Court of St. Louis County, MO, September 30, 1826, RSPP, Series 2, Accession #21182606 (first quote); William J. Anderson, *The Narrative of William J. Anderson, Twenty-Four Years a Slave* (Chicago: Daily Tribune Book & Job Printing Office, 1857), 30 (second quote).

mistreated him but who was simply "opposed to Freedom." William felt that he had as much a right to freedom and self-improvement as any white person, and that indeed his entire race deserved that right. In a letter of his own writing from Syracuse in 1858, he declared to abolitionist William Still in Philadelphia that he wished to "go to school at McGrowville & spend my winter their [sic]. I am going sir to try to Prepair myself for a Lecturer, I am going sir By the Help of god to try and Do something for the Caus [sic] to help my Poor Breathern that are suffering under the yoke." Ideological convictions constituted an important motivation for many enslaved people to flee.[16]

The life story of the infamous refugee-turned-abolitionist Henry Bibb, a Kentucky slave who ran north and then returned to the South several times in desperate attempts to rescue his family before ultimately losing track of them, provides a similarly interesting example of an enslaved man's revolutionary ideas about his own right to freedom and self-improvement. Like Matilda Lawrence and William Cooper, the fact that Bibb was the son of a slaveholder and light-skinned enough that he could almost pass for white was doubtless a factor in the formation of his opinions, but what really hardened his ideological convictions and his commitment to freedom was his continual subjection to abuse at the hands of his many owners as well as having to witness the abuse of his own wife. Bibb wrote in his memoir that "the circumstances in which I was then placed, gave me a longing desire to be free." Crucially, it was not just the abuse itself that sparked his demand for freedom – it was the *faulty ideology of slavery* that made such abuse possible, even standard. Bibb understood that he was "a slave, a prisoner for life." His suffering "kindled a fire of liberty" within him, he claimed, convincing him that God had created all human beings equal, and that "every man has a right to wages for his labor; a right to his own wife and children; a right to liberty and the pursuit of happiness; and a right to worship God according to the dictates of his own conscience." Bibb's clear references to the Declaration of Independence and the values laid out in the Bill of Rights underscore his understanding of freedom as a universal moral, legal, and political right. Unlike his fellow bondsmen who ran away to

---

[16] William Cooper to William Still, June 9, 1858, reprinted in Still, *The Underground Railroad*, 108 (quote). S. Charles Bolton recently argued that runaways "were exercising the entire triad of natural rights that Thomas Jefferson claimed for Americans, 'life, liberty, and the pursuit of happiness.'" See Bolton, *Fugitivism*, 8.

nearby southern towns and cities in attempts to navigate lives of informal freedom, Bibb would settle for nothing less than a *legal* recognition of his humanity and his natural rights as a human being.[17]

Like Bibb, many northbound refugees from slavery testified that the excessive physical and psychological suffering they had endured during slavery had ultimately convinced them of their right to seize their freedom. Beatings and whippings caused freedom seekers to attempt to *take control of their own bodies* from those who claimed ownership over them. Most were men, and notions of masculinity and the humiliation of not being allowed to "be their own man" clearly informed their decisions to escape. Suffering abuse at the hands of another man was experienced as an insult to their manhood and to their humanity. James Currey, a refugee from North Carolina whose story was published in the *Liberator* in 1840, claimed that ever since childhood "the desire for freedom" had so dominated his thoughts that he resolved that "if I was ever whipped after I became a man, I would no longer be a slave," a resolution he eventually felt compelled to make good by fleeing to Pennsylvania and removing himself from a master who claimed ownership over his adult body. Another Virginia refugee likened the abuse he experienced to dehumanization, telling an interviewer that his master treated his slaves "worse than a horse or a hog ought to be treated; so, seeing what I was coming to, I wished to get away." William, a thirty-four-year-old runaway to Philadelphia from Cambridge, Maryland, told an agent of the city's Vigilance Committee in 1854 that he "was used very hard, which was the cause of his escape, though that he was entitled to his freedom had been entertained for the previous twelve years." Excessive physical abuse was often compounded by the torture and humiliation of having to witness loved ones being abused as well. One Virginia runaway to Pittsburgh claimed that his master "whipped my wife and children … I could not stand this abuse of them, so I made up my mind to leave." The refugee's original plan had been to bring his family with him, but when his wife became nervous and failed to join him, he left anyway rather than suffer such assaults on his family. The conviction that all people had a right to own their own bodies and should enjoy the right to protection from physical abuse at the hands of people who under slavery claimed

---

[17] Henry Bibb, *Narrative of the Life and Adventures of Henry Bibb, an American Slave, Written by Himself* (New York: The Author, 1849), 17 (quotes).

absolute authority over those bodies served as a powerful motivation to flee north.[18]

Testimonies of enslaved women who escaped to the northern states – although they form only a small minority of such sources – also frequently mention a desire to take back ownership of their own bodies, especially those who had suffered physical abuse. Perhaps the most famous example was the North Carolina slave Harriet Jacobs, who after years of sexual abuse by her master felt compelled to go into hiding in her free grandmother's garret for seven years before ultimately being smuggled out of the South on board a vessel bound for Philadelphia in 1842. Like the abovementioned Matilda, Jacobs appears to have felt some claim to freedom long before her escape in the sense that in her narrative she made a specific point of underscoring the fact that she was light-skinned (although not herself the child of a slaveholder); that she had free family members (including her maternal grandmother – meaning that she only narrowly missed manumission herself, since slave status was passed down through the maternal line); that her father was highly skilled and had saved all his life to purchase his family's freedom but had never managed; and that she was literate from an early age. Her desire – demand – to be free, however, arose from her desire to wrest back control of her own body after years of relentless sexual abuse and persecution at the hands of her master James Norcom, which convinced her that all enslaved people should own themselves. Jacobs had indeed known others in her immediate circle who had fled for that very reason, even before her own flight attempt. In her narrative she openly expressed admiration for her uncle Benjamin, for example, who "dared feel like a man" and resolved to escape to New York. Harriet wished to live like a woman, with a right to her own body and the right to raise her own children. After seven years in a suffocating attic, a scheme was finally concocted to have her smuggled north and her children to follow, upon which Harriet admitted that "the anticipation of *being a free woman* almost proved too much for my weak frame. The excitement stimulated me ..."[19]

The records of northern vigilance committees also attest to the desire of female northbound runaways to escape physical abuse at the hands of

[18] James Curry, "Narrative of James Curry, a Fugitive Slave," *The Liberator*, January 10, 1840; James Adams, in Drew, *North-Side View of Slavery*, 19; Still, *The Underground Railroad*, 97 (quote); Dan Josiah Lockhart, in Drew, *North-Side View of Slavery*, 46–50. See also Franklin and Schweninger, *Runaway Slaves*, 42–48; and Kennedy, "Northward Bound," 58.

[19] Harriet Jacobs, *Incidents in the Life of a Slave Girl* (1861; New York: Barnes & Noble, 2005), 11–14, 23–33, 42–45, 165–166 (quote).

their masters. Hannah, a "hearty looking" Maryland slave woman from Caroline County, about twenty-three or twenty-four years of age, escaped to Philadelphia and claimed to agents of William Still's Vigilance Committee of Philadelphia that she left because her master used her "so bad, beat and knocked" her about. Mary Elizabeth, another Maryland refugee who presented herself to the committee, explained that she had run away because of "hard treatment." Jane Clark, yet another enslaved woman from Maryland who escaped to New York in 1859, similarly claimed to have fled after years of floggings and abuse at the hands of her owner.[20]

As with enslaved people who fled within the South, bondspeople confronted with the threat or reality of sale and forced separations from loved ones often felt compelled to undertake risky flight attempts to safer territory in the free states. The psychological trauma of losing loved ones to the domestic slave trade, in particular, stands out as a grievance that spurred many to flee. William Still cited the domestic slave trade as one of the most important factors in stimulating slave flight to Philadelphia from the Upper South. "The slave auction block indirectly proved to be in some respects a very active agent in promoting travel on the U.G.R.R.," he wrote in 1872. Specific examples can be found throughout Still's records as well as in other slave testimonies. One Maryland man named Henry, for example, fled to Philadelphia not complaining of any "bad usage" by his master, but rather because of a deep conviction that "every man should have his liberty," an opinion he developed after his wife was sold away to Georgia. Other slave narratives similarly point to forced separation as a catalyst for flight. Henry Brown, the Virginia enslaved man who famously had himself shipped in a crate to Philadelphia in 1849, had not considered fleeing the slave South until his wife and children were sold to North Carolina, a traumatic event made him become "weary of my bonds" and desirous of possessing the freedom from which "I, and millions of my fellow-men, had been robbed." Others fled when their own numbers were called. Even in these desperate situations, runaways often referred specifically to perceived legal protections in the northern states to justify their decision for removing their valuable bodies from the South. One Virginia runaway who eventually ended up in Canada after living as a refugee in the northern states told an interviewer in the 1850s

---

[20] Still, *The Underground Railroad*, 104 (first quote); Ibid., 146 (second quote); Robin Bernstein, "Jane Clark: A Newly Available Slave Narrative," *Common-place.org* 18, no. 1 (2018), http://common-place.org/book/vol-18-no-1-bernstein/; Kennedy, "Northward Bound," ch. 2.

that his tipping point was the news that he was to be sold south, "which would separate me from my family, and knowing no law which would defend me, I concluded to come away."²¹

The role that family and kinship ties played in slave flight to the northern states differed in important respects to slave flight within the South itself. While runaways who fled to southern towns and cities often fled either with the intention of remaining close to family still in slavery or were drawn to urban areas because they already had spouses or family members living there – or both – freedom seekers who fled north more often fled with the intention or hope of *freeing their families as well as themselves*. This was true for enslaved people who fled the South in groups, which often constituted family units, but also for single escapees, who upon arrival in the North sometimes enlisted the help of abolitionists to help them "rescue" or even purchase their wives and children still in slavery. Court records as well as northern vigilance committee records provide numerous examples of both types of "family flight."

Flight attempts in collective family units are overwhelmingly attested to in the sources. In 1854, for example, a mulatto enslaved man from Louisiana named Enos, along with his wife Phillis and their two children, secreted themselves onboard a northbound steamboat called the *Eldorado*. Having all fled together, they were discovered only one day after departing New Orleans during a stop in Plaquemines Parish and returned to their owner. That same year the Vigilance Committee of Philadelphia recorded the arrival of a large group of runaways from Cambridge, Maryland, which included several couples and family groups: "Aaron Cornish and wife, with their six children; Solomon, George Anthony, Joseph, Edward James, Perry Lake, and a nameless babe, all very likely; Kit Anthony and wife Leah, and three children, Adam, Mary, and Murray; Joseph Hill and wife Alice, and their son Henry; also Joseph's sister." Another group of refugees from Maryland arrived in Pennsylvania consisting of a thirty-five-year-old man who not only emancipated himself, but, "through great perseverance, secured the freedom of his wife and six children; one child he was compelled to leave behind."²²

---

²¹ Still, *The Underground Railroad*, 2 (first quote); Ibid., 97 (second quote); Henry Brown, *Narrative of the Life of Henry Box Brown, Written by Himself* (Manchester: Lee & Glynn, 1851), 49–50 (third quote); David West, in Drew, *North-Side View of Slavery*, 87–88 (fourth quote; italics mine). See also Franklin and Schweninger, *Runaway Slaves*, 43–74; Kennedy, "Northward Bound," 55–56.

²² Petition of Dr. Henry Daret to 2nd District Court of New Orleans, May 2, 1854, RSPP, Series 2, Accession #20885453; Still, *The Underground Railroad*, 99–101, 99 (first

"Rescue" flight attempts, whereby one family member ran north with
the intention of engaging help and returning to free loved ones, can also
be found in court records, slave narratives, and the records of northern
vigilance committees. In 1848, a Missouri slave named John Walker fled
across the border into Iowa, found safety in the town of Salem (a strong-
hold of Quaker abolitionists), and subsequently crossed back into
Missouri with a group of abolitionist helpers in order to rescue his wife
and children. They also managed to rescue another fellow enslaved man
from the same farm along with his wife and children. Such actions were
extremely dangerous, as they could result in the recapture of the runaways themselves. Thomas Rice and Hiram Good crossed the border
from Pennsylvania to Maryland in the summer of 1855 claiming to be
"free negroes from Pennsylvania," for example, but were ultimately
arrested as runaway slaves and thrown into a Washington County jail
before they could reach their home communities. Harriet Tubman – the
most famous example of a runaway "rescuer" – returned several times to
her native Maryland to rescue enslaved family members, among others,
after her own successful flight in 1849. Far safer (but more difficult) was
to engage the assistance of abolitionists and try to get them to go south on
the runaway's behalf in an attempt to try and purchase the freedom of a
loved one. One woman named Arrah, who had to leave one of her
children behind in slavery when she fled to Philadelphia in 1857, engaged
the help of abolitionists connected with the Philadelphia Vigilance
Committee in order to raise funds to buy her child and bring him north.
In a letter filed with the committee one sympathetic agent who was
working closely with Arrah proposed that a "journey be made by her or
someone else, in order to take the other [child]," adding that he hoped
"that our friends in Philadelphia and New York will assist her to make up
the full amount required for the purchase of the boy."[23]

quote); Ibid., 103 (second quote). In their analysis of more than 2,000 runaway slave
advertisements, Franklin and Schweninger found that "in most instances runaway families included a husband and wife and one or two children," adding that "usually it was
the fear of being separated that prompted families to run away." See Franklin and
Schweninger, *Runaway Slaves*, 66–67.

23 *Fugitive Slave Case: District Court of the United States for the Southern Division of Iowa,
    Burlington, June Term 1850, Ruel Daggs v. Elihu Frazier, et als., Reported by Geo.
    Frazee* (Burlington, Iowa: Morgan & M'Kenny, 1850); Petition from Thomas Rice and
    Hiram Good to the Circuit Court of Washington County, MD, December 18, 1855,
    RSPP, Series 2: County Court Petitions, Accession #20985537; E. L. Stevens to William
    Still, July 13, 1857, in Still, *The Underground Railroad*, 156 (quote); Catherine Clinton,
    Harriet Tubman: The Road to Freedom (New York: Little, Brown & Co., 2004).

Even when rescue attempts failed – and they usually did – it is significant that many fugitive slaves living in the northern states fled there with
the intention to somehow become reunited with loved ones still in slavery.
The story of Charles Ball, whose gripping narrative was originally published in 1836 and later republished and more widely distributed in 1859,
is illustrative of a failed attempt. Ball had been born enslaved in Maryland
but sold as a young adult to South Carolina, ultimately ending up on a
cotton plantation in Georgia. The forced move separated him from his
wife and children back in Maryland, a situation he described as agonizing
and unbearable. He managed to escape, making his way all the way back
to Maryland on foot, where he was reunited with his family and settled
down near Baltimore, passing for free and living a life of informal
freedom like so many of his counterparts. His first wife died a few years
later but Ball remarried and continued to live a clandestine life within the
slave South. The precarious nature of his life as a "free man," however,
manifested itself when he was captured one day in 1830 and sold back
into slavery, once again separating him from his loved ones. Resolving to
escape the South altogether this time, he secreted himself onboard a vessel
to Philadelphia, reaching free soil and a place of far greater safety and
freedom than his native Maryland. Tellingly, his first order of business
upon arrival in Philadelphia was to get settled and immediately return to
Baltimore to try and rescue his family. Only when he learned that they
had been sold in the meantime did he go back to the North and resign
himself to life as a castaway from his native land and family.[24]

The dangers involved in running north were numerous. Runaways
who made for the free northern states navigated a daunting and dangerous borderland in which they always ran the risk of being pursued and
recaptured by their owners, heavily armed slave catchers (who often
unleashed "negro dogs" to hunt them down), or ordinary citizens. The
violence that this often entailed was enough to deter even the toughest
freedom seekers. Robert Churchill indeed recently noted that the theme of
violence constitutes "a current that runs through every fugitive account
and every Underground activist reminiscence." Brutal stories of bloody
pursuits were widely publicized and well-known in slave quarters
throughout the South. They even appear in court records. One runaway
from Delaware who fled to Pennsylvania in 1805, for example, was
ruthlessly hunted down by violent slave catchers and returned to his

---

[24] Charles Ball, *Fifty Years in Chains; or, The Life of an American Slave* (New York: Asher
& Co., 1859).

owner so badly beaten that he was "altogether blind," for which his owner sought compensation.[25]

Many runaways absconded well prepared to fight would-be captors to death, taking guns and other weapons with them. William Anderson, a northbound runaway from Mississippi to Indiana, claimed to have "procured a long knife previous to my starting, knowing it to be an indispensable article to a man in my situation." A group of Maryland runaways arrived in Philadelphia in 1854 even more heavily armed, as the city's Vigilance Committee quickly discovered. One was "armed with a six-barreled revolver, a large knife, and a determined mind"; another "was armed with two pistols and a dirk to defend himself"; and a third had "brought with him a butcher-knife." The most unfortunate runaways actually had to use their weapons in harrowing and sometimes deadly skirmishes. In 1831, for example, "a party of runaway Virginia negroes," some "11 or 12 in number, two of whom were women," attempted to reach the North by fleeing in an open boat up the coast. Finding themselves in hot pursuit by a group of white Delawareans in a whaleboat near Cape May on the southern tip of New Jersey, the group ended up in a firefight in which they successfully held their ground. The whaleboat "fired [a gun] with a view to frighten them," but the runaways "returned with a volley" of their own, striking one Mr. Hand, who "received a ball in his forehead which caused immediate death; another of the party had his hat brim pierced by a ball." The runaways were able to escape, and "when last seen, were shaping their course for New-York." Another group of runaways from Georgia, who found themselves pursued by officers just outside the District of Columbia one night in 1850, had revolvers on them and engaged in a gun battle with the white men, unloading literally all of their bullets, despite it being pitch black and reportedly impossible to see their targets. Even so, the slave catchers suffered casualties that included "Mr. Butts receiving a bullet in the arm; Smithey one through his hat; Capt. Goddard's eyebrow scorched ... [and] Cox a slight wound in the right cheek." As for the runaways, one made his escape into the murky night but left behind a coat so bloodied that he was presumed to be mortally wounded. Another was "shot in the back, and a bullet went through his watch ... and lodged

[25] Churchill, *The Underground Railroad and the Geography of Violence*, 3 (first quote); Petition of Richard Howard to the Sussex County Court, DE, April 19, 1808, RSPP, Series 2: County Court Petitions, Accession #20380801 (second quote); Franklin and Schweninger, *Runaway Slaves*, 149–181.

under the face, which no doubt saved his life." A third was taken into custody.[26]

It took a certain will and character to risk a flight attempt across heavily guarded state borders. Various studies have analyzed the profiles of freedom seekers and the logistics of running away from the antebellum South. Examinations of newspaper advertisements and notices have demonstrated that most runaways tended to be young men who were physically capable of undertaking prolonged journeys – Franklin and Schweninger estimated that as many as 80 percent of runaways were men, most under thirty – and that most fled alone or at most in very small groups. Most were also to some extent skilled or semi-skilled, were described as artful or cunning, demonstrated self-confidence, were intelligent and resourceful, and possessed an enormous amount of courage. In short, most northbound freedom seekers tended to be in the prime of their life and possess a fiery will to succeed in their endeavor. Descriptions of runaways in various sources tend to underscore their value and intelligence. Ben, an enslaved man from Kentucky who fled to Indiana in 1827 but was caught and returned to the South, was described in court records as a "skilled carpenter, worth between $175 and $200 a year in hire," for example. Two runaways from Richmond who arrived in Philadelphia in 1854 were described as so valuable that they would have "sold for $1200 each." The first, named James, was described as "thirty-two years of age, of dark complexion, well made, good-looking, reads and writes, is very fluent in speech, and remarkably intelligent." He was hired out every year by his mistress. His companion, named William and owned by the same woman, was described as twenty-five years of age, hired out for $125 per year, a "tip-top baker" as well as a wagoner, and altogether a "valuable piece of property."[27]

Like their counterparts who made for sites of informal freedom within the South, northbound freedom seekers knew that successful flight

---

[26] Anderson, *Narrative of William J. Anderson*, 34 (first quote); Still, *The Underground Railroad*, 97–98 (second quotes); *The Liberator*, June 11, 1831 (third and fourth quotes); *The Courier*, August 23, 1850 (fifth and sixth quotes).

[27] Kennedy, "Northward Bound," 59–61; Frankling and Schweninger, *Runaway Slaves*, 210–212, 224–228; John Hope Franklin and Loren Schweninger, "The Quest for Freedom: Runaway Slaves and the Plantation South," in Gabor S. Boritt and Scott Hancock, eds., *Slavery, Resistance, Freedom* (New York: Oxford University Press, 2007), 28; Petition of John L. Murray to Jefferson County Court, KY, July 9, 1827, RSPP, Series 2, Accession #20782711 (first quote); Still, *The Underground Railroad*, 55–57 (second quote).

entailed disguising their identities and their slave status as they made their way across a dangerous landscape. It is a common assumption that most runaways fled through forests by night wearing only the ragged clothing they had on their backs. In fact, however, only those who lived so near the border that they could attempt to flee in a beeline under cover of darkness appear to have arrived in the North looking like impoverished runaway slaves. One enslaved family who fled across the Pennsylvania border in the "dead of night" from neighboring Frederick County, Maryland, in 1858, for example, arrived at the offices of the Philadelphia Vigilance Committee described as wearing "rags [that] were not really worth the price that a woman would ask for washing them," and so were outfitted with completely new apparel by abolitionists. Another enslaved man from Martinsburg, (West) Virginia, fled to Pennsylvania during the Christmas holiday of 1857, having wandered through woods and fields on foot for two days in a region "where it was quite unsafe to make known his condition and wants." He ultimately arrived in Harrisburg shoeless – "his feet were literally worn out." Such "dashes to freedom" were only possible for those who lived along the border, however. For those whose journeys entailed more than a couple of nights of travel, disguising their appearance and engaging in elaborate "performances" were crucial to navigating the dangerous southern landscape. Falsified free papers or slave passes, different garb, aliases – these were just some of the standard weapons in their arsenal. Henry, an enslaved man from North Carolina, was caught with false freedom papers in an attempt "to escape to some non slaveholding state" in 1858. William Gales, a Maryland slave who openly told his master that he "would not stay with him," reportedly "shaved off his whiskers & moustache" in order to conceal his identity before he "ran off with out provocation" in 1859. Ben, a Virginia slave who ran to Alexandria in 1828 with the intention of "try[ing] to make his escape for New York or Boston," fled his master's residence dressed like a free man, donning "a black fur hat, with a sash round it, a grey cazinett roundabout blue vest do. and pantaloons, he also took with him a white pair of corded pantaloons." The infamous Frederick Douglass used his earnings from hiring stints to purchase free papers from a sympathetic free black sailor; armed with false documentation, he dressed up in "a red shirt and a tarpaulin hat and black cravat, tied in sailor fashion," boarded a train, and traveled unmolested from Baltimore to Philadelphia and on to New York.[28]

---

[28] Kennedy, "Northward Bound," 67–129; Still, *The Underground Railroad*, 109 (first quote); Ibid., 121 (second quote); Petition of David W. Bell to Craven County Court of Common Pleas, NC, September 1858, RSPP, Series 2, Accession #21285833 (third

Like Douglass, many northbound runaways secured the assistance of others to help them finalize their escape plans. The networks that many enslaved people from the Upper South utilized to help them escape via overland routes often included other enslaved people, free blacks, and even sympathetic whites who lived along the route. Some communities – especially cities and port towns – indeed served as common pit stops for northbound freedom seekers. One "valuable mechanic" from Virginia named William, who was caught planning his escape in 1856, was described as having "numerous acquaintances and relatives" in the city of Petersburg who were apparently preparing to have William passed along "to one of the northern states, and then be a total loss to his owner." Many runaways from Virginia and Maryland deliberately passed through Washington and Baltimore – with their large free black populations and extensive interracial UGRR networks – on their way to Pennsylvania. These cities thus served not only as magnets for runaways who intended to remain in the South, but they also served as conduits for those seeking to cross the Mason–Dixon line. In Baltimore, especially, runaways could make contact with potential helpers who could provide them with information, advice, false papers, or day labor to earn some extra money for the journey. Some stayed for months while making preparations. Richard, an enslaved man from Maryland, ran away from his master in 1859 "for the purpose of leaving the state of Maryland," but was caught in Baltimore and thrown into jail. Richard's owner alarmingly testified in a petition to a Baltimore county court that there were "letters and papers which has been found upon the person of the said Negro Boy which clearly shews a conspiracy between the Said Boy and Some other person or persons for the purpose of aiding the Escape of the said Boy." Another enslaved family from Anne Arundel County, Maryland, fled to the North via Baltimore. In that city the runaways had been directed to the address of a white family, where they were "sheltered by two occupants, who were ardent supporters of the Underground Railroad," as one of the family members later recalled in a Federal Writers' Project (FWP) interview. Free black churches in Washington also harbored and assisted untold numbers of northbound runaways, sometimes keeping them

quote); Petition of James S. Wilson to the Orphans Court of Anne Arundel County, MD, September 15, 1859, RSPP, Series 2: County Court Petitions, Accession #20985958 (fourth quote); *Alexandria Gazette*, January 1, 1828 (fifth quote); Frederick Douglass, *Life and Times of Frederick Douglass: His Early Life as a Slave, His Escape from Bondage, and His Complete History to the Present Time* (Hartford, CT: Park Publishing Co., 1881), 198–201.

hidden for months until safe passage could be arranged. One freedom seeker was discovered in the attic of a Methodist church in DC in 1858, for example, after hiding there for "four or five months, unsuspected." Apparently, he "had used up the communion wine, and picked up his food by nightly sorties into the neighboring pantries." Besides sympathetic supporters of the Underground Railroad, both Baltimore and DC also had active "smugglers" who promised runaways safe passage to Pennsylvania for a less noble ideal: profit. In 1850 one William D. Chaplin, a white resident of DC, was accused of running one such smuggling operation for a group of runaways from Georgia. "The plan seemed to be," as the press related, "for him [Chaplin] to have a two-horse carryall or carriage, and start early in the night. He would take two or three and proceed through Maryland by the way of Sandy Spring to Pennsylvania, they paying him $20 to $25 a piece."[29]

Whether free blacks, sympathetic whites, or profit-seeking human smugglers, contacts and social networks allowed some runaways to be "transported" to free soil through coordinated plans, often concealed or disguised in private wagons or even stagecoaches. The abovementioned family from Anne Arundel County, for example, was concealed in a "large covered wagon to transport merchandise from Baltimore to different villages along the turnpike to Hanover, Pa." One of the interviewed refugees, a child at the time, remembered that "on our way to Pennsylvania, we never alighted on the ground in any community or close to any settlement, fearful of being apprehended by people who were always looking for rewards." Another Maryland woman from Montgomery County, Maryland, ran to Washington, where she was assisted by members of a UGRR network, who helped disguise her as a man and formulated a plot to have her conveyed by carriage to New York in 1855. Occasionally, runaways' contacts devised more unconventional means of travel for freedom seekers. The infamous Henry "Box" Brown had sympathetic helpers pack him into a crate and ship him from Richmond, Virginia, to Philadelphia, where he was received and

---

[29] Kennedy, "Northward Bound," 67–129; Petition of William M. Everett to Southampton County Court, November 8, 1856, RSPP, Series 2, Accession #21685407 (first quote); Petition of George H. Carman to the Orphans Court of Baltimore County, MD, November 15, 1859, RSPP, Series 2: County Court Petitions, Accession #20985921 (second quote); Interview with Caroline Hammond (1936), in Born in Slavery: Slave Narratives from the Federal Writers' Project, vol. 8 (www.loc.gov/item/mesno80/) (third quote); *Democratic Watchman*, August 4, 1858 (fourth quote); *The Courier*, August 23, 1850 (fifth quote). See also Franklin and Schweninger, *Runaway Slaves*, 133–134.

"unpacked" by abolitionists after having spent part of the journey upside down. Although theirs were atypical experiences for northbound runaways as a whole – despite its legendary status, most runaways were not conveyed north by UGRR agents or other organized networks – such stories do underscore the importance of social contacts and networks in the runaway strategies of many freedom seekers.[30]

Most northbound runaways, however, were not "transported" in such an organized fashion, and most had little choice but to rely on their own wits and courage to reach freedom, taking advantage of ad hoc opportunities and slowly making their way to free soil by any means necessary. They ran, they walked, they stole horses, they disguised themselves as free blacks or slaves running an errand. The logistics were considerable and likely daunting to people who had never traveled beyond a radius of a few dozen miles from their homes. Simply securing enough provisions to make an extensive journey on foot involved careful planning, dependence on strangers along the way, or theft. Court records attest that one Isaac, a Delaware slave, ran away to Philadelphia in 1801 after having robbed a neighboring farm for provisions, for example. Then there were the difficulties of simply navigating the southern landscape in the literal sense of finding one's way. Slave testimonies of northbound runaways who fled alone underscore the confusion and practical difficulties involved in traversing the southern landscape to the free states. Charles Ball recalled that he made his way northward from Georgia mostly by stumbling through woods during the night, "with the stars for my guide, keeping the north-star over my left eye." At one point in North Carolina he had even gotten lost and found himself so far west that he was at the foot of the Appalachians, and had to correct his course by traveling due east. During the entire journey he was plagued by hunger, cold, and misery. The abolitionist and writer James Pennington, who escaped from Maryland, admitted in his 1849 memoir that when he fled he doubted his ability to actually reach safety, having had "no knowledge of distance or direction." As he described it, his mindset at the time was: "I know that Pennsylvania is a free state, but I know not where its soil begins, or where that of Maryland ends." Pennington indeed only knew for certain that he

---

[30] Interview with Caroline Hammond; Stanley Harrold, "Freeing the Weems Family: A New Look at the Underground Railroad," *Civil War History* 42, no. 4 (1996): 289–306; Brown, *Narrative of the Life of Henry Box Brown*; Manisha Sinha, *The Slave's Cause: A History of Abolition* (New Haven, CT: Yale University Press, 2017), 536; Kennedy, "Northward Bound," 67–129; Foner, *Gateway to Freedom*, 91–118.

was in Pennsylvania when he happened upon a Quaker couple in Adams County, who took him in and provided him with shelter and assistance. Rebecca Ginsburg has argued that most overland runaways forged a route northward by utilizing a "black landscape," consisting of a "system of paths, places and rhythms," created by enslaved people "often as a refuge." Linking up "black landscapes" across the counties of the Upper South, freedom seekers navigated their way to northern free states, sometimes zigzagging across the landscape to do so.[31]

As transportation links between the southern and northern states expanded in the nineteenth century – especially with the advent of railroads – growing numbers of runaways attempted to flee by rail. The southern states indeed desperately attempted to curb this alarming trend through legislation. In 1837 Virginia passed a law requiring enslaved people to produce written permission to use public transportation, whether stagecoach, train, or maritime vessels, for example. Maryland followed suit the following year with "An Act to Prevent the Transportation of People of Colour upon Railroads or Steamboats." North Carolina, Kentucky, Tennessee, and Louisiana passed similar measures at around the same time. Despite their best efforts, however, southern lawmakers were unable to prevent slave flight by modern transportation. Determined freedom seekers circumvented such obstacles by procuring falsified free papers (like Frederick Douglass) or otherwise disguising themselves as free black passengers. Some took more unconventional approaches. One young man named John – only nineteen years old – was sold away from his native Faucquier County, Virginia, to a cotton planter in Alabama. After two years of extreme physical abuse at the hands of his master John decided to strike for freedom by taking a series of northbound trains. This entailed getting "on the top of the car, instead of inside it, and thus ride of nights, till nearly daylight, when, at a stopping-place on the road, he would slip himself off the car, and conceal himself in the woods until under cover of the next night he could manage to get on the top of another car." The route included mountains and tunnels. By such means he got as far as Alexandria, Virginia, before being caught and sent back to his master. Jeremiah Colburn, "a bright mulatto,

[31] Petition of Sally Russ, to Sussex County Court, DE, November 26, 1801, RSPP, Series 2: County Court Petitions, Accession #20380110; Ball, *Fifty Years in Chains*, 364–365 (first quote); James W. C. Pennington, *The Fugitive Blacksmith: or, Events in the History of James W. Pennington, Pastor of a Presbyterian Church, New York, Formerly a Slave in the State of Maryland, United States* (London: Charles Gilpin, 1849), 13 (second quote); Ginsburg, "Escaping through a Black Landscape," 54 (third quote).

of prepossessing appearance, reads and writes, and is quite intelligent," fled to Philadelphia in 1858 from his native Charleston, South Carolina, daringly disguising himself as a white man and traveling by rail in broad daylight. Colburn was reportedly "fair enough to pass for white, and actually came the entire journey from Charleston to this city under the garb of a white gentleman." As long as it got them north, no scheme was out of bounds, however audacious or perilous.[32]

Maritime routes of escape were especially popular, and indeed many runaways to port towns and cities such as Baltimore, Norfolk, Charleston, Pensacola, Mobile, Natchez, and New Orleans fled there with the express purpose of fleeing the southern states altogether. Escaping the South by smuggling oneself on board vessels docked at the South's major port cities – often with the assistance of free black crew members – occurred regularly enough that southern states attempted to legislate against allowing enslaved people to board vessels without special permission, as stated above. Indeed, some states and cities went a step further and undertook to thoroughly inspect all out-of-state vessels and prevent free black crew members from having any contact at all with local enslaved people. Black mariner laws, which prohibited free black crew members from freely disembarking in southern ports, were passed across the South. South Carolina passed a law in 1823 that required all "persons of color" who arrived in Charleston as crew members of vessels from the Northern United States or anywhere else in the Atlantic world to be taken into the custody of the sheriff – at the expense of the ship captain – and to remain there until their ships left port. It was a measure much protested by ship captains and even members of Charleston's own Chapter of Commerce. In 1841 South Carolina passed another stringent law, specifically designed at preventing "citizens of New York" from helping slaves flee to the North, which required merchant ships from New York to have their vessels inspected by port authorities in Charleston at their own expense of ten dollars. The law further threatened captains with a fine of $500 if any runaway was found to be hiding on board, no matter "how innocent and ignorant the Captain Owners, and all concerned may be." Black mariner laws infuriated northern and foreign (especially British)

---

[32] Still, *The Underground Railroad*, 106–107 (first quote); Ibid., 108 (second quote); Ibid., 81–86; Jenny Bourne Wahl, *The Bondman's Burden: An Economic Analysis of the Common Law of Southern Slavery* (New York: Cambridge University Press, 1998), 95; Franklin and Schweninger, *Runaway Slaves*, 290; Kennedy, "Northward Bound," 67–129.

ship captains. The British press widely publicized outrageous incidents in which black seamen in the employ of British vessels were wrongfully arrested as fugitive slaves at southern port towns, forcing captains to have to go to great pains to get them released. In at least one case from 1847 – some thirteen years after slavery had been abolished in the British Empire – a British sea captain reportedly had to trick a southern jailor into believing that he was the rightful owner of a seized black British mariner in order to get him out of jail.[33]

Even the most stringent measures did not deter flight via sea and river, however. Southern runaway slave ads from the entire antebellum period routinely warned masters of vessels not to harbor transport runaway slaves, and both northern abolitionist records and southern court records are replete with references to runaways who fled (or intended to flee) north onboard ships. As early as 1792 a plot was uncovered in North Carolina involving "a Number of Negro Slaves" who were planning to flee by boat to "the Northern States." Jack, a Delaware slave, ran away by hiring himself out as a free black crew member in 1805, leaving not only the state but indeed the United States altogether. When he returned to the United States two years later, he settled in New Jersey, where he was eventually discovered by his former owner. In 1814 one Louisiana slave named Ned smuggled himself onboard a US naval ship docked at New Orleans that was captained by a northerner who refused to give Ned back to his master before setting sail for the North. In 1828 the owner of one enslaved man named Ben, from Kentucky, accused the two owners of the steamboat *Cincinnati* of permitting Ben to board their ship and then letting him ride with them to Pittsburgh, where he disembarked and disappeared. The slaveholder demanded the ship be impounded and that he be paid "damages for carrying him away." In 1834 one Hiram, a Virginia slave, was captured on board a vessel docked on the James River in Richmond "in the effort as it is confidently believed, to escape to some

---

[33] Petition of David Alexander et al., to the House of Representatives of South Carolina, November 1826, RASP, Series 1: Legislative Petitions, Accession #11382603; Petition of T. Street et al., to the Senate of South Carolina, n.d. 1845, RASP, Series 1: Legislative Petitions, Accession #11384505; *Caledonian Mercury* (Edinburgh), October 24, 1847. See also Matthew J. Clavin, *Aiming for Pensacola: Fugitive Slaves in the Southern and Atlantic Frontier* (Cambridge, MA: Harvard University Press, 2015); Thomas C. Buchanan, *Black Life on the Mississippi: Slaves, Free Blacks, and the Western Steamboat World* (Chapel Hill: University of North Carolina Press, 2004); David C. Cecelski, *The Waterman's Song: Slavery and Freedom in Maritime North Carolina* (Chapel Hill: University of North Carolina Press, 2001).

Northern State." Prince, a Louisiana slave, was "Carried away" onboard a steamboat docked at New Orleans and bound for New York in 1837; he never returned. Peter, an enslaved man from Louisiana, passed himself off as a free black and escaped from New Orleans by illegally hiring himself as an assistant to the steamboat *Tiger* in 1838. In 1854 three men from Richmond escaped to Philadelphia by smuggling themselves onboard a steamer "in a space, not far from the boiler, where the heat and coal dust were almost intolerable." In the most audacious maritime escape attempt of the antebellum period, seventy-seven freedom seekers attempted to escape from Washington to New Jersey aboard the vessel *The Pearl* in 1848, but were captured when the captain was forced to land at Point Lookout, Maryland, due to stormy weather. However tortuous the journey or great the risks, port towns and cities in both the Upper and Lower South served as magnets for northbound runaways.[34]

Enslaved people who were hired out to steamboats and other vessels, especially those that plied the Mississippi and Ohio rivers, were arguably in the best position to flee via maritime routes. This category of runaway appears frequently in court cases related to northbound runaways. The records from New Orleans in particular are illustrative. In 1817 one Louisiana slave named Jack was hired out as an assistant onboard a vessel that was to "make a voyage" from "the port of New Orleans to Louisville in Kentucky & back." The vessel returned without Jack, who had jumped ship while docked at Cincinnati, on the free side of the river. His owner demanded compensation from the ship's owner. An almost identical incident took place in 1835, when a Louisiana slave woman named Eliza, valued at $1,000, was hired out to serve as a chambermaid onboard a steamboat ironically named the *Freedom*. While docked at

---

[34] Petition of J. Banks et al., to Pasquotank County, NC, December 6, 1792, RSPP, Series 2, Accession #21279202 (first quote); Petition of Kensey Johns to New Castle County Court, DE, December 23, 1809, RSPP, Series 2, Accession #20380901; Petition of Jeremiah Spiller to District Court of Louisiana, December 5, 1814, RSPP, Series 2, Accession #20881437 (second quote); Petition of James McGregor et al., to Jefferson County Court, KY, July 2, 1828, RSPP, Series 2, Accession #20782810 (third quote); Petition of Mary D. Hite to Henrico County Court, VA, n.d. 1834, RSPP, Series 2, Accession #21683430 (fourth quote); Metition of Ahimaaz Buel to Parish Court of New Orleans, March 29, 1837, RSPP, Series 2, Accession #20883739 (fifth quote); Petition of Louis Emmerling to District Court of Louisiana, July 16, 1838, RSPP, Accession #20883886 (sixth quote); Still, *The Underground Railroad*, 54 (seventh quote); *Port Tobacco & Charles Town Advertiser*, April 26, 1848; Mary Kay Ricks, *Escape on the Pearl: The Heroic Bid for Freedom on the Underground Railroad* (New York: William Morrow, 2007); Kennedy, "Northward Bound," 67–129.

Cincinnati, Eliza seized her own freedom and ran away, never to be heard from again. Dennis, a Louisiana slave man, was hired out as a cabin waiter and captain's servant onboard the steamer *J. M. White* in the summer of 1847. During a stop at St. Louis, Dennis was apparently left "without care or protection," and disappeared from his employer, presumably having made his way across the river to the free soil of Illinois. Charles, another slave from Louisiana, was hired out to the steamboat *Empire* in 1850, and successfully made his escape while his vessel was stopped at Cincinnati, where slavery is not "permitted." Charles' owner sued the steamboat captain for "Carelessness and negligence."[35]

MAROONED IN THE FREE STATES

Reaching the free states was only half the battle. Settling in, making a living, and evading recapture in a strange environment – especially after a harrowing and risky journey across a heavily patrolled borderland – must have been daunting for even the most determined freedom seekers. Marcel van der Linden recently argued that in preindustrial societies deserters of all kinds, including runaway slaves, "basically had three options ...: blend in with the locals, find a hiding place, or try to go far away, to a place where different authorities were in control ..." Freedom seekers in the Northern United States employed all three of these strategies at the same time, a complicated and often confusing affair. Some scholars such as Steven Hahn and Ira Berlin have indeed argued that runaways in the free states faced a *permanent* struggle to navigate free society, and that most essentially resembled "maroons" who lived not only severed from their home communities but also relegated to the shadowy margins of largely indifferent and sometimes openly hostile receiving communities. Caution and distrust toward most people were characteristic of the ways in which they navigated free society. Only in their dealings with people whom they knew or believed to be sympathetic

---

[35] Petition of Thomas Dunford to District Court of Louisiana, May 7, 1817, RSPP, Series 2, Accession #20881706 (first quote); Petition of Eliza Burks to District Court of Louisiana, January 12, 1836, RSPP, Series 2, Accession #20883622 (second quote); Petition of James A. Lusk to 5th District Court of New Orleans, October 30, 1848, RSPP, Series 2, Accession #20884857; Petition of Robert G. Beverley to 3rd District Court of New Orleans, January 11, 1851, RSPP, Series 2, Accession #20885153 (third quote).

to their plight – especially other runaways, free blacks, and abolitionists (both black and white) – did they dare let their guard down.[36]

Northbound runaways who set foot on free soil were indeed usually very much aware that their status in the free states was quite uncertain, although there is evidence that at least some refugees believed that they were legally "free" as soon as they crossed the border. One runaway slave advertisement for a forty-year-old woman from Maryland who ran away to Pennsylvania, for example, specifically stated that she had "been taught to believe that she is entitled to her freedom in that state." William Anderson, who successfully fled from Mississippi to Indiana in 1836, similarly claimed in his 1857 memoir that when he landed on free soil he rejoiced, thinking "that only a few moments ago I was a slave on yonder boat, but now free! free forever! ... In the State of Indiana I felt light and comfortable; the small obstacles I had to encounter I did not fear." But there is overwhelming evidence that most runaways arrived in the North with a more accurate understanding of their precarious status. They knew about slave catchers, had heard about rendition cases, were uncertain about the extent to which their freedom would be recognized (and by whom), and distrustful of the white population. Many appear to have fully expected to have to live in the shadows or at least disguise their true identities. Indeed, much like their counterparts who fled to southern cities, many northbound runaways fled with the aim of "passing" as free blacks in the free states, often changing their names and acquiring false documents to do so, as is evident from runaway slave ads. In other words, runaways not only often acquired falsified free papers in order to traverse the heavily patrolled borderlands, but also to disguise their true identities *after arrival* in the North. One Virginia runaway named Isaac fled across the Mason–Dixon line in 1832; his owner learned that he would likely "alter his name as I think he obtained a free pass from a fellow by the name of John Beeson, & is in Pennsylvania from every information I can get." Isaac did not change his name and acquire forged free papers in order to cross the border – he lived very near the border – but in order to navigate *northern* society. Such behavior underscores the extent to which

---

[36] Van der Linden, "Mass Exits," 39 (quote); Steven Hahn, *The Political Worlds of Slavery & Freedom* (Cambridge, MA: Harvard University Press, 2009), 29, 32; Ira Berlin, "North of Slavery: Black People in a Slaveholding Republic," unpublished paper given at the American Slavery Conference, Gilder Lehrman Center, Yale University, September 26–27, 2002.

refugees in the northern states sought to keep secret the fact that they were runaways from the South, at least to the general public.[37]

The fact that many fugitive slaves immediately sought out either known personal contacts or sympathetic – read: antislavery – organizations and individuals upon arrival in the northern states speaks volumes to how vulnerable they must have felt. Runaways did not simply cross the border and present themselves to local authorities as refugees seeking protection from slavery. Quite the contrary. They arrived in disguise, cautiously presenting themselves to people whom they thought would help them without blowing their cover. Most initially sought the assistance of northern free blacks, both known and unknown to them personally. When Charles Ball, who fled from Savannah to Philadelphia smuggled on board a ship, disembarked on free soil, he stopped a black stranger on the street to ascertain if he was indeed in Philadelphia. The man realized immediately that Ball was a runaway slave and directed him to the house of another free black, who harbored him and furnished him with a new set of clothes. Certain free black communities indeed developed a reputation for receiving and assisting runaway slaves. In southern Pennsylvania, established free black communities in towns such as Gettysburg, York, Harrisburg, Carlisle, and Lancaster became major destinations for runaways from Virginia and Maryland. Similar strategies were employed by freedom seekers who crossed the Ohio River borderland into Illinois, Indiana, and Ohio. Hundreds of freedom seekers from Kentucky crossed the river to Madison, Indiana, for example, sailed to free soil by a well-known Virginia-born free black named George DeBaptiste, who operated his rescue operations from there and helped organize assistance from the town's free black community. Ohio's border communities, especially, absorbed thousands of runaways. Cincinnati's black communities became such popular beacons of freedom for runaways (especially from Kentucky) that historians have frequently referred to the city as a "frontier of freedom," and the Ohio River on which it lies as a "River Jordan" for refugees from the South. Indeed, the Ohio Anti-Slavery Society estimated in 1835 that over half of the city's black population had been enslaved in the South. And not just Cincinnati, but other black communities in Ohio border towns such as New Richmond, Moscow, Manchester, Portsmouth, Ironton, Gallipolis, Point Pleasant,

[37] *Adams Sentinel* (Gettysburg, PA), November 26, 1828 (first quote); Anderson, *Narrative of William J. Anderson*, 35 (second quote); *Star and Republican Banner*, February 28, 1832 (third quote); Kennedy, "Northward Bound," 67–129.

and Marietta received regular streams of freedom seekers. Black freedom networks and active agents of the UGRR were especially active throughout the borderland, although they were more extensive in the eastern free states than in the former Northwest Territory.[38]

Abolitionist organizations and black churches (to which the former were often formally or informally connected) were the most prominent, best organized, and most trusted recipients of runaway slaves from the South, certainly in the late antebellum period. The well-preserved records of the Vigilance Committee of Philadelphia – run by free blacks such as Robert Purvis and later William Still – provide a glimpse into how such societies worked in practice. With full knowledge that the status of slave refugees from the South was very much contested and precarious in Pennsylvania – and that actively aiding refugees was a criminal offense – agents of the Vigilance Committee went about their work with painstaking care and a good measure of secrecy. Interestingly, most refugees who sought help from the VCP knew exactly where to find them and directed themselves to specific addresses of committee members upon arrival, suggesting that they arrived in the city with clear knowledge of assistance networks. One group of three runaways from Richmond, for example, arrived onboard a steamer one night in February 1854 and walked through the pouring rain directly to the "house of one of the Committee," arriving around 3 a.m. Others were "picked up" at the harbor by free blacks who worked as agents of the committee, many of whom were women. Purvis claimed that "the most efficient persons were women agents who brought the slaves," and that during his tenure two women in particular directed dozens of runaways to his door: one a "black woman, the other a mulatto."[39]

---

[38] Ball, *Fifty Years in Chains*, 425; Bordewich, *Bound for Canaan*, 202–205; David G. Smith, *On the Edge of Freedom: The Fugitive Slave Issue in South Central Pennsylvania, 1820–1870* (New York: Fordham University Press, 2013), 27–31; Blackett, *Captive's Quest for Freedom*, 142–143; Kelly M. Kennington, *In the Shadow of Dred Scott: St. Louis Freedom Seekers and the Legal Culture of Slavery in Antebellum America* (Athens: University of Georgia Press, 2017); Kennedy, "Northward Bound," 67–129; Ann Hagedorn, *Beyond the River: The Untold Stories of the Heroes of the Underground Railroad* (New York: Simon & Schuster, 2002), 41; Nikki M. Taylor, *Driven toward Madness: The Fugitive Slave Margaret Garner and Tragedy on the Ohio* (Athens: Ohio University Press, 2016), 58–59; Nikki M. Taylor, *Frontiers of Freedom: Cincinnati's Black Community, 1802–1868* (Athens: Ohio University Press, 2005), 22, 28–29, 51–54, 81–83; Joe William Trotter, Jr., *River Jordan: African American Urban Life in the Ohio Valley* (Lexington: University Press of Kentucky, 1998), 26–27.

[39] Robert Purvis to Wilbur H. Siebert, December 23, 1895, cited in Kennedy, "Northward Bound," 91 (first quote); Still, *The Underground Railroad*, 55 (second quote); Jesse

The following letter, written by one of William Still's contacts in Wilmington, Delaware, describes how cross-border networks functioned in practice to arrange for refugees to be "picked up" at the harbor or train station upon arrival in Philadelphia:

"WILMINGTON, 2 mo. 5m, 1858. Esteemed Friend:–William Still:—I have information of 6 able-bodied men that are expected here to-morrow morning; they may, to-morrow afternoon or evening, take the cars at Chester, and most likely reach the city between 11 and 12 at night; they will be accompanied by a colored man that has lived in Philadelphia and is free; they may think it safer to walk to the city than to go in the cars, but for fear of accident it may be best to have some one at the cars to look out for them. I have not seen them yet, and cannot certainly judge what will be best. I gave a man 3 dollars to bring those men 15 miles to-night, and I have been two miles in the country this afternoon, and gave a colored man 2 dollars to get provisions to feed them. Hoping all will be right, I remain thy friend,

HUMANITAS[40]

Once safely at the address of a VCP agent refugees were subsequently taken in or dispersed among various safe houses in the city, sometimes literally hidden in attics and basements until the coast was clear. Purvis, for one, hid recently arrived freedom seekers in a secret room in his basement, for example. VCP agents also conducted interviews with runaways, aimed at ascertaining their needs and the best means of assisting them. According to William Still, these were always conducted in a spirit of "sympathy," and without agents or runaways ever learning the names of their interviewers or helpers. In the earliest days of the organization, no notes at all were taken for fear they might be discovered by federal authorities. Later it was decided that notes should be taken in order to facilitate family reunifications, but these potentially damning records were kept under lock and key until after the Civil War.[41]

Similar operations were reported in Cincinnati, which also had an active network of prominent Quaker abolitionists and agents of the UGRR, including Levi and Catherine Coffin, who moved there in 1847 from Indiana (where they had incidentally also assisted countless

Olsavsky, "Women, Vigilance Committees, and the Rise of Militant Abolitionism, 1835–1859," *Slavery & Abolition* 39, no. 1 (2018): 357–382; Margaret H. Bacon, *But One Race: The Life of Robert Purvis* (Albany: State University of New York Press, 2007).
[40] Thomas Garnett to William Still, February 5, 1858, reprinted in Still, *The Underground Railroad*, 445; Kennedy, "Northward Bound," 90–93.
[41] Robert Purvis to Wilbur H. Siebert, December 23, 1895, in Kennedy, "Northward Bound," 91; Still, *The Underground Railroad*, 55.

runaways from the South). According to Levi, Cincinnati received a continual and ever-increasing flow of runaways from across the river in Kentucky in the late antebellum period, and "hardly a fugitive came to the city without applying to us for assistance." Like their Philadelphia counterparts, the Coffins harbored runaways by hiding them in their large house for days and sometimes weeks until safer quarters could be arranged. Sometimes entire groups of refugees from Kentucky or Virginia were hidden upstairs without visitors even knowing that anyone else was home. Local antislavery women met tri-monthly at the Coffin household, "to spend a day in making and repairing clothing for fugitive slaves," as one female abolitionist later recalled. This was done not only to provide assistance but also to help disguise refugees' ragged appearance, which might raise suspicions about their true backgrounds. Tellingly, Coffin himself admitted that most runaways "took refuge among the colored people" of the city, and he revealed his prejudices when he complained that free blacks were far "too careless" in their efforts to harbor refugees, and that their lack of caution sometimes resulted in recapture. Whether they sought assistance from the Coffins or free blacks, however, runaways to Cincinnati apparently knew that they could call at various addresses throughout the city where sympathetic opponents of slavery would take them in, keep secret their true identities, and help them in their quest to forge lives of freedom.[42]

Even cities farther away from the border such as New York – which received countless slave refugees via both maritime and overland escape routes (often passing first through Philadelphia) – were home to highly organized vigilance committees by the 1830s, predominately led by free blacks who were willing to violate federal laws and provide shelter and assistance to runaways with whom they felt a measure of racial solidarity and common cause. The vulnerability of runaways indeed exposed the vulnerability of all blacks in the North, as it threatened even free blacks with unjust search, seizure, and enslavement – whether by kidnapping or botched (and corrupt) rendition hearings. Such vulnerability spurred free blacks – along with abolitionists and northern state governments – to

---

[42] Salafia, *Slavery's Borderland*, 199–203; Kennedy, "Northward Bound," 106–113; Levi Coffin, *Reminiscences of Levi Coffin, the Reputed President of the Underground Railroad* (Cincinnati, OH: Robert Clarke & Co., 1880), 299 (first quote); Ibid., 297–298 (third quote); Laura Smith Haviland, *A Woman's Life-Work, Labors and Experiences of* (Cincinnati, OH: Waldron & Stowe, 1882), 112 (second quote). See also William Birney, *Sketch of the Life of James G. Birney* (Chicago: National Christian Association, 1884).

mobilize and organize to actively assist runaways from the South, as explained in Chapter 1. In a very literal sense, their own liberty was at stake. David Ruggles, the African-American founder of the New York City Committee of Vigilance (NYCCV) in 1835, exhibited a clear example of such racial solidarity with runaways in an editorial published in the *Liberator*, arguing that "we must no longer depend on the inter-position of the Manumission or Anti-Slavery Societies, in the hope of peaceable and just protection … We must look to our own safety." Research by Eric Foner has shown that even though the NYCCV was officially a biracial organization, most of its active members "were black New Yorkers." The efforts of its members helped hundreds of runaways and in so doing provided the city's free black population with a measure safety from southern enslavers and corrupt officials of justice. As early as 1837 the committee declared at its annual meeting that "there are multi-tudes of fugitive slaves who take refuge here," reiterating that the aim of the organization was to "throw a shield of protection around the fireside of the free colored man, and to aid the poor fugitive slave in escaping to a land of freedom."[43]

Many freedom seekers journeyed even further north upon arrival in the free states, whether upon the advice of abolitionist organizations (espe-cially after 1850) or of their own accord. Thousands of runaways who crossed the Mason–Dixon line from Maryland or Delaware into Pennsylvania, or who arrived in New York harbor smuggled onboard Atlantic vessels, for example, pressed on to towns and communities in upstate or western New York and Massachusetts. From Syracuse to Boston, towns and cities throughout these states were widely known as bulwarks of abolitionism, populated by activists who were sympathetic to the cause of runaway slaves. Many of those who crossed the Ohio River likewise sought refuge further away from the border, especially the towns and cities of Ohio's Western Reserve on Lake Erie, an abolitionist strong-hold. Places such as Cleveland and Oberlin were safer for permanent

---

[43] *Liberator*, August 6, 1836 (first quote); Graham Russell Gao Hodges, *David Ruggles: A Radical Black Abolitionist and the Underground Railroad in New York City* (Chapel Hill: University of North Carolina Press, 2010), 88; Foner, *Gateway to Freedom*, 63–90; Leslie M. Harris, *In the Shadow of Slavery: African Americans in New York City, 1626–1863* (Chicago: University of Chicago Press, 2003), 210; Bordewich, *Bound for Canaan*, 171–176; Don Papson and Tom Calarco, *Secret Lives of the Underground Railroad in New York City: Sydney Howard Gay, Louis Napoleon and the Record of Fugitives* (Jefferson, NC: McFarland, 2015); *New York Evangelist*, May 20, 1837 (second quote).

settlement than the border communities along the Ohio River. For one thing they were less vulnerable to borderland slave catchers, but they were also attractive destinations because they were close enough to Canada to provide runaways with a viable escape route if threatened with rendition. For the same reason, Michigan became an increasingly popular destination for runaways from the South – especially the border city of Detroit.[44]

The settlement experiences of runaways in the Northern United States differed dramatically, depending on how they fled, where they ended up, and the nature of their assistance networks. Finding boarding and employment were clearly the most pressing challenges for recent arrivals. Most runaways arrived in the North destitute. William Wells Brown, the famous abolitionist who was born a slave in Kentucky but successfully fled to the North as a young man, crossed the border and made his way through Ohio surviving on little more than what he was offered by Quaker abolitionists along the way, who furnished him with food, advice, and sometimes a few cents. He arrived at his destination of Cleveland "a stranger ... [with] no money," a common experience. Some runaways managed to save up meager earnings from extra work during slavery in order to help fund their journey north, but only a lucky few had more than a coin in their pocket when they arrived on free soil. Those who did were in a far better position to start their new lives than those who did not. William and Ellen Craft, for example, the Georgia couple who daringly fled to Boston by rail in 1849 – disguising the light-skinned Ellen as a male slaveholder and William as her personal servant – noted in their narrative that "our little earnings in slavery were not all spent on the journey," and so they were able to "[get] on very well" once they got settled in. Others prepared for their journeys by stealing goods or cash that were meant to help them make a new start upon arrival at their destination, a risky strategy that is sometimes referred to in runaway slave ads and court records. Harrison and Aimée, two mulatto slaves from Louisiana, for example, stole several pieces of valuable gold and diamond

---

[44] Kennedy, "Northward Bound," 67–129; J. Brent Morris, *Oberlin, Hotbed of Abolitionism: College, Community, and the Fight for Freedom and Equality in Antebellum America* (Chapel Hill: University of North Carolina Press, 2014); Roy E. Finkenbine, "The Underground Railroad in 'Indian Country,'" in Damian Alan Pargas, ed., *Fugitive Slaves and Spaces of Freedom* (Gainesville: University Press of Florida, 2018), 70–92; Tiya Miles, *The Dawn of Detroit: A Chronicle of Slavery and Freedom in the City of the Straits* (New York: The New Press, 2017), 152–153; Carol E. Mull, *The Underground Railroad in Michigan* (Jefferson, NC: McFarland, 2010).

jewelry (valued at an exorbitant $3,375) from their master before con-
cealing themselves on board the ship *Tecumseh* in 1840, bound for New
York. Refugees who arrived in the North with valuables and starting
capital were clearly exceptions to the rule, however.[45]

Social networks in northern communities were a tremendous asset to
refugees seeking financial assistance and employment in the northern
states. Those who arrived in the North with sympathetic free black and/
or white abolitionist contacts – whether individuals or organizations –
utilized these networks to help them find the means to make a living as
free people. Vigilance committees across the northern states were active in
not only receiving, harboring, and clothing recent arrivals from the South,
but also in helping them find work. William and Ellen Craft were brought
into contact with some of Boston's most active abolitionists upon arrival
in the city. These contacts helped set William up as a carpenter and
furniture maker (his trade during slavery) and Ellen as a seamstress. As
mentioned in the Introduction, Matilda Lawrence likewise quickly found
employment as a domestic in the house of James Birney, a renowned
abolitionist, after her escape in Cincinnati. Birney later claimed that he
did know she was a runaway slave, but it is unlikely that he did not at
least suspect her true background, since he was actively involved in the
UGRR in Cincinnati. Indeed, many abolitionists and agents of the UGRR
were known to have employed runaways from the South themselves as a
means of assisting them in their plight. Abolitionist activists like Laura
and Charles Haviland, who owned a farm in Lenawee County, Michigan,
for example, were known to have not only helped harbor freedom seekers
who were passing through the region (on their way to Detroit or Canada)
but also temporarily employ them in their agricultural operations in order
to help them save money to start their new lives.[46]

Whether they tapped into social networks or went about making a
living on their own, urban areas were especially attractive destinations for
runaway slaves, not only because of the anonymity and institutional

---

[45] William Wells Brown, *Narrative of William Wells Brown, an American Slave* (Boston:
The Anti-Slavery Office, 1847), 106 (first quote); William and Ellen Craft, *Running a
Thousand Miles to Freedom: Or, the Escape of William and Ellen Craft from Slavery*
(London: William Tweedie, 1860), 86 (second quote); Petition of François Barthelemy
LeBeau to District Court of Louisiana, February 18, 1840, RSPP, Accession #20884009.

[46] Craft, *Running a Thousand Miles to Freedom*, 86; Birney, *Sketch of the Life of James
G. Birney*; Stacey Robertson, *Hearts Beating for Liberty: Women Abolitionists in the Old
Northwest* (Chapel Hill: University of North Carolina Press, 2010), 167; Haviland,
A Woman's Life-Work.

assistance provided by their free black communities, but also because of opportunities to find employment and eke out a living. Although rural black farming communities were certainly not unknown in the northern states – many of which were indeed founded by free-born or legally manumitted black settlers from the southern states, especially Kentucky, Virginia, and North Carolina – land ownership and even tenancy was out of reach for most refugees from slavery, certainly for recent arrivals. Most felt compelled out of necessity to try their luck in urban society. An important advantage that slave refugees in the North had over their counterparts who ran to urban areas within the South was that they could quite *openly* seek employment, even if they did not have falsified documents. In other words, they dared walk up to a hotel or a harbormaster and ask for work, since they were presumed free. Even refugees who arrived penniless and as complete strangers were able to quickly find low-paying jobs in towns and cities across the North, including relatively small towns. One runaway who crossed the Ohio River and arrived in Madison City, Indiana, in the summer of 1836 claimed that he stumbled into town nearly penniless but was able to find work right away. Upon arrival

my funds in pocket amounted to one dollar, which I advanced for my board. I sought employment immediately, and soon engaged to work for Messrs. F. Thompson and E. D. Luck, carrying the hod for a dollar a day. This, of course, was new and rather severe labor for me at this time; but it was far better than toiling in the cotton or corn field, for a reward of a scanty meal of corn and the lash.

He ended up saving enough money to eventually – years later – buy land, a rare luxury. The abovementioned William Wells Brown arrived in Cleveland with no specific contacts and without a dollar to his name, but, "believing myself to be somewhat out of danger, I secured an engagement at the Mansion House, as a table waiter, in payment for my board." He was later properly hired by the proprietor at $12 a month, where he remained until the spring, when he "found good employment on board a lake steamboat."[47]

In major urban centers such as Boston, Philadelphia, New York, and Cincinnati – constituting the largest metropolitan areas in the North

[47] Frank M. Matthias, "John Randolph's Freedmen: The Thwarting of a Will," *Journal of Southern History* 39, no. 2 (1973): 263–272; Anderson, *Narrative of William J. Anderson*, 35 (first quote); Brown, *Narrative of William Wells Brown*, 106–107 (second quote).

during the antebellum period – opportunities for refugees and other newcomers appeared even more promising, certainly by the latter decades of the antebellum period. As the Industrial Revolution took root in these areas, the surging industrial economy created an atmosphere of endless activity – bustling streets, busy docks, new businesses and factories, new railroad and steamboat transportation networks – that must have seemed exciting to recent arrivals. While success stories among freedom seekers were not unknown, however, it is important to remember that most African Americans (both free people and refugees from slavery) occupied the bottom rung of the economic and social ladder in every northern city. Men typically found day labor and short-term employment on docks and at ports, in factories, as peddlers and in a wide variety of other menial occupations. They spent their days as draymen, carters, waiters, servants, cooks, dock workers, boatmen, sailors, and day laborers on construction projects and other works. Only a small proportion found better paying work as carpenters, blacksmiths, shopkeepers, tailors, or barbers. Women, meanwhile, were usually relegated to positions as domestics and seamstresses. African Americans in northern cities may have indeed suffered more from economic segregation than their counterparts in southern cities. In antebellum southern cities black people – whether slave or free – performed *most* occupations, so finding employment in a wide variety of low-paying sectors was possible if armed with falsified documents. In antebellum northern cities, by contrast, African Americans always constituted only a small minority of the urban population and working class black laborers faced stiff competition for unskilled employment from white laborers, especially Irish and German immigrants. As James and Lois Horton have argued, a racially restricted system of employment caused entire sectors of the industrializing northern urban economy to be effectively shut off to black workers.[48]

In Philadelphia, for example, blacks were largely excluded from the industrializing textile, shoe, and metal sectors. The Pennsylvania Abolition Society compiled a census of black families in the city in

---

[48] Kennedy, "Northward Bound," 133–138; Harris, *In the Shadow of Slavery*, 79–81; Stephen Kantrowitz, *More Than Freedom: Fighting for Black Citizenship in a White Republic, 1829–1889* (New York: Penguin, 2013), 20; Gary Nash, *Forging Freedom: The Formation of Philadelphia's Black Community, 1720–1840* (Cambridge, MA: Harvard University Press, 1988), 214–217, 251–252; Gary Collison, *Shadrach Minkins: From Fugitive Slave to Citizen* (Cambridge, MA: Harvard University Press, 1997), 67; James O. Horton and Lois E. Horton, *In Hope of Liberty: Culture, Commerce and Protest among Northern Free Blacks, 1700–1860* (New York: Oxford University Press, 1997), 110, 114–117.

1838 and found that most were relegated to low-paid work as day laborers, porters, waiters, carters, coachmen, sailors, and cooks. A New York city directory for 1840 reveals similar employment patterns. In Boston most African Americans were listed in the 1850 census as common laborers, and as many as a quarter of African-American men were employed at the docks or on (dangerous) seafaring vessels during the antebellum period. Cincinnati city directories similarly indicate that black men mainly worked as sailors, dockers, and stewards, but also as cooks, porters, waiters, carters, barbers, and day laborers. Women worked at domestic occupations. Freedom seekers from the southern states were forced into urban economies that relegated them to the very bottom of the pecking order and excluded them from the most promising lines of work in newly industrializing urban centers.[49]

Most African Americans in Boston, New York City, Philadelphia, and Cincinnati suffered from structural poverty and lived in impoverished and virtually segregated black neighborhoods. In Boston, they clustered around Beacon Hill (often referred to as "Nigger Hill" by whites); in New York, they congregated around the Fifth and Sixth Wards; in Cincinnati they were mostly confined to the First and Fourth Wards. Cramped conditions were the norm. Most free blacks – let alone slave refugees – were forced to share rooms and accommodations with others. Young, single men, who made up the bulk of runaways from the South, typically became boarders in black households or lodged in boarding houses that catered to temporary residents such as seamen. In Boston, many households in black neighborhoods counted more than twenty African-American residents. In Philadelphia, black newcomers in the 1820s lived in crowded alleys and courtyards throughout the city; most were relegated to tenements and shanties in South Philadelphia.[50]

---

[49] Horton and Horton, *In Hope of Liberty*, 110, 114–117; Nash, *Forging Freedom*, 214–217, 251–252; Collison, *Shadrach Minkins*, 67; Kennedy, "Northward Bound," 133–138; Pennsylvania Abolition Society, Committee to visit the Colored People, vol. 1–5 (1838), *Slavery, Abolition and Social Justice* database (Leiden University). See also Erica Armstrong Dunbar, *A Fragile Freedom: African American Women and Emancipation in the Antebellum City* (New Haven, CT: Yale University Press, 2011); Taylor, *Frontiers of Freedom*, 25–29; Nancy Bertaux, "Structural Economic Chance and Occupational Decline among Black Workers in Nineteenth-Century Cincinnati," in Henry Louis Taylor, ed., *Race and the City: Work, Community, and Protest in Cincinnati, 1820–1970* (Urbana: University of Illinois Press, 1993), 132–134.

[50] Kennedy, "Northward Bound," 136; Taylor, *Frontiers of Freedom*, 25–29; Collison, *Shadrach Minkins*, 64; Horton and Horton, *In Hope of Liberty*, 110, 114–117; Nash, *Forging Freedom*, 248.

The hardships experienced by northern black communities were severe, even more so for refugees from slavery who arrived in the North virtually penniless and had to start from scratch. Abolitionists highly praised the work ethos of runaway slaves from the South. Frederick Douglass, who visited Cincinnati in 1850, for example, declared that nowhere had he "met with a more industrious, enterprising and public-spirited community of colored people." He was impressed by black men's willingness to "do true men's work, which requires hard hands and rugged frames," even going about their labor "cheerfully." To be sure, refugees from slavery had extra incentives to pull themselves up by their bootstraps and do whatever was necessary to make a living on free soil. But it cannot be denied that freedom seekers throughout the North often found themselves in dire straits, dependent as they were on day labor and seasonal employment, highly vulnerable to economic fluctuations, and sometimes without means to pay for the roof over their heads. Some were indeed lured into lives of theft and crime, while others were compelled to solicit aid from almshouses and benevolent organizations during times of economic setbacks. James and Lois Horton have argued that structural racism and disadvantages in the economic sphere, combined with harsh living conditions, "practically guaranteed that many free blacks would become poor, dependent, and, perhaps, criminal." One Delaware slave who ran to Philadelphia in 1806 was discovered by his master eighteen years later to have spent at least part of that time incarcerated, laboring as a convict in Pennsylvania prisons.[51]

Records of relief societies throughout the North illustrate the desperate circumstances in which some freedom seekers found themselves. The admission books of almshouses in Massachusetts in the 1850s, such as the Danvers Alms House just outside of Boston, record the admission of several fugitive slaves or presumed fugitive slaves (African Americans born in the South, for example). In Cincinnati, various reports indicate that many black residents made regular requests for aid to local alms-houses, mutual aid societies, and other charitable organizations. Poor relief for blacks indeed became a controversial subject among Cincinnati's white population, many of whom believed blacks should be

---

[51] Frederick Douglass, "Character and Condition of the Colored People of Cincinnati," *Anti-Slavery Bugle*, August 10, 1850 (first quote); Horton and Horton, *In Hope of Liberty*, 110 (second quote), 114–117; Petition of Ezekiel Anderson to Kent County Court, DE, May 20, 1823, RSPP, Series 2, Accession #20382302. See also Kennedy, "Northward Bound," 138–143; Taylor, *Frontiers of Freedom*, 36–38.

excluded from relief funds. Benevolent societies and "colored orphan asylums" were established by abolitionist societies throughout the North in order to care for African-American children whose parents were financially unable to do so. Parents were compelled to relinquish all custody of their children, who were taken in and educated by Quakers and other activists. The Samaritan Asylum for Colored Orphans in Boston, established in 1834, aimed to provide disadvantaged children "an education that will enable them to procure a respectable maintenance." The Colored Orphan Asylum in New York, established by Quaker women in 1836, similarly aided more than 1,000 children, including many children of fugitive slaves – some of whom were "orphaned" when their parents were captured and sent back to the South. In Philadelphia and New York, black mutual aid societies such as the Free African Society and the New York African Society for Mutual Relief helped provide crucial assistance to those in need within their communities, including refugees from slavery. To be sure, northern free soil was a far cry from Canaan land for runaway slaves. Tellingly, however, as Gary Nash has noted, "Not one man or woman, as far as is known, voluntarily returned to slavery in order to escape the miseries of northern urban life."[52]

Compounding the miseries of northern urban life, refugees from slavery also had to endure periodic outbursts of racial conflict and violence in their new communities. Most northern whites were of course not abolitionists – the vast majority were at best indifferent to the plight of runaway slaves and at worst openly hostile. The constant influx of slave refugees from the South exacerbated an already acute anxiety among northern whites about the growing black populations in their midst, and this anxiety regularly spilled over into mob violence. In the 1820s and 1830s black communities in Providence were attacked multiple times – on one occasion in 1831 the state militia had to be called in to restore order. Waves of lawless violence poured over Cincinnati's black community between the 1820s and 1840s. One particular incident in 1829 entailed hundreds of whites attacking African-American homes, institutions, and businesses in the Fourth Ward. In 1834 white New Yorkers launched a series of attacks against African Americans, attacking

[52] Kennedy, "Northward Bound," 138–140; Taylor, *Frontiers of Freedom*, 36–38; Julia Winch, *Philadelphia's Black Elite: Activism, Accommodation, and the Struggle for Autonomy, 1787–1848* (Philadelphia: Temple University Press, 1998), 5–8; Harris, *In the Shadow of Slavery*, 82–88; *The Liberator*, August 2, 1834 (first quote); Nash, *Forging Freedom*, 247–248 (second quote).

churches and the houses of abolitionists like Lewis Tappan. Weeks later
Philadelphia became the site of mob violence in which hundreds of people
were involved. Fighting in the city erupted again in 1838 and 1842.[53]

Racial violence became so alarming that some northern states and
cities responded by introducing restrictions on black settlement. Even
Massachusetts formed a committee to investigate the possibilities of
prohibiting further black migration into the state as early as 1821, believing African-American newcomers to be "dangerous to order and a burden
on public charity," as James and Lois Horton have argued. A similar bill
was introduced in the legislature of Pennsylvania in 1831 which specifically referred to the rising tide of refugees from Virginia and Maryland as a
potential threat to public order. The states of the Old Northwest, where
attitudes were even more staunchly opposed to black settlement, restrict-
ive "Black Laws" were implemented and revised on a regular basis,
starting with Ohio in 1804. Indiana and Illinois followed suit in subsequent decades. These states, partly populated by settlers from Virginia
and Kentucky, passed laws that limited black immigration from other
states, required black settlers to provide legal proof of freedom to county
clerks, and demanded black newcomers to pay registration fees and bonds
to guarantee good behavior (ranging from 12 cents in Ohio to $500 in
Indiana). These measures were poorly enforced, however, and both free
blacks and slave refugees continued to pour into the free soil border
states, avoiding hefty bonds by simply not registering with city or county
authorities. In this respect they actually resembled the African-American
communities in southern cities like Richmond, Virginia, where many
legally manumitted free blacks resided illegally in the state of Virginia,
and therefore lived "undocumented" lives, much like their runaway slave
counterparts.[54]

---

[53] James J. Gigantano, *The Ragged Road to Abolition: Slavery and Freedom in New Jersey,*
1775–1865 (Philadelphia: University of Pennsylvania Press, 2014), 208; Christy Clark-
Pujara, *Dark Work: The Business of Slavery in Rhode Island* (New York: New York
University Press, 2016), 101–109; Taylor, *Frontiers of Freedom,* 63–64; *Liberator,* July
12, 1834, July 19, 1834; *Emancipator,* July 15, 1834, July 19, 1834, August 26, 1834;
Kennedy, "Northward Bound," 67–129; Horton and Horton, *In Hope of Liberty,*
102–104.

[54] Kennedy, "Northward Bound," 67–129; Horton and Horton, *In Hope of Liberty,*
102–104, 102 (quote); Eric Ledell Smith, "The End of Black Voting Rights in
Pennsylvania: African Americans and the Pennsylvania Constitutional Convention,"
Pennsylvania History: A Journal of Mid-Atlantic Studies 65, no. 3 (1998): 282;
Middleton, *The Black Laws,* 44–60.

Indeed, however poor or desperate their circumstances, and despite periodic outbursts of racial violence and measures enacted to prevent their settlement, refugees from slavery were determined to make the northern states their permanent home. This entailed more than finding employment and housing; it also meant rebuilding a sense of community. Like their southern counterparts, runaway slaves in the North lived in black communities, attended black churches, visited the same shops and barbers and grog shops as their free black counterparts, married northern blacks and established families. They navigated black life in the free states by becoming part of black life in the free states, as dozens of slave narratives vividly illustrate. That does not mean that they intentionally severed all ties with their home communities in slavery, however. Indeed, runaways lived with one foot in the North and one foot in the South, and exhibited a dual orientation to family and community. They may have lived with and like free blacks in the North, but their backgrounds in slavery made them different from their free black counterparts. This is evident in both their attempts to effect family reunifications with southern family members and their active role in the abolitionist movement. As discussed above, the first order of business for many runaways who directed themselves to friendly organizations such as the Philadelphia Vigilance Committee or the Quakers in Cincinnati was to try to engage help to establish contact with – or organize the rescue of – loved ones left in slavery. Such cases reveal volumes about not only the primary motivations and expectations of northbound runaways from slavery, but also about how they did not consider their migration to free soil "complete" until every possibility for family reunification had been exhausted. One young slave mother named Emeline Chapman, who changed her name to Susan Bell in order to avoid detection, felt forced to flee from her home in Washington to Philadelphia in September 1856, after hearing that she was to be sold away from her husband and children. Upon arrival she begged the local vigilance committee's agents to see about rescuing her children. Fearing recapture by slave catchers, the committee forwarded Emeline to Syracuse for her own safety, but even from there she had agents bombard William Still with letters inquiring as to whether or not he had been able to establish contact with her family and when they were coming. The same was true for Oscar Ball, a runaway from Virginia who passed through Philadelphia and ended up in Oswego, New York. Having changed his name to John Delaney, he got on as best he could as a day laborer in the cold northern city, despite sometimes having to go weeks at a time with no work. However difficult his circumstances, however, he continued to send regular letters to the Philadelphia Vigilance Committee to inquire about possibility of getting his brothers and other members of his family out of slavery. Even as Emeline and Oscar were getting themselves established in new community in the North, in other words, they actively lobbied and negotiated their own family reunification from the South.[55]

It was precisely their personal ties to the South and their stake in the future of both slavery and federal fugitive slave laws that led many refugees from slavery to play an active role in abolitionist movements throughout the northern states. It is no coincidence that abolitionism in the United States – including militant abolitionism – featured so many prominent African-American members who were themselves runaways from slavery. Frederick Douglass, Harriet Tubman, James Pennington, Henry Bibb – these are only a few of the most famous. Northbound runaways fled the South with strong convictions about what freedom should entail, and upon arrival they found themselves in a part of the country where they could mobilize and try to do something about it. Although they did *not* enjoy the political rights and privileges accorded to white citizens and residents – indeed, after the Dred Scott decision of 1857 African Americans lost even the most basic claims to civil rights – they *were* politically active at the grassroots level. Once becoming established in their new communities, thousands of runaways – men and women – did what they could to assist other fugitive slaves, serve as agents for vigilance committees and other abolitionist organizations, and join broader (often biracial) movements aimed at advancing equal rights for African Americans, abolishing federal fugitive slave laws, and ending slavery in the South. A few spoke of their stories in public or narrated their stories for publication – often using false names – in newspapers and even as books. Most, however, worked behind the scenes, keeping the motor of abolitionism running. Their lives, liberty, and loved ones were at stake. In a very real sense, northern abolitionism

---

[55] Kennedy, "Northward Bound," 67–129; J. W. Loguen to William Still, October 5, 1856, in Still, *The Underground Railroad*, 158 (quote), 440. The records of abolitionist Sydney Howard Gay, for example, reveal several examples of freedom seekers escaping the slave South with the intention of reuniting with family members still in slavery at a later date (and with the help of abolitionists). See Sydney Howard Gay, "Record of Fugitives, Book 1" (n.p.), Columbia University Libraries Online Exhibitions (https://dlc.library.columbia .edu/record_of_fugitives). See also Foner, *Gateway to Freedom*, 190–215.

would have been unthinkable without runaway slaves. Their plight, eyewitness accounts of slavery, and the very fact of their flight educated northerners to the realities and horrors of southern slavery. Manisha Sinha has recently argued that refugees from slavery were so essential to the antislavery movement in nineteenth-century America that they advanced a new culture of black politics: "fugitive slave abolitionism." Most importantly, runaway slaves helped turn parts of the North into de facto sanctuary spaces for refugees from slavery.[56]

THE THREAT OF RENDITION

As noncitizens in a part of the country where formal protection from reenslavement coud not be guaranteed, runaway slaves in the Northern United States navigated a precarious freedom that owed much to luck, assistance, and local authorities' interpretation of federal and state law. As Matthew Salafia has argued, "Everyone involved [in fugitive slave cases] knew that the meaning of the law depended on who enforced it, and they tried to manipulate the legal system to further their own ends." Despite the abolition of slavery and the designation of the northern states as "free soil" territories, refugees from slavery could be recaptured and sent back to their owners in the South on the basis of federal fugitive slave laws, especially after the Fugitive Slave Act of 1793 and its revised, more draconian 1850 version, as explained in Chapter 1. And although rendition was never a simple affair, its threat constantly loomed over runaways' heads like a Damocles sword.[57]

---

[56] Sinha, *The Slave's Cause*, ch. 13; John Stauffer, *The Black Hearts of Men: Radical Abolitionists and the Transformation of Race* (Cambridge, MA: Harvard University Press, 2002); Hodges, *David Ruggles*; Foner, *Gateway to Freedom*; Kennedy, "Northward Bound," 269–318. On black women's abolitionism, see Shirley J. Yee, *Black Women Abolitionists: A Study in Activism, 1828–1860* (Knoxville: University of Tennessee Press, 1992); Manisha Sinha, "Coming of Age: The Historiography of Black Abolitionism," in Timothy Patrick McCarthy and John Stauffer, eds., *Prophets of Protest: Reconsidering the History of American Abolitionism* (New York: The New Press, 2006), 23–38.

[57] Salafia, *Slavery's Borderland*, 140–141 (quote); Kennedy, "Northward Bound," 205–268; Jonathan Daniel Wells, *Blind No More: African American Resistance, Free-Soil Politics, and the Coming of the Civil War* (Athens: University of Georgia Press, 2019); Delbanco, *The War before the War*, 164–186; Foner, *Gateway to Freedom*, 119–150.

Most unnerving for refugees in the northern states was not knowing who might spot them or turn them in. Slave catchers and kidnappers were active in the border regions, and southern slaveholders frequently sent agents of their own to northern towns and cities when they thought they had a good lead. Stories of sudden and terrifying arrests (or attempted arrests), many of which were publicized in newspapers across the North, struck fear into the hearts and minds of African Americans living throughout the free soil states. Matilda Lawrence was tracked down and captured by an agent sent to Cincinnati by her master in a case that not only horrified the city's black community but also commanded national attention, as explained above. Oney Judge, the enslaved woman owned by George and Martha Washington who fled to Portsmouth, New Hampshire, in 1796, was recognized by port officials and eventually pursued by "a man by the name of Basset," who was sent by the Washingtons to recover her and bring her back to Virginia (in this case unsuccessfully because she was smuggled away and hidden by friends). Another runaway who fled to Boston in 1850 named Shadrach Minkins, from Norfolk, Virginia, was arrested in a case that provoked outrage across the North. Minkins had found employment at Taft's Cornhill Coffee House, a popular establishment that was frequented by southern businessmen visiting the city. Apparently recognized by an acquaintance of his master, who subsequently mobilized a recapture effort, Minkins was arrested by two men posed as customers at his place of employment. The horrifying case of Margaret Garner, an enslaved woman from Kentucky who fled with her husband and children to Cincinnati in 1856, "struck most deeply into the national psyche," as Andrew Delbanco put it. The Garners fled with the assistance of Underground Railroad agents connected to Levi Coffin, including other fugitive slaves living in and around the city and even Margaret's own uncle. The family was tracked down by a posse consisting of slave catchers and US federal marshals, however, who found the runaways barricaded in the uncle's house. Upon storming the residence Margaret's husband, Robert, fired a gun at the slave catchers, wounding one, and Margaret took a knife and killed her own daughter rather than let her be returned to slavery. She intended to kill her other children and herself as well, but was subdued by the posse. Tragic stories like these were known and talked about by African Americans throughout the free states. The arrival of a southerner or group of southerners in any northern town consequently threw black communities into a state of alarm. Indeed, formal alarm systems were put in place in many northern towns – the distribution of handbills, the tolling of church bells, and the grapevine telegraph warned African Americans that slave catchers had been spotted in the vicinity.[58]

And then there were ordinary *northern* white citizens to be cautious of. While some white northerners went to great lengths – even risking legal jeopardy – to protect runaway slaves from reenslavement, others were disgusted by the influx of blacks from the South and proved all too willing to report the refugees in their midst to the authorities, especially in the border region along the Mason–Dixon line and Ohio River, as Robert Churchill has recently argued. In 1812, for example, an enslaved man from Delaware named Prince took flight from his owner, one Alexander Laws, who "traced and pursued" his slave as far as Marcus Hook, Pennsylvania, where he was forced to turn back "without success." Prince may have seemed safe at this point, but in fact he continued to be pursued on several fronts. Laws ran a series of runaway slave ads in local newspapers and posted handbills around the region in an effort to locate his slave. In 1813, a resident of Chester County, Pennsylvania, wrote to Laws and reported that "a strange negro man" had recently begun to work for his neighbor, and that he matched "the description in the advertisement." Laws made haste to Chester County but upon arrival found that the "strange" black man was not Prince at all. Serendipitously for him, however, he later learned that the real Prince had been turned in as a runaway by another Pennsylvania resident and was now "in jail in Philadelphia." Three years after Prince struck for freedom, he was finally returned to slavery, betrayed by an ordinary white resident of a Pennsylvania farming community. Indeed, runaways in the Northern United States were never completely safe, even years after their initial flight attempts. No statute of limitations protected fugitive slaves living in the free states, and slaveholders certainly appeared to have the law on their side. Any news or rumors regarding the precise whereabouts of their runaways could spur them to action, no matter how much time had elapsed since their escape. One enslaved man named Thomson who fled

---

[58] Wells, *Blind No More*, 19; *Liberator*, August 22, 1845 (first quote); Collinson, *Shadrach Minkins*, 66–67; Gordon S. Barker, *Fugitive Slaves and the Unfinished American Revolution: Eight Cases* (Jefferson, NC: McFarland, 2014), 37–53, 160–180; Delbanco, *The War before the War*, 319 (second quote); Taylor, *Driven toward Madness*. See also Franklin and Schweninger, *Runaway Slaves*, 156–160; Stanley Harrold, *Border War: Fighting over Slavery before the Civil War* (Chapel Hill: University of North Carolina Press, 2010), 108–147.

to Pennsylvania in 1811 was not discovered and recaptured until 1818, after seven years of living in freedom.[59]

Although federal law seemed to uphold slaveholders' right to recover their runaway slaves in the free states, however, in practice the logistics, cost, and legal aspects of actually doing so constituted formidable challenges from the earliest years of the republic, as argued in Chapter 1. The Fugitive Slave Act of 1793 placed the burden of finding and apprehending a runaway slave squarely with the slaveholder, a difficult and expensive process. Northern officers and civilians were not required to assist slaveholders in this process, and indeed according to some local interpretations of federal law were even prohibited from doing so. The border states complained incessantly about the unreliability of northern officers and authorities in assisting or even allowing the recapture of runaways in the free states, a stance that frequently resulted in de facto freedom for fugitive slaves who were known to have fled north of the Mason–Dixon line and Ohio River. Maryland's House of Delegates highlighted as early as 1798 that its state's slaveholders were subjected to "great loss and inconvenience for the escape of slaves to Delaware, Pennsylvania, and New Jersey, where they remained concealed and protected by the whites." Some twenty years later the same legislative body charged that "every possible difficulty is thrown in the way" of slaveholders who traveled to Pennsylvania to reclaim their runaway slaves. The US Congress even drafted a southern-sponsored bill in 1818 that would have required state officers to participate in the arrest of fugitive slaves, but the bill was rejected on the grounds that it violated the principle of dual sovereignty and separate spheres between state and federal government. The principle of northern noncooperation with federal fugitive slave laws was indeed later upheld by the US Supreme Court in the *Prigg* v. *Pennsylvania* verdict of 1842.[60]

---

[59] Churchill, *The Underground Railroad and the Geography of Violence*, 88–111, 139–170; Salafia, *Slavery's Borderland*, 165–184; Petition of Alexander P. Laws to Kent County Court, December 4, 1816, RSPP, Series 2, Accession #20381603 (quote); Petition of James Frazer to New Castle County Court, June 2, 1818, RSPP, Series 2, Accession #20381801.

[60] Harrold, *Border War*, 23–25 (quotes), 73–77; Foner, *Gateway to Freedom*, 38–39; Morris, *Free Men All*, 94; Sinha, *The Slave's Cause*, 390; Kennedy, "Northward Bound," 207–209; Paul Finkelman, "The Kidnapping of John Davis and the Adoption of the Fugitive Slave Law of 1793," *Journal of Southern History* 56, no. 3 (1990): 397–422; Stephen Lubet, *Fugitive Justice: Runaways, Rescuers, and Slavery on Trial* (Cambridge, MA: Harvard University Press, 2012), 20–22.

Northern anti-kidnapping statutes and personal liberty laws, moreover – which were designed to obstruct the execution of federal fugitive slave law, as explained in Chapter 1 – complicated procedures by severely circumscribing the conditions for the lawful seizure of African Americans and their transportation across state borders. From the earliest days of the republic southern slaveholders had aimed for *recaption* – the simple common-law seizure of a lost piece of property, like a strayed horse – rather than the legally more complicated rendition. And to be sure, many slaveholders flouted the law and committed (or attempted to commit) recaption when they thought they could get away with it. There is no evidence that suggests that this was as easy as grabbing them off the street and throwing them into a wagon headed back south, however. The simple apprehension of suspected fugitive slaves in the northern states could result in state prosecution for attempted kidnapping – as indeed occurred in the case of Edward Prigg, which led to the *Prigg* verdict of 1842 in the first place – as well as writs of habeas corpus and demands for state hearings for residents who were presumed free unless proven otherwise. The Pennsylvania General Assembly passed a sweeping personal liberty law in 1826 that established procedures for a court hearing to determine the status of the alleged fugitive slave, gave the accused the time necessary to prove their freedom, and authorized Pennsylvania justices to issue warrants for arrest. In 1828, New York outlawed private recaption and established a procedure that demanded state involvement in the judicial disposal of fugitive slave cases. The Massachussetts "Latimer Law" of 1843 – a direct response to the *Prigg* decision – not only prohibited state officials from assisting in federal fugitive slave cases, but also prohibited the use of state jails for the apprehension of runaway slaves. All of the northern states passed similar personal liberty laws and anti-kidnapping statutes in the antebellum period. Such statutes often resulted in the legal acquittal of the accused. In 1840, for example, one James Turner was arrested in Reading, Pennsylvania, as a "fugitive from service" and, according to state personal liberty laws, brought before the local justice. The presiding judge allowed Turner to call a witness – a free black man – to testify on his behalf, and subsequently determined that the slaveholder who claimed Turrner as his slave had insufficient evidence. Turner was released as a free man. Such cases infuriated southern slaveholders.[61]

---

[61] H. Robert Baker, "The Fugitive Slave Clause and the Antebellum Constitution," *Law and History Review* 30, no. 4 (2012): 1150; William R. Leslie, "The Pennsylvania Fugitive Slave Act of 1826," *Journal of Southern History* 18, no. 4 (1952): 429–445; Don

Northern noncooperation with – and legal obstruction of – federal fugitive slave laws constituted formidable challenges for slaveholders and their agents, even before the Fugitive Slave Law of 1850. A case that came before the Virginia General Assembly in 1838 provides an interesting glimpse into how complicated such recovery efforts could be in a part of the country where public opinion was strongly opposed to the rendition of slave refugees. During the previous year a group of Virginia runaways had managed to collectively steal a whaling boat docked in Northampton County and made for New York. Given the unusual nature of the crime – running away *and* grand theft – the Governor of Virginia intervened, fearing that the incident might set a dangerous precedent, and appointed a special agent named Edward Waddy to travel to New York and recover the "fugitives from justice." Waddy encountered difficulties almost from the start. Upon arrival in New York City, he immediately presented himself to local police officers and requested their assistance, but they refused, even after receiving an order from the Governor of New York to do so because the case involved theft. Interestingly, the reason the officers gave for their refusal was "the great odium which any of them must incur by being engaged in the apprehension of slaves." In other words, they risked resistance and possible physical harm from local New Yorkers if they carried out such an unpopular task. In the end the officers agreed to cooperate only if they received extra pay for their services. In what amounted to a bribe, Waddy was forced to advance the exorbitant sum of $2,720 of his own money just to get the New York officers to help him carry out his charge. With their assistance he ultimately managed to recapture ten of the runaways, but as the mission dragged on he found it

E. Fehrenbacher and Ward M. McAfee, *The Slaveholding Republic: An Account of the United States Government's Relations to Slavery* (New York: Oxford University Press, 2001), 215–216; Paul Finkelman, "*Prigg v. Pennsylvania* and Northern State Courts: Anti-Slavery Use of a Pro-Slavery Decision," in John R. McKivigan, ed., *Abolitionism and American Law* (New York: Garland, 1999), 215; *Pennsylvania Freeman*, March 5, 1840; Carol Wilson, *Freedom at Risk: The Kidnapping of Free Blacks in America, 1780–1865* (Lexington: University of Kentucky Press, 1994), 67–68; Andrew K. Diemer, *The Politics of Black Citizenship: Free African Americans in the Mid-Atlantic Borderland, 1817–1863* (Athens: University of Georgia Press, 2016), 51–52; Salafia, *Slavery's Borderland*, 154–156; Richard Newman, *The Transformation of American Abolitionism: Fighting Slavery in the Early Republic* (Chapel Hill: University of North Carolina Press, 2002), 40–44; Hyon Hur, "Radical Antislavery and Personal Liberty Lawsin Antebellum Ohio, 1803–1857" (PhD diss., University of Wisconsin-Madison, 2012); Stanley W. Campbell, *The Slave Catchers: Enforcement of the Fugitive Slave Law, 1850–1860* (Chapel Hill: University of North Carolina Press, 1970), 184–185; Morris, *Free Men All*, 94.

"more and more difficult" to execute the rendition process due to local hostility to his mission. During the trial of the ten fugitives the courthouse was indeed surrounded by an angry mob of protesters. Waddy claimed that he was "hazarding his life," and at one point he himself was arrested and "actually incarcerated within the walls of the City Jail." To make matters worse, he received only $975 in rewards from the runaways' owners when he returned them to Virginia, leaving him $1,745 in the hole. He sued the state for financial compensation.[62]

At best – when it did not involve the threat of violence or potential incarceration by state authorities – the retrieval of fugitive slaves who were living in the free states was an expensive and complicated affair. Numerous complaints in court records related to the recapture of north-bound runaways testify specifically to the trouble and expense involved in even successful rendition cases. In 1829 "several slaves" belonging to the estate of Sherwood Haywood in North Carolina escaped to a free state (the records do not mention which state), the heirs complaining in an equity case that Haywood's widow had had to expend a "large sum" to capture them and secure their rendition. When the slaves were subsequently sold, they brought in less than it cost to recover them in the North, leaving the estate with a net loss. The exquisitely named Pleasant H. Harbour, a slaveholder from Louisiana, sued a steamboat captain in 1842 after his slave George escaped up the Mississippi River to Illinois by concealing himself onboard the vessel. George was eventually recovered by his master but only "after great trouble & loss," and he therefore demanded compensation. Indeed, virtually all southern sources related to the recapture of runaways in the North employ terms like "trouble," "loss," and "expense." Northern resistance, civil disobedience, and the risk of state prosecution under personal liberty laws and kidnapping statutes rendered even covert attempts at recapture a difficult undertaking.[63]

The 1850 Fugitive Slave Law was supposed to make things easier for slaveholders, but in fact the successful recapture and rendition of fugitive slaves remained an expensive and complicated affair even after its

---

[62] Petition of Edward R. Waddy to the General Assembly of Virginia, January 1, 1838, RSPP, Series 1: Legislative Petitions, Accession #11683807 (quotes). See also Franklin and Schweninger, *Runaway Slaves*, 160.

[63] Petition of William A. Blount Jr. et al., to Equity Court of Wake County, NC, December 1858, RSPP, Series 2, Accession #21285612 (first quote); Petition of Pleasant H. Harbour to District Court of Louisiana, November 14, 1842, RSPP, Accession #20884243 (second quote); Franklin and Schweninger, *Runaway Slaves*, 160.

passage. Section 6 of the 1850 law explained in detail the procedure prescribed for recovering a fugitive slave in a northern state. Slaveholders or their authorized agents were required to either request formal arrest warrants from federal commissioners and then seize their runaways or seize their runaways and bring them before a federal commissioner. In both cases written proof – in the form of a sworn affidavit and other documents such as wills or certificates – was required to establish both the identity and the slave status of the alleged runaway, a process that in some cases took considerable time because such materials had to be acquired and collected, and then submitted and processed by the circuit or district courts. When Catherine Gaston, a slaveholder and resident of the District of Columbia, learned that her runaway slave Isaac Starkey was living in New York in 1851, she had to submit "full and satisfactory proof" to the Circuit Court of DC that she was indeed the owner of Isaac and that he had unlawfully fled her residence, as well as a formal request for the necessary papers to reclaim him in New York. The Maryland owner of three runaways – brothers named Stephen, Robert, and Jacob Pembroke – had to submit repeated requests for legal documents between 1854 and 1857. The three had fled in May 1854 and were presumed to be living in either New York City or Brooklyn, but even as late as May 1857 their owner was still pleading with the US Commissioners in the District of Maryland to open a formal file and take depositions and affidavits to prove the identities of his runaway slaves so that he could receive the "benefit" of the 1850 Fugitive Slave Law in tracking them down. Only after the identity and status of the runaway had been established could a federal commissioner issue a certificate of removal. Federal commissioners were authorized to force any bystanders or local police forces to assist them, and – in a particularly corrupt bargain with slaveholders – they were to be paid $10 if the verdict favored rendition of the fugitive slave, but only $5 if the defendant was released.[64]

---

[64] Matthew Pinsker, "After 1850: Reassessing the Impact of the Fugitive Slave Law," in Damian Alan Pargas, ed., *Fugitive Slaves and Spaces of Freedom in North America* (Gainesville: University Press of Florida, 2018), 93–94; Delbanco, *The War before the War*, 226–228; Petition of Catherine Gaston to the Circuit Court of the District of Columbia, April 1, 1851, RSPP, Series 2, Accession #20485102 (quote); Files of Stephen Pembroke and Robert & Jacob Pembroke, Records of the US Commissioners, 1837–1860, of the US District Court for the Southern District of New York (microfilm), Roosevelt Institute for American Studies, Middelburg, Netherlands; Delbanco, *The War before the War*, 226–227.

In practice the legal procedures set out in the law were confusing at best, even to lawyers and judges. Although traditional scholarship by historians such as Stanley Campbell often portrayed the law as largely successful – arguing that most judges and commissioners faithfully executed their duties and that northern public opinion more or less accepted it – a more recent generation of scholars have complicated this view. Matthew Pinsker recently argued that "the 1850 Fugitive Slave Law might well be the worst piece of legislation in American history." It was certainly a "spectacular failure in its actual operations," not only due to its sporadic enforcement and massive resistance by northerners, but also because it was a "legal mess," according to Pinsker. The numbers alone suggest that the law fell far short of recovering a majority of freedom seekers in the northern states. Campbell calculated that 332 fugitive slaves were brought before federal commissioners between 1850 and 1861. Some of them were arrested in groups, however, so in fact Campbell identified only 125 actual rendition hearings. The majority of the fugitive slaves brought before federal commissioners were sent back into slavery, indicating that most federal commissioners indeed dutifully executed their duties. But, as Pinsker argues, not all of the trials resulted in favor of the claimant, and the fact that so few cases came to a hearing at all speaks volumes to the complications involved in successfully applying the law and securing formal rendition in the 1850s. By way of comparison, three times as many runaways were formally arrested and returned to slavery from the District of Columbia alone during the same period. Slaveholders themselves indeed loudly complained that the federal government had failed to uphold their constitutional rights to retrieve runaway slaves, even after 1850.[65]

Just one month after the passage of the Fugitive Slave Law of 1850 the city of Philadelphia was confronted with its first case, one that very well illustrates the challenges involved for southern slaveholders looking to retrieve their runaway slaves. Henry Garnet, a hod carrier, was arrested on his way to work on October 17, accused of being the runaway slave of

<hr>

[65] Pinsker, "After 1850," 109–110; Campbell, *The Slave Catchers*; Blackett, *Captive's Quest for Freedom*, 3–87; Delbanco, *The War before the War*, 262–316; Foner, *Gateway to Freedom*, 119–150; Fehrenbacher and McAfee, *The Slaveholding Republic*, 231–232; Scott J. Basinger, "Regulating Slavery: Deck-Stacking and Credible Commitment in the Fugitive Slave Act of 1850," *Journal of Law, Economics, & Organization* 19, no. 2 (2003): 307–342; William Link, *Roots of Secession: Slavery and Politics in Antebellum Virginia* (Chapel Hill: University of North Carolina Press, 2003), 107. For the DC arrest figures, see Chapter 2 of the present volume.

one Thomas P. Jones of Maryland. The new US fugitive slave commissioner was not even in place yet, so Supreme Court Justice Robert Grier had to preside over the rendition trial. Despite legal statutes that supposedly limited due process for accused fugitive slaves and prevented their testimony in court, Garnet was allowed to be represented by four attorneys and call witnesses – in other words, he employed legal rights that were supposedly denied to him by federal law. In the end, Justice Grier not only allowed the alleged fugitive to act as a legal person, but he ruled in favor of the accused, releasing him on a technicality that, according to Pinsker, was "borne out of the complicated and poorly followed procedures that had been detailed in the sixth section of the new law." The claimant had produced wills to prove that Henry was his slave, and he had brought witnesses, but the wills appeared to have an illegible state seal and were therefore rejected. The claimant's witnesses had moreover failed to have their affidavits preapproved by a magistrate. Grier essentially ruled that the claimant had not followed the required procedure for reclaiming his runaway slave under the new 1850 law. When the claimant requested a postponement in order to correct his errors, Grier denied it, arguing that Jones should have come better prepared and that Pennsylvania state law did not allow state jails to be used in fugitive slave cases, so he had no choice but to allow Garnet to exit the courthouse a free man. Legal technicalities sometimes even backfired on slaveholders and their agents from the law's earliest days, due to ambiguities between federal and state law regarding the lawful seizure of African Americans. In some cases, if an alleged fugitive slave was dragged before the federal commissioner but ended up being acquitted, the slave catcher could be tried under state law for attempted kidnapping. This occurred in the spring of 1851 – only months after the passage of the Fugitive Slave Law – when one professional slave catcher in Pennsylvania made a huge mistake by seizing the free-born child of an alleged fugitive for federal rendition to Maryland, apparently thinking that the child of the fugitive also belonged to that fugitive's master. Not only was the agent unsuccessful, but he was subsequently arrested by *state* officials on child kidnapping charges and sentenced to ten years of hard labor in prison and a $1,000 fine. Such cases did more than frustrate southern slaveholders – they put them on guard.[66]

---

[66] Pinsker, "After 1850," 93 (first quote), 101–103, 102 (second quote); *Philadelphia Evening Bulletin*, October 18, 1850; *Philadelphia Public Ledger*, October 18, 1850. See also Delbanco, *The War before the War*, 262–316; Foner, *Gateway to Freedom*,

At worst, attempts to recover fugitive slaves in the northern states were not only complicated and expensive, but indeed dangerous and even life-threatening, as they incensed northerners – both black and white – to commit acts of civil disobedience and even outright mob violence in defense of the runaways in their midst. Acts of violence were indeed already commonplace long before the deeply unpopular Fugitive Slave Law of 1850 was passed; the controversial law therefore did not consti-tute any neat turning point in the strategies employed by northerners to prevent the rendition of runaway slaves. Indeed, a large body of scholar-ship has emphasized that violent resistance to the execution of fugitive slave laws throughout the antebellum period was common. Stanley Harrold has argued that the states of the Lower North constituted a theater of "border war" over slavery that raged for decades before the Civil War. Robert Churchill has identified at least eighty "fugitive slave rescue attempts" in the northern states between 1794 and 1850, which he defines as any "incident in which activists used force or intimidation either to prevent the recapture of individuals claimed as fugitive slaves who had reached the North or to rescue such individuals from the custody of slave catchers, masters, or officers intent on returning them to slavery." Some sixty-nine of these rescue attempts – nearly 87 percent – were successful. Obstruction tactics, violence and the threat of violence, rescues of pursued and even arrested individuals, and counter-prosecution of slave catchers were common long before 1850 (Figure 3.1).[67]

Consider the case of Francis Giltner, a Kentucky slaveholder who traveled to Michigan to recover several of his runaway slaves in 1848. Having tracked his bondspeople down in the town of Marshall, Giltner showed up on the morning of January 27 and entered the house where the runaways were presumed to be living, accompanied by the local deputy sheriff and three Kentuckians. Upon entry the group "found six fugitive slaves, the property of Giltner," according to a newspaper report. The runaways were immediately rounded up and ordered to accompany the

119–150; Blackett, *Captive's Quest for Freedom*, 3–87; Kennedy, "Northward Bound," 232–254.
[67] Harrold, *Border War*; Robert H. Churchill, "Fugitive Slave Rescues: Toward a Geography of Northern Antislavery Violence," *Ohio Valley History* 14, no. 2 (Summer 2014): 51–75, esp. 53 (quote) and 54; Blackett, *Captive's Quest for Freedom*, 3–87; Delbanco, *The War before the War*, 262–316; Kennedy, "Northward Bound," 205–254. The pamphlet literature produced as a result of fugitive slave cases can be found in Paul Finkelman, ed., *Fugitive Slaves and American Courts: The Pamphlet Literature*, 4 vols. (Clark, NJ: Lawbook Exchange, 2012).

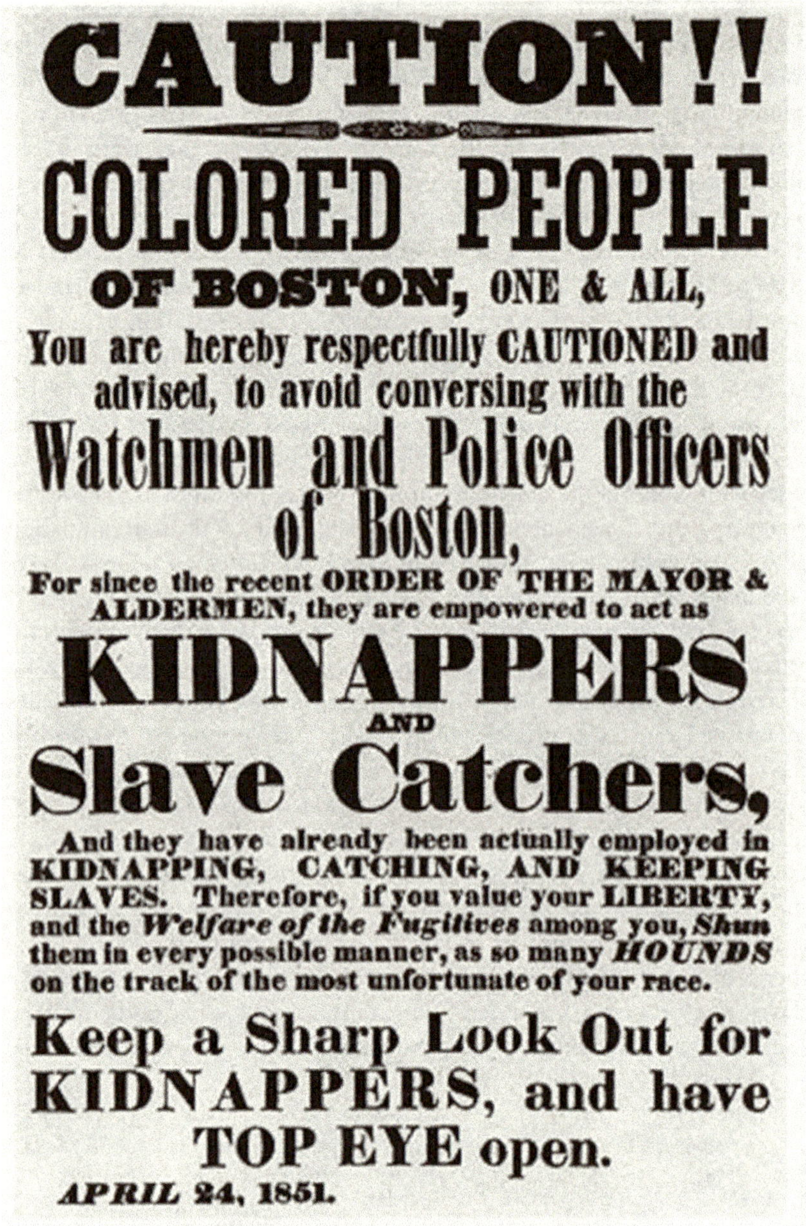

CAUTION!!

COLORED PEOPLE

OF BOSTON, ONE & ALL,

You are hereby respectfully CAUTIONED and advised, to avoid conversing with the

Watchmen and Police Officers of Boston,

For since the recent ORDER OF THE MAYOR & ALDERMEN, they are empowered to act as

KIDNAPPERS

AND

Slave Catchers,

And they have already been actually employed in KIDNAPPING, CATCHING, AND KEEPING SLAVES. Therefore, if you value your LIBERTY, and the *Welfare of the Fugitives* among you, *Shun* them in every possible manner, as so many *HOUNDS* on the track of the most unfortunate of your race.

Keep a Sharp Look Out for KIDNAPPERS, and have TOP EYE open.

APRIL 24, 1851.

FIGURE 3.1 Handbill warning of slave catchers in Boston, 1851.

white men to the office of the magistrate, but before they could get them out of the door the group "was surrounded by a mob, which, by its violent threats, menaces, and assaults, prevented the removal of the slaves to the office of the magistrate." Panicking, Giltner shouted to the deputy sheriff "time after time, to discharge his duty," but "so great was the excitement and violence of the mob, that the officer was afraid to seize the slaves." The mob, which consisted of some 200–300 local residents, included not only committed white abolitionists but also "forty to fifty" African Americans, "many of whom [were] fugitive slaves from Kentucky." They refused to back down. Newspaper reports stated that many in the mob had guns and "pledged their lives" to defend the runaways from being sent back to Kentucky, even if Giltner "proved his right to do so." The standoff lasted hours, and the situation finally took an interesting turn when some leading townsmen arranged for a warrant to arrest the *Kentuckians* for trespassing, for which they were indeed subsequently dragged in front of a local magistrate, "who was an abolitionist," and fined $100. Giltner got away with his life, but without his slaves and $100 in the hole, not to mention the cost and trouble of his journey to Michigan in the first place. The story of this incident was published in newspapers as far away as South Carolina, effectively warning southerners of what they were potentially getting themselves into if they went north to try to recover their runaway slaves, whatever the letter of federal law.[68]

As is clear from the report of the Marshall incident, runaways themselves played an active role in such incidents. In small communities such as Marshall, but also in major cities such as Philadelphia, Boston, New York, and Cincinnati, refugees from slavery fought to obstruct justice and help black-led and biracial vigilance committees create and defend free soil. They pledged their lives to do so because their very lives were at stake. Major abolitionist activists such as David Ruggles, William Still, William Lloyd Garrison, and Levi Coffin could not have been as effective as they were if they had not had the support of fiercely determined runaway slaves who were willing to risk their lives and their freedom in order to protect members of their community from reenslavement. Together with sympathetic free black and white members of their adopted communities, they helped thwart the execution of fugitive slave laws and create sanctuary spaces for other runaways from slavery. Importantly,

[68] *Edgefield Advertiser* (SC), May 24, 1848.

their efforts often paid off in at least two ways. First, recent estimates suggest that the assistance of black-led and biracial vigilance committees made freedom seekers in the northern states *at least ten times likelier to succeed (in other words, to permanently escape slavery) than fail (be returned to slavery)* during the 1850s. Consider the abovementioned figure of 332 fugitive slaves dragged before federal commissioners between 1850 and 1861. For the same period, the records of vigilance committees in New York, Boston, and Philadelphia alone record 1,250 successful covert escapes. And those are just the records of the three vigilance committees in the three biggest cities. If the northern states are taken in their entirety, estimates must surely reach a few thousand. Second, the obstructionist tactics of the defenders of runaway slaves were only very rarely punished throughout the antebellum period. Whatever the letter of the law stated, few abolitionists or fellow refugees who harbored or helped fugitive slaves were ever even fined – and when they were the fines were rarely paid in full – let alone sentenced to jail. Indeed, the handful or so of criminal convictions that resulted from civil disobedience to federal fugitive slave laws throughout the North were largely symbolic, even after the 1850 law, which explicitly criminalized not only civil disobedience but even the refusal to assist in recapture. One such case in Indiana in 1854, involving a man who was tried for obstructing the Fugitive Slave Law of 1850, was sentenced to one hour in prison and a $50 fine. Another Illinois abolitionist was imprisoned for ten days in Chicago in early 1860, but the jailors let him out every night to dine with antislavery supporters. Defenders of fugitive slaves – with fugitive slaves themselves on the front lines – were truly a force to be reckoned with in the northern states, mainly because they found themselves in states where key members of the community – from judges to jailors – often deeply opposed federal fugitive slave laws on their free soil.[69]

---

[69] See, for example, Andrew Diemer, "'Agitation, Tumult, Violence Will Not Cease': Black Politics and the Compromise of 1850," in Van Gosse and David Waldstreicher, eds., *Emancipations, Reconstructions, and Revolutions: African American Politics and U.S. History from the First to the Second Civil War* (Philadelphia: University of Pennsylvania Press, 2020); Pinsker, "After 1850," 108–109. Eric Foner's discovery of Sydney Howard Gay's "Record of Fugitives" documents 200 successful individual runaways. For the same period there are at least 250 cases from Boston vigilance records and more than 800 from William Still's records for the Philadelphia vigilance committee. See Foner, *Gateway to Freedom*, 190–215; Larry Gara, "William Still and the Underground Railroad," *Pennsylvania History* 28 (January 1961): 33–44.

Fugitive slave trials – when rendition cases came to trial at all – not only galvanized support for stricter personal liberty laws, but also further mobilized civil society to organize mass civil disobedience, widely publicized protests, and daring rescue attempts that caused such a sensation that they led many slaveholders throughout the South to openly question whether federal laws upholding their right to recover runaway slaves were enforceable at all. In one rendition case in Henry County, Iowa, in 1848, for example, the Missouri owner of nine escaped slaves was obstructed in every possible way from recovering his human property. The slaveholder, one Ruel Daggs, had tracked down the party of runaways across the Des Moines River in free soil Iowa. Together with an armed posse he crossed the border, located the runaways, and attempted to seize them, but local Quaker abolitionists, led by Elihu Frazier, prevented him from doing so. Daggs then stepped to the local magistrate to ask for assistance, but the magistrate refused to hear the case because the "Negroes were not properly before him," a legal technicality designed to obstruct the slave catchers. He also demanded proof of ownership in the form of a sealed certificate from the clerk of the court in Missouri. In the meantime, the runaways managed to escape the region with the assistance of the abolitionists. Eventually Daggs attempted to sue Frazier and other local abolitionists for "rescuing" the runaways and obstructing their rendition. During the trial the defense attorney demanded that Daggs not only prove ownership of the accused runaways, but indeed "prove the existence of Slavery in Missouri, and that the negroes were slaves" at all. Daggs replied that he had no evidence with him just then and there. Justice Nelson Gibbs, who presided over the trial, proceeded to put Daggs and his men on the spot himself by interrogating them at length about their "legal agency." Gibbs demanded to know upon what grounds Daggs and his posse had crossed state lines and attempted to personally seize the African Americans they claimed were runaway slaves. The men were forced to admit that they had had no legal authority to cross state lines for the purpose of detaining anyone, as they were not officers of the law. As a crowd of angry community residents gathered around the courthouse, the defense attorney delivered a powerful speech to the jury in which he underscored the crux of the matter: that in Iowa "we recognize no person as a slave. The presumption of freedom is universal." Even then the jury ultimately found the abolitionists guilty on some (but not all) counts of obstruction and awarded Daggs a compensation settlement of $2,900 – he had demanded $10,000 – but Daggs never received a cent, the abolitionists were never imprisoned, and the slaves were never recovered.[70]

The Daggs case was argued just before passage of the 1850 Fugitive Slave Law, but that act did not put an end to daring fugitive slave rescues – rather quite the opposite. Churchill identified seventy-four fugitive slave rescue attempts in the 1850s, fifty of which were successful (a success rate of 68 percent). The well-known trial of William Henry – who went by the name Jerry – who was arrested as a fugitive slave in Syracuse, New York, demonstrated that the 1850 Fugitive Slave Law would be obstructed by any means necessary in a part of the country where the population was virulently opposed to it. Jerry was a runaway from Missouri who had been working as a cooper in Syracuse for some time before he was quietly manacled and taken into custody by US Deputy Marshall Henry Allen on the morning of October 1, 1851. In the carriage ride to the office of the US Commissioner downtown, his plight caught the attention of city residents. Syracuse was coincidentally "crowded with citizens of the county" that morning, "who were attending their County Fair." Even more coincidentally, the Liberty Party happened to be holding a state convention in Syracuse at the same time, swelling the number of committed abolitionists in town. A manacled slave was not something local citizens were used to seeing in their city, and according to court records "an immediate and intense excitement ensued. Citizens and strangers flocked to the Commissioners [sic] Office – the bells of the churches were tolled – Counsel volunteered to defend the person claimed." During the trial itself, enraged local citizens encouraged Jerry to make "an effort to escape" while the commissioner recessed for dinner, which he did, but once out of the door he was overtaken by city police, beaten, and dragged back to the Commissioner's Office. The crowd surrounding the building grew larger and angrier. Stones were thrown and a commotion ensued. Under the circumstances the nervous commissioner decided to adjourn and postpone the trial until the following morning. Henry was left imprisoned in the jail attached to the Commissioner's Office, under the supervision of Deputy Marshall Allen, but Allen left the building in order to prepare for the following day's proceedings. At "about nine o'clock in the evening, the doors and windows of the Police Office were forced, and Henry [Jerry] rescued and sent to Canada." The full story of the rescue was even more sensational – a band of black and white citizens, including other

---

[70] *Fugitive Slave Case: District Court of the United States.*

slave refugees and members of the Syracuse Vigilance Committee, executed an elaborate plan by which they stormed the building and gained
entry by smashing windows, removing their casings, and even removing
bricks from the wall. Once inside they attacked the jail cell with a
battering ram, seized the prisoner, and spirited him away in a carriage
under cover of darkness.[71]

The rescue caused such outrage among southern slaveholders, and
such embarrassment among federal authorities, that it quickly resulted
in demands for retribution and retaliatory arrests. In the end twenty-six
rescuers were tried – even Deputy Marshall Allen was arrested and
charged with kidnapping for "allowing" Jerry to be rescued – but only
one black man was convicted and fined. (Members of the community paid
the fine for him.) Nine others were charged in absentia but had already
long fled to Canada. Southern slaveholders were incensed – the "Jerry
Rescue" suggested that federal law was potentially a dead letter in abolitionist country and that even fugitive slaves *in custody* could be rescued
by antislavery activists.[72]

Sensational rescues and rescue attempts continued to make the head-
lines in the 1850s, causing the fugitive slave issue to truly reach fever
pitch. Sometimes they had serious legal repercussions that only furthered
the abolitionist cause of turning the North into a sanctuary space for
refugees from slavery. One such rescue turned Wisconsin into a legal
asylum for runaway slaves for a period of four years, for example.
Joshua Glover, a fugitive slave who escaped from St. Louis to
Wisconsin but was caught and incarcerated in Milwaukee in 1854, was
rescued when twenty men bashed the jail door down with a twenty-foot
log. The incident resulted in the Wisconsin Supreme Court declaring the
Fugitive Slave Law of 1850 unconstitutional and thus nullified throughout the state (a ruling overturned in 1859 by the US Supreme Court). Even
when rescue attempts were *un*successful and the runaways were in fact
returned to their masters, southern slaveholders found that the rage they

---

[71] Churchill, "Fugitive Slave Rescues," 54; Barker, *Fugitive Slaves and the Unfinished American Revolution*, 96–117; Angela F. Murphy, *The Jerry Rescue: The Fugitive Slave Law, Northern Rights, and the American Sectional Crisis* (New York: Oxford University Press, 2016); *Trial of Henry W. Allen, U.S. Deputy Marhsal, for Kidnapping, with Arguments of Counsel & Charge of Justice Marvin, on the Constitutionality of the Fugitive Slave Law, in the Supreme Court of New York* (Syracuse: Power Press of the Daily Journal Office, 1852).

[72] Barker, *Fugitive Slaves and the Unfinished American Revolution*, 96–117; Murphy, *The Jerry Rescue*; *Trial of Henry W. Allen, U.S. Deputy Marshal*.

sparked when they attempted to apply the federal fugitive slave law was far more than they bargained for. Indeed, as Andrew Delbanco recently argued, the "anger ignited in the North" that resulted in actual rendition cases helped push the northern and southern states closer to war. The infamous trial of Anthony Burns, a runaway slave from Alexandria, Virginia, at a Boston courthouse in 1854, serves as an interesting case in point. The arrest of Burns mobilized civic reactions reminiscent of (and no doubt influenced by) the Jerry trial in Syracuse a couple of years earlier. Such was the fury it sparked among abolitionists and concerned citizens – especially African Americans – that the Burns trial resulted not only in the counter-arrest of Burns' master on charges of attempted kidnapping but also led to mass rallies and ultimately a nighttime mob raid on the courthouse to try and liberate Burns and secret him away. Some of the mob were armed with "new axes, and many of them had pistols, stones and brickbats." The rescue attempt failed; instead, it ended in a major riot that witnessed officers having their badges torn off by black protesters, axes being freely handed out by abolitionists, and at least one officer – a member of the US Marshal's posse – fatally stabbed. At its peak the angry mob had reportedly swelled to between 2,000 and 3,000, and the governor of Massachusetts was forced to call in federal troops to restore order. In the end, Burns lost the case and was returned to Virginia, but at such risk and cost that the drama stoked fear and outrage among slaveholders throughout the South. (Burns was later bought and freed by abolitionists from Massachusetts.)[73]

Remarkably, many fugitive slaves who were successfully returned to their masters by legal means did not give up. In other words, rendition – when it did occur – was not always the end of the story for northbound freedom seekers. Many tried again, and again. Southern runaway slave ads and court records widely attest to the problem of *habitual* runaways: Those who fled north, were recaptured and sent back to the South, and then ran away again. Habitual runaways had basically lost the fear of recapture and were determined to win their freedom – do or die. As Franklin and Schweninger argued, they so longed for their liberty that they simply "refused to capitulate," no matter what the consequences. One Maryland slaveholder complained to the Anne Arundel Court in

---

[73] Delbanco, *The War before the War*, 316–317, 316 (quote); Barker, *Fugitive Slaves and the Unfinished American Revolution*, 136–159; Gordon S. Barker, *The Imperfect Revolution: Anthony Burns and the Landscape of Race in Antebellum America* (Kent State University Press, 2010); *Baltimore Sun*, May 29, 1854.

1856 that his slave Robert had a habit of running away to the North via Baltimore, adding that the runaway was by no means "ignorant of consequences nor of the Law" but seemed not to care. As Robert "by his conduct seems desirous of leaving the State without permission," the slaveholder requested permission to sell him out of state. Another habitual runaway from Maryland named Robinson was described in court as "of a surly, morose and discontented disposition ... he is greatly dissatisfied with his state of servitude." Yet another habitual runaway from Maryland, a nineteen-year-old term slave named Amelia, fled on three separate occasions in the late 1850s. Each time she was caught and sent back to her owner, one William Ghent, who suffered "much expenses in loss of her service & in recovering said slave," as he declared to a Baltimore County judge. Indeed, Amelia helped her own sister run away as well. Upon Amelia's third recapture she "vow[ed] & declare[d] that she will not stay with your Petitioner but will run away from him if he takes her home." Considering her "dangerous" to remain in the neighborhood, Amelia's owner requested permission to have her sold out of state. The owner of George and Jane, an enslaved couple from Virginia, similarly requested permission to sell his bondspeople after they had been caught trying to smuggle themselves on board a vessel bound for New York. The slaveholder declared that the two were "difficult to manage & in the habit of frequently running away."[74]

Widely publicized fugitive slave trials, the rampant problem of habitual runaways, and preventive alarm systems in northern communities that were aimed at obstructing slave catchers, convinced many slaveholders that the successful retrieval of fugitive slaves in the free states was nearly impossible, a testament to not only the dizzying bureaucracy involved in federal rendition but also to the effectiveness of efforts by northern lawyers, abolitionists, fellow fugitive slave activists, and ordinary citizens in protecting the refugees living in their midst. This is especially clear in southern county court records related to fugitive slaves. Slaveholders

---

[74] Franklin and Schweninger, *Runaway Slaves*, 38 (first quote); Petition of Thomas R. Carey to the Orphans Court of Anne Arundel County, MD, November 26, 1856, RASP, Series 2: County Court Petitions, Accession #20985644 (second quote); Petition of John M. Timanus to the Orphans Court for Baltimore, MD, RASP, Series 2: County Court Petitions, Accession #20986110 (third quote); Petition of William C. Ghent to the Orphans Court of Baltimore County, MD, October 26, 1859, RSPP, Series 2: County Court Petitions, Accession #20985920 (fourth quote); Petition of Thomas Cowles to Henrico County Court, VA, August 7, 1833, RSPP, Series 2, Accession #21683321 (fifth quote).

often petitioned county courts for permission to sell slaves whom they feared might try to escape to the North, because they viewed their chances of successful recapture as close to zero. In 1860 one M. Banner, a Maryland slaveholder, petitioned an Anne Arundel court for permission to sell his slave named Samuel Hodge. Samuel had absconded and been caught, but it had cost Banner "great expense to have Hodge captured and placed in jail." Banner believed that if released from confinement, Hodge "would again run away ... and escape to some free state *where your petitioner would not be able to recover him.*" Other cases reveal that many slaveholders indeed regarded runaways to the North a total loss, and undertook virtually no steps to even try to find or retrieve them, even before Fugitive Slave Law of 1850 that provoked such massive resistance among northerners. Tellingly, examples of such exasperation especially abound in court cases from the border states, where slaveholders were arguably in the best position to recover their runaways compared to their southern counterparts. In 1835 an enslaved man from Kentucky named Bailey, valued at $700 and described as "a young man of good health & of good constitution – Stout and active," absconded to the North onboard the steamboat *Splendid* and was reported to be living just across the river in Cincinnati. Bailey's owner declared to a Jefferson County court that he had "wholly lost sd. Negro" and undertook no steps to even try to recapture him. Instead, he sued the owner and commandant of the steamboat that carried him across the river for financial compensation. In 1845 one William Rew, a resident of Virginia, similarly petitioned the state for a refund after an enslaved man he had purchased at a sheriff's auction for $526 "ran off from your Petitioner and ... gone to the State of New York." Considering it "virtually impossible to retrieve slave property in the North," he demanded his money back. A mulatto slave man from Missouri named Carter, who was valued at $1,000, illegally boarded the steamboat *Timoleon* at St. Louis in 1849 and was transported across the river to "a Town in the State of Illinois." Carter's owner complained to a Missouri court that his slave "hath been wholly lost and [is] of no value to said Plaintiff," and demanded compensation from the owner of the steamboat. For the owners of runaways from further South, recapture was even more expensive, time-consuming, and complicated. If they could somehow recover the costs of northbound runaways by stepping to the courts, then that was preferable to a drawn-out slave hunt. Dunham Spalding, a Louisiana slaveholder and owner of one twenty-three-year-old bondsman named Felix, sued a Missouri steamboat captain after Felix smuggled himself onboard and fled to the North, after which he "has never, since, been in your petitioner's possession." Spalding did not even try to recover Felix, despite the enslaved man being valued at an exorbitant $1,500.[75]

Enslaved people who fled to the northern free states essentially fled to spaces of semi-formal freedom, where slavery was formally abolished but where their protection from reenslavement was highly contested between federal and state authorities' respective interpretations of both fugitive slave laws, which dictated the conditions under which enslaved people could be returned to their masters, and personal liberty laws, which stipulated the circumstances under which African Americans could be legally apprehended and transported out of the state to slavery. Unlike their counterparts who fled to spaces of informal freedom in towns and cities across the South, refugees from slavery in the North were presumed free unless proven otherwise, even by local authorities. They were therefore legally protected from informal recaption (even if this did sometimes occur illegally), and they were afforded certain rights even when they were formally apprehended under fugitive slave laws, such as the right to habeas corpus and the right to counsel. Although southern slaveholders appeared to have the weight of federal law on their side, in practice northern officials and civilians – both black and white, including runaway slaves themselves – went to great lengths to uphold the principle of free soil in their states. Indeed, they often simply obstructed federal fugitive slave laws that they disagreed with and that they felt violated state sovereignty. Their actions helped create and defend sanctuary spaces throughout the free states, and in turn protect the vast majority of refugees from slavery who crossed the Mason–Dixon line and Ohio River to freedom.

Northbound runaways appear to have known very well that their chances of successfully escaping slavery in the free states were especially strong, despite fugitive slave laws, and to have been strongly motivated by a desire to not only extricate themselves from slavery, but indeed flee

---

[75] Petition of M. Banner to the Orphans Court of Anne Arundel County, MD, January 31, 1860, RASP: Series 2: County Court Petitions, Accession #20986032 (quote, italics mine); Petition of Bailey Riley to Jefferson County Court, KY, May 27, 1836, RSPP, Series 2, Accession #20783514 (first quote); Petition of William Rew to the Legislature of Virginia, January 1845, RASP, Series 1: Legislative Petitions, Accession #11684508 (second quote); Petition of Fleming Calvert to Circuit Court of St. Louis County, MO, October 19, 1849, RSPP, Series 2, Accession #21184901 (third quote); Petition of Dunham Spalding to Parish Court of Orleans, LA, July 19, 1843, RSPP, Series 2, Accession #20884301.

slaveholding society altogether. Their active cooperation with vigilance societies and participation in abolitionist movement testifies to their commitment to keeping the free states free, and to striking a blow at the institution that had forced them to leave families and communities behind. Semi-formal freedom in the North did *not* translate into freedom from discrimination or anything approaching citizenship rights and privileges, however. While most refugees from slavery in the northern states found themselves relatively safe from reenslavement, they struggled to settle in their new societies, were usually relegated to the bottom rungs of northern urban economies, sometimes had to depend on alms and charities, and were forced to live in overcrowded and substandard conditions. Even so, not one voluntarily returned to the South. To refugees from slavery, semi-formal freedom in the northern states was infinitely better than no freedom at all.

4

"Departure from the House of Bondage"

Spaces of Formal Freedom in British Canada and Mexico

Townsend Derricks, a twenty-five-year-old runaway slave from Alexandria, Virginia, had few bad words for his former master, a German by the name of Gotlieb Appich, whom he described as a "tolerably fair man." In a statement made before the Vigilance Committee of Philadelphia (VCP), which received Townsend as a refugee in the fall of 1857, he admitted that his master had been abusive toward another slave in their household, an older woman whom he often beat over the head in "the most savage manner." He also conceded that Appich's wife – "a great swabby, fat woman" – was of a particularly "ill disposition" because she drank too much. Townsend himself, however, had "not suffered much" in the way of physical abuse. The reason he had been "induced to peril his own life" and undertake a dangerous "effort to obtain his own freedom" was not because of any ill-treatment but rather because of a looming threat of forced separation from his young wife, Mary.[1]

Upon arrival in Philadelphia Townsend had been a married man for only seven months. Mary had been owned by a Loudoun County slaveholder named Caldwell Carr, who had recently died and whose estate was now in the process of being divided among several heirs. The family member who was to receive Mary lived "some fifty miles distant into the country," where, as Townsend's interviewer noted, "the chances for

---

[1] "Arrived from Alexandria, VA, 1857: Townsend Derrix," in William Still, *The Underground Railroad: A Record of Facts, Authentic Narratives, Letters, etc.* (Philadelphia: Porter & Coates, 1872), 442–443. In the records of the Vigilance Committee of Philadelphia Townsend's surname is erroneously spelled "Derrix" and later "Derrit," and his master is recorded as being called "Gallipappick," providing interesting insight into how Townsend must have pronounced "Gotlieb Appich" during his interview.

intercourse between husband and wife would be no longer favorable."
For the young couple, this news was the tipping point whereby life under
the yoke of slavery had become unbearable. "Rather than submit to such
an outrage," the VCP interviewer recorded, "Townsend and his wife
made the attempt aforementioned."[2]

Both Townsend and Mary were extremely valuable slaves, however,
and their owners did everything in their power to obstruct their flight to
free soil. Right from the start "the pursuers were on their track."[3] On
October 7, 1857 the *Alexandria Gazette* ran a glaring ad that read in full:

$500 REWARD – Ranaway from the subscriber, on Sunday, 27th inst., my negro
man, who calls himself TOWNSEND DERRICKS. He is about 5 feet 10 inches
high, tolerable stout built, of dark or black color, age about 25 years – took with
him a good supply of clothing. Said Townsend took in company with him his wife
MARY, the property of the estate of Caldwell Carr, dec'd, who has been hired for
several years, and was then living, with James H. McVeigh, of this city. Said Mary
is a bright mulatto and good looking, and is about 25 years of age. She also took
with her a good supply of clothing. The above reward of $500 will be paid for the
apprehension and delivery of the said Townsend, or secured in jail so that I get
him; and in addition, a liberal reward will be paid for the arrest and delivery of his
wife Mary, or secured in jail so that she can be recovered by her owner.

Gotlieb Appich [4]

The reward offered for Townsend alone was astronomical for the 1850s,
amounting to approximately half his market value. It must have immediately caught the attention of slave catchers operating in the region,
because Townsend and Mary were hunted down and eventually confronted in an incident whereby "the wife was captured and carried back,
but the husband escaped." Under the circumstances, and with such a high
price on Townsend's head, remaining in Philadelphia was judged to be
too dangerous by the VCP. Plans were made to send him to Canada,
where he would be beyond the reach of slave catchers and US fugitive
slave laws. As chance would have it, Townsend was already well connected with a few runaways who had gone before him and who had
ended up at a US-Canada crossing point at Oswego, New York – including Oscar Ball, a.k.a. John Delaney, mentioned in the previous chapter.
Delaney was a relative of Mary, and in a letter to William Still dated
November 21, 1857 he revealed that he had heard about Townsend's
recent escape and was arranging with Philadelphia agents to get
Townsend and a few other runaways up to Oswego "in the spring,"

[2] Still, *The Underground Railroad*, 442–443.
[3] Still, *The Underground Railroad*, 443 (quote).
[4] *Alexandria Gazette*, October 7, 1857.

when the danger of frostbite was over, from where they could be ferried across to Canada.[5]

With the help of his contacts in Philadelphia and Oswego, Townsend succeeded in removing his valuable body from the grips of southern slaveholders once and for all. He next appears in the historical record in the 1860 marriage records of Toronto, having remarried a woman from Quebec in 1860, and subsequently in the 1861 Canadian census, listed as "Townsend Derrick" (having apparently dropped the -s), born in Alexandria, Virginia, now a resident of Toronto and employed as a tobacco peddler in that city. Townsend eventually relocated to Hamilton, where he continued to work as a "tobacconist," had children, remarried after his second wife died, and lived out the rest of his life in Canada, never returning to the United States. He died in Hamilton in 1910. In a symbolic final act, Townsend had his official birthdate – which was clearly unknown to him and was variously listed as simply "circa" 1830, 1831, and 1833 in the Canadian vital records – registered as July 4, 1830, which is how it is listed in his death record.[6]

The story of Townsend Derricks was repeated tens of thousands of times during the antebellum period, and it reveals both the limits of semi-formal freedom for refugees from slavery and the advantages of seeking out formal freedom beyond the borders of the United States. Even if a vast majority of runaways who fled to free soil in the Northern United States succeeded in permanently escaping slavery, the threat of recapture always loomed large in their minds. Periodic rendition trials, sensational news stories, and tales of illegal recaption by slave catchers and kidnappers reminded them again and again that reenslavement was a very real possibility. Southern slave communities were aware of the national controversies surrounding fugitive slaves and, as argued in the previous chapter, even those who fled to the free states knew that they remained in a precarious and vulnerable position as long as they stayed within the

---

[5] John Delaney to William Still, Esq., November 21, 1857, reprinted in Still, *The Underground Railroad*, 400.

[6] Marriage of Townsend J. Derrick and Sarah Ward, January 2, 1860, Toronto, Ontario, County Marriage Registers, 1859–1869 (familysearch.org); Census of Canada, 1861, Board of Registration and Statistics, Public Archives of Canada (digitized at familysearch.org); Census of Canada, 1871, Board of Registration and Statistics, Public Archives of Canada (digitized at familysearch.org); Marriage of Townsend J. Derrick and Julia Flanigan, November 16, 1880, Hamilton, Wentworth, Ontario, County Marriage Registers, 1869–1927 (familysearch.org); Death of Townsend J. Derrick, November 30, 1910, Hamilton, Wentworth, Ontario, Ontario Deaths, 1869–1937 (familysearch.org). I am grateful to Melani Carty for making some of the records relating to Townsend Derricks available to me.

jurisdiction of federal fugitive slave laws. For many runaways, the most sure-fire way to escape slavery forever was to leave the United States.

Canada was not the only international destination for fugitive slaves from the southern states – although as a space of formal freedom it was numerically the most important and the most well-connected with abolitionist networks in the Northern United States, and has therefore also received the most attention from scholars. Thousands of enslaved people living in the Deep South throughout the antebellum period, especially Louisiana and Texas, however, pointed their compasses south, avoiding the Northern United States altogether and fleeing across the nearby Mexican border to free soil. Other runaways utilized maritime escape routes and successfully smuggled themselves onboard vessels that brought them to post-abolition Haiti, the Bahamas, and even as far away as England. Black refugees from American slavery turned up like castaways all over the Atlantic world, where various foreign governments offered them asylum and protection from extradition and reenslavement, at least on paper. Historians have produced many fine local studies of fugitive slaves beyond the borders of the United States, but few have approached foreign destinations collectively as a distinct category for refugees from slavery – as spaces of *formal* freedom, where asylum for slave refugees was unconditional and legal protections from extradition and reenslavement uncontested – or considered their relation to spaces of informal and semi-formal freedom within the United States.[7]

How and why did runaway slaves from the US South escape to spaces of formal freedom during the antebellum period, and how were their experiences compared to those of their counterparts who fled *within* the United States? This chapter will examine slave flight to British Canada

---

[7] Franklin and Schweninger briefly touch upon Canada and Mexico as destinations for runaways, but do not delve into the legal regimes of freedom in either. See John Hope Franklin and Loren Schweninger, *Runaway Slaves: Rebels on the Plantation* (New York: Oxford University Press, 1999), 116–123. Jeffrey Kerr-Ritchie examined slave flight to various destinations in North America, including Canada and Mexico, in his seminal article "Fugitive Slaves across North America," in Leon Fink, ed., *Workers across the Americas: The Transnational Turn in Labor History* (New York: Oxford University Press, 2011). Kerr-Richie's other work deals more specifically with spaces of freedom in different parts of the (British) Caribbean. See for example: Jeffrey Kerr-Ritchie, "The US Coastal Passage and Caribbean Spaces of Freedom," in Damian Alan Pargas, ed., *Fugitive Slaves and Spaces of Freedom in North America* (Gainesville: University Press of Florida, 2018); Jeffrey Kerr-Ritchie, *Rebellious Passage: The Creole Revolt and America's Coastal Slave Trade* (New York: Cambridge University Press, 2019). Matthew Clavin similarly examines the post-emancipation circum-Caribbean as a broad destination for runaway slaves from the United States. See Matthew J. Clavin, *Aiming for Pensacola: Fugitive Slaves on the Atlantic and Southern Frontiers* (Cambridge, MA: Harvard University Press, 2015).

and Mexico, two popular but also very different North American spaces of formal freedom for freedom seekers from the United States. Its focus lies on the period roughly between the 1830s and 1860, with particular emphasis on the last two decades, during which each of these respective destinations constituted spaces of formal legal sanctuary for runaway slaves from the southern states (and from the Republic of Texas, 1836–1845). For British Canada, the 1830s constituted the decade in which US officials lost hope in securing an extradition treaty for the rendition of runaway slaves (especially after 1829), as well as the decade in which British abolition unequivocally proclaimed its territory free soil (effective 1834). In the case of Mexico, the 1830s constituted the first full decade of federal abolition (proclaimed in 1829), as well as the establishment of the Rio Grande as a borderline that separated Mexican free soil from Texan slavery (in 1836; later US slavery after annexation in 1845). Both of these parts of the continent became increasingly popular destinations for fugitive slaves in the 1840s and especially the 1850s, and both aroused the ire of southern slaveholders, who fumed about the inability to legally retrieve runaways. One Texas slaveholder indeed spoke for his class when he complained in a scathing editorial in 1848: "Slaves escaping to the free states of the Union, are continually recaptured and restored to their masters; but they are never recovered from Mexico or Canada." This chapter will discuss the motivations and networks that facilitated flight beyond the borders of the United States, and it will juxtapose the fates of these international refugees with those of runaways who fled to spaces of informal and semi-formal freedom.[8]

ESCAPING TO BRITISH CANADA AND MEXICO

Refugees from slavery who crossed international land borders and settled in either British Canada or the Republic of Mexico in the late antebellum period can be roughly divided into three categories: first, those who aimed

---

[8] *The Civilian and Galveston Gazette*, April 28, 1848 (quote). Two recent PhD dissertations examine the development of free soil in Canada and Mexico, respectively, and the experiences of runaway slaves there before the US Civil War. See Thomas Mareite, "Conditional Freedom: Free Soil and Fugitive Slaves from the US South to Mexico's Northeast, 1803–1861" (PhD diss., Leiden University, 2020); Oran Patrick Kennedy, "Northward Bound: Slave Refugees and the Pursuit of Freedom in the Northern US and Canada, 1775–1861" (PhD diss., Leiden University, 2021). A note on terminology: The region of present-day Ontario where most refugees from slavery settled was called Upper Canada until 1841, and Canada West after that. Both names were used interchangeably well into the 1850s and 1860s, however.

for these respective destinations in the first place; second, those who aimed for other destinations within the United States but were encouraged – or felt compelled – en route to keep going; and third, those who actually *settled* in other destinations within the United States but lifted stakes and fled again as a result of oppression or heightened fears of recapture.

Many freedom seekers who fled north of the border clearly set out to do so from the start, intentionally traversing the northern free states merely as places of transit to formal freedom on British soil. Representatives of the Freedmen's Inquiry Commission charged with investigating the conditions of slave refugees in Canada in 1864 admitted that as Canada solidified its commitment to free soil in the first decades of the nineteenth century, "the rumor gradually spread among the slaves of the Southern States, that there was, far away under the north star, a land where the flag of the Union did not float; where the law declared all men equal, where the people respected the law, and the government, if need be, enforced it." The prospect of full legal freedom convinced many runaways to bypass the trouble and ambiguity of northern free soil altogether. Indeed, the records of northern vigilance committees refer to innumerable cases of recently arrived refugees who actively sought assistance for onward travel to Canada rather than settlement in northern cities. The black-led Vigilance Committee of Philadelphia provides an interesting case in point, as its records from William Still's directorship in the 1850s – when the Fugitive Slave Law had convinced many freedom seekers that the northern states were no longer safe – are full of cases of "fugitives in transit" who were "making their way from Slavery to Freedom, with the horrors of the Fugitive Slave-law staring them in the face." The interviews conducted with these runaways unveil important information about enslaved people's geopolitical literacy and how they conceived of Canada as a land of freedom, especially in the late antebellum period. Not all of them explained to VCP interviewers how they had heard about Canada or where they got their information from, but they all implicitly or explicitly revealed a strong conviction that *real* freedom from slavery could not be found within the United States (Figure 4.1).[9]

---

[9] G. Howe, *The Refugees from Slavery in Canada West: A Report to the Freedmen's Inquiry Commission* (Boston: Wright & Potter, 1864), 11; Still, *The Underground Railroad*, 5 (second quote). See also Kennedy, "Northward Bound," 116–129, for a brief examination of northbound runaways who fled directly to Canada via the Detroit and Niagara borderlands. For more on "geopolitical literacy," see Philip Troutman, "Grapevine in the Slave Market: African American Geopolitical Literacy and the 1841 *Creole* Revolt," in Walter Johnson, ed., *The Chattel Principle: Internal Slave Trades in the Americas* (New Haven, CT: Yale University Press, 2004), 203–233.

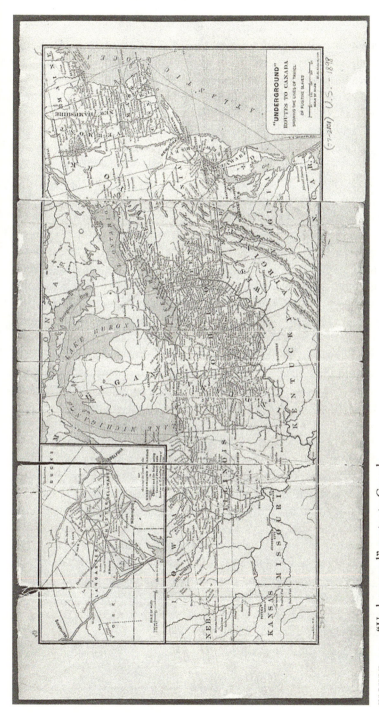

FIGURE 4.1. "Underground" routes to Canada.
Source: New York Public Library Digital Collections.

A few examples are illustrative. One Maryland runaway named
Abram passed through the offices of the VCP in March 1857, claiming
to have followed the north star for nine days, out of which for three days
he had been without food. Having heard of an Underground Railroad to
Canada, he sought to continue north. The VCP "furnished [him] with a
free ticket and other needed assistance," and Abram was "sent on his way
rejoicing," traveling "Canada-ward without delay." Upon arrival in the
British provinces he had a letter sent back to Philadelphia ensuring his
helpers that he was "in good health" and happy to be "in a land of
liberty! I am a man among men!" A few months later, in July 1857, a
Virginia runaway named Charles Thompson arrived in Philadelphia, also
seeking assistance for onward travel to Canada. In an extensive interview
he related to the VCP that he had "made up my mind not to stop short of
the British protection; to shake hands with the *Lion's* paw ... live or die."
In February 1858 the committee received a party of six runaways from
Virginia, who had traveled through Maryland and Delaware partly with
the assistance of UGRR agents. All of them likewise intended to get to
Canada from the start. One man, a forty-four-year-old named Horatio
Wilkinson, admitted to committee agents that his master had recently
warned his slaves that Canada is "the meanest part of the globe" for black
people, and that all black people from the South who moved there were
subsequently shipped off around Cape Horn and sold, but the slaves
believed the story "to be a lie." The others in Horatio's party were less
specific about their knowledge of Canada, but simply claimed that they
wished to live there because it appeared to afford them a life of dignity
and freedom. John Mitchell, for example, stated that he was motivated to
move to Canada because his mistress continually and openly reminded
her enslaved people that they would never be free, and that she did not
believe in black freedom. "I thought if I could make my escape to Canada,
I would do it," he told interviewers, implying that black freedom could
only be found there. A third member of the party named Josiah similarly
sought "refuge in a foreign clime" because he had set his mind on
freedom. Slavery, he claimed, denied him "his manhood." A fourth
named George simply stated that slavery "was nothing more nor less
than downright robbery," and therefore preferred to try and make a
respectable living in Canada.[10]

---

[10] Still, *The Underground Railroad*, 52–54 (first quotes); Ibid., 149 (second quote); Ibid.,
   446–448 (third quotes); Kennedy, "Northward Bound," 91–93; Julie Roy Jeffrey,

All of these freedom seekers stopped in Philadelphia because they were in need of assistance, including information regarding the proper route and money to travel through the northern states, but none of them intended to remain in Pennsylvania or anywhere else in the Northern United States. The initiative to flee the country stemmed from the refugees themselves. Much of the internal correspondence of the VCP and other abolitionist organizations indeed dealt with establishing and maintaining safe routes to the Canadian border for those who sought to emigrate, not just arranging for the settlement and protection of runaways within the northern states. One letter from the tireless UGRR agent Seth Concklin – who was shortly thereafter murdered for his efforts in assisting fugitive slaves – to William Still in 1851 outlined a reconnaissance mission undertaken by the former in order to assist an enslaved family from Alabama that wanted to get to Canada. Writing from Indiana, Concklin specifically stated in his letter that "the plan is to go to Canada, on the Wabash, opposite Detroit. There are four routes to Canada. One through Illinois, commencing above and below Alton; one through to North Indiana, and the Cincinnati route, being the largest route in the US. I intended to have gone through Pennsylvania," the fourth route, Concklin claimed, but the risk of boat crossings of Lake Erie had been too risky of late, as "many get lost." Another letter on file in Still's VCP records came from an abolitionist and UGRR agent named Miss G. A. Lewis, from Kimbleton, Pennsylvania, who in 1855 received a group of eleven runaways from Delaware who wanted to get to Canada. She wrote to Still "to get any advice if you have any to give, as to the best method of forwarding them, and assistance pecuniarily, in getting them to Canada." In the 1850s the VCP was thus particularly active in assisting runaways who wished to leave the country from the outset.[11]

Abolitionists Remember: Antislavery Autobiographies and the Unfinished Work of Emancipation (Chapel Hill: University of North Carolina Press, 2008), 61–96.

[11] Seth Concklin to Wm. Still, February 18, 1851, in Still, *The Underground Railroad*, 28 (first quote); G. A. Lewis to Wm. Still, October 28, 1855, in ibid., 39–40 (second quote). Various northern vigilance committees in New York state, including Rochester, Albany, and Buffalo, coordinated together to help runaways who passed through Pennsylvania reach Canada. Between 1855 and 1856, for example, the Albany Vigilance Committee claimed that "287 fugitive slaves passed through the city of Albany, *en route* to Canada" (*Fremont Journal*, November 7, 1856). See Kennedy, "Northward Bound," 97–99; Dann J. Broyld, "The 'Dark Sheep' of the Atlantic World: Following the Transnational Trail of Blacks to Canada," in Benjamin Talton and Quincy T. Mills, eds., *Black Subjects in Africa and Its Diasporas: Race and Gender in Research and Writing* (New York: Palgrave Macmillan, 2011), 95–108; Dann J. Broyld, "'Over the Way': On the Border of Canada

Boston abolitionist Benjamin Drew's interviews with slave refugees living in various communities scattered along the borderlands of Canada West, published in 1856, also provide an interesting glimpse into the intentions of runaways who ended up north of the border. At the time Canada numbered some 30,000 black residents, of whom "nearly all the adults, and many of the children, have been fugitive slaves from the United States." Many of the recent arrivals whom Drew interviewed saw the Northern United States as little more than a transit region on the way to safer ground in Canada. Indeed, out of 114 black immigrants in Canada whom Drew interviewed, fully 67 (or 59%) claimed to have either fled directly to Canada or made no mention of first trying to settle in the Northern United States. George Johnson, who was interviewed two hours after his arrival in the border town of St. Catherines on April 17, 1855, for example, recounted how he had escaped from Virginia because of his "love of liberty." From the start, his intention was to make for Canada. One of his friends had recently escaped the fate of being sold to the Deep South by fleeing to Toronto; from there he sent a letter "home," so that his friends and family would know where he had ended up. Johnson claimed that when he heard this, he wasted no time in gathering some food and starting off, together with "two comrades." Upon reaching Pittsburgh – already comfortably in free soil territory – Johnson remained only two nights, and then only because he lost track of his two friends while purchasing groceries. By the second night he gave up trying to find them and crossed into Canada by himself, convinced that they had gone before him. Johnson's nervousness about spending even two nights in a city in a free state speaks volumes to his ideas about his own freedom and safety as a fugitive slave in the Northern United States.[12]

Similar examples of runaways who were convinced that legal freedom could only be found under British protection can be found throughout Drew's interviews. Henry Gowens, who had escaped from Alabama

before the Civil War," in Paul Lovejoy and Vanessa S. Oliveira, eds., *Slavery, Memory, Citizenship* (Trenton, NJ: Africa World Press, 2016), 109–128.

[12] Benjamin Drew, *A North-Side View of Slavery: The Refugee, or the Narratives of Fugitive Slaves Living in Canada, Related by Themselves* (Boston: John P. Jewett & Co., 1856). Drew cites an 1852 report of the Canadian Anti-Slavery Society to provide his estimate of the black population of Canada (p. v). A later report submitted to the Freedmen's Inquiry Commission in 1864 admitted that it was difficult to ascertain the precise number of fugitive slaves living in Canada because the census data was inaccurate. The report claims that "intelligent people, acquainted with the matter, estimate the present population at between 20,000 and 30,000. Our own calculation is, that it does not fall short of 15,000, nor exceed 20,000." George Johnson, in Drew, *A North-Side View*, 52–54 (quote).

sixteen years before his interview with Drew, claimed to have gone directly to Canada, choosing not to settle in the Northern United States because "even in free States [black people] are accounted as nothing, or next to nothing. But in Canada, all are really free and equal." John Warren, who fled from Tennessee in 1854, wrote himself a false pass and hired himself aboard a vessel that took him to Cincinnati. Believing that the northern states were not real free soil, however, Warren "stopped for two or three days, and then left for Canada," settling in London. John Little, originally from North Carolina but sold several times throughout the South, effected his escape from Jackson, Mississippi, along with his wife. In an exhausting journey up through Illinois and Michigan, the couple finally crossed over to Windsor from Detroit. Little tellingly remarked that "that was the first time I set my foot on free soil," despite having traversed hundreds of miles through the northern free states. Isaac Williams, another refugee from Virginia who fled in December 1854, recounted traveling through Pennsylvania with a small party of fellow runaways and not stopping along the way, mentioning only that "we reached Canada the morning after Christmas, at three o'clock." Interestingly, his notion of freedom for black people on the Canadian side of the border was clearly influenced by stories of British evacuations of Virginia slaves during the Revolution and the War of 1812, which must have still been talked about in slave quarters throughout the state. Williams remarked that in Virginia, "they [the slaves] think that if Great Britain were to get into a war with America, it would be the means of freeing them. They would slip round and get on the English side."[13]

Mexico also became linked with formal freedom for enslaved people living in the southwestern slave states during this period, and fleeing south of the border from various communities in Texas and Louisiana could be undertaken relatively directly, without having to traverse spaces of semi-formal freedom along the way. Kyle Ainsworth, in his recent quantitative analysis of the Texas Runaway Slave Project database (which documents more than 2,000 individual runaway slaves for the period 1835–1865), found that Mexico was by far the most cited presumed destination (amounting to 54.9 percent). The next most cited destinations were spaces of informal freedom within Texas (22.9 percent). Suspected flight to northern free soil or beyond was cited for only nine individual runaways (less than 1 percent) before the outbreak of the Civil War – indeed, one

---

[13] Henry Gowens, in Drew, *A North-Side View*, 142 (quote); John Warren, in ibid., 185 (quote); John Little, in ibid., 216 (quote); Isaac Williams, in ibid., 54–67, 67 (quote).

runaway slave ad from 1856 was for a freedom seeker who had previously tried to flee to Ohio but been caught, and had now taken off for Mexico. Direct flight to Mexico was clearly the intention of a substantial proportion of runaways in the southwestern borderlands.[14]

Successful escapes were never as easy as making a beeline for the border, however. Traversing the Texan landscape was a dangerous affair – perhaps even more so than northbound flight to Canada, not only because of the risk of recapture but also because of the hostile natural environment, with its exceedingly hot and dry climate, lack of shade for long stretches, sparse water sources, and vast distances between settlements. Disorientation and heat exhaustion in the Texas-Mexican borderlands could prove deadly. Runaways who intended to reach the southern border quickly and directly did well to adequately prepare for the journey – most took with them shotguns for self-defense and to hunt for food – and, if possible, secure a means of transportation that would reduce their travel time. Scholars have recently underscored the importance of horses and mules in aiding slave flight in the Texan borderlands, which according to Ainsworth are mentioned in 18.6 percent of all escape attempts documented in Texan newspapers (far more than in similar studies of runaway slaves in neighboring slave states such as Louisiana, Arkansas, and Mississippi). A smattering of examples are illustrative. On the night of July 20, 1852, four enslaved men from Hodges Bend in Fort Bend County fled their respective masters, riding off on "a Bay, Roan, Dun Pony, and a Dun Mare Mule," and "making their way for Mexico." In 1853 a "fine looking bright mulatto" named Lucy fled Cedar Lake with her "small boy child" on a stolen "American horse," likewise endeavoring "to make her way into Mexico." Charlie, a nineteen-year-old enslaved man from Grayson County, fled in 1858 on "a yellow Spanish horse," also "making his way for Mexico."[15]

---

[14] Mareite, "Conditional Freedom," ch. 1; Kyle Ainsworth, "Advertising Maranda: Runaway Slaves in Texas, 1835–1865," in Damian Alan Pargas, ed., *Fugitive Slaves and Spaces of Freedom in North America* (Gainesville: University Press of Florida, 2018), 208–209; *The True Issue*, December 20, 1856, in the Texas Runaway Slave Project, https://digital.sfasu.edu/digital/collection/RSP (hereafter TRSP), (quote); Alice L. Baumgartner, *South to Freedom: Runaway Slaves to Mexico and the Road to the Civil War* (New York: Basic Books, 2020), 165–184; Mekala Audain, "'Design His Course to Mexico': The Fugitive Slave Experience in the Texas-Mexico Borderlands, 1850–1853," in Pargas, ed., *Fugitive Slaves and Spaces of Freedom*, 232–250.

[15] For more on the deadliness of the Texan landscape, see Mareite, "Conditional Freedom," 77–79; Ainsworth, "Advertising Maranda," 216; James David Nichols, *The Limits of Liberty: Mobility and the Making of the Eastern US-Mexico Border* (Lincoln: University

Even with the aid of horses, direct flight attempts across the Mexican borderlands could turn into prolonged and potentially life-threatening journeys. Frederick Law Olmsted, traveling through the region in 1854, struck up a conversation with a refugee from slavery in Mexico who related that "a good many [runaways] got lost and starved to death, or were killed on the way, between the settlements and the river." Tales of fatal and near-fatal escape attempts can be found in Texas newspapers. One runaway named Gin who tried to flee to Mexico from Fayette County in 1851, riding on a "grey stallion with a rifle gun," somehow got "lost and nearly starved," and succumbed to turning himself in to a white man, but escaped again once he had recovered his strength. A runaway who fled in 1858 with two companions, all "on their way to Mexico," became "so starved as to decline going any further." A San Antonio newspaper reported that he "left the gang, and came into the plantation of one of the settlers ... for something to eat, where he still is." A party of three wandering runaways from Mississippi ended up in such dire straits in the Texan borderlands in 1851 that two of them killed the third in order to eat him. They were captured in a state of "dreadful extremity produced by hunger."[16]

Spaces of informal freedom, especially urban areas within Texas, were scattered along most routes leading south, but the ads and articles in the Texas Runaway Slave database suggest that it was not uncommon for runaway slaves in the region to traverse urban spaces as mere stepping stones to formal freedom in Mexico, rather than as potential destinations in their own right. Just as northbound freedom seekers from Virginia and Maryland often passed through Baltimore and Philadelphia on their way to Canada, so did southbound freedom seekers pass through San Antonio and Houston on their way to Mexico. Considering the risks involved in wandering long distances through the desert landscape, this strategy was undoubtedly safer than avoiding inhabited areas altogether, despite the heightened risk of recapture in more densely populated towns. Passing

of Nebraska Press, 2018), 140; *The Texas Monument*, July 28, 1852, in TRSP (first quote); *Colorado Tribune*, September 10, 1853, in TRSP (second quote); *Dallas Herald*, September 15, 1858, in TRSP (third quote).
[16] Frederick Law Olmsted, *A Journey through Texas: Or a Saddle-Trip on the Southwestern Frontier* (New York: Dix, Edwards & Co., 1857), 323 (first quote); *The Texas Monument*, January 29, 1851, in TRSP (second quote); *The San Antonio Herald*, January 7, 1858, in TRSP (third quote); *The Northern Standard*, April 12, 1851 (fourth quote).

through towns allowed runaways to secure supplies and provisions, get vital information, earn a bit of money through day labor, and even link up with other freedom seekers bound for the border. The roads that connected towns across the borderlands, moreover, greatly simplified navigation. Dan and Eliza, who ran away from their master in 1843, "started on the road to Houston" and were "on their way to Mexico." Frank, who fled from the vicinity of Montgomery with a stolen horse and a considerable amount of stolen cash in December 1848, was presumed to be aiming for Mexico "by [way of] Bastrop or San Antonio." Henry fled his master near Port Lavaca in 1853 and was supposed to be traveling "by the way of San Antonio to Mexico."[17]

Whatever the routes taken, direct flight attempts to the southern border speak volumes to enslaved people's geopolitical literacy and suggest that slaves living in or near the southwestern borderlands conceived of Mexico as a land of freedom from slavery, and as a safe destination for runaways from the United States. This notion is amply confirmed by southern newspapers as well as post-emancipation interviews with former slaves from the region. In print, southern slaveholders decried the proximity of foreign free soil to the slave states because they found it encouraged slave flight. One concerned southerner wrote in an 1855 newspaper editorial that "nearly all the negroes of Texas, have some ideas, more or less extensive, of the general disposition of the Mexican people toward them, and, I believe, it is only a matter of expediency with more than half of the slave population of Texas, that they do not raise in a body and go over to the Mexican side of the Rio Grande." Former slaves from Texas attested to interviewers that they indeed knew about the free status of runaway slaves south of the border. Felix Heywood, who grew up in slavery in Texas and was interviewed by the Federal Writers' Project in the mid-1930s, related that there "wasn't no reason to run up North. All we had to do was walk, but walk South, and we'd be free as soon as we crossed the Rio Grande. In Mexico you could be free." James Boyd likewise claimed that "iffen a nigger want to run away, he'd light out

---

[17] Thomas Mareite has mapped various approximate southern routes to freedom that pass through "transit" towns such as Austin, San Antonio, El Paso, and Galveston. Mareite, "Conditional Freedom," 77–79; Ainsworth, "Advertising Maranda," 209; *Telegraph and Texas Register*, July 5, 1843, in TRSP (first quote); *Democratic Telegraph and Texas Register*, January 3, 1849, in TRSP (second quote); *San Antonio Ledger*, December 8, 1853, in TRSP (third quote).

for ole Mexico. That was nigger heaven them days, they thought." Such notions spurred direct flight across the southern border.[18]

The second category of runaways to formal freedom (both northbound and southbound) consisted of freedom seekers who did not necessarily aim directly for foreign soil initially, but who ended up deciding en route to flee the United States, either because slave catchers were in pursuit or they were encouraged to keep going by sympathetic helpers, or – as in the case of Townsend Derricks – both. These refugees from slavery often initially aimed for places of informal or semi-formal freedom, but felt compelled to make a haphazard bid for formal freedom due to circumstances encountered during their flight attempts. Networks were important for these runaways, as they were often encouraged or assisted by opponents of slavery who believed in their right to live in legal freedom, and who pointed them in the direction of international border crossings.

Canada, for example, clearly developed a reputation as a place of safety and legal freedom among northerners who sympathized with the plight of runaway slaves, and who helped them get there or advised them to go there. The question arises why these runaways did not aim for Canada in the first place. In testimonies many admitted to have been apprehensive about leaving the country, while others simply did not appear to have Canada on their radars – one runaway in Toronto claimed that back in his home community in Maryland "a great many slaves know nothing of Canada." Still others simply hoped to find safety in a northern city that they had heard about or where they had contacts. As argued in the previous chapter, most runaways to the Northern United States succeeded in escaping slavery, after all, despite federal fugitive slave laws. In any case, it is clear that many refugees who ended up in Canada did not initially set out for the British provinces, but were pressured to do so by northerners.[19]

The records of the Vigilance Committee of Philadelphia describe various cases of runaways who arrived in Pennsylvania in grave danger of recapture, and who – like Townsend Derricks – were "forwarded" to Canada for that reason. One party that came before the committee from

---

[18] Mareite, "Conditional Freedom," 38; *The Washington American*, November 22, 1855 (first quote); Felix Heywood, in Federal Writers' Project, *Slave Narratives: A Folk History of the United States of America from Interviews with Former Slaves*, vol. 16/2 (Washington, DC: Works Progress Administration, 1941), 132 (second quote); John Boyd, in Andrew Water, ed., *I Was Born in Slavery: Personal Accounts of Slavery in Texas* (Winston-Salem: John Blair, 2003), 6 (third quote).

[19] John A. Hunter, in Drew, *A North-Side View*, 115 (quote).

Virginia in November 1853, led by one Wesley Harris, had undergone a harrowing flight across the Mason–Dixon line, in which they had been hotly pursued by slave catchers and ultimately forced to engage in a firefight with them. Two of the runaways were "almost fatally wounded," including Harris, whose condition upon arrival in Philadelphia was "most fearful indeed." The VCP provided medical services and allowed the party "time for recuperation," before sending them on to Canada for their own safety. Another group of three runaways from Maryland's Eastern Shore arrived in Philadelphia in 1853, "having been led to believe that they could enjoy the freedom they had in mind in New Jersey." As slave catchers were in "hot pursuit," however, the VCP strongly advised them to make for Canada. The runaways were made to understand that "in view of the imminent dangers existing under the fugitive slave law … that if they were captured they would have themselves the most to blame." The runaways were "very much alarmed" at this advice, but accepted their "folly." The VCP furnished them with disguises, financial means, and instructions, and "admonished them not to stop short of Canada."[20]

Drew's interviews with refugees from slavery living in Canada provide similar examples. James Adams, a runaway from Virginia who fled to St. Catherines as a seventeen-year-old in 1824, for example, admitted in an interview to Benjamin Drew that he "wished to get away" from Virginia, but that he initially aimed for the northern states as a destination. In a gripping escape account, he related that he and his cousin originally aimed for Cleveland, but some of the people who assisted them through Ohio advised them to keep going. One man warned them that five fugitive slaves had recently been captured while making their way through his wheat field. Later they encountered a preacher who told them not to go to Cleveland "as we would be taken up." The preacher passed them on to a friend, who arranged for their passage onboard a schooner to Buffalo, under the close supervision of the captain, who was "an Englishman." When they got to Buffalo the captain first got off to walk through town and check that there were no "problems" – slave catchers or handbills calling for the arrest of the two boys. Finding the coast clear, he then walked with James and his cousin "as far as Black Rock Ferry" – the vessel that plied back and forth across the river to Canada – "giving us

---

[20] Still, *The Underground Railroad*, 48–51 (quote); Ibid., 204–205 (quote); Kennedy, "Northward Bound," 97–99; Broyld, "The 'Dark Sheep' of the Atlantic World," 95–108; Broyld, "'Over the Way,'" 109–128.

good advice all the way, how we should conduct ourselves through life in Canada . . .." For James and his cousin, both the decision and the means to flee to Canada were provided by northern and Canadian opponents of slavery.[21]

Other testimonies of refugees in Canada similarly reveal an initial desire to flee to the Northern United States but a change of plans upon arrival. William Grose, an enslaved man originally from Virginia but sold to New Orleans, ultimately decided that he was willing to risk his life to reach free soil, a place where he could be "perfectly safe." He related to Benjamin Drew: "I said to myself – I recollect it well – I can't die but once; if they catch me, they can but kill me." Armed with a razor to defend himself, he successfully made it upriver to free soil. Grose originally "intended to stay in my native country," but upon arrival in the North he saw too many "mean-looking men," by which he presumably meant slave catchers. As he became increasingly nervous about settling in the United States, he ultimately made a friend who advised him to continue north, and "who helped me on the way to Canada, which I reached in 1851." Joseph Sanford recounted a similar story, having fled Kentucky in a large group that consisted of thirteen runaways, all of whom collectively "resolved to run away, hit or miss, live or die." Originally intending to settle across the river in Cincinnati, the group found itself relentlessly pursued by slave catchers, whom they managed to evade only because abolitionists helped conceal them for two weeks. After that the group was guided by abolitionists to Michigan, but there they were again pursued and even arrested by local authorities as fugitive slaves. Fortunately, recalled one of their free black helpers, "before they got off before a judge, [they] were sent over the line into Canada."[22]

Records of slave flight in the southern borderlands also reveal haphazard escape routes that only indirectly led runaways to the Mexican border. In virtually all of these cases, some form of assistance or advice was provided by networks or contacts forged en route, including other runaway slaves and free blacks, as well as antislavery settlers and Mexican peons. Perhaps most unusual were cases of runaways whose initial destinations were unclear but who eventually joined up with free blacks who were migrating to Mexico. As Mekala Audain has recently argued, free blacks living in the US South – especially the Deep

[21] James Adams, in Drew, *A North-Side View*, 19–28, 27–28 (quotes).
[22] William Grose, in Drew, *A North-Side View*, 85–86 (quotes); John Sanford, in ibid., 362 (quote); John Hatfield, in ibid., 364 (quote).

South – increasingly came to see the neighboring republic to the south as a "Mexican Canaan" in the 1840s and especially the 1850s. Free black migration south of the border indeed increased in the late antebellum period to the point that slaveholders feared a "negro stampede for Mexico." Runaways sometimes attached themselves to migrating groups of free blacks, passing for free as they traversed the southern landscape until they reached free soil. In 1851, for example, some twenty runaways from Arkansas joined a company of free Black Seminoles who were on their way to Coahuila. A few years later, in 1857, more than 100 free blacks from Louisiana emigrated to Veracruz and established the Donato colony at Tlacotalpan – their company included runaway slaves who had joined the migrating settlers.[23]

More common, however, was a course readjustment as a result of contact with antislavery whites or Mexican peons, who often encouraged runaways to pursue southern routes to freedom or even actively served as conductors, although nowhere near to the same extent or with the same ideologically charged organizational efficiency as northern conductors of the Underground Railroad. Nervous slaveholders throughout the region certainly appear to have believed that their counties were crawling with abolitionists dedicated to helping slaves reach Mexican free soil. As one Dallas newspaper put it, "Freesoilers and Runaways" plagued the southern borderlands. Texan newspapers regularly referred to abolitionist "plots" to assist or conduct runaway slaves to Mexican free soil, and both ordinary citizens and Texan courts ruthlessly punished individuals deemed to be even tangentially connected to slave escapes. In 1848, for example, a settler captured and confined a white man and a runaway slave who had trespassed on his land – the white man was held on suspicion of conducting the slave toward Mexico. In 1858, a white man was labeled an "abolitionist" and charged with "negro stealing" for leading a group of runaway slaves whom he had encountered toward Mexico with the "promise of freeing them."[24]

---

[23] Mekala Shadd-Sartor Audain, "Mexican Canaan: Fugitive Slaves and Free Blacks on the American Frontier, 1804–1867" (PhD diss., Rutgers University, 2014), 127–161; Mareite, "Conditional Freedom," 86; Kenneth Porter, *The Black Seminoles: History of a Freedom-Seeking People* (Gainesville: University Press of Florida, 1996), 133; Sidney L. Jemelle, "The 'Circum-Caribbean' and the Continuity of Cultures: The Donato Colony in Mexico, 1830–1860," *Journal of Pan African Studies* 6, no. 1 (2013): 65.

[24] *Dallas Herald*, November 9, 1859, in TRSP (first quote); *The Northern Standard*, March 11, 1848, in TRSP (second quote); *Dallas Herald*, July 31, 1858, in TRSP (third quote); Mareite, "Conditional Freedom," 88–89; Ainsworth, "Advertising Maranda," 211–212.

In runaway slave ads and capture notices throughout the region slave-holders often implicated the assistance of abolitionist guides. In 1845, an advertisement for three runaways from Brazos who had made off with four valuable horses stated that "it is supposed that there is some white man or Mexican at their head." In 1851, an entire party of runaway slaves was captured near the Mexican border, having been led there by "a white man, whom they called Gee," and who had made his escape across the river during the arrest. During the Christmas holidays of 1852 an announcement was placed in the *San Antonio Ledger* warning that "twenty-three slaves" had recently been spotted passing through "the neighborhood of Austin, accompanied by one white man. They were on their way to Mexico, and refugees from bondage." In 1857, an exorbitant $500 reward was offered "for the apprehension of any white man, provided evidence is furnished sufficient to convict him of having stolen or seduced away" a certain runaway slave from DeWitt County named Abraham.[25]

Certain groups of settlers, in particular Germans, were placed under considerable scrutiny by other white Texans for their presumed antislav-ery sentiments and assistance to runaway slaves. As historians such as Kyle Ainsworth, Thomas Mareite, and others have argued, proslavery Texans widely feared "meddlesome intruders" – white settlers who did not wholeheartedly support the dominant proslavery ideology and who at times even appeared to actively oppose it by providing information and material assistance to runaway slaves in the borderlands. German new-comers, most of whom were small non-slaveholding farmers with critical views on slavery, were particularly suspect in the eyes of local slave-holders. Evidence indeed suggests that some German farmers did help direct runaway slaves to the southern border. Frederick Law Olmsted recounted one such case during his travels through Texas, whereby a German man encountered a half-starved runaway, bound up his wounds and gave him food, and sent him "on his way" to Mexico. A writer for the *New-York Daily Tribune* who visited the region in 1855 similarly claimed that "no German will deliver a fugitive slave to his owner" and that the German population often helped runaways reach free soil.[26]

[25] *Texas National Register*, January 11, 1845, in TRSP (first quote); *The Civilian and Galveston Gazette*, January 24, 1851, in TRSP (second quote); *The San Antonio Ledger*, December 30, 1852, in TRSP (third quote); *The Galveston News*, February 21, 1857, in TRSP (fourth quote); Mareite, "Conditional Freedom," 88–89.

[26] Mareite, "Conditional Freedom," 94–95; Ainsworth, "Advertising Maranda," 210–211; Baumgartner, *South to Freedom*, 263; Olmsted, *A Journey through Texas*, 327–328 (first quote); *New York Daily Tribune*, January 20, 1855 (second quote).

Yet little evidence suggests the existence of even a semi-organized southern version of the Underground Railroad. As several historians have noted, the proslavery culture and ideology in Texas was so hegemonic, antislavery sentiments (and actions) were so harshly punished by legal and extra-legal means, and the free black population was numerically so inconsequential, that formalized support networks for runaways in the southern borderlands never fully developed. Even most German settlers in the southern borderlands feared openly expressing their antislavery views or helping runaway slaves, in contrast to their Quaker counterparts in Pennsylvania and other northern states, as Sean Kelley has pointed out. Furthermore, no abolitionist organizations existed on the Mexican side of the border to coordinate escapes, as they did in Canada and the Northern United States. The networks that facilitated haphazard escapes across the Mexican border tended to be just that: haphazard. They were indeed not even limited to groups and individuals who sympathized with the plight of runaway slaves for ideological reasons, but also included ad hoc helpers who saw some kind of financial stake in assisting runaways across the border.[27]

Low-skilled Mexican laborers constituted the most "dangerous classes" – from the perspective of slaveholders – that assisted or encouraged runaways to cross the border, in particular because they not only often held ideological objections to slavery and closely identified with bondspeople, but also had material incentives to help fugitive slaves reach Mexico, as they often charged runaways a fee for their services or participated in the theft of horses and other valuable goods along the way. In the sources that link slave escapes across the southern border with Mexican assistance – including travel narratives and Texan newspapers – the term "Mexican" does not necessarily refer to legal nationality but rather a perceived ethnicity, with no distinction between Mexican Texans and Mexican migrants from the republic to the south. Although legally free, indebted Mexican peons and other low-skilled Mexican workers were poor and mobile, crisscrossing the borderlands in search of work and escaping debtors, and they tended to sympathize with African-American

---

[27] Mareite, "Conditional Freedom," 88–89; Sean M. Kelley, *Los Brazos de Dios: A Plantation Society in the Texas Borderlands, 1821–1865* (Baton Rouge: Louisiana State University Press, 2010), 174–177; Audain, "Mexican Canaan," 2; Ainsworth, "Advertising Maranda," 211. Alice Baumgartner has recently similarly argued that "there was no official Underground Railroad to Mexico, only the occasional ally; no network, only a set of discreet, unconnected nodes." See Baumgartner, *South to Freedom*, 2.

slaves based on their shared conditions as marginalized manual laborers. They indeed often worked side by side with slaves, and socialized with them to a great extent. In so doing, Mexican laborers became essential sources of information and inspiration for the slave population throughout the region – they transmitted geographic information about routes to Mexico and their own tales of escape from various employers and debtors inspired would-be runaways. Among white settlers, itinerant Mexican laborers developed a stubborn reputation for spreading the notion of freedom among the slave population and were ruthlessly attacked in the Texan press for encouraging slave flight to Mexico. Covering a debate on the issue at the state convention in 1854, the *Texas State Times* complained that "by placing themselves on an equality with the slave, they stir up among our servants a spirit of subordination." Another newspaper proclaimed that same month that the "inducements for a negro to run off to Mexico" were fueled by the idea that "he will there be on a footing with the peon Mexican whom he sees here, and with whom he associates on a perfect equality."[28]

Even more infuriating for Texan slaveholders, Mexican laborers actively served as guides and intermediaries for runaway slaves whom they encountered throughout the borderlands. Slaveholders publicly denounced Mexican accomplices to slave flight as "highway robbers, horses and cattle thieves, and idle vagabonds" who would "scruple at nothing, and a few dollars from a negro, is sufficient to secure their services." One newspaper editorial decried that Mexican peons were "at the command of the slave for a small bribe, and the latter relies upon a peon as capable of running him successfully into Mexico." Runaway slave ads frequently reported bands of runaway slaves being "piloted to Mexico by Mexican peons," and even visitors to the region such as George Featherstonhaugh commented that smuggling slaves was one of many "modes of getting a livelihood" for peons. Slaveholders' frustration and often outright paranoia about Mexican "conductors" of runaway slaves to Mexico often erupted in violence or threats of violence. In 1853,

---

[28] Nichols, *The Limits of Liberty*, 166; James D. Nichols, "The Line of Liberty: Runaway Slaves and Fugitive Peons in the Texas-Mexico Borderlands," *Western Historical Quarterly* 44, no. 4 (2013): 413–433; Mareite, "Conditional Freedom," 89–91; Jeffrey Kerr-Ritchie, *Freedom's Seekers: Essays on Comparative Emancipation* (Baton Rouge: Louisiana State University Press, 2014), 25; Baumgartner, *South to Freedom*, 165–184; *Texas State Times*, October 14, 1854, in TRSP (first quote); *The Standard*, October 21, 1854, in TRSP (second quote).

white residents of Matagorda ordered "every Mexican to leave the county." Accusing peons and other itinerant workers of helping runaway slaves to get to Mexico, local whites threatened "an appeal to Lynch law" if the order was not respected. In the 1850s, Mexican *carreteros*, cartmen who traded across the borderlands, were accused of smuggling runaway slaves "out of the State in the oxteams." In the so-called Cart War of 1857, some seventy-five suspected *carreteros* conductors were murdered near San Antonio.[29]

The third category of runaways to sites of formal freedom consisted of refugees who had already settled in places of semi-formal freedom in the northern states, but who felt compelled to flee again because of ill-treatment or for fear of recapture and rendition, revealing and illustrating the vulnerability and insecurity of semi-formal freedom in the northern states. Some received word that their masters were in pursuit; others were actually arrested and managed to make their escape; and still others became exceedingly nervous after the passage of the controversial 1850 Fugitive Slave Law, which – even though it largely failed, as discussed in the previous chapter – scared many refugees (and even free blacks) living in the northern states. All of these runaways were already one step removed from slavery and living in semi-formal freedom, and most had initially not exhibited any particularly strong desire to live outside of the United States *per se*, but uncertainty, prejudice, and the threat of reenslavement in the Northern United States made them change their minds and make for formal freedom. Most runaways who fall into this category removed to neighboring Canada.

A few examples from St. Catherines – a village in the Niagara region that Drew described as a place of "refuge for the oppressed" for its 800 black residents – are illustrative. Alexander Hemsley, for example, fled slavery in Maryland at the age of twenty-three, "not owing to any

[29] "Seguin, Texas Citizens circular regarding proceedings of a meeting to discuss the end of slave trafficking," 1854, University of Houston, Digital Library (first quote); *The Standard*, October 21, 1851, in TRSP (second quote); *Indianola Bulletin*, May 31, 1855, in TRSP (third quote); George W. Featherstonhaugh, *Excursion through the Slave States, from Washington on the Potomac to the Frontier of Mexico* (New York: Harper & Brothers, 1844), 64 (fourth quote); *Indianola Bulletin*, September 6, 1853, in TRSP (fifth quote); *The Washington American*, November 22, 1856, in TRSP (sixth quote); Elisha M. Pease, *Informe del gobernador del estado de Tejas: y documentos relativos a los asaltos contra los carreteros mejicanos* (Austin, TX: John Marshall & Co., 1857); Mareite, "Conditional Freedom," 93.

sudden impulse or fear of present punishment," as he recounted to Benjamin Drew years later, "but from a natural wish to be free," which he eloquently defined as "liberty for the mind ... that, if I thought of anything beneficial for me, I should have liberty to execute it." Like many of his counterparts, he made for free soil in the nearby northern states, specifically in New Jersey, where he "had been told people were free, and nobody would disturb me." His flight across the borderlands was a relatively quick affair – he lived only 33 miles from Pennsylvania, and after a brief stay in hiding with a Quaker family continued on to New Jersey. Upon arrival he successfully settled into his new community, married a local woman in Evesham, had three children, and "spent eight or nine years" there, "being hired and getting my money." After receiving a favorable job offer in Northampton, Hemsley removed there, where he also lived unmolested and carried on building his life in freedom. This peaceful state of affairs changed in October 1836, however, when a group of five southern men visiting the region found out that he was a runaway, contacted his master's family in Maryland (his master had been dead some six or seven years by then) and arranged for a warrant at the Court of Common Pleas to arrest him. He was taken into custody one morning while leaving his house to go to work, marking the beginning of a long and excruciating ordeal. His friends in Northampton mobilized and secured legal counsel for him, so at least Hemsley was not without assistance, but initially his case did not look favorable. The hearing took place three weeks after his arrest, and on the basis of testimony from a Maryland man who swore to the runaway's true identity, a local judge declared Hemsley a fugitive slave and ordered him sent back to the rightful heirs of his master in Maryland. Luckily for Hemsley, however, his lawyers had secured a trump card just in case, and immediately upon announcement of the verdict they handed the judge a writ of habeas corpus – doubtless inspired by the Matilda Lawrence case in Ohio just months earlier – sending the case into the appeals process. Three months later, in February 1837, the Supreme Court of New Jersey at Trenton declared the evidence against Hemsley insufficient and ordered him released from custody. Even then, his lawyers and friends "were afraid that my claimants would waylay and smuggle me, and thought I had better leave for the North, which I did." Passing through Oswego and then Rochester, New York, Hemsley and his family eventually crossed over to Canada "on board a British boat, *The Traveller*, for Toronto." From there he went to St. Catherines and settled permanently. Upon reaching "English territory," he later recalled, "I had a comfort in the law – that my shackles were struck off, and that a man was a man by law."[30]

Dan Josiah Lockhart, another St. Catherines resident who had originally been enslaved in Frederick County, in northern Virginia, recounted a similar story. Lockhart was already married and had children by the time he made his escape in 1847, and it was with a mind of "rescuing" his family from slavery that he fled the South in the first place. He had witnessed his loved ones being whipped, and he claimed to Drew that he "could not stand this abuse of them, and so I made up my mind to leave." Like so many northbound runaways, Lockhart aimed to go first, settle in the northern states, and then send for his wife and children. It was not that he had never heard of Canada – he told Drew that in Virginia he had often heard the white people warn their slaves that Canada was a terrible place, that the wild geese were so numerous and so bad "that they would scratch a man's eye out; that corn wouldn't grow there, nor anything else ..." Whether he believed these stories or not, he did not say, but he clearly did not intend to go all the way to Canada. Disguised as a free black, Lockhart slipped away one day while his master was away on business, and made it to Pennsylvania by the following day. He "got employment in Pittsburgh," and subsequently "wrote to a friend to tell my wife that I was there," setting the wheels in motion to have her and the children join him on free soil. Lockhart's master got ahold of the letter, however, and immediately dispatched two agents to Pittsburgh, where they found and tried to quietly apprehend the runaway at the Crawford Hotel. Lockhart was able to get away only because he made a ruckus – screaming "murder!" and "fire!," he created quite a scene. The owner of the hotel threatened the agents to let him go "or there'll be bloodshed here," adding that it would "ruin" his establishment if word got out "that there are kidnappers here." Meanwhile, Lockhart's friends had mobilized and surrounded the hotel; they seized him and secreted him away to a nearby house. Shaken and "fatigued," he was cautioned by sympathetic members of the community that he "could be carried back if I remained in the United States," so he "started off to Canada by the underground railroad" and settled in St. Catherines.[31]

---

[30] Drew, *A North-Side View*, 17 (first quote); Rev. Alexander Hemsley, in ibid., 33–38 (quotes). See also Kennedy, "Northward Bound," 178.

[31] Dan Josiah Lockhart, in Drew, *A North-Side View*, 45–50 (quotes). Lockhart claimed that he had learned to read and write in Virginia because the "children showed me." See p. 50.

Many of the fugitive slave rescues that commanded such national attention in the 1840s and especially the 1850s indeed concerned apprehended runaways who were already living in the northern states, and who were "liberated" from arresting officers, jails, and courtrooms across the northern states and smuggled to Canada for their own safety. The Christiana Rescue in Pennsylvania 1851 (during which southern claimants were killed by a mob that defended four runaways from Maryland); the Shadrach Minkins rescue in Boston in 1851; the infamous "Jerry Rescue" in Syracuse in 1851; the Joshua Glover rescue in Milwaukee in 1854 – these and countless other daring acts entailed smuggling runaways who were already living in the Northern United States and who found themselves threatened with recapture to safer ground in British Canada.[32]

The mere passage of the 1850 Fugitive Slave Law and subsequent accounts of sensational arrests, trials, riots, and rescues compelled many runaway slaves living in the northern states to flee again, this time beyond the borders of the United States. Indeed, the Fugitive Slave Law spawned the settlement of entire black communities north of the border. The "Elgin Settlement," a prosperous farming community of black residents in Buxton – most of them former slaves from the United States – was settled mainly by people who had "resided in the free States before entering Canada" in the early 1850s, according to Drew. The Refugees' Home, a tract of land near Windsor that accommodated twenty black families on small 25-acre plots each, was purchased and set up (by an association set up by the tireless Henry Bibb) soon after the passage of the Fugitive Slave Bill with an aim to help "refugees from American slavery" who could now no longer count on safety in the Northern United States. William Jackson, one of the original settlers of Queen's Bush – a tract of wilderness in Canada West settled mainly by black people, especially

[32] Gordon Barker, *Fugitive Slaves and the Unfinished American Revolution: Eight Cases, 1848–1856* (Jefferson, NC: McFarland, 2013); Thomas P. Slaughter, *Bloody Dawn: The Christiana Riot and Racial Violence in the Antebellum North* (New York: Oxford University Press, 1991); "New Man-Hunting Atrocities at Harrisburg," *Pennsylvania Freeman*, October 2, 1851; "GREAT RIOT: Awful Loss of Life in an Attempt to Capture Fugitive Slaves," *The Sun*, September 13, 1851; Gary Collison, *Shadrach Minkins: From Fugitive Slave to Citizen* (Cambridge, MA: Harvard University Press, 1997); Angela F. Murphy, *The Jerry Rescue: The Fugitive Slave Law, Northern Rights, and the American Sectional Crisis* (New York: Oxford University Press, 2015); H. Robert Baker, *The Rescue of Joshua Glover: A Fugitive Slave, the Constitution, and the Coming of the Civil War* (Athens: Ohio University Press, 2006), 1–26; Robert Churchill, "Fugitive Slave Rescues in the North: Toward a Geography of Antislavery Violence," *Ohio Valley History* 14, no. 2 (2014): 51–75.

fugitive slaves from the United States – claimed to Benjamin Drew in
1855 that "some colored people have come in from the free States, on
account of the fugitive slave bill, and bought land."[33]

Of the black immigrants in Canada who claimed to Drew in 1855 that
they had first lived in the Northern United States, over one-quarter (11
out of 41) specifically cited the Fugitive Slave Law as their prime motivation for leaving the country altogether. One woman who wished to
remain anonymous told Benjamin Drew in 1855 that she had escaped
slavery years before and had been living in the Northern United States.
(She would not say which city or state, for fear of endangering loved ones
who were still there.) She related that she had "married a free colored
man" and that she and her husband had been "comfortably settled in the
States, [but] were broken up by the fugitive slave law, – compelled to leave
our home and friends, and to go at later than middle life into a foreign
country among strangers." Another woman living in St. Catherines
named Nancy Howard recounted a similar story. After fleeing her master
in Maryland she settled into a quiet life in Lynn, Massachussetts, where
she lived for seven years, "but I left there through fear of being carried
back, owing to the fugitive slave law." Charles Peyton Lucas, a blacksmith from Virginia, likewise originally fled to the Northern United States
in 1841 after finding out that he was to be sold. He settled in Geneva,
New York, "until the passage of the fugitive slave law, when my friends
advised me to go to Canada, and which advice I complied, at a great
sacrifice." He ended up in Toronto. Nelson Moss, also from Virginia, had
fled to Pennsylvania and had been living there for three years when he felt
compelled to lift stakes and move on to London, Canada. "I did not leave
Pennsylvania so much on account of the prejudice," he told Drew in
1855, "as on that of the fugitive slave bill. I did not like to live in a
country which was governed by a partial law." The move had cost him
"considerable sacrifice," but at least in Canada he felt safe. William
Humbert, who fled from Charleston in 1853, "lived in the free States
some months, but finally left on account of the Fugitive Slave Bill,"
claiming that he "had to come to Canada to avoid the ten dollar commis-

---

[33] Drew, *A North-Side View*, 291 (first quote); Ibid., 323–324 (second quote); William
Jackson, in ibid., 190 (quote). One resident of the small community of Queen's Bush said
that he knew of only one free-born black living in the area, a man "from Pennsylvania,
and that is myself." The rest were fugitive slaves.

sioner" (a reference to the fee that federal commissioners were paid for every fugitive slave they sent back to the South).[34]

Slave refugees living in the North also left for Canada because of discriminatory and oppressive state laws, as well as the everyday prejudice they experienced living in northern communities. George Williams, who fled from Kentucky as a young man, told Benjamin Drew that he lived in Ohio for six years and, despite suffering "on account of my color," was doing well there. He even had a farm. But when a state law was passed requiring black residents to produce a certificate of good behavior, Williams, being a fugitive slave, was frightened into leaving for Canada. He claimed to have been partly duped: "A white man represented it worse than it was, so as to take advantage, as myself and two others had a heavy crop standing." He left a valuable harvest behind and resettled in the town of Sandwich. David Grier, who also fled from Kentucky to Ohio, similarly claimed to have emigrated to Canada in 1831 "on account of the oppressive laws demanding security for good behavior" in Ohio. Ephraim Waterford, born a term-slave in Virginia and promised freedom at age twenty-one, left his native state and settled in Indiana at first, but decided to move again to Canada "on account of oppression in Indiana ... A law was passed that a colored man could not devise real estate to his wife and children, and there were other equally unjust laws passed."[35]

Mexico similarly commanded the attention of free black emigrants from the northern states who wished to escape excessive discrimination and the constant threat of fugitive slave laws, especially after the passage of the 1850 Fugitive Slave Law. It is unclear how many ultimately removed to Mexico, nor how many of these were in fact slave refugees from the southern states, however, as no slave testimonies of runaways in Mexico survive and free black emigrants are indistinguishable from runaways who had been living in semi-formal freedom. Yet it is illustrative to consider how free black communities in the Northern United States – virtually all of which included at least some fugitive slaves – thought about Mexico as a potential destination for resettlement. Abolitionists in the Northern United States – both black and white – pushed the idea of

---

[34] Thomas L. Wood Knox, in Drew, *A North-Side View*, 191; Mrs.—, in ibid., 31 (quote); Nancy Howard, in ibid., 50 (second quote); Charles Peyton Lucas, in ibid., 109 (quote); Nelson Moss, in ibid., 153 (quote); William L. Humbert, in ibid., 333 (quote).
[35] George Williams, in Drew, *A North-Side View*, 343–344 (quote); David Grier, in ibid., 372 (quote); Ephraim Waterford, in ibid., 373 (quote).

black emigration to Mexico as early as the 1830s. In a series of articles on emigration possibilities published in the *Liberator* in 1832, for example, free blacks living in Cincinnati were cited who stated that they would "never remove to Africa" but contemplated moving to either "Canada or Mexico, as countries far more congenial to our constitutions, and where our rights as freemen are secured." At the 1833 Convention for the Improvement of the Free People of Color, held in Philadelphia, emigration possibilities to Mexico were also openly discussed. Throughout the late antebellum period, romanticized depictions of Mexico as a land of freedom indeed continued to appear in the black abolitionist press and at conventions aimed at exploring possibilities of emigration. After the passage of the 1850 Fugitive Slave Law, interest in Mexico as a destination for resettlement spiked. At the 1854 National Emigration Convention of Colored People, held at Cleveland, fugitive slaves were explicitly advised to consider moving to Mexico, where they would be safe from the clutches of "miserable, half-starved, service Northern slave catchers by the way, waiting cap in hand, ready and willing to do the bidding of their contemptible southern masters."[36]

Whether they fled directly or indirectly to spaces of formal freedom in Canada and Mexico, all three categories of runaways shared important motivations to flee slavery and seek refuge outside of the United States. Northbound runaways who ended up in Canada, in particular, shared many of the same motivations to flee the South as their counterparts who remained in the northern states. Indeed, as stated above, there was some overlap between these two groups, as some fugitive slaves in Canada had already been refugees in the northern states. The prospect of sale, forced migration, and excessive abuse spurred thousands to undertake a flight to freedom. Like other northbound runaways, however, runaways in Canada also often expressed a *positive desire to live in a land of freedom*, including many who claimed to have had decent masters or never suffered severe abuse. Virtually all of the runaways interviewed by northern vigilance committees or in Canada expressed an ideological revulsion of slavery and a commitment to revolutionary principles of freedom and equality – as well as a willingness to risk death to achieve it. They simply

---

[36] *The Liberator*, February 4, 1832 (first quote); Mareite, "Conditional Freedom," 32–35; National Emigration Convention of Colored People, *Proceedings of the National Convention of Colored People: Held at Cleveland, Ohio, Thursday, Friday and Saturday, the 24th, 25th and 26th of August 1854* (Pittsburgh, PA: A. A. Anderson, 1854), 69 (second quote).

found the reward of freedom worth whatever physical risks were involved. Henry Banks, who ran from Virginia directly to Canada and was shot during a pursuit, related to Benjamin Drew that he "caught the shot from my legs to my shoulders – all over my back. About a hundred shot holes were counted in my back." He thought it was worth it to live in freedom, however, as he did "not think it was intended for any man to be a slave. I never thought so, from a little boy. The slaves are not contented. They can't be: I never knew one to be so where I was."[37]

Like their counterparts in the Northern United States, moreover, many runaway slaves in Canada were "unusual" in ways that may have influenced their opinion that they were especially deserving of, and suited for, freedom. Indeed, they even had a reputation for being unusual among the slave population. Samuel Howe's report on the condition of slave refugees in Canada West in 1864 admitted that "it is commonly said that the Canadian refugees are 'picked men'; that the very fact of their escape from slavery, is proof of their superiority." He found such claims exaggerated, adding that the refugees constituted a fairly accurate representation of the American slave population, but individual portraits of many runaways suggest that their reputation for being unusual may not have been completely invented. Some refugees were described in interviews and other records as particularly light-skinned, for example. Others could read and write; still others were skilled or experienced in hiring their own time; and several had been promised freedom by their masters or had some other legal claim to freedom. Many runaways indeed embodied a combination of several of these characteristics. John Lindsay, who ultimately fled to Canada and settled in St. Catherines, told Benjamin Drew that he had been born free but was illegally sold and carried to Tennessee, where he lived enslaved until he was twenty-five years old. Tellingly underscoring the fact that he "was whiter then than I am now," and that "a person across the street could not tell whether I were a white or colored man," he related that in the South "justice was refused me, [so] I resolved to free myself." Williamson Pease, a mulatto man with blue eyes who escaped Tennessee in 1854, similarly made a point of emphasizing to his

---

[37] Christopher Nichols, in Drew, *A North-Side View*, 70–71 (first quote); Henry Banks, in ibid., 76 (second quote). See also Still, *The Underground Railroad*, 2; Kennedy, "Northward Bound," 57–64; S. Charles Bolton, *Fugitivism: Escaping Slavery in the Lower Mississippi Valley, 1820–1860* (Fayetteville: University of Arkansas Press, 2019), 8 (second quote); Eric Foner, *Gateway to Freedom: The History of the Underground Railroad* (New York: W. W. Norton, 2016), 12; Franklin and Schweninger, *Runaway Slaves*, 37–42, 116.

interviewer how light-skinned he was; he added that he had a bit of education, and was supposed to have been manumitted but never was. Back in the South, Pease claimed, he had "passed for a white man when among strangers," and his owners "tried to teach me at home, but never sent me to school." He was promised his freedom someday but his master never delivered on that promise, and he eventually walked away to freedom – he was so light-skinned that nobody questioned him. William Howard, a runaway from Baltimore County, Maryland, claimed to have lived more or less like a free man during slavery. He had had a kind mistress who allowed him to "hire my time, giving her seven dollars a month, although I could earn a great deal more." He even married a free woman and had two children. Howard only decided to escape when his mistress died and the estate was to be sold. Knowing that he risked a forced separation from his family and a new owner who would probably not allow him to live as freely as he was accustomed to, he arranged to take his family to Canada. John Pettifoot, a runaway from Richmond, Virginia, who passed through the care of the VCP seeking assistance to get to Canada, was described as "Anglo-African and Anglo-Saxon ... about equally mixed," and quite "bright in color and intellect," having "managed to steal the art of reading and writing, to a certain extent." The runaway told his interviewer that he had been hired out for years at a tobacco factory, but believed "'no right' to work for anybody for nothing." And although his mistress had supposedly "willed" him free, he was not willing to wait for her "motions to die." He was convinced "that if Providence would aid him, and he could get a conductor to put him on the right road to Canada, he would be alright."[38]

Similar characteristics can be found among runaways who headed across the southern borderlands for Mexico. Short-term triggers such as physical abuse, overwork, or the threat of sale undoubtedly prompted many to flee their masters – runaway slave ads from the region are full of references to scars and mutilations, and the number of runaways structurally peaked during the cotton harvest – but an underlying desire to live in free territory motivated their decisions to ultimately cross the Rio Grande. Even without any surviving interviews or oral testimonies, the unshakable determination of southbound refugees to risk death in order

---

[38] Howe, *Refugees from Slavery in Canada West*, iii (first quote); John Lindsay, in Drew, *A North-Side View*, 77 (second quote); William Howard, in ibid., 111 (third quote); Williamson Pease, in ibid., 123–130 (fourth quotes); Still, *The Underground Railroad*, 153–154 (fifth quotes).

to live in freedom can be gleaned from the very nature of their escape attempts, considering how treacherous and deadly the landscape in the border regions was. Indeed, not only did runaways risk disorientation and starvation in the desert, as discussed above, but many also fled under the most desperate circumstances in order to reach free soil at all costs. Reports of runaways attempting to flee to Mexico while wounded or chained, or committing desperate acts of violence along the way to avoid recapture, were not uncommon. One freedom seeker from a plantation north of Houston, for example, who was described as unusually "determined to make his way to Mexico," had already made a previous escape attempt but had been caught near Columbus, and had now run off again with an "Iron collar around his neck and shackles on his feet." Two runaways who were eventually caught and jailed near Brenham, in Washington County, in 1860, committed the capital crime of murdering their master before slipping away, apparently in an effort to win time before their absence was detected, knowing full well that they would be executed if caught. Both admitted to their captors that their owner, one Thomas Erwin, was "a very kind master," but that "they had some two years since resolved to go to Mexico, and they believed if Erwin was out of the way, they would have no difficulty in getting away." They shot him with a double-barrelled shotgun late one night and disappeared into the darkness. Another "desperate encounter" took place near Goliad that same year, whereby a party of runaways stopped a white man and unabashedly asked him "how far it was to the Rio Grande, and how to ask for water, bread, &c. in Spanish," then shot both him and his horse, though not mortally, resulting in a chaotic firefight. Such cases reveal a "liberty or death" mentality among runaways across the southern borderlands.[39]

The profiles of some runaways who attempted to reach Mexico were also "unusual" in the same ways as their northbound counterparts – ways that doubtless made them more confident of their ability (and right) to live in freedom. Some were light-skinned, for example, while others were highly skilled or could read and write. Frank, a twenty-year-old runaway from a plantation on the Guadalupe River who was described as "a very

---

[39] Mareite, "Conditional Freedom," 40–52; Kelley, *Los Brazos de Dios*, 106–120; Andrew J. Torget, *Seeds of Empire: Cotton, Slavery and the Transformation of the Texas Borderlands, 1800–1850* (Chapel Hill: University of North Carolina Press, 2015), 83–84; *Galveston Weekly News*, September 28, 1858, in TRSP (first quote); *The Weekly Telegraph*, July 8, 1860, in TRSP (second quote); *Texas Republican*, June 16, 1860, in TRSP (third quote).

bright Mulatto," rode off one night on his master's horse, his intention to "aim for Mexico, and try to pass for a white man." The runaway slave ad for another freedom seeker named Frank, who fled his master's plantation in Montgomery County in 1849 on "a stolen horse" with "considerable cash, likewise stolen," mentioned that he "can read tolerably well and writes legibly." Frank had indeed fled with "a pass of his own writing," and took with him "ink and paper, and some books." His intention was to "try to pass as free." Elleck, who ran away with his brother from Harrison County during the Christmas holidays of 1854, was similarly described as "bright complexioned [and] very intelligent for a negro, can read and make figures." John, a runaway of a "mulatto color" who escaped his master in Bell County in 1858, was described as a "sensible negro and reads a little." Such references are relatively rare compared to sources for northbound runaways, however.[40]

Where southbound freedom seekers differed from their northbound counterparts was in their apparent lack of family ties and in family considerations as a factor in their decision to flee to free soil. There are of course exceptions – cases of entire families fleeing together, siblings (usually brothers), and couples with children fleeing to Mexico can be found in newspapers throughout the region. Yet such cases appear to have been relatively uncommon. Moreover, runaway slave ads rarely make reference to family ties or suspicions of assistance from family networks on the route to Mexico, unlike ads from virtually all other parts of the South. As Thomas Mareite has recently argued, "The *absence* of family ties ... spurred bids for self-emancipation across the border." The average runaway in the Texan borderlands, according to Kyle Ainsworth's statistical analysis of runaway slave ads, was a twenty-eight-year-old man who escaped by himself. Those who escaped in groups tended to escape with other unattached young men. Indeed, 91 percent of runaways were male, an unusually high percentage compared to all other destinations in North America. The reason for the overwhelming prevalence of apparently unattached young men among southbound runaways must be sought in the fact that Texas and its neighboring slave states constituted the furthest destinations for enslaved people forcibly transported from other regions in the domestic slave trade. According to Michael Tadman, the net balance of enslaved people imported to Texas

---

[40] *San Antonio Texan,* January 6, 1859, in TRSP (first quote); *Democratic Telegraph and Texas Register,* January 3, 1849, in TRSP (second quote); *The Standard,* January 13, 1855, in TRSP (third quote); *State Gazette,* June 19, 1858, in TRSP (fourth quote).

between 1840 and 1859, for example, amounted to 127,812, a figure even higher than that of neighboring Louisiana (124,001), which suffered negative population growth and served as the final depot for most domestic slave-trading firms operating from the Upper South. Whereas many victims of the domestic slave trade made desperate attempts to traverse truly vast distances in order to either return home or reach northern free soil, as argued in the previous chapters, those who ended up in the Texan borderlands appear to have often judged such prospects unfavorably, and decided to make for nearby Mexican free soil instead. By doing so they effectively "gave up" on the hope of ever being reunited with loved ones.[41]

BLACK REFUGEES ABROAD

How did freedom seekers fare in British Canada and Mexico in the three decades preceding the Civil War? How did they settle into new communities and make a living? The nature of formal freedom beyond the borders of the United States allowed refugees from slavery to undergo settlement processes that differed by degrees – sometimes markedly – from those who remained in the United States, whether in the northern free states or in the urban South. Differences were also discernible between different spaces of formal freedom, however, with British Canada generally constituting a safer and more amenable destination for refugees from slavery than Mexico, where runaways' experiences of freedom tended to be conditional on various social, economic, and legal factors.

Unlike runaways who settled in spaces of informal and semi-formal freedom, black newcomers in Canada could rebuild their lives in the open, without having to hide their true identities or their backgrounds. In theory and in law, they found themselves in a part of the continent where they could seek formal employment, purchase land, build and attend churches and schools, and enjoy the same citizenship rights shared by other free British subjects throughout the empire. In practice, life in Canada was far from easy for many refugees. Economic setbacks,

---

[41] Mareite, "Conditional Freedom," 41–43, 41 (first quote); Ainsworth, "Advertising Maranda," 207; Michael Tadman, *Speculators and Slaves: Masters, Traders, and Slaves in the Old South* (Madison: University of Wisconsin Press, 1989), 12; Damian Alan Pargas, *Slavery and Forced Migration in the Antebellum South* (New York: Cambridge University Press, 2014).

prejudice and distrust of the white population, and widespread homesickness for family and community left behind weighed heavily on the collective and individual experiences of runaways who emigrated north of the
border, even those who ended up making out relatively well in a material
sense. Virtually all, however, succeeded in their quest to attain permanent
freedom from slavery.[42]

Like their counterparts who fled to both northern and southern towns
and cities, making a living was the most important point of business for
refugees in Canada. Most accounts suggest that recent arrivals were able
to find employment and secure housing relatively quickly. Benjamin Drew
admitted that life for black people in Canada had certain drawbacks –
especially white prejudice – but he made a point of portraying the refugees
whom he spoke to as thrifty, honest, and hard-working, assuring readers
that in Canada they made a decent living and did not live in squalor. His
objective was to counter southern arguments that free black people were
incapable of sustaining themselves in a respectable manner. In St.
Catherines, for example, he underscored that "houses occupied by the
colored population are neat and plain without; tidy and comfortable
within." In the "wealthy, enterprising, and beautiful city" of Toronto,
he claimed that most black people resided in the northwestern section of
the city, but that their neighborhoods were a far cry from the impoverished black neighborhoods of cities in the Northern United States. "The
houses resemble those of the same class in St. Catherines: but as they have
not so generally extensive gardens, more time can be allotted to the
beautifying and general care of their dwellings than in St. Catherines."
He found the black population of the city "on the whole, remarkably
industrious." Many of the refugees living in Hamilton he similarly
described as "'well off'; are good mechanics, and good 'subjects' in the
English sense of that word." In Galt he visited a boarding house where
recent arrivals were accommodated until they could find more permanent

---

[42] For more on the legal development of freedom in the British colonies, see Christopher
Leslie Brown, *Moral Capital: Foundations of British Abolitionism* (Chapel Hill:
University of North Carolina Press, 2006); Van Gosse, "'As a Nation, the English Are
Our Friends': The Emergence of African American Politics in the British Atlantic World,
1772–1861," *American Historical Review* 113, no. 4 (2008): 1003–1028; Joseph
Murphy, "The British Example: West Indian Emancipation, the Freedom Principle, and
the Rise of Antislavery Politics in the United States, 1833–1843," *Journal of the Civil War
Era* 8, no. 4 (2018): 621–646; Gordon S. Barker, "Revisiting 'British Principle Talk':
Antebellum Black Expectations and Racism in Early Ontario," in Damian Alan Pargas,
ed., *Fugitive Slaves and Spaces of Freedom in North America* (Gainesville: University
Press of Florida, 2018), 34–69.

housing; the owner assured Drew that "they have all got employment." In Chatham he claimed that during a stroll through town he saw black immigrants from the United States industriously employed everywhere he looked, "building and painting houses, working in mills, engaging in every handicraft employment," and even "a street occupied by colored shopkeepers and clerks." Those who were at home seemed to be "busy upon their gardens and farms." In Windsor, Drew reported that "the general appearance [of the black population] is very much in their favor. There are many good mechanics among them: nearly all have comfortable homes, and some occupy very neat and handsome houses of their own." Such positive impressions of black settlements in Canada were echoed by other reporters' accounts in the 1850s.[43]

Most of the refugees whom Drew interviewed – who were overwhelmingly men – claimed to be able to sustain themselves and even live well in the British provinces, despite having arrived destitute and in dire straits. They found work in unskilled and semi-skilled professions, in construction; on the railroads; as mechanics of all sorts; as farm hands; as peddlers of various wares; in shops; and as sailors and on steamboats on the Great Lakes. Henry Willimason, who settled in Hamilton after fleeing from Maryland along with his wife and wife's family in the early 1850s, told Drew that "we came like terrapins – all we had on our backs." He continued:

We had neither money nor food. It was in the fall: we gathered chips and made a fire. That is the way the principal part of our people come: poor, and destitute, and ignorant … In the face of these drawbacks, they have to do the best they can. I went to work on the railroad, – to which I was wholly unused, having been a waiter. I worked at it till I found something I could do better.

Stitching together odd jobs, Williamson claimed that after only two years he was "in a good situation and doing well," and that nothing could induce him to go back to the South. "I would rather be wholly poor and free," he reasoned.[44]

---

[43] Drew, *A North-Side View*, 18 (first quote); Ibid., 94 (second quote); Ibid., 119 (third quote); Ibid., 173 (fourth quote); Ibid., 234 (fifth quote); Ibid., 321 (sixth quote). See also "A Recent Tour," *Provincial Freeman*, March 24, 1853, which describes St. Catherines; or "The Negroes of Toronto," *Friends' Intelligencer*, October 31, 1857. Samuel Howe similarly claimed in his report to the Freedmen's Inquiry Commission that the refugees from slavery in Canada West were particularly hard-working: "No sensible people in Canada charge the refugees with slothfulness." See Howe, *Refugees from Slavery in Canada West*, 55.

[44] Henry Williamson, in Drew, *A North-Side View*, 134–135 (quotes); Kennedy, "Northward Bound," 161–183.

Williamson's experiences were echoed by other testimonies of refugees living in Canada West in the 1850s, both those interviewed by Drew and those found among the correspondence of northern vigilance committees. In Colchester, Drew found that "there is not one who cannot find work within a few hours after he gets here," a claim he made for several other communities he visited as well. Aby Jones, a runaway from Kentucky who settled in London, told Drew that when he arrived he "was not worth one cent," but he "neither begged nor received a farthing of money. I went to work at once." Sam Davis, a recent arrival from Virginia who had settled in Toronto only "a few months" before Drew interviewed him in 1855, reported that he had fled with seven dollars and spent every last penny on the journey to Canada, arriving completely destitute. "I have had work enough to support myself since I have been here," he boasted, however. "I intend to work, and save all I can." Henry Morehead, who fled Kentucky with his wife and children about a year before relating his story to Drew, similarly claimed that in London he was "making out very well," adding that he had "not been in the country long enough to accumulate any wealth, but I am getting along as well as the general run of people. It stands to reason, that a man must be doing something to pay a rent of five dollars a month, and support a family of four besides himself." Robert Jackson, a runaway from Maryland who was forwarded by the VCP to Canada in the fall of 1853, reported to his helpers in Philadelphia soon after arrival that he was now "a brakesman on the Great Western R.R.," and that he was making out well. Richard Edons, who fled together with his friend Abram from North Carolina in the summer of 1857, similarly wrote a letter in his own hand to his helper William Still upon arrival in Canada, informing him that "we arived in King[ston] all saft Canada West[.] Abram Galway gos to work this morning at $1 75 per day and John pediford is at work for mr george mink and I will opne [sic] a shop for my self in a few days[.]"[45]

Not all refugees in Canada found themselves in a position to sustain themselves immediately, however, and it is important to consider how difficult it was for tired and penniless newcomers to adjust quickly to their new communities and earn a bit of money, however willing they were to do so. As one refugee in Hamilton tellingly put it: "My people come into this country with nothing, and they have to work for what they do get.

---

[45] Drew, *A North-Side View*, 368 (first quote); Aby B. Jones, in ibid., 150 (second quote); Sam Davis, in ibid., 117 (third quote); Henry Morehead, in ibid., 181–182 (fourth quotes); Still, *The Underground Railroad*, 51 (fifth quote); Richard Edons to William Still, July 20, 1857, in Still, *The Underground Railroad*, 152 (sixth quote).

One cannot expect a great deal at once from such people." Much day labor tended to be seasonal, and those who arrived in the freezing winter often found it difficult to find work quickly. The VCP in Philadelphia, for example, received some letters from refugees they had sent to Canada in the winter who claimed to be safe and happy to live in freedom, but who were also clearly struggling to get settled. Edmund Turner, who fled Virginia in December 1857 and passed through the care of the VCP before ending up in Hamilton, wrote to William Still in his own hand three months later that he was "doing as well as I can at this time but I get no wages[.] But my Bord that is satfid at that thes hard time and glad that I am Hear [sic] and in good helth." During his travels through the border communities in Canada West Drew also found and heard about cases of recent arrivals who were having considerable difficulty. Most "of the cases of suffering and destitution" he witnessed were attributed to "sickness and improvidence." For some, the journey itself physically weakened runaways to the point of hampering their ability to work immediately upon arrival. William Johnson, a recent arrival who had fled from Virginia when Drew interviewed him in 1855, claimed that he had "been able to do no work on account of my frozen feet – I lost two toes on my right foot." He explained that his "feet were frostbitten on my way North, but I would have rather died on the way than to go back." Johnson's intention was to "go to work as soon as I am able," but for the time being he had little choice but to accept help from others. Many refugees indeed depended on local charities – most of it organized and distributed by other black residents – as a vital lifeline upon arrival in Canada. Drew noted the existence of at least fourteen "True Band" societies in Canada West, black-run and -organized relief organizations that collected donations for fugitive slaves, cared for those who were sick or injured, and helped them find homes and jobs. Robert Nelson, a runaway from Virginia who arrived in Colchester "without a shilling," told Drew that if people "wish to give money to the fugitives and the sick, it should be given to the True Band societies, who can distribute it as it is wanted. The Band will attend to the fugitives." Similar associations sprang up throughout the Canadian borderlands, some of them with the assistance of white abolitionists, including the Refugee Slaves' Friend Society in St. Catherines and the Toronto Ladies' Association for the Relief of Destitute Colored Fugitives.[46]

[46] Rev. R. S. W. Sorrick, in Drew, *A North-Side View*, 120–121 (first quote); Edmund Turner to William Still, March 1, 1858, in Still, *The Underground Railroad*, 119 (second quote); William Johnson, in Drew, *A North-Side View*, 29–30 (third quotes); Drew,

Women were essential contributors to refugee families' household income in Canada – indeed, some were single mothers and therefore the sole breadwinners. They, too, found it difficult to earn money to sustain themselves upon arrival in Canada. Most accepted what work they could find, and, like their counterparts in the northern states and in southern cities, they found themselves limited by gender norms to certain sectors of the economy. They worked as seamstresses, domestics, washerwomen, and selling garden produce and handicrafts at marketplaces. Those whose husbands managed to lease or purchase land performed the backbreaking work of homesteading. Drew interviewed very few women living in Canada West – only 18 out of the 114 interviews he conducted were with women – and most of those he did speak to said little about their work, but some provided interesting clues to the challenges experienced by female refugees. Single mothers, in particular, arrived desperate to find work as soon as possible in order to care for their dependent children. Sarah Jackson, a single mother who was interviewed a week after arriving in London, told Drew optimistically: "I expect to work for a living, and I am trying to get a house." Some of her peers who had been there longer, however, made it clear that life as a single mother was a continual struggle, and that finding well-paid work was no easy task. One "Mrs. Ellis" fled Delaware with her two children after learning that her master intended to sell her, settling in St. Catherines about a year before Drew interviewed her in 1855. Making no mention of a husband – either in Canada or in Delaware – she admitted that she struggled to sustain her small family. "Rent and provisions are dear here, and it takes all I can earn to support myself and my children," she related. "I could have one of my children well brought up and taken care of, by some friends in Massachusetts, which would much relieve me, – but I cannot have my child go there on account of the laws, which would not protect her." Calling her life in Canada "a hardship," she nevertheless felt that she had "had to struggle much harder" when she lived in slavery, and so she stood by her decision to flee, however difficult her present circumstances were. The abovementioned refugee from Maryland "Mrs. Nancy Howard," who initially fled to Massachusetts and lived there for seven years before ultimately removing again to Canada on account of the Fugitive Slave Law, had also been living in St. Catherines for only a year before Drew interviewed her. She, too, made no mention of a husband – Drew appears

A North-Side View, 236–239; Robert Nelson in Drew, *A North-Side View*, 371–372 (fourth quote).

to have affixed the title "Mrs." to all of the women he interviewed, regardless of their marital status – and she admitted she had trouble finding work in her new community. Back in Maryland she had been a domestic slave, and it is likely that she worked in a domestic capacity in Massachusetts as well. In St. Catherines, however, she found it "harder to get work ... than I did in Massachusetts."[47]

As a rule, couples and family groups fared better, and over time some refugee families acquired capital and considerable property. John Little, a runaway from North Carolina, arrived in Canada with his wife and settled in the bush with virtually no means at all. "Myself and my wife built us here a little log hut amid the snow," he told Drew. Over the next few years they continually cleared and planted the land, and managed to settle on 100 acres, 50 acres of which they formally owned. Little hired himself out in the beginning to supplement their income. When Drew interviewed the couple, they had a respectable farm with "fifty acres of wheat, eighteen acres of oats, one acre of potatoes, and twenty acres of meadow grass." They also had "horses, oxen, cows, hogs, sheep, and poultry in abundance." John Little's advice to other runaways from slavery was to "go into the backwoods of Queen Victoria's dominions, and you can secure an independent support." His wife added that she was "proud" of the backbreaking work she had performed to "help get cleared up, so that we could have a home, and plenty to live on. I now enjoy my life very well." Alexander Hamilton, who fled from St. Louis to London in 1834, similarly told Drew that when he arrived he had "only a dollar and a half." He "found no need to beg," however, "for I found work at once. I have done well since I came here. I have made a good living and something more. I own real estate in London – three houses and several lots of land." He added that "the colored people in London are all making a living: there is no beggar among them." The above-mentioned Philip Younger, who fled Alabama and ended up settling in Chatham, claimed that black refugees "are placed in different circum-stances here – some drag along, without doing much, – some are doing well. I have a house; I have taken up fifty acres of land, and have made the payments required. I have other property besides." His neighbors were also doing well. "Here is Henry Blue, worth twelve thousand dollars; Syddles, worth a fortune; Lucky, worth a very handsome fortune;

<hr />

[47] Mrs. Sarah Jackson, in Drew, *A North-Side View*, 179 (first quote); Mrs. Ellis, in Drew, ibid., 44 (second quote); Mrs. Nancy Howard, in ibid., 51 (third quote); Kennedy, "Northward Bound," 161–183.

Ramsay, a great deal of land and other property, at least twelve thousand dollars; all these were slaves at some time."[48]

Success stories such as these took considerable time to develop, however, and were often scarred with setbacks along the way. The process of "settling" should indeed not be seen as a linear process, but rather as a series of ebbs and flows whereby newcomers struggled to get ahead as well as they could, sometimes falling into debt or bad luck along the way. The experiences of some of the older black residents of Canadian border communities are illuminating. The abovementioned Alexander Hemsley, who had fled Maryland as a young man and settled into life as a free black in New Jersey before finding himself forced to uproot and move again to Canada in 1836, concluded his interview with Drew in 1855 by relating that he was now "about sixty years of age, and have been lying sick about nine months." Looking back upon his life in Canada he admitted that "my pay has been poor, for our people all start poor, and struggle to support themselves." He at least had a "house and a quarter acre of land," but his estate was incumbered with $200 of debt. Hemsley had "had a great deal of sickness in my family, and it has kept me comparatively poor," he claimed. Had it not been for various incumbrances, his property would have been paid for "long ago." Some older residents viewed their struggles as a long process of redemption from slavery. James Adams, also mentioned above, who fled Virginia and arrived in Canada in 1824, related proudly to Drew more than thirty years later that "I am now buying this place," indicating his house. For Adams, the fact that it took more than three decades to finally be able to afford a house did not concern him. "My family are with me, – we live well, and enjoy ourselves." His life in slavery, which he described as "the most disgusting system a man can live under," would have been much worse.[49]

Reconstructing the early settlement experiences of slave refugees in Mexico is a far more challenging task, given the scarcity of source material and the lack of testimonies from runaways themselves. Because of the

---

[48] John Little, in Drew, *A North-Side View*, 217–219 (quotes); Mrs. John Little, in ibid., 233 (quote); Alexander Hamilton, in ibid., 178 (quotes); Philip Younger, in ibid., 250 (quotes); Kennedy, "Northward Bound," 161–183.

[49] Rev. Alexander Hemsley, in Drew, *A North-Side View*, 40 (first quotes); James Adams, in ibid., 28 (second quotes). Samuel Howe was adamant that the slave refugees in Canada West in 1864 were often poor but also slowly but surely upwardly mobile. He encountered "signs of extreme poverty among those recently arrived, [but] we did not see such marks of utter destitution and want, as may be found in the lower walks of life in most countries." See Howe, *Refugees from Slavery in Canada West*, 57–58.

highly charged nature of the fugitive slave issue in antebellum America, moreover, many editorials and reports on the material conditions of runaways on Mexican free soil are heavily tainted by politicized exaggerations. Falling into proslavery and antislavery camps, respectively, they essentially propound "two conflicting myths," as Thomas Mareite recently argued. On the one hand, in much the same way that slaveholders from the Upper South depicted Canada as a frozen and inhospitable wasteland to their slaves, Texan slaveholders consistently claimed that Mexico was an impoverished and inhospitable destination for runaways, and that most refugees south of the border suffered a fate that was far worse than slavery. Such views were indeed widely published in Texan newspapers as paternalistic arguments for not only maintaining racial slavery but also banishing Mexican peons from Texan communities. One slaveholder penned an editorial on "Runaways in Mexico" in the *Standard* in 1854 in which he claimed that "when the negro gets to Mexico he ... finds nothing but the most squalid wretchedness, poverty, and starvation for his lot. Some become peons as a matter of self-preservation ... [W]hile in Mexico, they are brutally used, not half-clothed, have no physicians, are regarded with jealousy by the peons, and have nothing but corn dodgers, and few of them to eat." Cloaked in paternalistic self-righteousness, the author declared the presence of peons "among us" as "decidedly injurious to our slave population," because they lured enslaved people to a fictitious freedom on the other side of the border. On the other hand, American abolitionists and free soil activists insisted that Mexico was a heaven on earth for runaways from slavery. One Republican member of Congress claimed in 1858 that black migrants in Coahuila were well settled in a region with a "beautiful climate" and "a rich, productive soil," adding that it was fully understandable that so many "determined to locate their new homes in this most romantic portion of Mexico."[50]

The truth appears to have been less extreme than either of these conflicting myths would have us believe. Evidence suggests that many southbound runaways indeed struggled to sustain themselves immediately

---

[50] Mareite, "Conditional Freedom," 40, 171–172 (first quote); *The Standard*, October 21, 1854 (second quote); Joshua R. Giddings, *The Exiles of Florida: Or the Crimes Committed by Our Government against the Maroons, Who Fled from South Carolina, and Other Slave States, Seeking Protection under Spanish Laws* (Columbus, OH: Follett, Foster & Co., 1858), 325 (third quote); Nichols, *The Limits of Liberty*, chs. 3, 6, 7. See also Sarah E. Cornell, "Citizens of Nowhere: Fugitive Slaves and Free African Americans in Mexico, 1833–1857," *Journal of American History* 100, no. 2 (2013): 351–374.

upon arrival in Mexico, and they also appear to have been confronted with more formidable challenges to making a living than their counterparts in Canada, where wages were not only higher but where black communities were better organized in accommodating newcomers and helping them get settled. Mexico was clearly not a land of abundance for a vast majority of refugees from American slavery. Virtually none, however, stumbled back into Texas half-starved and half-clothed in an attempt to reclaim any "superior" living conditions under slavery.

For refugees from slavery in northeastern Mexico, the ability to get settled and physically sustain oneself immediately upon arrival depended much on networks and adequate preparations made before fleeing. Arriving at the Mexican border penniless and friendless – although it occurred often enough – was to be avoided if possible, as there were virtually no formal organizations or sympathetic abolitionist households to receive or assist anonymous refugees. Instead, many fled with specific contacts and some kind of starting capital, which often consisted of cash or stolen goods that could be traded either upon arrival or along the way. Frederick Law Olmsted, traveling through the borderlands in 1854, commented that most runaways "brought with them money, which they had earned and hoarded for the purpose, or some small articles which they had stolen from their masters." Other southbound runaways fled with rather large articles from their masters. Six enterprising young men who fled together from Texas to Mexico in the winter of 1845, for example, somehow managed to make off with twenty-five horses – "four ... fine blooded mares, a large pacing horse, and about twenty head of common horses." The runaway slave ad that announced their flight included the presumption that the runaways had a contact in Mexico – "some white man or Mexican" – and implied that they intended to sell the animals upon arrival. In 1856 five runaways similarly fled south of the border in the company of three Mexicans, all "well armed and mounted," and herding no less than twelve valuable horses, clearly with the intention of selling them for cash. Such cases suggest that at least some runaways sought to arrive on free soil with sufficient means to get settled and make a realistic attempt at sustaining themselves.[51]

By the late 1830s and early 1840s most southbound refugees crossed into Mexico at Matamoros, in Tamaulipas, which quickly developed a

---

[51] Olmsted, _A Journey through Texas_, 324 (first quote); _Texas National Register_, January 11, 1845, in TRSP (second quote); _Texas State Times_, November 15, 1856, in TRSP (third quote).

reputation as the main gateway to liberty for runaways from north of the Rio Grande. By 1853 the city indeed listed some 450 black and mulatto residents out of a total population of roughly 11,000. It was an attractive destination for recent arrivals for two reasons. First, it was an expanding port city with various opportunities for both skilled and unskilled labor. And second, the population of Matamoros, especially wary of Texan and American incursions and raids, appears to have been particularly sympathetic to the plight of runaway slaves. One US consul lamented in 1860 that locals were "deadly hostile to every American unless he is a negro or mulatto." Such sentiments undoubtedly proved advantageous to recent arrivals who sought work or assistance in getting settled. Although southerners who passed through Matamoros often claimed, as Thomas Green did in 1845, for example, that the condition of the "negroes who had absconded from Texas" was "vastly worse" in Matamoros, city records suggest otherwise. A survey of the city's population from 1841 listed black men engaged in various occupations, including as barbers, carpenters, masons, tailors, coachbuilders, and general laborers. Most had lived in the city an average of five years when the survey was conducted, and were thus clearly runaways.[52]

Other border towns such as Piedras Negras in Coahuila similarly became popular destinations for refugees from slavery. Thriving mainly as a trade conduit to and from neighboring Texas, Piedras Negras provided runaways – especially men – opportunities to earn money in a variety of low-skilled occupations, mainly as casual laborers, herders, carriers and *carreteros* for the transit trade in cotton, corn, wool, lead, hides, and manufactured goods. Most appear to have lived in makeshift huts or rented rooms and basements in town. When Olmsted visited Piedras Negras in 1854, he painted an ambiguous portrait of the slave refugee population there. Conversing with one runaway, originally from Virginia but sold to Texas, who had fled there four or five years earlier, he discovered that the man made his living as a "mechanic, and could earn a dollar very easily, every day," although he sometimes earned extra as a muleteer or servant. The refugee "could speak Spanish fluently," and was generally "very well satisfied with the country." The man did comment,

---

[52] Mareite, "Conditional Freedom," 172–174; Nichols, *The Limits of Liberty*, 73–75; US Consul, "Fitzpatrick to Cass, January 6, 1860," cited in Mareite, "Conditional Freedom," 173 (first quote); Thomas J. Green, *Journal of the Texian Expedition against Mier* (New York: Harper & Brothers, 1845), 124 (second quote), 431 (third quote). Only men were listed in the city survey. See Mareite, "Conditional Freedom," 173.

however, that many other recent arrivals struggled to get settled, claiming that "they had never been used to taking care of themselves, and when they first got here they were so excited with being free, and with being made so much of by these Mexican women, that they spent all they brought very soon; generally they gave it all away to the women, and in a short while they had nothing to live upon." The refugee underscored that most recent arrivals also could not speak Spanish, which hampered their ability to find work, and "often they were poor and miserable." After a short while, however, "if they chose to be industrious," he insisted, "they could live very comfortably." Wages were low, but "they had all they earned for their own, and a man's living did not cost him much here." He added that many were industrious, saved their money, and "could make money faster than the Mexicans themselves could." He knew of a few who had settled further from the border who had acquired "wealth, and positions of honor." Olmsted found the particulars of the refugee's testimony confirmed by "every foreigner I saw" in that region, as well as "by the Mexicans themselves."[53]

Throughout the borderlands, runaway slaves with particular skills sought employment as craftsmen in some of the better-paying niches of the nineteenth-century economy. Mexican residence permits (*cartas de seguridad*) were issued to refugees whose occupations included coach-builder and carpenter, for example. For unskilled newcomers, however, jobs were sought wherever they were to be had, whether in town or outside of it. Undoubtedly collecting advice and tips from the people they met in various border towns and crossing points, many recent arrivals in search of employment gravitated to ranches and *haciendas* in the imme-diate hinterlands, most of which were dedicated to animal husbandry but also commercial agriculture, especially wheat, maize, cotton, peans, agave, and even sugarcane. Slave refugees – mainly men but also some women – appear to have worked on such establishments in low-wage capacities as farmhands, often listed in sources as "*sirvientes a sueldo y ración*" (literally "servants at wage and ration"), or more generally a *jornaleros* and *labradores* (laborers). Most were single men but occasion-ally entire families turn up, such as one couple with their four children on the ranch of one Juan Longoria Tijerrina in Tamaulipas. Working conditions at these establishments were far from ideal and often entailed some form of dependency. Some scholars have underscored that fugitive slaves who became farmhands on Mexican *haciendas* essentially traded one master for another, often entering into labor arrangements that closely resembled some form of debt peonage. Research by James David Nichols has found that even Mexican officials – including the governor of Coahuila – remarked upon such arrangements throughout the state. It is the situation of these runaways that Texan slaveholders referred to in their widespread propaganda about the horrible fate of runaway slaves in Mexico. Clearly, the vulnerability and desperation of many fugitive slaves upon arrival in Mexico provided them with particularly weak bargaining power to negotiate for decent working conditions.[54]

Indeed, not all newcomers succeeded in finding legitimate employment at all upon arrival in Mexico, and some who crossed into the country with smuggled horses and peon contacts quickly gravitated to illegal smuggling as a means of survival. As argued by Nichols, the sharp increase in smuggling activities – either led by runaway slaves or with the participation of runaways – at Piedras Negras threatened to strain relations between black newcomers and Mexican authorities and residents in the 1850s. One band of horse and cattle thieves led by a runaway named Francisco, in particular, sowed resentment among locals. Runaways who had joined free black migrants in Mexico, especially the Black Seminoles, similarly earned such a stubborn reputation as cattle smugglers that Governor Santiago Vidaurri advised Black Seminoles to distance themselves from them. Rumors even spread of a plan to potentially relocate them to the Pacific coast. Slave refugees who settled in and around the town of Múzquiz, in Coahuila, were described as dangerously drawn to vagrancy and vice, and characterized by city officials as petty thieves. The state government urged the municipality to either encourage them to find formal employment or take action against them. Such cases suggest that many newcomers – especially single young men without ties to family – found it difficult to find legitimate means of subsistence upon arrival in Mexico, and gravitated to illegal activities and criminal networks.[55]

---

[54] Mareite, "Conditional Freedom," 180–181, 185; Nichols, *The Limits of Liberty*, 188; James David Nichols, "Freedom Interrupted: Runaway Slaves and Insecure Borders in the Mexican Northeast," in Damian Alan Pargas, ed., *Fugitive Slaves and Spaces of Freedom in North America* (Gainesville: University Press of Florida, 2018), 254; Cornell, "Citizens of Nowhere," 351–374.

[55] Mareite, "Conditional Freedom," 182–183; Nichols, *The Limits of Liberty*, 135–136; Porter, *The Black Seminoles*, 156.

Black emigrants to both Canada and Mexico – and runaway slaves in general – placed great value in self-sufficiency. Acquiring land was the ultimate goal of most emigrants to Canada, but with virtually no means with which to purchase land outright, many recent arrivals settled on patches of wilderness, which they turned into homesteads by the sweat of their brow. Essentially squatting on what seemed like unused forest land, refugees exhibited remarkable initiative and independence, but this practice also made them vulnerable to formal claims and evictions by local authorities and land agents. The small settlements at Queen's Bush serve as an interesting case in point. In 1846 refugees from slavery began to trickle into the "bush," the name given to a "large, unsurveyed tract of land, now comprising the townships of Peel and Wellesley, and the country extending thence to Lake Huron." As one original resident named William Jackson put it, "Fugitive slaves came in, in great numbers, and cleared the land." When they inquired about obtaining proper titles, they were informed that it was clergy land, and none could be given. By the time the land was formally surveyed two years later, "there were as many as fifty families." The arrival of the land surveyor made many refugee families panic, however, as they heard rumors that they would soon be forced to purchase the land at a price most could not afford, a rumor apparently spread by a greedy and deceiving land speculator who wanted them to sell the land to him at an artificially low price. Jackson recalled that "they were afraid they would not be able to pay when pay-day came. Under these circumstances, many of them sold out cheap," and removed to other communities. John Francis, a refugee from Virginia who arrived in Queen's Bush in 1846, related to Drew: "We settled down where we saw fit. We knew nothing about price nor terms." When the land agent arrived, he "put up public notices, that the settlers who had made improve-ments were to come and pay the first instalment, or the land would be sold from under them. It was hard times in Canada, and many could not meet the payment. ... Fearing that the land would be sold ... they sold out for very little and removed to other parts." Some sold out for as little as ten dollars, and Francis himself had sacrificed two cows to make the payment. In the end, however, both Jackson and Francis claimed that the black settlers had all been duped, as they never heard from the land agent again. Some of the families who refused to sell out were never forced to pay anything, and were still residing there when Drew passed through in 1855.[56]

---

[56] Drew, *A North-Side View*, 189 (quote); William Jackson, in ibid., 190 (quotes); John Francis, in ibid., 196 (quotes); *National Anti-Slavery Standard*, July 29, 1847; Linda Kubisch-Brown, *The Queen's Bush Settlement: Black Pioneers, 1839–1865* (Toronto:

Those who were eventually able to purchase land tended to do well for themselves. Canada West offered rich and fertile soil, where black farmers could grow hemp, flax, wheat, corn, oats, potatoes, and raise poultry and livestock for market. It was also covered in valuable woodland that could be sold as timber. The *Voice of the Fugitive*, a local periodical set up by runaway slave and abolitionist Henry Bibb, regularly informed readers about the availability of cheap land for sale in the Western District in the early 1850s, in particular Essex and Chatham-Kent Counties, which saw their black populations swell with refugee crossings at the Detroit River. In 1851 the *Voice* reported that the Canada Company was offering "700,000 acres of land in blocks containing from 2000 to 9000 acres each, situated in the Western Distrrict, and scattered lots in almost every township in Canada West." The average price was between two and four dollars per acre, and the land was "rich and generally well stocked with valuable timber." In Colchester, the *Voice* similarly reported in 1851 that "there is about 6000 acres of Canada Company land for sale ... [the] price of which is from $2 to $2.50 per acre," particularly suitable to abundant harvests of hemp and flax. Trade between local farmers and nearby Detroit merchants appears to have thrived in the 1850s. The *Voice* related in 1852 that "many come from Detroit here to trade," and reported one black merchant who crossed on the ferry with "almost 200 dozen of eggs, six or eight turkeys with chickens and butter." A journalist from Ohio who visited Windsor a few years later, in 1859, claimed that many of the black residents in the region had once been slaves in the South, but were "now hard at work for their wives and little ones, owning a good property and continually accumulating."[57]

Collective purchases of land and even organized utopian communities for black refugees from the United States had begun in Canada long before the 1850s, although most were relatively short-lived and hampered with difficulties. Many of the third category of refugees discussed

57 "Canada Lands," *Voice of the Fugitive*, June 1, 1851 (first quote); "Hemp and Flax Growing," *Voice of the Fugitive*, March 12, 1851 (second quote); "Progress of Improvement in Windsor," *Voice of the Fugitive*, June 3, 1852 (third quote); *Cleveland Morning Herald*, December 7, 1859 (fourth quote); Kennedy, "Northward Bound," 161–183. Samuel Howe reported in 1864 that the slave refugees who lived on farmsteads "generally own the land which they occupy; and in many cases they have paid off the mortgages, and hold a clear fee." See Howe, *Refugees from Slavery in Canada West*, 65.

above – those who first settled in the Northern United States and then lifted stakes and moved on to Canada – emigrated to join such enterprises. The Wilberforce settlement roughly 20 miles north of London was one such community, settled mainly by black migrants from Ohio. Following the Cincinnati riots of 1828, two prominent African-American leaders named Israel Lewis and Thomas Crissup were sent to Upper Canada to negotiate the purchase of 4,000 acres for the purpose of establishing a formal colony for African Americans who wished to leave the United States. Permission from the Lieutenant Governor was secured relatively quickly, but raising enough funds to effect the purchase and help settlers get started proved a challenge. In the end they were aided by Ohio Quakers and a new black abolitionist organization founded in Philadelphia called the "American Society of Free Persons of Color, for improving their condition in the United States; for purchasing lands; and for the establishment of a settlement in the Province of Upper Canada." Settlers began to trickle in by 1829, bringing with them few provisions and scant financial means, but high hopes for converting the wilderness into a peaceful community and achieving a real freedom and independence that was denied to them in the Northern United States. By 1832 the abolitionist periodical the *Genius of Universal Emancipation* described the settlement as rich with the possibility of economic development: "It is covered with a heavy growth of timber," and the soil was "extremely fertile. All kinds of grain, &c., produced north of the Carolinas, succeed well here." There was moreover an abundance of wildlife – including bear, deer, and wolves – and many settlers began hunting and selling animal skins and furs to traders. At its height, Wilberforce comprised a few hundred dedicated and hard-working settlers and was praised as a model community, complete with neat log cabins, a Sunday school, three saw mills, and a grist mill. By the 1840s, however, the colony had fallen into disarray. Fundraising campaigns in the United States and Great Britain failed to generate the necessary funds to keep the settlement running and attract new settlers, and in-fighting between the board of managers and Lewis – who was accused of embezzling funds meant for the colony – destroyed the credibility of the community. In the end many settlers moved away, some of them indeed to Queen's Bush.[58]

[58] Kennedy, "Northward Bound," 161–183; Nikki M. Taylor, *Frontiers of Freedom: Cincinnati's Black Community, 1802–1868* (Athens: Ohio University Press, 2005), 61–80; *Genius of Universal Emancipation*, July 1, 1830; Marilyn Baily, "From Cincinnati, Ohio to Wilberforce, Canada: A Note on Antebellum Colonization,"

A more successful utopian community was the Elgin settlement at Buxton, established in 1849 by Irish-born Presbyterian minister William King. King had married into a slaveholding family from Louisiana and inherited his wife's enslaved people when she died. Committed to liberating them, he developed plans to resettle them in Canada, and negotiated to that end the purchase of 9,000 acres close to the shore of Lake Erie. King's intentions went further than to simply resettle his own bondspeople – the idea was to create a peaceful community for hard-working black migrants that would, according to the settlement's own constitution, "improve the racial and moral condition of the coloured population of Canada. To induce them to settle in rural districts ... to educate their children, and generally to protect their rights, and advance their interests." The settlement was placed under the authority of a supervisory board, with King acting as managing director. Refugees from slavery were among the first to move to Elgin, including those who had initially settled elsewhere in Canada but removed to Buxton when they heard about the new community being established. Throughout the 1850s and into the Civil War years, the Elgin settlement received glowing reviews. In 1851 one writer for the *Frederick Douglass' Paper* reported that the land had been divided into 50-acre plots and "offered for sale to colored persons of approved moral character, who will become settlers upon their lots." He took specific note of the "wholesome spirit of industry and enterprise throughout the settlement." Most homes were "built of logs," the land was being "adapted for the culture of wheat; but it also produces corn, tobacco, and hemp," and there was even a grist mill and brickyard. A few years later Drew claimed that settlers were "characterized by a manly, independent air and manner ... they have purchased homes for themselves, paid the price demanded by the government, erected their own buildings, and supported their own families by their own industry." Churches and schools had been established. The abolitionist press in the United States pointed to Buxton as a model community.[59]

Journal of Negro History 58, no. 4 (1973): 427–440; "Wilberforce Settlement," *Genius of Universal Emancipation*, reprinted in *Liberator*, May 12, 1832; Austin Steward, *Twenty-Two Years a Slave, and Forty Years a Freeman; Embracing a Correspondence of Several Years, While President of the Wilberforce Colony, London, Canada West* (Rochester, NY: William Alling, 1857).

[59] Sharon A. Roger Hepburn, *Crossing the Border: A Free Black Community in Upper Canada* (Urbana: University of Illinois Press, 2007); "Constitution of the Elgin Settlement," Buxton Mission and Elgin Settlement Papers, *Slavery, Abolition & Social Justice* (database), Leiden University; "Register of Lands," in ibid.; Samuel J. May,

Similar projects and planned communities for runaway slaves in Mexico were virtually nonexistent, although some American abolitionists did go to great lengths to advocate and even raise funds for their development. Abolitionists such as Samuel Webb and David Lee Child corresponded with Mexican officials to inquire about the possibility of black settlement in the early 1830s, for example. Benjamin Lundy, the editor of the *Genius of Universal Emancipation*, was perhaps the most vocal and tireless champion of Mexico as an asylum for runaway slaves. Lundy visited the country three times in order to scout out a tract of land for a black colony. Encouraged by the respectable appearance and relatively peaceful lives of the runaways and free black migrants he met during his travels, he concluded that in Mexico "one complexion is as much respected as another." In March 1835 Lundy signed a contract with the state of Tamaulipas for the settlement of about 250 black families over the next two years, but the plan was killed by the outbreak of the Texan Revolution just months later, and thus never came to fruition. In November that same year another celebrated abolitionist, Massachusetts ship captain Jonathan Walker, who was known for helping to smuggle fugitive slaves to safety via maritime routes in the circum-Caribbean, also visited Matamoros with the intention of helping to establish a haven for runaways from the United States. He found the border region in a state of chaos with the recent outbreak of hostilities, however, and both he and his son were even shot during their stay. Like Lundy, Walker's plans for an asylum colony came to naught.[60]

After the Texan Revolution abolitionist interest in promoting black settlements and colonies south of the Rio Grande was renewed, especially after passage of the Fugitive Slave Law in 1850, but rarely went beyond strong admonitions to runaways to consider running south rather than north. At the National Emigration Convention of Colored People, held in Cleveland in 1854, for example, speakers acknowledged that Mexico was as safe a destination for fugitive slaves as Canada, but did not develop any plans for organized settlements south of the border. The only runaways

---

"Condition and Prospect of Fugitives in Canada," *Anti-Slavery Bugle*, October 4, 1851 (quotes); Drew, *A North-Side View*, 297.

[60] Mareite, "Conditional Freedom," 32–37; *Genius of Universal Emancipation*, November 27, 1829; Thomas Earle, *The Life, Travels and Opinions of Benjamin Lundy, Including His Journeys to Texas and Mexico, with a Sketch of Contemporary Events, and a Notice of the Revolution in Hayti* (Philadelphia: W. D. Parrish, 1847), 54 (quote); Jonathan Walker, *Trial and Imprisonment of Jonathan Walker, at Pensacola, Florida, for Aiding Slaves to Escape from Bondage* (Boston: Anti-Slavery Office, 1845), 108–110.

who probably ended up in organized settlements were those who attached themselves to free black migrants, such as the *mascogos* migrants (mainly Black Seminoles) who migrated to Coahuila in 1851. Runaways who either migrated with the *mascogos* or fled to their settlement at Nacimiento de los Negros in the 1850s benefitted from the privileges and infrastructure of that community, which included land and farming instruments to cultivate maize and sugarcane. Similarly, the runaways who attached themselves to the groups of free blacks (mainly *gens de colours*) from Louisiana who established the Eureka colony and the Donato colony in Tlacotalpan (Veracruz) in 1857, found themselves in organized farming communities dedicated itself to producing maize and sugarcane for export via Veracruz. The fate of runaways, specifically, in these settlements is virtually unknown.[61]

Whether they lived in newly established black farming settlements, informal black communities on the outskirts of towns, or in towns themselves, refugees from slavery tended to rely on themselves as much as possible. A clear distinction can be made, however, between the extent to which refugees in Canada and Mexico, respectively, attempted to – or were able to – integrate into local communities. In general, refugees in Canada tended to self-segregate more than their counterparts in Mexico.

No racist laws in the British Dominion forced black residents to segregate from the white population, whether in their places of residence or in public schools and facilities. Yet black settlements throughout Canada went to great lengths to facilitate collective self-help and independent institutions – including schools and churches – a kind of self-segregation deeply rooted in not only a desire for independence but also a widespread distrust of the white population. That distrust was not unfounded, as black settlers suffered prejudice, manipulation, and social rejection in many border communities. Even the Elgin settlement faced massive resistance from white Canadians in Kent County, that latter of whom did their best to prevent it from being established at all. Local whites indeed collectively petitioned the provincial government in 1849 to block the land purchase, as they believed "such a settlement in any part of this District would be highly deleterious to the morals and social condition of the present and future inhabitants of this District, as well as to its

---

[61] Mareite, "Conditional Freedom," 35–37; *Proceedings of the National Emigration Convention of Colored People* (Pittsburgh, PA: A. A. Anderson, 1854); Porter, *Black Seminoles*, 133; Jemelle, "The 'Circum-Caribbean' and the Continuity of Cultures," 65–69.

prosperity in every other respect." Hundreds gathered at a Chatham hotel
to protest the settlement, and shouted down King when he tried to address
the crowd. Their cries ultimately went unheeded, but serve as a powerful
example of how "welcome" refugees from American slavery were in some
of the Canadian townships.[62]

Drew commented abundantly on the prevalence of white prejudice
against black residents of Canada West in the 1850s – a feature of life
that, much to his dismay, caused refugees from slavery to turn inward. In
Hamilton, for example, he was surprised to see that only a handful of
refugees sent their children to the public school, and was vexed to learn
that the reason had more to do with the ire of the local white population
than with any lack of interest in education among the black residents.
"It is much to be regretted that the colored people do not to a greater
extent avail themselves of the advantages presented by the perfect equality
of the English laws," he lamented. "Yet it is scarcely to be wondered at,
when we consider that prejudice against them prevails and to too great an
extent in Hamilton." One local resident whom he interviewed claimed
that the "main obstacle" to living there was the "prejudice existing
between colored and white." Another resident complained that local
blacks were often "insulted" by "the ruffians of Canada." Yet another
refugee from slavery admitted to Drew that "there is some prejudice here
among the low class of people," but relativized that prejudice by compar-
ing it to what he had seen in the Northern United States, adding that
"it has not the effect here it has in the States, because here the colored man
is regarded as a man, while in the States he is looked upon more as a
brute."[63]

Similar experiences were reported in London, Colchester, and elsewhere. In London, only a handful of black residents sent their children
to the public schools because, as Drew reported, "many of the whites
object to having their children sit in the same forms as the colored pupils."

[62] Kennedy, "Northward Bound," 196 (quote); *Kent Advertiser*, August 23, 1849; Peggy
    Bristow, "'Whatever You Raise in the Ground You Can Sell It in Chatham': Black
    Women in Buxton and Chatham, 1850–1865," in Peggy Bristow, ed., *"We're Rooted
    Here and They Can't Pull Up": Essays in African Canadian Women's History* (Toronto:
    University of Toronto Press, 1994), 75–78; Sharon A. Roger Hepburn, "Crossing the
    Border from Slavery to Freedom: The Building of a Community at Buxton, Upper
    Canada," *American Nineteenth Century History* 3, no. 2 (2002): 25–68.

[63] Drew, *A North-Side View*, 118 (first quote); Rev. R. S. W. Sorrick, in ibid., 121 (second
    quote); Edward Patterson, in ibid., 121 (third quote); Williamson Pease, in ibid., 130
    (fourth quote).

Although the schools were legally open to all regardless of color, some of the "lower classes" refused to send their children to school at all if blacks were admitted. Under the circumstances, it was "unpleasant to the colored children to attend the public schools." In the "beautiful farming town" of Colchester, Drew likewise lamented that the school situation for refugees was far from ideal – "sectarianism and prejudice interfere too much." The town clerk told Drew that black residents "ought to be by themselves," adding that "if we try to encourage them, we shall have to mix with them." Although the refugees he spoke to were making an honest living and "improving" themselves in every way possible, he found it a pity that they had "but few friends among the white settlers." Less than a decade, later, Samuel Howe, in his US government report to the Freedmen's Inquiry Commission on the condition of slave refugees in Canada West in 1864, similarly highlighted the *"Prejudice of the Whites against Negroes"* as a defining feature of their lives, lamenting that English Canadians "manifest it just as brutally as Americans do." Howe's report cited several interviews with local citizens and public officials who deemed the presence of African Americans in their communities as regrettable – in the words of one hotel clerk: "Niggers are a damned nuisance."[64]

Unlike in the Northern United States, refugees from slavery were not confronted with race riots and mob violence in Canada. But the cold shoulder they received from white settlers compounded the distrust of white people that they had already developed under slavery. Some individuals fought for the equal treatment accorded to them under British law, but most black communities in the Canadian borderlands simply developed their own institutions and community life. As the mayor of Chatham admitted to representatives of the Freedmen's Inquiry Commission, "The colored people generally live apart," because there had been "a very strong prejudice against them." They established schools and churches, organized their own charity relief, mobilized to engage with the abolitionist cause in the United States, and even published their own newspapers. *The Provincial Freeman*, a black newspaper founded in 1853 by Mary Ann Shadd Carey – a free black woman from Delaware who moved with her family to Canada and became a tireless activist, abolitionist, and advocate of black emigration to Canada West – and co-edited by Samuel Ringgold Ward, a slave refugee from Maryland,

[64] Drew, *A North-Side View*, 147 (first quotes), 368 (second quotes); Howe, *Refugees from Slavery in Canada West*, 37–50, quotes on pp. 37, 39, and 40.

specifically addressed the problems of prejudice and operated under the motto "Self-Reliance is the True Road to Independence." In some of their endeavors black leaders were greatly assisted by white abolitionists, but even then, the institutions they developed were primarily meant to serve the needs of their own community, rather than constitute color-blind alternatives to public institutions per se.[65]

Education – especially learning to read and write – was taken seriously by refugees from slavery, not only as an avenue to self-improvement for themselves and their children, but also as a means of protection from manipulation at the hands of dishonest merchants, land agents, and government officials. It was taken even more seriously because of the widespread prejudice among white Canadians against blacks attending "their" public schools. One refugee from Maryland who ultimately settled in Dresden in 1851 commented to Drew that "there is a great deal of prejudice here. Statements have been made that colored people wished for separate schools; some did ask for them, and so these have been established, although many colored people have prayed against them as an infringement of their rights." Indeed, some sent their children to the public schools anyway; a few went so far as to bring lawsuits against local schools that outright refused admission to black students. William Thompson, who migrated from Virginia and settled in the small settlement of Galt around 1830, told Drew that "when I came here, colored children were not received into the schools. I fought, and fought, and fought, and at last it got to the governor, and the law was declared, that all had equal rights." Despite such cases, however, many leading members of black communities in Canada recognized the need for black newcomers to be educated in a way that catered to their own needs, in a safe and uplifting environment, and expended considerable effort in either petitioning local authorities for separate schools, or establishing educational facilities themselves that would free them from having to suffer white resentment at the public schools. In the latter they were often assisted by white abolitionist sympathizers.[66]

[65] Mayor Cross, of Chatham, quoted in Howe, *Refugees from Slavery in Canada West*, 44 (quote); Jane Rhodes, *Mary Ann Shadd Cary: The Black Press and Protest in the Nineteenth Century* (Bloomington: Indiana University Press, 1998); Jason H. Silverman, "Mary Ann Shadd and the Search for Equality," in Leon Litwack and August Meier, eds., *Black Leaders of the Nineteenth Century* (Urbana: University of Illinois Press, 1991), 87–102.

[66] William Henry Bradley, in Drew, *A North-Side View*, 313 (first quote); William Thompson, in ibid., 137 (second quote); Kennedy, "Northward Bound," 184–203. A member of Parliament from Toronto, the Honorable George Brown, admitted to representatives of the Freedmen's Inquiry Commission in 1864 that when he was candidate for parliament "150 people signed a paper, saying that if I were to agree to urge the

The most prominent and formal of such undertakings were connected to organized black settlements. The British-American Institute at the Dawn settlement for fugitive slaves, established by abolitionist Hiram Wilson and runaway slave Josiah Henson, was a well-known example. The idea for the institute was conceived during a convention for black people in Canada in 1838, when Henson and Wilson proposed establishing a school to provide a means for black refugees and their children to receive not only a basic education (especially reading and writing) but also specialized vocational training in manual labor, such as blacksmithing, millworking, carpentry, various farming skills, and – for girls – the domestic arts. By 1840 they had raised enough money from Quakers in England to purchase 200 acres of wilderness along the Sydenham River for the purpose; the institute formally opened in 1842, and by 1845 it counted some seventy students. Refugees specifically settled in and around Dawn – which in the 1840s and 1850s had some 500 black residents – in order to attend or send their children to the institute. Financial troubles and management difficulties stunted the development of the institute in the late 1840s, and by 1848 Wilson had resigned and moved to St. Catherines, but it continued to function into the 1860s. At the Elgin settlement, the Buxton Mission School fared even better. With more than seventy pupils enrolled in 1852, "and the number ... increasing," the school earned such a reputation for quality teaching that it – quite uniquely – began to attract *white* students, even though it was established specifically for black residents. Black abolitionist William Cooper Nell visited the school and remarked that it "has become so much superior to the one which was mostly attended by white children of Buxton, that the latter has been discontinued, and the school at the Elgin Settlement is attended not only by the children of settlers, but also indiscriminately by the white children of Buxton." By 1854, almost 150 students were enrolled in the school; a separate Sabbath school had been established, attended by another 120 students. The annual report of the directors of the settlement for 1854 proudly proclaimed that "progress has been made in secular and scriptural knowledge." Like Dawn, the Elgin settlement attracted scores of black refugees who specifically

passage of a law that the negro should be excluded from the common schools, and putting a head-taks upon those coming into the country, they would all vote for me; otherwise they would vote for my opponent." See Howe, *Refugees from Slavery in Canada West*, 43.

settled there to send their children to school. Isaac Riley, a runaway from Missouri, had originally settled in St. Catherines, but removed to Buxton when he heard of the Elgin settlement, explaining to Drew that "my children can get good learning here."[67]

Smaller-scale undertakings were far more common throughout the Canadian borderlands, however, and took a variety of forms, from Sunday schools and night schools, to book clubs and even neighborly instruction. Wilson and his wife opened an American Missionary Association night school for refugees from slavery after removing to St. Catherines, providing many newcomers with a Bible and a spelling book upon arrival. In Toronto, black students could be found in the public schools and even at the university, but the black community also established its own lyceum, which was "attended by both sexes" and more closely resembled a debating club or literary society than a formal school, according to Drew. Informal private tutoring and auto-didactic efforts were undertaken by adults who were unable to attend formal schooling or who felt unwelcome at public schools. One refugee and resident of Hamilton, where prejudice put most blacks off from attending formal schooling, told Drew that he was "learning to write" in his own time. Another black settler and preacher claimed that in Oro township the refugees from the United States had "been instructed by the missionaries to read and write." Aby Jones, a runaway from Tennessee who settled in London, claimed that he had never been sent to school but had "learned to read and write" since coming to Canada. Not all had the time or the energy to devote to education, however, and some openly admitted as much in their interviews with Drew. Philip Younger, for example, who was seventy-two years old and had been living in Canada for almost twenty years when Drew interviewed him, and who was by all accounts doing well financially, remarked that looking back on his years in

---

[67] Drew, *A North-Side View*, 310–312; Jason H. Silverman, *Unwelcome Guests: Canada West's Response to American Fugitive Slaves, 1800–1865* (Millwood, NY: Associated Faculty Press, 1985), 63–64; Kennedy, "Northward Bound," 184–203; Jacqueline L. Tobin and Hettie Jones, *From Midnight to Dawn: The Last Tracks of the Underground Railroad* (New York: Doubleday, 2007), 170–171. For the Buxton Mission School, see Hepburn, *Crossing the Border*, 164; William C. Nell, "Impressions and Gleanings of Canada West," *Liberator*, December 24, 1858 (quote); Fifth Annual Report of the Directors of the Elgin Association, September 1854, quoted in Drew, *A North-Side View*, 295 (first quote); Isaac Riley, in Drew, *A North-Side View*, 298 (second quote).

freedom he "suffered from want of education. I manage by skill and experience and industry – but it is as if feeling my way in the dark."[68]

Churches served a central function in virtually all aspects of community self-help, from schooling to poor relief to purchasing land to mobilizing for abolitionist causes in the United States. Although black residents in Canada were not formally excluded from any churches, and a number of white Quakers set up missionary organizations and Sunday schools to specifically assist refugees from slavery, black communities in Canada also pooled together to establish their own churches and congregations. St. Catherines in the 1850s, for example, not only had a Sunday school for refugees run by the tireless Quaker abolitionist Hiram Wilson and his wife, but also a separate Methodist church where many black residents worshiped. In Toronto there were three black churches – one Baptist and two Methodist. London had a Baptist and Methodist church "exclusively for colored people," although, according to one resident, "colored people attend at every church in London." Organized communities such as Buxton's Elgin settlement and the Dawn settlement constructed their own meeting houses for their members. Sandwich had separate churches for refugees from the United States, including worship services held by the Refugees' Home Society. The black community at Amherstburg established First Baptist Church, attended by more than 100 worshippers. So it was throughout the borderlands.[69]

By the 1850s black residents in townships across Canada were formally mobilizing to advance and defend their interests. True Band Associations, the first of which was founded in Malden in 1854 and within a year had mushroomed into fourteen across Canada West, were perhaps the most active and committed self-help organizations established by and for black refugees from the United States in the years just before the outbreak of the Civil War. Drew first learned about these associations while visiting Chatham, a town where he claimed black residents suffered

---

[68] Tobin and Jones, *From Midnight to Dawn*, 170–171; Drew, *A North-Side View*, 94–95 (first quote); Henry Williamson, in ibid., 135 (second quote); Rev. R. S. W. Sorrick, in ibid., 120 (quote); Philip Younger, in ibid., 251 (third quote).

[69] For St. Catherines, see James Adams, in Drew, *A North-Side View*, 28. For Toronto, see Drew, ibid., 94. For London, see John Holmes, in ibid., 173 (quote). For Elgin and Dawn, see Drew, ibid., 294 and 311. For Sandwich, see Drew, ibid., 342, and David Cooper, in ibid., 335. For Amherstburg, see Rev. William Troy, in ibid., 355. See also Adrienne Shadd, "Extending the Right Hand of Fellowship: Sandwich Baptist Church, Amherstburg First Baptist, and the Amherstburg Baptist Association," in Karolyn Smardz Frost and Veta S. Tucker, eds., *A Fluid Frontier: Slavery, Resistance, and the Underground Railroad in the Detroit River Borderland* (Detroit, MI: Wayne State University Press, 2016), 120–132.

from prejudice and where whites complained about black "sauciness." The refugee population wasted little time in establishing its own institutions – "they maintain separate churches, and attend a separate public school," according to Drew – but they also established an overarching association that effectively served as a mutual aid society and even informal government. Of the 800 total black residents in Chatham, including children, 375 were paying members of the local True Band, which Drew described as follows:

A True Band is composed of colored persons of both sexes, associated for their own improvement. Its objects are manifold: mainly these: – the members are to take a general interest in each other's welfare; to pursue such plans and objects as may be for their mutual advantage; to improve all schools, and to induce their race to send their children into the schools; to break down all prejudice; to bring all churches as far as possible into one body, and not let minor differences divide them; to prevent litigation by referring all disputes among themselves to a committee; to stop the begging system entirely; (that is, going to the United States, and there by representing that the fugitives are starving and suffering, raising large sums of money, of which the fugitives never receive the benefit, – misrepresenting the character of the fugitives for industry, and underrating the advance of the country, which supplies abundant work for all at fair wages;) to raise such funds among themselves as may be necessary for the poor, the sick, and the destitute fugitive newly arrived; and to prepare themselves ultimately to bear their due weight of political power.

It is clear that True Bands arose at least in part out of a distrust of the white population of Canada, as many of their aims focused specifically on grievances that they had suffered at the hands of whites – including prejudice in local schools and the widely reported "begging scams" whereby people posed as abolitionists went around the borderlands (in Canada and the United States) collecting money for refugees and then made off with the money.[70]

By contrast, self-help organizations and formal mobilization for the advancement of black refugees' education and mutual interests were nonexistent in Mexico. Indeed, although sources are extremely limited, self-segregation appears to have barely been an issue among runaways in Mexico, many of whom succeeded in integrating with the local population, overcoming formidable barriers of language and faith to do so. Part of the explanation must lie in the less rigid attitudes of Mexicans toward race and their relatively welcoming attitudes toward African Americans. In the

[70] Drew, in *A North-Side View*, 235–236; Michael Hembree, "The Question of 'Begging': Fugitive Slave Relief in Canada, 1830–1865," *Civil War History* 37, no. 4 (1991): 314–327; Kennedy, "Northward Bound," 174–175.

wake of the Texan Revolution, Mexican public opinion on slavery became ever more closely intertwined with anti-US sentiment, and the country's abolition of slavery and free soil policy became increasingly viewed as evidence of Mexico's moral superiority over slaveholding Texas and the United States. The Mexican press continually denounced slavery and the oppression of African Americans north of the border. Although formal abolitionist organizations to assist black refugees from the United States and Texas were virtually absent in Mexico, locals across the borderlands and down the Gulf Coast appear not to have shunned or protested their arrival, as they often did in Canada, and the Mexican press generally approved of the government's policy of accepting freedom seekers from the US South.[71]

Indeed, black refugees in Mexico were generally spared significant objections to either their presence or their social integration, save for the ire some aroused who engaged in illegal smuggling or horse rustling, as stated above. Contrasting Benjamin Drew's scathing descriptions of racial prejudice in Canada West, travel narratives from Mexico provide interesting references to runaways' *inclusion* in Mexican society. During a visit to Mexico's Gulf Coast on the eve of the US Civil War, for example, ethnologist Edward Taylor spoke to a former Texan slave named Sam, who told him that refugees from the United States often intermarried with local Mexicans and European immigrants. Olmsted spoke to a runaway slave in Piedras Negras who "could speak Spanish fluently" and "had joined the Catholic True Church." The refugee further claimed that Mexican women made "much" of African-American men – meaning that male newcomers were popular with local women – and that most newcomers settled into their new communities relatively quickly, learning the language and marrying into Mexican families, including prominent ones. Even in the sparse established free black communities, such as that of the Black Seminoles in Coahuila – which most resembled self-segregated black settlements in Canada – residents intermingled with Mexicans, eventually converted to Catholicism, and Hispanicized their names.[72]

That is not to suggest that all runaways adapted so quickly or even wanted to integrate into Mexican society. There were surely exceptions.

[71] Mareite, "Conditional Freedom," 163–164; Nichols, "The Limits of Liberty," 71–72. For examples of positive Mexican press coverage of the republic's asylum policy for runaway slaves from the United States, see, for example, *El Indicador*, February 23, 1846; *El Siglo XIX*, November 21, 1850 and January 1, 1851.

[72] Mareite, "Conditional Freedom," 175–177; Edward Taylor, *Anahuac: Or Mexico and the Mexicans, Ancient and Modern* (London: Longman, Green, Longman & Roberts, 1861), 36, 307–308; Olmsted, *A Journey through Texas*, 324–325 (quotes).

Some runaways indeed appear to have sought to settle together in the hinterlands rather than within established Mexican communities. Whether they did so because they felt uncomfortable in Mexican towns, or distrusted their Mexican neighbors, or feared slave catchers in border communities, the existence of isolated runaway encampments is reported in some travel narratives from the late antebellum period. Olmsted reported the existence of a "gang of runaways" that had "settled together within a few days' walk of Eagle Pass." Tellingly, he noted that the newcomers were "not generally able to speak Spanish," and that their refusal to establish networks and connections within Mexico left them isolated and impoverished – in his words the runaways were "in a more wretched and desperate condition than any others."[73]

Scholars such as Sarah Cornell have emphasized, moreover, that African-American newcomers *were* subject to a certain degree of discrimination as "a sometimes-racialized other in Mexico." Cornell warns that interpretations of Mexican society as welcoming and inclusive may be overstated. Discrimination was especially evident in legal procedures aimed at acquiring official residency – a view broadly shared by other scholars, as will be discussed below – but to a lesser extent also in African-Americans' attempts at acquiring "cultural citizenship." Black newcomers had clear imperatives to want to integrate into Mexican society upon arrival, whether through conversion, marriage, employment, or other means. Their vulnerability as refugees – who often arrived with few or no contacts or resources – rendered the establishment of networks and acceptance by locals essential to their successful navigation of Mexican free soil. According to Cornell, however, "Mexican racism posed a significant challenge to black claims of social and cultural belonging." In border communities, especially, tensions about the influx of black refugees from the United States began to rise in the 1850s. In 1855, residents of Tamaulipas even petitioned the government to extradite fugitive slaves (unsuccessfully). While such incidents were relatively rare, they do indicate that social integration was a more complicated affair than more optimistic accounts of Mexico's racial fluidity would suggest.[74]

---

[73] Olmsted, *A Journey through Texas*, 326 (quotes). Thomas Mareite recently argued that some runaways "formed new beacons of freedom for themselves from scratch, especially in the northeastern borderlands." See Mareite, "Conditional Freedom," 179–180.

[74] Cornell, "Citizens of Nowhere," 351 (first and second quotes), 354 (third quote), 366–374; Paul Foos, *A Short, Offhand, Killing Affair: Soldiers and Social Conflict during the Mexican-American War* (Chapel Hill: University of North Carolina Press, 2002), 146;

EXTRADITION AND REENSLAVEMENT

Runaways' acceptance – or lack thereof – by receiving societies could have important consequences for their risk of extradition and reenslavement. Well-connected refugees in both Canada and Mexico were simply better insulated from slave catchers than were isolated newcomers. They also had better access to legal recourse in the event of a dispute regarding their status or residence on foreign soil. Crucially, however, social integration was far more important for slave refugees in Mexico – where legal residence and protection from slave catchers often depended on the actions and cooperation of local communities and officials – than it was in Canada, where the safety of black newcomers was more secure, despite widespread prejudice.

As in the Northern United States, refugees from slavery in Canada were well connected with the abolitionist cause, but unlike in the Northern United States, they rarely had to mobilize or engage legal counsel to prevent extradition or rendition to slavery. As argued in Chapter 1, those in Upper Canada (where the vast majority settled) found themselves in a part of the continent where the government refused to extradite freedom seekers from as early as the late eighteenth century, eventually coming to interpret the 1772 Somerset case in England as applying to Canada as well. By the 1820s and 1830s British free soil was unequivocally understood as a space of formal freedom for fugitive slaves, where no fugitive slave laws or extradition treaties could reach them. Although refugees in Canada were legally quite safe from reenslavement, however, it is important to acknowledge that the extradition "issue" continued to flare up throughout the antebellum period, as angry American slaveholders and governments demanded a return of their valuable human property. The difference with the Northern United States is that in Canada they only succeeded once – and even then only because the runaway was accused of a crime in the United States, not because he had fled slavery. The British were under no legal obligation to acknowledge slaveholders' "right" to reclaim runaway slaves on their soil. Indeed, they were prohibited from doing so.[75]

Rosalie Schwartz, *Across the Rio to Freedom: US Negroes in Mexico* (El Paso: Texas Western Press, 1975), 45.

[75] Brown, *Moral Capital*, 78, 96–98; Barker, "Revisiting 'British Principle Talk,'" 34–69; Don E. Fehrenbacher and Ward M. McAfee, *The Slaveholding Republic: An Account of the United States Government's Relations to Slavery* (New York: Oxford University

Southern slaveholders did *try* to recover fugitive slaves in Canada. As early as the 1790s, in the wake of the American Revolution, in the wake of the War of 1812, and well into the 1820s, southerners implored the federal government to negotiate an extradition treaty with British officials in London and in Upper Canada for the recovery of fugitive slaves. In 1819, when Secretary of State John Quincy Adams was charged with negotiating one such extradition arrangement with Britain, the impetus was a vocal group of Tennessee slaveholders who had recently "lost" their slaves to Canada, the latter having taken refuge in Malden. Adams failed, as did his successors in the 1820s. Petitions by the US ambassador in London were repeatedly rejected or shelved. In 1826, a renewed attempt to secure a treaty with Great Britain failed, the main US negotiator Albert Gallatin writing back to Washington that "it was utterly impossible for them to agree to a stipulation for the surrender of fugitive slaves." By 1829, American officials had begun to give up that they would ever secure any such treaty with the British. Martin Van Buren, then serving as Secretary of State, wrote in a letter to a colleague that an "arrangement" by which "the surrender of fugitive slaves … taking refuge in the neighbouring Provinces" seemed "a little doubtful," considering "the entire failure of the repeated efforts which were made by the late Administration of this Government to effect that object."[76]

As the federal government failed to arrange any type of formal treaty with Great Britain for the return of runaway slaves in Canada, slaveholders took matters into their own hands and petitioned the government of Upper Canada directly. In each case, they employed a clever strategy: they petitioned for the return of runaway slaves whom they charged with having committed some kind of crime. In other words, they petitioned for the extradition of *criminals*, rather than runaway slaves, at least in a legal sense. In 1833 Upper Canada enacted the Fugitive Offenders Act, which allowed for the extradition of individuals charged with "Murder, Forgery, Larceny or other crime." This became the loophole through which slaveholders hoped to recover fugitive slaves living in Canada. The Fugitive

---

Press, 2001), 91–98; Kennedy, "Northward Bound," 254–267; Kathryn Smardz Frost, *I've Got a Home in Glory Land: A Lost Tale of the Underground Railroad* (New York: Farrar, Strauss, and Giroux, 2007), ch. 11.

[76] Fehrenbacher and McAfee, *The Slaveholding Republic*, 93–98, 102–103; Communication of Albert Gallatin, cited in Howe, *Refugees from Slavery in Canada West*, 13 (first quote); Martin Van Buren to W. T. Barry, August 12, 1829, cited in Kennedy, "Northward Bound," 256–257 (second quote).

Offenders Act was tested several times – unsuccessfully – during the 1830s. In 1834, for example, a runaway from Virginia named Abraham Johnson was accused of having stolen his master's horse, but the Executive Council of Upper Canada denied the request for extradition. More publicized and controversial was the 1837 case of Solomon Moseby and Jesse Happy, two runaways from Kentucky who also stole their masters' horses in order to effect their escape to Niagara. The Executive Council turned down the request to extradite Happy, citing insufficient grounds to indict, as Happy had written to his master and informed him where the horse was. Moseby had sold the horse, however, and the council agreed to extradite him to stand trial. In a scene that very much resembled a fugitive slave rescue in the Northern United States, black residents in Canada mobilized to save Moseby from reenslavement. Several hundreds gathered around the jail where he was being held and demanded his release. When the crowd eventually rushed to the jail, police and soldiers opened fire, killing two and wounding one. Moseby escaped in the chaos, fleeing to Toronto and subsequently to England.[77]

The Moseby case demonstrated that the refugee population in Canada would go to great lengths and mobilize to protect any members of their community from extradition to the United States – which by extension threatened their own freedom and safety. It also scared them into active political participation in their host society. In 1839 black activists met in London to draft a petition that would formally protect refugees in Upper Canada from extradition to the United States. Residents of Upper Canada themselves wrote letters and held public meetings in which they underscored their status as equal subjects of the British Crown and deserving of the protection of the metropole – appealing to "metropolitan whites' self-image as benevolent emancipators," according to Ikuko Asaka.

---

[77] Legislature of Upper Canada, "An Act to Provide for the Apprehending of Fugitive Offenders from Foreign Countries, and Delivering Them Up to Justice" (1833); David Murray, *Colonial Justice: Justice, Morality, and Crime in the Niagara District, 1791–1849* (Toronto: University of Toronto Press, 2002), 118; Frost, "Forging Transnational Networks for Freedom," in Frost and Tucker, eds., *A Fluid Frontier*, 53–58; Bradley Miller, *Borderline Crime: Fugitive Criminals and the Challenge of the Border, 1819–1914* (Toronto: University of Toronto Press, 2016), 118; Jason H. Silverman, "Kentucky, Canada, and Extradition: The Jesse Happy Case," *Filson Club History Quarterly* 54 (1980): 50–60; David Murray, "Hands across the Border: The Abortive Extradition of Solomon Moseby," *Canadian Review of American Studies* 3, no. 2 (2000): 187–209; Kennedy, "Northward Bound," 257–259.

The British government ignored their calls, however, and never pledged to enact any additional protections for slave refugees in Canada.[78]

Black newcomers' fear of extradition and reenslavement truly reached fever pitch with the Nelson Hackett case of 1841, the only case in which a runaway slave was indeed extradited and sent back into slavery from Canadian soil. During his escape from Arkansas, Hackett had stolen his owner's horse, gold watch, and an expensive beaver topcoat. Months later his master discovered him living in Chatham and had him arrested for theft. In December 1841, Sir Charles Bagot, Governor-General of Upper Canada, approved the extradition request because of the gold watch, which, according to Bagot, exceeded what was necessary for Hackett to effect his escape. As British diplomat Lord Ashburton later explained to American abolitionist Lewis Tappan, "had he only taken the horse ... he would not probably have been surrendered, for you know the horse was necessary for his escape." The watch, however, was simply theft. Hackett was sent back to slavery in Arkansas, from where he was sold to Texas. African Americans on both sides of the US-Canadian border were appalled. The *National Anti-Slavery Standard* warned that the case set "a most dangerous and alarming precedent."[79]

Only months later the issue of extradition resurfaced in the Webster-Ashton Treaty, signed between Great Britain and the United States in 1842. The treaty settled several outstanding border disputes between Canada and the United States, but it also revised the conditions of criminal extradition. Article 10 of the treaty specified that henceforth extradition would only be approved for "the crime of murder, or assault with intent to commit murder, or piracy, or arson, or robbery, or forgery, of the utterance of forged paper." It made no mention of fugitive slaves living in Canada – nor, for that matter, did it mention the recent mutiny on board the slave trading vessel the *Creole*, which had resulted in the liberation and protection of most of the enslaved in the British Bahamas – and US negotiators agreed not to press the issue. The revised conditions were not tested until 1860, when the final extradition case of a runaway

[78] Ikuko Asaka, "'Our Brethren in the West Indies': Self-Emancipated People in Canada and the Antebellum Politics of Diaspora and Empire," *Journal of African American History* 97, no. 3 (2012): 219–220, 223 (quote); Kennedy, "Northward Bound," 256–263.

[79] Bryan Prince, "The Illusion of Safety: Attempts to Extradite Fugitive Slaves from Canada," in Frost and Tucker, eds., *A Fluid Frontier*, 67–80; "Editorial Summary," *Philanthropist*, January 11, 1843; Lewis Tappan, "Interview with Lord Ashburton," *Liberator*, September 16, 1842 (first quote); "The Governor of Canada," *National Anti-Slavery Standard*, September 1, 1842 (second quote).

in Canada came before the courts. The case revolved around one John Anderson, who had fled from Missouri in 1853 with the aim of reaching Canada. During his escape he had been discovered and pursued by a white farmer, whom he had stabbed to death in an altercation. Anderson successfully reached Canada and lived in relative security for six years, but he was arrested in 1860 threatened with extradition on the grounds that he was charged with murder in the United States. His extradition request was approved, but, in another episode that recalled similar fugitive slave activism in the Northern United States, a crowd of black residents and white abolitionists assembled in Toronto to protest the extradition. Under sustained pressure, British officials eventually freed Anderson on a technicality.[80]

Refugees from slavery who settled in British Canada therefore enjoyed considerable protection from formal extradition and reenslavement, with only one documented case of a slave being legally returned to the South in the antebellum period. Refugees in Canada remained vulnerable to reenslavement in two ways, however. First, they could be kidnapped by slave catchers or ruffians, and returned to the United States. Although it is impossible to confirm how often this actually occurred, a handful of attempted kidnappings were reported. During his travels through the border region in the late 1820s, William Lyon Mackenzie reported two such incidents: one involving a girl in Queenstown who was seized "in broad daylight ... by two hired scoundrels," who accused her of having stolen $500 and forced her onto a ferry to the United States; and another involving a man who was seized "by a band of slaveholding ruffians from the south, and conveyed across the Niagara River gagged and pinioned." The second man managed to escape and return to the Canadian side. By the 1830s such cases were exceedingly rare, however, as the growth of black communities and abolitionism in Upper Canada created a hostile environment to would-be abductors. Indeed, one case reported in the *Buffalo Daily Gazette* in 1843 described an incident during which slave catchers in pursuit of two runaways in Sandwich were "met by a mob [of]

---

[80] Prince, "The Illusion of Safety," 71; Fehrenbacher and McAfee, *The Slaveholding Republic*, 108–109; Robin W. Winks, *The Blacks in Canada: A History* (Montreal: McGill-Queen's University Press, 1971), 172–173; Thomas Clarkson, "Ashburton Treaty: The Tenth Article," *British and Foreign Anti-Slavery Reporter*, November 2, 1842; Jeffrey Kerr-Ritchie, *Rebellious Passage: The Creole Revolt and America's Coastal Slave Trade* (New Yok: Cambridge University Press, 2019); Kennedy, "Northward Bound," 257–267; Jeannine Marie DeLombard, "Making Waves on the Black Atlantic: The Case of John Anderson," *Slavery & Abolition* 33, no. 2 (2012): 191–204.

armed runaway negroes and severely beaten, being forced to return without their property."[81]

Second, runaways living in Canada could be seized crossing the border back into the United States, which, although rare, did sometimes occur at both the Detroit–Windsor border as well as the Niagara region. The main purpose for dangerously returning to the United States was to rescue loved ones still in slavery, or engage help in rescuing loved ones still in slavery. Indeed, like their counterparts in the Northern United States, many slave refugees in Canada testified that their separation from wives, children, other family members, and friends in the South constituted a source of overwhelming and lasting anguish. Henry Atkinson, a refugee from Virginia who was interviewed by Benjmain Drew in St. Catherines in 1855, became emotional when he mentioned having left his wife and baby, explaining that he "never expect to see her again in this world – nor our child." Drew wrote an aside in brackets: "[Here Atkinson's eyes filled with tears.]" David West, another refugee in St. Catherines, left behind a wife and four children when he fled, admitting to Drew that his "family are perpetually on my mind. I should be perfectly happy if I could have my wife and the four children." It was not uncommon for recent arrivals in Canada to immediately go about making plans to have friends and loved ones join them. Most did so by writing letters, or having letters written for them, to abolitionists in the United States. The correspondence of the VCP contains some illuminating examples. One man named John Hill, who had fled from Virginia to Hamilton and subsequently worked as an agent of the VCP to "receive" refugees in Canada, wrote to William Still in 1856, imploring him to arrange for a friend to be rescued from Petersburg: "Kind Sir, as all of us is concerned about the welfare of our enslaved brethren at the South, particularly our friends, we appeal to you your sympathy to do whatever is in your power to save poor Willis Johnson from the hands of his cruel master." Another refugee from Maryland sent a letter from St. Catherines addressed directly to his wife (which was unable to be delivered), explaining his sorrow at having hastily left her and beseeching her to come to Canada, writing "don't be Descurredged[,] I was sory to leave you . . . you must not think that I did

---

[81] William L. Mackenzie, *Sketches of Canada and the United States* (London: Effingham Wilson, 1833), 21–23 (first quotes); *Buffalo Daily Gazette*, August 19, 1843 (second quote); Kennedy, "Northward Bound," 266–267. See also reports of kidnapping in the *National Anti-Slavery Standard*, April 5, 1856; and the *Anti-Slavery Bugle*, April 22, 1857.

not care for you ... Do not Bee afraid to come But start and keep trying ... and I will take care of you and treat you like a lady ..."[82]

Others, however, more daringly crossed back into the United States to arrange for family reunification, or were duped into doing so. The case of Henry Goings, who penned his own story without the help of abolitionists during the Civil War, serves as an illuminating example. Goings was born in Virginia but had been sold and forcibly migrated all over the South before finally fleeing from Alabama as a young man in the 1840s. He crossed into Canada from Michigan, settled in Chatham, and gained employment on the steamers that plied the River Thames and the lakes. Only a month after his arrival, Goings formed an acquaintance with a free black Canadian, who disingenuously duped Goings into giving him $150 to travel back to Alabama to recover his wife. When the man finally arrived back in Chatham six months later, he told Goings "that he had fetched my wife to a town which was about a day's travel from Detroit. She was taken sick and could travel no further," and Goings was summoned to travel with the man back across the border to see her. Instead of crossing directly at Detroit, the man led Goings through a complicated detour, landing him eventually at Perrysburg, Ohio, where he was met not by his wife but by the constable, who promptly arrested him as a fugitive slave. The entire plan had been a trap. Luckily for Goings, the Perrysburg community rallied to his defense and secured a capable lawyer for him, who successfully convinced the magistrate that the constable had no federal jurisdiction to arrest fugitive slaves. The case ended in a "nonsuit," and before it could be appealed, Goings was shuttled back to Canada.[83]

Cases like these were surely exceptional, but they also underscore the extent to which refugees in Canada lived with one foot still in the United States. With friends and family members still living in southern slavery, a fiery commitment to abolition, and strong connections and working relationships with abolitionists in the Northern United States (who aided runaways in reaching Canada in the first place), many runaway slaves in Canada resembled political exiles rather than immigrants. Some scholars

---

[82] Henry Atkinson, in Drew, *A North-Side View*, 81–82 (quote); David West, in ibid., 88–89 (first quote); John H. Hill to Wm. Still, September 15, 1856, reprinted in Still, *The Underground Railroad*, 41 (second quote); James Massey to Wife, April 24, 1857, reprinted in ibid., 143–144 (third quotes).

[83] Henry Goings, *Rambles of a Runaway from Southern Slavery*, ed. Calvin Shermerhorn, Michael Plunkett, and Edward Gaynor (Charlottesville: University of Virginia Press, 2012), 48–54, 49 (quote).

have indeed dubbed them "trans-border citizens" or "continental abolitionists." Their trans-border orientation is most evident in their involvement with the abolitionist movement, which was focused on liberating
their homeland from the oppressive institution that had forced them to
flee and that still held their loved ones in bondage. Some of the most
prominent refugee activists in Canada, including figures like Henry Bibb
and Harriet Tubman, crossed and recrossed the border several times in
their efforts to assist other runaways, coordinate with abolitionists in the
United States, participate in abolitionist lecture circuits, and – in the case
of Tubman – "rescue" enslaved people in the South. Abolitionist organizations that included or were initiated by slave refugees sprang up across
the Canadian borderlands as early as the 1820s. Black residents in
Windsor set up an antislavery organization in 1827 that collaborated
with (and was eventually eclipsed by) partner organizations across the
river in Detroit. The most active organizations were established in the
1850s, however, when the Fugitive Slave Law sent thousands of refugees
northward bound to British free soil. The biracial Anti-Slavery Society of
Canada was founded in Toronto in 1851, with Henry Bibb on its executive board, committed itself to "the extinction of Slavery" by means of
"tracts, newspapers, lectures, and correspondence, and by manifesting
sympathy with the houseless and homeless victims of Slavery flying to our
soil." Local chapters and similar antislavery organizations were established throughout the borderlands, and were well connected with abolitionist organizations in the United States. Bibb himself founded the black
newspaper the *Voice of the Fugitive* from his home base in Sandwich in
1851, which advocated "the immediate and unconditional abolition of
chattel slavery everywhere, but especially on American soil." The newspaper was distributed throughout Canada West but also in many
Northern US states, including Michigan, Ohio, Pennsylvania, and New
York. By the 1850s black abolitionists in Canada – most of them refugees
from slavery – were so thoroughly embedded in the abolitionist activism
of their neighbors in the Northern United States that they held joint
meetings and conventions, and even hosted John Brown in 1858 to
develop strategies for the raid on Harpers Ferry that would ultimately
spark the Civil War.[84]

[84] Tobin and Jones, *From Midnight to Dawn*, 181; Winks, *The Blacks in Canada*, 253–267;
Catherine Clinton, *Harriet Tubman: The Road to Freedom* (New York: Little, Brown and
Company, 2004); *Constitution and By-Laws of the Anti-Slavery Society of Canada*
(Toronto: George Brown, "Globe" Office, 1851), 3–5 (first quote); Henry Bibb, in

Slave refugees in Mexico were more vulnerable to recapture and reen-slavement than their counterparts in British Canada, despite finding themselves on free soil and under the jurisdiction of a national govern-ment that purported to refuse their extradition. To be sure, runaway slaves in Mexico enjoyed far greater protection – both legally and prac-tically – than did runaways in, for example, the Northern United States. But in Mexico the fugitive slave issue was complicated by two important factors that were virtually absent in other spaces of formal freedom such as Canada. First, the poorly guarded border between Mexico and Texas facilitated regular illegal slave-catching raids. Second, male runaways' ambiguous legal status as protected refugees from slavery but also undocumented immigrants set limits to their "freedom" in Mexico, and made them vulnerable to potential harassment and prosecution by local authorities.

The practical enforcement of Mexico's official free soil policy – announced in 1829 and further cemented in the Constitution of 1857 – was undermined by illegal incursions into Mexican territory by slave catchers out to recover runaway slaves. As James David Nichols has forcefully argued, the international border could prove to be a swinging door for fugitive slaves. Nichols underscores that "Mexican law and even the loftiest principles espoused by the independent government [of Mexico] could be abjured through simple force majeure." The porous and poorly guarded border that facilitated southbound slave flight also facilitated organized raids by slaveholders and reward-seeking bounty hunters, many of which even included the assistance of hired Mexican nationals. The extent of the problem is illustrated in the efforts of federal and local authorities to combat abductions of African Americans throughout the borderlands. Local authorities were most active in attempting to combat illegal slave-raiding in their communities, often pursuing both foreigners and Mexicans who carried out or assisted in attempted abductions, as well as providing overt support to slave refugees when danger lurked. When Manuel Flores, a head official in the munici-pality of Guerrero, heard that a local African American (referred to as "Manuel" in the records) had been abducted by a Texas slaveholder named James Bartlett in 1851, and was being dragged back to Texas roped behind Bartlett's horse, for example, Flores immediately mobilized three volunteers to go after them. In a tense confrontation, Bartlett

Voice of the Fugitive, January 1, 1851 (second quote); Kennedy, "Northward Bound," 276–292.

refused to surrender, and the Mexicans fatally shot him through the chest, saving Manuel from reenslavement. The incident generated widespread attention in both the northern and southern US press, with northern abolitionists hailing it as a sign of Mexican commitment to liberty and southerners denouncing it as murder. For Flores and other Mexican officials, however, such actions were necessary to defend free soil and protect African Americans from would-be kidnappers. Indeed, local authorities also often prosecuted Mexican collaborators who were hired by slaveholders to help track down runaways. In 1855 two Mexicans in Guerrero were prosecuted for trying to forcibly carry two runaway slaves back across the river to Texas. In Matamoros in 1859 two brothers similarly received four-year prison sentences for conspiring to abduct a runaway slave and return him to slavery, having been hired to do so by a slaveholder in Texas.[85]

Local officials' attempts to combat abductions and illegal incursions into Mexican territory by slave catchers were often supported or even instigated by their counterparts at the state level, especially in Nuevo León y Coahuila. In 1859, for example, the state government of Nuevo León y Coahuila reminded its *alcaldes* (mayors) to enforce the free soil provision in the Mexican constitution and recommended severe punishments for Mexican residents who served as accomplices in such crimes, including the seizure and sale of their properties, the proceeds of which could then be reserved for future rescue missions. State authorities also consistently reminded American settlers who sought permission to immigrate to the northern borderlands of Mexico's free soil policy and warned that any African-American laborers who worked on their farms and ranches would be legally free. Finally, state officials demonstrated a commitment to protecting refugees from slavery by helping to coordinate and effect the evacuation and resettlement of African Americans deemed to be at risk of abduction. In 1846, for example, a hotly pursued runaway from Texas reached Laredo and was removed to Mier (Tamaulipas), further from the border, at the behest of state officials. On a larger scale, state officials proved critical in the removal of runaway slaves who were living in northern and central Coahuila to the southern part of the state in 1859, when local authorities sounded the alarm after military personnel learned

---

[85] Nichols, "Freedom Interrupted," 251–274, 252 (quote); Nichols, *The Limits of Liberty*, 147–169; Mareite, "Conditional Freedom," 186–190; Cornell, "Citizens of Nowhere," 353. For the James Bartlett case, see also *Galveston Weekly News*, May 6, 1851, TRSP; *The Texas Monument*, April 23, 1851, TRSP; *Anti-Slavery Bugle*, May 31, 1851.

of a large posse gathering at San Antonio with the intention of crossing the border and abducting African Americans. Fearing an incident that might provoke a border war, state officials ordered and helped coordinate the relocation of the African Americans to the towns of Parras and Múzquiz, further from the border.[86]

At the federal level, abductions sometimes resulted in military actions and official diplomatic complaints, as they constituted breaches of Mexican territorial sovereignty, an issue of particular sensitivity in the wake of the Mexican–American War of 1846–1848. Raids and abductions strained relations between the two countries and contributed to dangerously rising tensions in the 1850s, and military force was mobilized on numerous occasions to protect border communities from invasions. In 1859, when reports that more than 400 Americans were preparing to cross the border to abduct black residents from a settlement near San Fernando de Rosas, for example, the army quickly mobilized all local citizens between the ages of sixteen and sixty and defended the border against the invaders. Mexican diplomatic officials openly confronted their counterparts in Washington when abductions involved the participation of the US military. When a slave refugee named Antonio was captured by four US soldiers and with the assistance of three Mexican peasants in 1850, for example, Mexico's foreign minister demanded an explanation from the US government. The Americans dismissed the case as a private matter, however, despite the involvement of army personnel. US representatives in Mexico and the US government in general expressed little concern about slave-raiding in the borderlands or even further into Mexican territory, even when they involved US soldiers.[87]

To a certain extent, illegal incursions into Mexican territory to locate and remit – by force – runaway slaves after Texan annexation in 1845 were the result of repeated failures by both the Texan and the US governments to adequately prevent slave flight or secure an extradition treaty with the Mexican national government. In 1833 the Mexican government officially refused to extradite fugitive slaves, and it never altered its stance in the following decades, much to the chagrin of southern slaveholders, who often blamed their own governments for their

---

[86] The correspondence between various local officials in Northern Mexico – from the state government to the mayors, and among state officials themselves – reveals volumes on this topic. For an analysis of these sources and this topic, see Mareite, "Conditional Freedom," 187–189.

[87] Mareite, "Conditional Freedom," 186; Nichols, "Freedom Interrupted," 267–269.

losses. Indeed, one particularly disaffected planter addressed a crowd in Texas in 1858 and publicly blamed the federal government in Washington for the recent deaths of three slave catchers in Mexico, "valiant and worthy young men" who were "murdered and robbed in cold blood, while in pursuit of runaway slaves," an incident that would never have happened if Washington had succeeded in enacting some kind of extradition treaty with Mexico. The planter lamented that the "present fugitive slave law will not act in foreign governments in obtaining our rights and our property," and that Washington's failure had left Texan slaveholders particularly vulnerable to the free soil policies of their southern neighbors. His frustrations were shared by slaveholders across the state and the broader South.[88]

Influential slaveholders and private citizens exerted considerable pressure on state and national governments to secure the legal remission of fugitive slaves in Mexico, starting with the short-lived period of Texan independence. Texan President Mirabeau Lamar received petitions in 1840 from slaveholders who complained that their attempts at recovering runaways across the border were repeatedly frustrated by local authorities, and that only a demand from "the highest authority of the Government" would have any chance of alleviating the problem. In 1841, citizens of San Antonio similarly addressed the Texas Senate, complaining of constant streams of runaways crossing into Mexico. In 1843 newspapers such as the *Independent Chronicle* (based in Galveston) called on government to negotiate for the mutual restitution of criminals with Mexico, including peons and slaves. The period of Texan independence was too volatile for the government to negotiate effectively with the Mexican national government, however, and so citizens' requests for formal extradition of runaways generally went nowhere until after Texan annexation to the United States in 1845.[89]

The issue was given added impulse and urgency during and after the Mexican–American War of 1846–1848, which was at least partly

---

[88] Henderson McBride Pridgen, *Address to the People of Texas, on the Protection of Slave Property* (Austin, TX: n.p., 1859), 13 (first quote), 10 (second quote); *San Antonio Herald*, December 15, 1857; Mareite, "Conditional Freedom," 203–204; Cornell, "Citizens of Nowhere," 353.

[89] Silvanus Hatch to Pres. Lamar, May 5, 1840, cited in Charles Adam Gulick, Winnie Allen, Katherine Elliott, and Harriet Smither, eds., *The Papers of Mirabeau Buonaparte Lamar*, vol. 5 (Austin, TX: Pemberton Press, 1968), 426 (first quote); Joseph Milton Nance, *After San Jacinto: The Texas-Mexican Frontier, 1836–1841* (Austin: University of Texas Press, 1963), 472–473; *Independent Chronicle*, October 15, 1843.

justified by expansionists in the South as a means of securing slavery amidst rising sectional tensions. During the war, dozens of African-American slaves brought to the border by the invading US army effected their escape into Mexico, further incensing southern slaveholders. One journalist claimed that for troops stationed across from Matamoros, there was "great difficulty in keeping the slaves upon this river," while an army captain lamented that "several slaves belong to officers [had] left their masters and gone over to Matamoros." Indeed, many runaways joined the Mexican army and fought against the United States in the invasions of Monterrey and Veracruz, a curiosity seized upon in the US southern press and testimonies of soldiers. Jacob Oswandel, recounting the invasion of Veracruz and the capture of 6,000 prisoners, commented that "some were real negroes." After the capitulation of Monterrey in September 1846, one Texas soldier even recognized his own former slave, now a captain in the Mexican army, and attempted to seize him (unsuccessfully).[90]

The war not only compounded the fugitive slave problem in the borderlands, but also emboldened southern slaveholders, writers, and politicians – especially those from Texas – to demand formal rendition arrangements with Mexico. Throughout the 1850s, calls for increased security of slave property in Texas reached fever pitch. The Texas state legislature passed regular resolutions urging its federal representatives in Washington to press for an extradition treaty. Newspaper editors demanded the return of runaway slaves, underscoring that the absence of such a treaty would lead to the economic ruin of Texas and the South. *The Texas State Times* estimated that Mexican free soil had already cost slaveholders some $3.2 million in net losses (meaning slave escapes) by 1855.[91]

---

[90] Thomas B. Thorpe, *Our Army on the Rio Grande* (Philadelphia: Carey and Hart, 1846), 25 (first quote); Philip N. Barbour, in Martha Isabella Hopkins Barbour, ed., *Journals of the Late Brevet Major Philip Norbourne Barbour* (New York: Putnam's Sons, 1936), 28 (second quote); *Democratic Telegraph and Texas Register*, July 8, 1846; Jacob Oswandel, *Notes of the Mexican War, 1846-47-48* (Philadelphia: n.p., 1885), 99; *Nashville Patriot*, February 23, 1859. See also Mareite, "Conditional Freedom, 192–194; Robert E. May, "Invisible Men: Blacks and the U.S. Army in the Mexican War," *The Historian* 49, no. 4 (August 1987): 473; Nichols, *The Limits of Liberty*, 35.

[91] See for example: *Journal of the House of Representatives of the State of Texas: Fourth Legislature, Extra Session* (Austin, TX: J. W. Hampton, 1853), 227; *Journal of the Senate of the State of Texas, Sixth Legislature* (Austin, TX: Marshall & Oldham, 1855), 58; *Journal of the House of Representatives of the State of Texas at the Adjourned Session, Sixth Legislature* (Austin, TX: Marshall & Oldham, 1856), 17; *Texas State Times*, June 2, 1855; Mareite, "Conditional Freedom," 196–196.

By the 1850s, the Mexican government's refusal to consider a formal extradition treaty with the United States even led some overly frustrated proslavery advocates to call for yet another annexation or invasion of Northern Mexico, or at least to lend support to proslavery separatist projects in some northern Mexican states. In his recent analysis of diplomatic correspondence between Mexican and British officials in 1851, for example, Thomas Mareite revealed that Mexican ministers grew deeply alarmed at US slaveholders' interference in local politics in the states bordering the Rio Grande, in particular their attempts to get slavery reintroduced there and support independence movements. When in September 1851 José María Carbajal led an armed uprising in an attempt to establish the breakaway state República de Sierra Madre, he was openly and heavily endorsed by both the Texas press and by Texas officials (with whom he had considerable contact), among other reasons because he promised to extradite fugitive slaves as criminals. His guerrilla war failed, but proslavery southerners continued to fantasize about a proslavery buffer between Texas and Mexico. *The Texian Advocate* wrote in 1852 that free soil policies "may require the dismemberment of a Mexican State or two." By the late 1850s, more and more proslavery voices advocated simply swallowing up Northern Mexico altogether. The *Nueces Valley Weekly*, for example, openly supported extending the border between Mexico and the United States to the Sierra Madre. In 1859, Texas congressman Henry Jewett seriously proposed occupying the Mexican states adjacent to the Rio Grande frontier if Mexico City refused to formalize an extradition treaty. Some proslavery writers and politicians began to go even further, embracing grandiose visions of a vast slaveholding empire that would include Mexico, the Caribbean, and Central America. Paramilitary groups were established to that end, such as the Knights of the Golden Circle, which sent armed units to the Rio Grande in 1860 in preparation for an invasion of Mexico.[92]

Despite overt attempts by many Mexican officials to protect runaway slaves from illegal reenslavement by slave catchers, scholars such as Thomas Mareite, James David Nichols, and Sarah Cornell, among others,

---

[92] Mareite, "Conditional Freedom," 196–201; Nichols, *The Limits of Liberty*, 133–134; Schwartz, *Across the Rio to Freedom*, 34; Mike Dunning, "Manifest Destiny and the Trans-Mississippi South: Natural Laws and the Extension of Slavery into Mexico," *Journal of Popular Culture* 35, no. 2 (2004): 119; *The Texian Advocate*, November 27, 1852, TRSP (quote); *Nueces Valley Weekly*, April 3, 1858; *The Standard*, May 28, 1859; Robert E. May, *The Southern Dream of a Caribbean Empire, 1854–1861* (Gainesville: University Press of Florida, 2002), 136–162.

have warned against overestimating the safety and security of Mexican free soil for runaways. Not only were they vulnerable to kidnapping, but they were also vulnerable to legal complications, threats, and intimidation by local officials in their new communities. The legal status of male refugees from slavery was ambiguous, leaving open loopholes that caused great anxiety for freedom seekers. Put simply, until the new Mexican constitution of 1857 was ratified, Mexican laws required male foreigners to provide proof of national citizenship when applying for a legal residence permit, a *carta de seguridad*. (This requirement did not apply to female runaways, due to the laws of coverture.) While the Mexican government was clear and unyielding in its policy of refusing to formally extradite runaway slaves, US officials and consuls exploited Mexico's immigration laws by denying service to black residents seeking nationality certificates and by refusing to acknowledge that any runaway slaves from the United States were citizens or even US subjects. The US minister at Mexico City, Powhatan Ellis, explicitly stated in correspondence with local consuls in 1839 that "when [slaves] are found absconding from their owners, and seek refuge in another country, they are not to be protected by the Diplomatic Agents of the diplomatic agents from whence they flee." This led to a precarious situation for male runaways, as they found themselves on free soil but also lacking the formal documentation to legalize their residence in Mexico. Most did not even try to obtain legal residence, not wanting to tip off any American authorities to where they were.[93]

In practice, the legal limbo of male refugees from slavery made them dependent on winning the favor of local officials for *amparo* [refuge], and justifying their presence on the grounds that they could sustain themselves and become integrated into Mexican communities. Under such circumstances, social integration by means of, for example, converting to Catholicism, learning to speak Spanish, forging local relationships, and earning a livelihood became extremely pressing for southbound runaways. As Sarah Cornell has forcefully argued, male runaways in Northern Mexico, lacking the qualifications for legal citizenship rights, had to rely on developing their "cultural citizenship" as a way of proving their worthiness of living unmolested in local communities. And indeed,

---

[93] Cornell, "Citizens of Nowhere," 353–354, 361–363; Powhatan Ellis, quoted in Cornell, "Citizens of Nowhere," 362 (quote); Nichols, "Freedom Interrupted," 251–274; Mareite, "Conditional Freedom," 184–187; Kelley, "'Mexico in His Head,'" 709–723. The Mexican Constitution of 1857 abolished the requirement for a *carta de seguridad*.

for most refugees this was enough. Many Mexican officials essentially ignored the requirement that runaway slaves obtain a *carta de seguridad*, granting them *amparo* and carving out a space of legal exception for refugees from slavery. Other local officials granted *cartas de seguridad* to runaways who took up arms to help defend the border, as was the case with eight runaways who fled to Matamoros in 1843 and subsequently served in the National Guard, for example. Finally, some Mexican officials turned a blind eye to false information on the applications of runaways who were determined to obtain *cartas de seguridad* at any cost. There are documented cases of refugees, for example, who tried to circumvent the requirement of a certificate of nationality by claiming to be from countries that did not have consular representatives in the town or state. One recent study of local government records discovered several cases of African Americans being denied *cartas de seguridad* and then resubmitting their applications, claiming to be from "Africa" or – especially in the case of Louisiana runaways – Haiti.[94]

The problem was that such means of circumventing the residency requirements depended on the goodwill and cooperation of Mexican officials. Until the new Constitution of 1857 effectively abolished the requirement, no national policy was enacted to deal with the refusal of US consuls to recognize the citizenship of fugitive slaves living in Mexico. Instead, each case was treated individually by local authorities, who could demand foreigners' *cartas* at any time and imprison or fine those who failed to produce them. It is important to note that the arresting officials did *not* have any federal authority to extradite African Americans who were caught without papers, but recent research by James David Nichols has shown that they did sometimes *threaten* to send them back to Texas. Nichols discovered cases in which local authorities demanded that runaways participate in military campaigns against the Comanches and Apaches in exchange for *amparo* in the 1850s, for example. Those who did not go willingly were threatened with being returned to slavery.

---

[94] Cornell, "Citizens of Nowhere," 354, 367–369; Nichols, "Freedom Interrupted," 251; Jürgen Buchenau, "Small Numbers, Great Impact: Mexico and Its Immigrants, 1821–1873," *Journal of American Ethnic History* 1, no. 1 (2001): 23–49; Mareite, "Conditional Freedom," 184–186. One Cesario Rivier, born in New Orleans, originally registered in Matamoros in 1841 by claiming that he was French, circumventing the requirement for consular papers, since there was no French consul in the town. He later moved to Coahuila in 1850, where he applied for a *carta* as a US national, but was rejected. He finally applied in 1854, claiming that he was from Haiti. See Mareite, "Conditional Freedom," 185–186.

The considerable efforts that some runaways undertook to obtain *cartas* – even lying about their origins – certainly suggest that they feared their legal limbo could lead to reenslavement. At the very least, the insecurity and confusion of the residency requirements made male refugees vulnerable to harassment and extortion by local officials. When arrests were made, imprisoned refugees often depended on petitions submitted by family and friends, underscoring their value to the community, exceptional work ethic, or even military service, in order to save them from having to pay hefty fines for residing in Mexico without papers.[95]

Refugees from slavery in British Canada and Mexico in the decades preceding the US Civil War sought freedom in parts of the continent that were not only committed to enforcing free soil within their national territories, but were also, unlike the Northern United States, unencumbered by any legal requirements to allow for the legal remission of fugitive slaves to southern slaveholders. From the 1830s on, runaway slaves who crossed international borders to the north and south found themselves in spaces of *formal freedom* from slavery, as both the British and Mexican governments staunchly refused to even entertain the prospect of enacting fugitive slave legislation or signing extradition treaties with the United States. The legal regimes in British Canada and Mexico provided runaways with legal protections from legal reenslavement.

For runaways in Mexico, however, legal protections from reenslavement did not always translate into protection from reenslavement in practice, as the same open border that allowed refugees to cross over to free soil also allowed their enslavers to cross over to illegally try to recover them. Legal protections from reenslavement also did not protect male refugees from legal harassment and extortion for failing to produce the documents necessary for legal residency, moreover. Such threats and complications were absent in British Canada, but even there, freedom from slavery did not translate into freedom from harassment and discrimination from ordinary residents. Spaces of formal freedom in North America did *not* constitute spaces of equal opportunity or social harmony. For refugees from southern slavery, however, the relative safety they provided made them superior to spaces of informal and semi-formal freedom in the Southern and Northern United States, respectively.

---

[95] Cornell, "Citizens of Nowhere," 367–374; Nichols, "Freedom Interrupted," 251–274, esp. 253–254; Nichols, *The Limits of Liberty*, 170–188.

Conclusion

By the eve of the US Civil War, southern slaveholders had clearly reached a point somewhat beyond desperation in their efforts to counter slave flight. By then thousands of runaways lurked about anonymously in their towns and cities, passing for free and – armed with forged documents – remaining at large indefinitely. Untold numbers of enslaved people had taken refuge in the northern free states, where they not only proved extremely difficult to track down but also to reenslave, due to ineffective rendition procedures, legal challenges, and mass civil disobedience. Tens of thousands of refugees from slavery were legally out of reach in British Canada and Mexico, among other parts of the Atlantic world. In their frustration, southern politicians and state legislatures resorted to the enflamed and misguided politics of exasperation: they lashed out at all those whom they believed to be in conspiracy against them to steal their human property and undermine their most important institution. In 1859–1860, twelve southern states seriously considered proposals to expel free blacks or reenslave them, hoping to rid themselves of the confusion that made spaces of informal freedom possible. In the winter of 1860–1861, eleven southern states gave up on union with the northern free states, charging them with "deliberately refus[ing] for years past to fulfill their constitutional obligations" and specifically citing the refusal of northern states to comply with federal fugitive slave laws as the main reason for secession. Around the same time, armed militias mobilized along the southern border, poised to invade and occupy Northern Mexico after its latest refusal to extradite freedom seekers who had taken refuge within its territory. All of these efforts were in vain. As desperation spilled into a bloody civil war in the spring of 1861, southern slaveholders ironically opened the floodgates to an even greater slave refugee crisis, one that would help topple slavery once and for all.[1]

Runaways from slavery exploited the surge in black freedom in various parts of postrevolutionary North America, correctly identifying potential spaces of freedom throughout the continent and seeking refuge in those spaces by any and all means available to them. In so doing they essentially turned sites of black freedom into sites of refuge for runaways. Indeed, freedom seekers helped create and defend the very spaces of freedom to which they fled. When free black communities sprang up in towns and cities across the South in the postrevolutionary era, for example, they were not intended to be sanctuaries for runaways from the surrounding hinterlands. Freedom seekers turned them into sanctuaries for runaways. When the Northern United States, British Canada, and the Republic of Mexico abolished slavery within their borders, they did not do so in order to turn their territories into an asylum for fugitive slaves from the Southern United States. Freedom seekers turned them into an asylum for fugitive slaves. Whether hiding out in in the urban South, evading recapture in the antebellum North, or settling in beyond the borders of the United States, the actions of freedom seekers helped define black freedom throughout North America.

The three spaces of freedom to which enslaved people fled between the American Revolution and the outbreak of the Civil War differed by degrees and continuously evolved over time. The main differences in the experiences of runaways to spaces of informal, semi-formal, and formal freedom, respectively, ultimately come down to differences in their motivations, networks, visibility, and vulnerability.

---

[1] Only Arkansas actually passed a free black expulsion bill. The legislatures of Missouri and Florida passed similar bills but these were vetoed by the state governors. All other proposals failed. Act No. 151, "An Act to Remove the Free Negroes and Mulattoes from this State," February 12, 1859, *Acts of the General Assembly of the State of Arkansas* (Little Rock: General Assembly of the State of Arkansas, 1859), 175–178; Ira Berlin, *Slaves without Masters: The Free Negro in the Antebellum South* (New York: The New Press, 1974), 360–380; Jonathan M. Atkins, "Party Politics and the Debate over the Tennessee Free Negro Bill, 1859–1860," *Journal of Southern History* 71, no. 2 (2005): 245–278; Andrew Delbanco, *The War before the War: Fugitive Slaves and the Struggle for America's Soul from the Revolution to the Civil War* (New York: Penguin, 2018), 348; *Declaration of the Immediate Causes Which Induce and Justify the Secession of South Carolina from the Federal Union, and the Ordinance of Secession* (Charleston, SC: Evans & Cogswell, 1860), 7–8; Robert E. May, *The Southern Dream of a Caribbean Empire, 1854–1861* (Gainesville: University Press of Florida, 2002), 136–162.

The *motivations* of freedom seekers throughout North America naturally shared important similarities. They all sought to escape a life of
slavery. They all sought to live free of any master, make choices, and live
free from physical abuse and the threat of forced separations from loved
ones. Violence and forced separations – or the threat thereof – spurred
enslaved people to make risky bids of freedom in every direction.
Runaways' intentions and expectations of freedom from slavery, however, tended to differ by degrees, and these informed their escape
attempts. Freedom seekers from the Upper South, for example, were
within relatively easy reach of spaces of informal, semi-formal, *and*
formal freedom. Yet they all chose different destinations, at least in part
because they had different intentions. Runaways who fled to spaces of
informal freedom settled for a life of freedom in the shadows, with no
legal rights, status, or recourse. They had their reasons. Many placed
family over freedom elsewhere, seeking to remain close to loved ones still
in bondage. Others preferred places they knew, tapping into trusted
networks and settling into communities that they knew from hiring stints
or similar experiences. Freedom seekers who fled the South altogether, by
contrast, were often motivated by a desire to sever all ties with slaveholding society and reach free soil, where they hoped for a recognition of their
humanity and legal protections from reenslavement. Often risking their
lives and traveling under the most trying circumstances imaginable, runaways to spaces of semi-formal and formal freedom entertained notions
of reclaiming their rights as human beings and living beyond the sight and
reach of any slaveholder.

The *networks* of runaways in all three spaces of freedom were crucial
factors in their escape attempts. These, too, differed by degrees.
Runaways who fled to spaces of informal freedom almost always had
family, friends, or work contacts in urban areas who not only served as
beacons but also helped harbor them and get them settled in free black
communities. Runaways to spaces of semi-formal freedom in the
Northern United States similarly often knew family or friends who had
gone before them but often depended upon strangers to help them reach
free soil and provide assistance upon arrival. These strangers were frequently – though not always – organized or connected to vigilance committees, church groups, and other bastions of antislavery. Freedom
seekers beyond the borders of the United States, by contrast, relied less
upon contacts abroad, and were less likely to know many people upon
arrival at their destinations. A comparison between refugees from slavery
in British Canada and Mexico, however, reveals that the former were far

more successful in establishing their own separate communities and self-help organizations – often connected to abolitionist societies in the United States – than the latter, partly as a result of their being shunned by white society. The successful settlement of refugees in Mexico, on the other hand, was more conditional upon their integration within Mexican society, rather than the establishment of any separate or self-segregated communities.

A continental view of runaways from southern slavery reveals the importance of *visibility* as an important factor in slave flight. The revolutionary era disrupted the link between blackness and slavery that had hitherto been taken for granted among state and municipal authorities as well as the general public. For runaways to spaces of informal freedom within the antebellum South, where *many* but by no means *all* – nor even a majority – of black people were considered potentially free, the erasure of their visibility as slaves was the key to their successful navigation of city streets undetected. They had to not only look and act like free blacks, but they had to acquire false documentation to "prove" it in case they were questioned. Refugees in spaces of informal freedom were less dependent on disguises, as they lived in regions where black people were considered free unless proven otherwise. Yet they, too, had to be constantly on the alert for potential slave catchers and questioning of their origins. They, too, had to hide their true backgrounds and be discreet about where they came from and their previous condition of slavery. Refugees from slavery in spaces of formal freedom were on far safer ground and had less to fear about others knowing that they were runaway slaves. Even they, however, were affected by others' knowledge – or assumptions – of their backgrounds. In Canada, refugees from slavery were largely shunned by racist white settlers. In Mexico, runaway slaves suffered less from a rigid color line than their counterparts in the north, but they sometimes became targets for harassment by local authorities who issued threats or demanded bribes when refugees failed to produce *cartas de seguridad*.

Perhaps the greatest difference in freedom seekers' experiences in each of the three spaces of freedom was in their *vulnerability*, especially as it related to recapture and reenslavement. Hiding out within a slaveholding society, runaways in spaces of informal freedom were clearly the most vulnerable to arrest and reenslavement. Their lack of any legal rights or claims to freedom only exacerbated their already highly precarious situation. Runaways in spaces of semi-formal freedom were on far safer ground, but they had to be on guard for illegal slave catchers and, most terrifyingly, agents of the law itself. While antislavery lawyers, judges, activists, and ordinary civilians often obstructed the execution of federal fugitive slave laws in the northern states, they were not always successful, and the possibility of rendition to the South always loomed over runaways' heads as a very real possibility. Refugees from slavery in spaces of formal freedom were the least vulnerable to reenslavement, as both Canada and Mexico staunchly and consistently refused to extradite fugitive slaves to the United States. The porous and poorly guarded Mexican border made refugees there more vulnerable to illegal slave-catching raids than their counterparts in Canada, however.

When the US Civil War broke out, enslaved people fled en masse to Union lines, seeking asylum and protection, believing northern troops to constitute an army of liberation. And indeed, their actions ultimately convinced President Lincoln and his cabinet to embrace abolition as a central war aim, turning Union-occupied territory into new spaces of freedom in their own right. Following Lincoln's Emancipation Proclamation on September 22, 1862, refugees from slavery throughout the continent came out of the woodworks and joined the war effort. African Americans in southern cities attached themselves to the invading Union armies, providing crucial insider information and assistance; black men in the northern states lined up for military service; refugee communities in Canada expressed their support and helped recruit soldiers to send south; black resistance to the Confederacy in the US-Mexican borderlands peaked. Collectively, their actions helped destroy southern bondage forever, converting all of North America into a space of formal freedom from slavery.[2]

---

[2] Ira Berlin, Joseph P. Reidy, and Leslie S. Rowland, eds., *Freedom: A Documentary History of Emancipation, 1861–1867, Volume 1, Series II: The Black Military Experience* (New York: Cambridge University Press, 1983); Peter Kolchin, *American Slavery, 1619–1877* (New York: Hill & Wang, 2003), 200–238; Richard M. Reid, *African Canadians in Union Blue: Volunteering for the Cause in the Civil War* (Kent, OH: Kent State University Press, 2015); Thomas Mareite, "Conditional Freedom: Free Soil and Fugitive Slaves from the US South to Mexico's Northeast, 1803–1861" (PhD diss., Leiden University, 2020), 212–213; Andrew J. Torget, "The Problem of Slave Flight in Civil War Texas," in Jesús de la Teja, ed., *Lone Star Unionism, Dissent and Resistance* (Norman: University of Oklahoma Press, 2016), 37–59.

Bibliography

ARCHIVES

Archives of Ontario, Toronto, ON
Hill Memorial Library, Louisiana State University, Baton Rouge, LA
John F. Kennedy Institute for American Studies, Freie Universität, Berlin, Germany
Library of Congress, Washington, DC
Library of Virginia, Richmond, VA
National Archives and Records Administration, Washington, DC
Public Archives of Canada, Ottawa, ON
Roosevelt Institute for American Studies, Middelburg, Netherlands
Smithsonian Library, Washington, DC

DIGITAL ARCHIVES

Born in Slavery: Slave Narratives from the Federal Writers' Project, 1936–1938 (Library of Congress, Washington, DC), www.loc.gov/collections/slave-narratives-from-the-federal-writers-project-1936-to-1938/.
Chester County, PA, Fugitive Slave Records, 1820–1839, www.chesco.org/1722/Fugitive-Slave-Records-1820-1839.
Chronicling America (Library of Congress, Washington, DC), https://chroniclingamerica.loc.gov/.
Documenting the American South, North American Slave Narratives (University of North Carolina, Chapel Hill, NC), https://docsouth.unc.edu/neh/.
Family Search, www.familysearch.org.
Freedom on the Move (Cornell University, Ithaca, NY, etc.), https://freedomonthemove.org.
Louisiana Runaway Slave Advertisements, 1836–1865 (Louisiana Digital Library, Baton Rouge, LA), https://louisianadigitallibrary.org.
Portal to Texas History (University of North Texas, Denton, TX), https://texashistory.unt.edu/.

Race and Slavery Petitions Project (University of North Carolina, Greensboro, NC), https://library.uncg.edu/slavery/petitions/.

Race and Slavery Petitions Project, Slavery and the Law Collection (Roosevelt Institute for American Studies, Middelburg, Netherlands), www.roosevelt.nl/collections/digital-resources.

Slavery, Abolition, and Social Justice (Leiden University, Leiden, Netherlands), www.bibliotheek.universiteitleiden.nl/.

Slavery and Anti-Slavery: A Transnational Archive (Leiden University, Leiden, Netherlands), www.bibliotheek.universiteitleiden.nl/.

Sydney Howard Gay Papers (Columbia University, New York), https://exhibitions.library.columbia.edu/exhibits/show/fugitives/record_fugitives.

Texas Runaway Slave Project, East Texas Digital Archives (Stephen F. Austin State University, Nacogdoches, TX), https://digital.sfasu.edu/digital/collection/RSP.

University of Houston Digital Library (Univeristy of Houston, Houston, TX), https://digital.lib.uh.edu/.

NEWSPAPERS AND PERIODICALS

Adams Sentinel (Gettysburg, PA)

Alexandria Advertiser and Commercial Intelligencer (Alexandria, VA)

Alexandria Gazette (Alexandria, VA)

Anti-Slavery Bugle (New Lisbon, OH)

Arkansas Gazette (Little Rock, AR)

Augusta Chronicle (Augusta, GA)

Baltimore Sun (Baltimore, MD)

British and Foreign Anti-Slavery Reporter (London, UK)

Buffalo Daily Gazette (Buffalo, NY)

Caledonian Mercury (Edinburgh, UK)

Cape Fear Mercury (Wilmington, NC)

Carolina Centinel (Newbern, NC)

Charleston Courier (Charleston, SC)

Charleston Mercury (Charleston, SC)

The Civilian and Galveston Gazette (Galveston, TX)

Cleveland Morning Herald (Cleveland, OH)

Colorado Tribune (Denver, CO)

Couirier de la Louisiane (New Orleans, LA)

The Courier (Washington, DC)

Daily National Intelligencer (Washington, DC)

The Daily Picayune (New Orleans, LA)

Dallas Herald (Dallas, TX)

Democratic Telegraph and Texas Register (Houston, TX)

Democratic Watchman (Bellefonte, PA)

Edenton Gazette and North Carolina General Advertiser (Edenton, NC)

Edgefield Advertiser (Edgefield, SC)

El Indicador (Veracruz, Veracruz, Mexico)

El Siglo XIX (Mexico, DF, Mexico)
Emancipator (New York, NY)
Fayettesville Observer (Fayettesville, NC)
Frankfort Argus (Frankfort, KY)
Fremont Journal (Fremont, NY)
Friends' Intelligencer (Philadelphia, PA)
Galveston News (Galveston, TX)
Galveston Weekly News (Galveston, TX)
Genius of Universal Emancipation (Pleasant, OH)
Georgia Gazette (Savannah, GA)
Georgia Journal & Messenger (Macon, GA)
The Granite Freeman (Concord, NH)
Huntsville Democrat (Huntsville, AL)
Independent Chronicle (Galveston, TX)
Indianola Bulletin (Indianola, TX)
Kent Advertiser (Kent, OH)
Lexington Intelligencer (Lexington, KY)
The Liberator (Boston, MA)
Maryland Gazette (Annapolis, MD)
Mississippi and State Gazette (Jackson, MS)
Nashville Patriot (Nashville, TN)
National Anti-Slavery Standard (New York, NY)
Newbern Spectator and Literary Journal (Newbern, NC)
New York Daily Tribune (New York, NY)
New York Evangelist (New York, NY)
Norfolk Intelligencer (Norfolk, VA)
North Carolina Sentinel (Newbern, NC)
The Northern Standard (Clarksville, TX)
Nueces Valley Weekly (Corpus Christi, TX)
Pennsylvania Freeman (Philadelphia, PA)
Pennsylvania Gazette & Universal Daily Advertiser (Philadelphia, PA)
Philadelphia Evening Bulletin (Philadelphia, PA)
The Philanthropist (Cincinnati, OH)
The Planters' Gazette (Iberville, LA)
Port Tobacco & Charles Town Advertiser (Port Tobacco, MD)
Provincial Freeman (Windsor, ON)
Raleigh Register and North Carolina Gazette (Raleigh, NC)
The Reporter (Lexington, KY)
The San Antonio Herald (San Antonio, TX)
San Antonio Ledger (San Antonio, TX)
San Antonio Texan (San Antonio, TX)
South Carolina Gazette (Charleston, SC)
The Standard (Clarksville, TX)
Star and Republican Banner (Gettysburg, PA)
State Gazette (Austin, TX)
Tarboro Press (Edgecomb, NC)
Telegraph and Texas Register (Houston, TX)

Tennessee Republican Banner (Nashville, TN)
The Texas Monument (La Grange, TX)
Texas National Register (Washington, TX)
Texas Republican (Marshall, TX)
Texas State Times (Austin, TX)
The Texian Advocate (Victoria, TX)
The Times Picayune (New Orleans, LA)
Virginia Gazette (Williamsburg, VA)
Virginia Gazette & Petersburg Intelligencer (Petersburg, VA)
The Universal Asylum and Columbian Magazine (Philadelphia, PA)
Upper Canada Gazette (Toronto, ON)
Voice of the Fugitive (Windsor, ON)
The Washington American (Washington, TX)

PRIMARY PUBLISHED

Aikin, John G., comp., *A Digest of the Laws of the State of Alabama…etc.* Philadelphia: Alexander Towar, 1833.

Alden, T. J. Fox, and J. A. van Hoesen. *Digest of the Laws of Mississippi, Comprising All the Laws of a General Nature, Including the Acts of Session of 1839.* New York: Alexander Gould, 1839.

"An ACT to Amend the Several Laws Concerning Slaves" (1806), in *The Statutes at Large of Virginia, from October Session 1792, to December Session 1806,* comp. Samuel Shepherd. Richmond, VA: n.p., 1836, 252.

"An Act to Prevent the Further Introduction of Slaves and to Limit the Term of Contracts for Servitude within this Province" (July 9, 1793), in *A Collection of the Acts Passed in the Parliament of Great Britain, Particularly Applying to the Province of Upper-Canada, and of Such Ordinances of the Late Province of Quebec, as Have Force of Law Therein.* York: R.C. Horne, 1818, 30–32.

"An Act Related to Crimes and Misdemeanors Committed by Slaves, Free Negroes and Mulattoes," in *Acts of the Legislative Council of the Territory of Florida, Passed at Their Seventh Session.* Tallahassee, FL: William Wilson, 1828, 174–190.

"An Act to Remove the Free Negroes and Mulattoes from This State" (February 12, 1859), *Acts of the General Assembly of the State of Arkansas.* Little Rock, AR: General Assembly of the State of Arkansas, 1859, 175–178.

Anderson, William J. *The Narrative of William J. Anderson, Twenty-Four Years a Slave.* Chicago: Daily Tribune Book & Job Printing Office, 1857.

Andrews, Ethan Allen. *Slavery and the Domestic Slave Trade, in a Series of Letters Addressed to the Executive Committee of the American Union for the Relief and Improvement of the Colored Race.* First published 1836; reprint Freeport, NY: Libraries Press, 1971.

Ball, Charles. *Fifty Years in Chains; or, The Life of an American Slave.* New York: Asher & Co., 1859.

Barbour, Martha Isabella Hopkins, ed. *Journals of the Late Brevet Major Philip Norbourne Barbour*. New York: Putnam's Sons, 1936.

Benezet, Anthony. *Epistle of Caution and Advice Concerning the Buying and Keeping of Slaves*. Philadelphia: James Cattin, 1754.

Berlin, Ira, Joseph P. Reidy, and Leslie S. Rowland, eds. *Freedom: A Documentary History of Emancipation, 1861–1867, Volume 1, Series II: The Black Military Experience*. New York: Cambridge University Press, 1983.

Bernstein, Robin. "Jane Clark: A Newly Available Slave Narrative," *Common-place.org* 18, no. 1 (2018), http://common-place.org/book/vol-18-no-1-bernstein/.

Bibb, Henry. *Narrative of the Life and Adventures of Henry Bibb, an American Slave, Written by Himself*. New York: The Author, 1849.

Birney, William. *Sketch of the Life of James G. Birney*. Chicago: National Christian Association, 1884.

Blassingame, John W., ed. *Slave Testimony: Two Centuries of Letters, Speeches, Interviews, and Autobiographies*. Baton Rouge: Louisiana State University Press, 1977.

Brown, Henry. *Narrative of the Life of Henry Box Brown, Written by Himself*. Manchester: Lee & Glynn, 1851.

Brown, William Wells. *Narrative of William Wells Brown, an American Slave*. Boston: The Anti-Slavery Office, 1847.

Chase, Salmon P. *Speech of Salmon P. Chase in the Case of the Colored Woman, Matilda, Who Was Brought before the Court of Common Pleas of Hamilton County, Ohio, by Writ of Habeas Corpus, March 11th, 1837*. Cincinnati, OH: Pugh & Dodd, 1837.

Coffin, Levi. *Reminiscences of Levi Coffin, the Reputed President of the Underground Railroad*. Cincinnati, OH: Robert Clarke & Co., 1880.

"Commonwealth v. Jennison," April 20, 1783, *Proceedings of the Massachusetts Historical Society (1873–1875)*, XIII (1875): 292–294.

Constitution and By-Laws of the Anti-Slavery Society of Canada. Toronto: George Brown, "Globe" Office, 1851.

Craft, William, and Ellen Craft. *Running a Thousand Miles to Freedom: Or, the Escape of William and Ellen Craft from Slavery*. London: William Tweedie, 1860.

"Daybook of the Richmond, Virginia Police Guard, 1834–1844," trans. by Leni Ashmore Sorensen, "Absconded: Fugitive Slaves in the Daybook of the Richmond Police Guard." PhD diss., College of William & Mary, 2005.

Declaration of the Immediate Causes Which Induce and Justify the Secession of South Carolina from the Federal Union, and the Ordinance of Secession. Charleston, SC: Evans & Cogswell, 1860.

"Decreto del gobierno – Abolición de la esclavitud" (September 15, 1829), in Manuel Dublán et al., *Legislación mexicana; o colección completa de disposiciones legislativas expedidas desde la independencia de la República* (México: Imprenta de Comercio, 1876), vol. 2, 163.

Douglass, Frederick. *Life and Times of Frederick Douglass: His Early Life as a Slave, His Escape from Bondage, and His Complete History to the Present Time*. Hartford, CT: Park Publishing Co., 1881.

"What to the Slave Is the Fourth of July?" in John W. Blassingame, ed., *The Frederick Douglass Papers, Series 1: Speeches, Debates, and Interviews, vol. 2: 1847–1854*. New Haven, CT: Yale University Press, 1982, 359–387.

Drew, Benjamin. *A North-Side View of Slavery: The Refugee; or the Narratives of Fugitive Slaves in Canada*. Boston: John P. Jewett & Co., 1856.

Earle, Thomas. *The Life, Travels and Opinions of Benjamin Lundy, Including His Journeys to Texas and Mexico, with a Sketch of Contemporary Events, and a Notice of the Revolution in Hayti*. Philadelphia: W. D. Parrish, 1847.

Featherstonhaugh, George W. *Excursion through the Slave States, from Washington on the Potomac to the Frontier of Mexico*. New York: Harper & Brothers, 1844.

Federal Writers' Project, *Slave Narratives: A Folk History of the United States of America from Interviews with Former Slaves*. 17 vols. Washington, DC: Works Progress Administration, 1941.

Finkelman, Paul, ed. *Fugitive Slaves and Amerian Courts: The Pamphlet Literature*, 4 vols. Clark, NJ: Lawbook Exchange, 2012.

Frantel, Nancy C., comp. *Richmond, Virginia Uncovered: The Records of Slaves and Free Blacks Listed in the City Sergeant Jail Register, 1841–1846*. Richmond, VA: Heritage Books, 2010.

Fugitive Slave Case: District Court of the United States for the Southern Division of Iowa, Burlington, June Term 1850, Ruel Daggs *v.* Elihu Frazier, et als., Reported by Geo. Frazee. Burlington, IA: Morgan & M'Kenny, 1850.

General Assembly of Pennsylvania, *An Act for the Better Regulating of Negroes in This Province*, section V, passed March 5, 1725.

An Act for the Gradual Abolition of Slavery, passed March 1, 1780.

General Assembly of Virginia, "An Act for Suppressing Outlying Slaves (1691)." Reprinted in William Waller Hening, ed., *The Statutes at Large: Being a Collection of All Laws of Virginia, from the First Session of the Legislature, in the Year 1619*. Philadelphia: R. & W. & G. Bartow, 1823, vol. 3, 86–88.

"An Act to Authorize the Manumission of Slaves (May 1782)." Reprinted in William Waller Hening, ed., *The Statutes at Large; Being a Collection of All the Laws of Virginia from the First Session of Legislature, in the Year 1619*. Richmond, VA: George Cochran, 1823, vol. 11, 39.

Giddings, Joshua R. *The Exiles of Florida: Or the Crimes Committed by Our Government against the Maroons, Who Fled from South Carolina, and Other Slave States, Seeking Protection under Spanish Laws*. Columbus, OH: Follett, Foster & Co., 1858.

Goings, Henry. *Rambles of a Runaway from Southern Slavery*, ed., Calvina Schermerhorn, Michael Plunkett, and Edward Gayno. Charlottesville: University of Virginia Press, 2012.

Green, Thomas J. *Journal of the Texian Expedition against Mier*. New York: Harper & Brothers, 1845.

Gulick, Charles Adam, Winnie Allen, Katherine Elliott, and Harriet Smither, eds. *The Papers of Mirabeau Buonaparte Lamar*, vol. 5. Austin, TX: Pemberton Press, 1968.

Haviland, Laura Smith. *A Woman's Life-Work, Labors and Experiences of.* Cincinnati, OH: Waldron & Stowe, 1882.

Howe, G. *The Refugees from Slavery in Canada West: A Report to the Freedmen's Inquiry Commission.* Boston: Wright & Potter, 1864.

Hynson, Jerry M., trans., *District of Columbia Department of Corrections, Runaway Slave Book, 1848–1863.* Westminster, MD: Willow Bend Books, 1999.

Hynson, Jerry M., comp., *Absconders, Runaways and Other Fugitives in the Baltimore City and County Jail.* Westminster, MD: Willow Bend Books, 2004.

Jacobs, Harriet. *Incidents in the Life of a Slave Girl.* 1861; reprint New York: Barnes & Noble, 2005.

Johnson, Samuel. *Taxation No Tyranny: An Answer to the Resolutions and Address of the American Congress.* London: T. Cadell, 1775.

Journal of the House of Representatives of the State of Texas: Fourth Legislature, Extra Session. Austin, TX: J. W. Hampton, 1853.

Journal of the Senate of the State of Texas, Sixth Legislature. Austin, TX: Marshall & Oldham, 1855.

Journal of the House of Representatives of the State of Texas at the Adjourned Session, Sixth Legislature. Austin, TX: Marshall & Oldham, 1856.

Legislature of Upper Canada. "An Act to Provide for the Apprehending of Fugitive Offenders from Foreign Countries, and Delivering Them Up to Justice." 1833.

Mackenzie, William L. *Sketches of Canada and the United States.* London: Effingham Wilson, 1833.

Moore, George H. *Notes on the History of Slavery in Massachusetts.* New York: Appleton & Co., 1866.

National Emigration Convention of Colored People. *Proceedings of the National Convention of Colored People: Held at Cleveland, Ohio, Thursday, Friday and Saturday, the 24th, 25th and 26th of August 1854.* Pittsburgh, PA: A. A. Anderson, 1854.

Olmsted, Frederick Law. *A Journey in the Seaboard Slave States; with Remarks on Their Economy.* New York: Dix and Edwards, 1856.

A Journey through Texas: Or a Saddle-Trip on the Southwestern Frontier. New York: Dix, Edwards & Co., 1857.

Oswandel, Jacob. *Notes of the Mexican War, 1846–47–48.* Philadelphia: n.p., 1885.

Pease, Elisha M. *Informe del gobernador del estado de Tejas: y documentos relativos a los asaltos contra los carreteros mejicanos.* Austin, TX: John Marshall & Co., 1857.

Pennington, James W. C. *The Fugitive Blacksmith: or, Events in the History of James W. Pennington, Pastor of a Presbyterian Church, New York, Formerly a Slave in the State of Maryland, United States.* London: Charles Gilpin, 1849.

Pridgen, Henderson McBride. *Address to the People of Texas, on the Protection of Slave Property.* Austin, TX: n.p., 1859.

Proceedings of the National Emigration Convention of Colored People. Pittsburgh, PA: A. A. Anderson, 1854.

Schweninger, Loren, ed. *The Southern Debate over Slavery, Volume 2: Petitions to Southern County Courts, 1775–1867.* Urbana: University of Illinois Press, 2008.

Second Congress of the United States. "An Act Respecting Fugitives from Justice, and Persons Escaping from the Service of Their Masters." *Proceedings and Debates of the House of Representatives of the United States at the Second Session of the Second Congress, Begun at the City of Philadelphia, November 5, 1792.* (November 5, 1792 to March 2, 1793), 1414–1415.

Siebert, William H. *The Underground Railroad from Slavery to Freedom.* New York: Macmillan, 1898.

The Slavery Code of the District of Columbia. Washington, DC: L. Towers & Co., 1862.

Snethen, Worthington G. *The Black Code of the District of Columbia, in Force September 1st, 1848.* New York: A.&F., W. Harned, 1848.

Stanton, Henry B. *Remarks of Henry B. Stanton, in the Representatives' Hall, on the 23nd (sic) and 24th of February, before the Committee of the House of Representatives, of Massachusetts, to Whom Was Referred Sundry Memorials on the Subject of Slavery.* Boston: I. Knapp, 1837.

Steward, Austin. *Twenty-Two Years a Slave, and Forty Years a Freeman; Embracing a Correspondence of Several Years, While President of the Wilberforce Colony, London, Canada West.* Rochester, NY: William Alling, 1857.

Still, William. *The Underground Railroad: A Record of Facts, Authentic Narratives, Letters, etc.* Philadelphia: Porter & Coates, 1872.

Stirling, James. *Letters from the Slave States.* First published 1857; reprint New York: Negro Universities Press, 1969.

Taylor, Edward. *Anahuac: Or Mexico and the Mexicans, Ancient and Modern.* London: Longman, Green, Longman & Roberts, 1861.

Thirty-First Congress of the United States, Session I. *An Act to Amend, and Supplementary to, the Act Entitled 'An Act Respecting Fugitives from Justice and Persons Escaping from the Service of their Masters'* (September 18, 1850), 462–465.

Thorpe, Thomas B. *Our Army on the Rio Grande.* Philadelphia: Carey and Hart, 1846.

Trial of Henry W. Allen, U.S. Deputy Marhsal, for Kidnapping, with Arguments of Counsel & Charge of Justice Marvin, on the Constitutionality of the Fugitive Slave Law, in the Supreme Court of New York. Syracuse, NY: Power Press of the Daily Journal Office, 1852.

Tucker, St. George. *A Dissertation on Slavery: With a Proposal for the Gradual Abolition of It in the State of Virginia.* Philadelphia: Mathew Carey, 1796.

Walker, Jonathan. *Trial and Imprisonment of Jonathan Walker, at Pensacola, Florida, for Aiding Slaves to Escape from Bondage.* Boston: Anti-Slavery Office, 1845.

Water, Andrew, ed. *I Was Born in Slavery: Personal Accounts of Slavery in Texas.* Winston-Salem: John Blair, 2003.

SECONDARY PUBLISHED

Adams, Rachel. *Continental Divides: Remapping the Cultures of North America.* Chicago: University of Chicago Press, 2009.

Adelman, Jeremy, and Stephen Aron, "From Borderlands to Borders: Empires, Nation-States, and the People in between in North American History." *The American Historical Review* 104, no. 3 (1999): 814–841.

Ainsworth, Kyle. "Advertising Maranda: Runaway Slaves in Texas, 1835–1865," in Damian Alan Pargas, ed., *Fugitive Slaves and Spaces of Freedom in North America.* Gainesville: University Press of Florida, 2018.

Aptheker, Herbert. "Maroons within the Present Limits of the United States." *Journal of Negro History* 24 (April 1939): 167–184.

Asaka, Ikuko. "'Our Brethren in the West Indies': Self-Emancipated People in Canada and the Antebellum Politics of Diaspora and Empire." *Journal of African American History* 97, no. 3 (2012): 219–239.

Atkins, Jonathan M. "Party Politics and the Debate over the Tennessee Free Negro Bill, 1859–1860." *Journal of Southern History* 71, no. 2 (2005): 245–278.

Audain, Mekala. "Mexican Canaan: Fugitive Slaves and Free Blacks on the American Frontier, 1804–1867." PhD diss., Rutgers University, 2014.

"'Design His Course to Mexico': The Fugitive Slave Experience in the Texas-Mexico Borderlands, 1850–1853," in Damian Alan Pargas, ed., *Fugitive Slaves and Spaces of Freedom in North America.* Gainesville: University Press of Florida, 2018.

Bacon, Margaret H. *But One Race: The Life of Robert Purvis.* Albany: State University of New York Press, 2007.

Baily, Marilyn. "From Cincinnati, Ohio to Wilberforce, Canada: A Note on Antebellum Colonization." *Journal of Negro History* 58, no. 4 (1973): 427–440.

Baker, H. Robert. *The Rescue of Joshua Glover: A Fugitive Slave, the Constitution, and the Coming of the Civil War.* Cambridge, MA: Harvard University Press, 2010.

"The Fugitive Slave Clause and the Antebellum Constitution." *Law and History Review* 30, no. 4 (2012): 1133–1174.

Baringer, Willam E. "The Politics of Abolition: Salmon P. Chase in Cincinnati." *Cincinnati Historical Society Bulletin* 29, no. 2 (1971): 78–99.

Barker, Gordon S. *The Imperfect Revolution: Anthony Burns and the Landscape of Race in Antebellum America.* Kent: Kent State University Press, 2010.

Fugitive Slaves and the Unfinished American Revolution: Eight Cases, 1848–1856. Jefferson, NC: McFarland, 2013.

"Revisiting 'British Principle Talk': Antebellum Black Expectations and Racism in Early Ontario," in Damian Alan Pargas, ed., *Fugitive Slaves and Spaces of Freedom in North America.* Gainesville: University Press of Florida, 2018.

Barnett, Randy E. "From Antislavery Lawyer to Chief Justice: The Remarkable but Forgotten Career of Salmon P . Chase." *Case Western Reserve Law Review*, 63, no. 3 (2013): 653–702.

Barr, Alwyn. "Freedom and Slavery in the Republic: African American Experiences in the Republic of Texas," in Kenneth W. Howell and Charles Swanlund, eds., *Single Star of the West: The Republic of Texas, 1836–1845*. Denton: University of North Texas Press, 2017.

Basinger, Scott J. "Regulating Slavery: Deck-Stacking and Credible Commitment in the Fugitive Slave Act of 1850." *Journal of Law, Economics, & Organization* 19, no. 2 (2003): 307–342.

Baumgartner, Alice L. *South to Freedom: Runaway Slaves to Mexico and the Road to Civil War*. New York: Basic Books, 2020.

Beckert, Sven. *Empire of Cotton: A Global History*. New York: Vintage, 2015.

Bell, D. G., J. Barry Cahill, and Harvey Amani Whitfield, "Slavery and Slave Law in the Maritimes," in Barrington Walker, ed., *The African Canadian Legal Odyssey: Historical Essays*. Toronto: University of Toronto Press, 2012.

Berlin, Ira. *Slaves without Masters: The Free Negro in the Antebellum South*. New York: Pantheon, 1981.

  Generations of Captivity: A History of African-American Slaves. Cambridge, MA: Harvard University Press, 2003.

  The Making of African America: The Four Great Migrations. New York: Penguin, 2010.

  The Long Emancipation: The Demise of Slavery in the United States. Cambridge, MA: Harvard University Press, 2015.

Bertaux, Nancy. "Structural Economic Chance and Occupational Decline among Black Workers in Nineteenth-Century Cincinnati," in Henry Louis Taylor, ed., *Race and the City: Work, Community, and Protest in Cincinnati, 1820–1970*. Urbana: University of Illinois Press, 1993.

Blackburn, Robin. *The American Crucible: Slavery, Emancipation and Human Rights*. New York: Verso, 2011.

Blackett, Richard M. *Making Freedom: The Underground Railroad and Politics of Freedom*. Chapel Hill: University of North Carolina Press, 2013.

  The Captive's Quest for Freedom: Fugitive Slaves, the 1850 Fugitive Slave Law, and the Politics of Slavery (New York: Cambridge University Press, 2018.

Blythe, Nancy. "Fugitives from Servitude: American Deserters and Runaway Slaves in Spanish Nacogdoches, 1803–1808." *East Texas Historical Journal* 38, no. 2 (2000): 1–14.

Bolton, S. Charles. *Fugitivism: Escaping Slavery in the Lower Mississippi Valley, 1820–1860*. Fayetteville: University of Arkansas Press, 2019.

Bond, Richard E. "Ebb and Flow: Free Blacks and Urban Slavery in Eighteen-Century New York." PhD diss., Johns Hopkins University, 2005.

Bordewich, Fergus. *Bound for Canaan: The Epic Story of the Underground Railroad, America's First Civil Rights Movement*. New York: HarperCollins, 2005.

Brana-Shute, Rosemary, and Randy J. Sparks, eds. *Paths to Freedom: Manumission in the Atlantic World*. Columbia: University of South Carolina Press, 2009.

Bristow, Peggy. "'Whatever You Raise in the Ground You Can Sell It in Chatham': Black Women in Buxton and Chatham, 1850–1865," in Peggy Bristow, ed., *"We're Rooted Here and They Can't Pull Up": Essays in*

African Canadian Women's History. Toronto: University of Toronto Press, 1994.

Brooke, John L. *"There Is a North"*: *Fugitive Slaves, Political Crisis, and Cultural Transformation in the Coming of the Civil War*. Amherst: University of Massachusetts Press, 2019.

Brown, Christopher Leslie. *Moral Capital: The Foundations of British Abolitionism*. Chapel Hill: University of North Carolina Press, 2006.

Brown, Elsa Barkley, and Gregg Kimball. "Mapping the Terrain of Black Richmond." *Journal of Urban History* 21, no. 3 (1995): 296–346.

Broyld, Dann J. "The 'Dark Sheep' of the Atlantic World: Following the Transnational Trail of Blacks to Canada," in Benjamin Talton and Quincy T. Mills, eds., *Black Subjects in Africa and Its Diasporas: Race and Gender in Research and Writing*. New York: Palgrave Macmillan, 2011.

"'Over the Way': On the Border of Canada before the Civil War," in Paul Lovejoy and Vanessa S. Oliveira, eds., *Slavery, Memory, Citizenship*. Trenton, NJ: Africa World Press, 2016.

Buchanan, Thomas C. "Rascals on the Antebellum Mississippi: African American Steamboat Workers and the St. Louis Hanging of 1841." *Journal of Social History* 34 (Summer 2001): 797–817.

Black Life on the Mississippi: Slaves, Free Blacks, and the Western Steamboat World. Chapel Hill: University of North Carolina Press, 2004.

Buchenau, Jürgen. "Small Numbers, Great Impact: Mexico and Its Immigrants, 1821–1873." *Journal of American Ethnic History* 1, no. 1 (2001): 23–49.

Burton, H. Sophie, and F. Todd Smith, *Colonial Natchitoches: A Creole Community on the Louisiana-Texas Frontier*. College Station: Texas A&M University Press, 2008.

Camp, Stephanie M. H. *Closer to Freedom: Enslaved Women and Everyday Resistance in the Antebellum South*. Chapel Hill: University of North Carolina Press, 2004.

Campbell, James M. *Slavery on Trial: Race, Class, and Criminal Justice in Antebellum Richmond*. Gainesville: University Press of Florida, 2007.

Campbell, Randolph B. *An Empire for Slavery: The Peculiar Institution in Texas, 1821–1865*. Baton Rouge: Louisiana State University Press, 1991.

Campbell, Stanley W. *The Slave Catchers: Enforcement of the Fugitive Slave Law 1850–1860*. Chapel Hill: University of North Carolina Press, 1970.

Carey, Anthony Gene. *Sold Down the River: Slavery in the Lower Chattahoochee Valley of Alabama and Georgia*. Tuscaloosa: University of Alabama Press, 2011.

Cecelski, David C. *The Waterman's Song: Slavery and Freedom in Maritime North Carolina*. Chapel Hill: University of North Carolina Press, 2001.

Chaplin, Joyce E. "Creating a Cotton South in Georgia and South Carolina, 1760–1815." *Journal of Southern History* 57 (May 1991): 171–200.

Churchill, Robert H. "Fugitive Slave Rescues: Toward a Geography of Northern Antislavery Violence." *Ohio Valley History* 14, no. 2 (Summer 2014): 51–75.

The Underground Railroad and the Geography of Violence. New York: Cambridge University Press, 2020.

Clark-Pujara, Christy. *Dark Work: The Business of Slavery in Rhode Island.* New York: New York University Press, 2016.

Clavin, Matthew J. *Aiming for Pensacola: Fugitive Slaves on the Atlantic and Southern Frontiers.* Cambridge, MA: Harvard University Press, 2015.

Clinton, Catherine. *Harriet Tubman: The Road to Freedom.* New York: Little, Brown & Co., 2004.

Cole, Shawn. "Capitalism and Freedom: Manumissions and the Slave Market in Louisiana, 1725–1820." *Journal of Economic History* 65, no. 4 (2005): 1008–1027.

Collison, Gary. *Shadrach Minkins: From Fugitive Slave to Citizen.* Cambridge, MA: Harvard University Press, 1997.

Condon, Sean. "The Slave Owner's Family and Manumission in the Post-Revolutionary Chesapeake Tidewater: Evidence from Anne Arundel County Wills, 1790–1820," in Rosemary Brana-Shute and Randy J. Sparks, eds., *Paths to Freedom: Manumission in the Atlantic World.* Columbia: University of South Carolina Press, 2009.

Cooper, Afua. "Acts of Resistance: Black Men and Women Engage Slavery in Upper Canada, 1793–1803." *Ontario History* 99, no. 1 (2007): 5–17.

"The Secret of Slavery in Canada," in Margaret Hobbs and Carla Rice, eds., *Gender and Women's Studies in Canada: Critical Terrain.* Toronto: Women's Press, 2013.

Copeland, David A., ed. *Debating the Issues in Colonial Newspapers: Primary Documents on Events of the Period.* Westport, CT: Greenwood, 2000.

Cornell, Sarah E. "Citizens of Nowhere: Fugitive Slaves and Free African Americans in Mexico, 1833–1857." *Journal of American History* 100, no. 2 (2013): 351–374.

Crothers, A. Glenn. *Quakers Living in the Lion's Mouth: The Society of Friends in Northern Virginia, 1730–1865.* Gainesville: University Press of Florida, 2012.

Curry, Leonard P. *Free Blacks in Urban America, 1800–1850: The Shadow of the Dream.* Chicago: University of Chicago Press, 1981.

"Free Blacks in the Urban South, 1800–1850." *Southern Quarterly* 43, no. 2 (2006): 35–51.

Dain, Bruce. *A Hideous Monster of the Mind: American Race Theory in the Early Republic.* Cambridge, MA: Harvard University Press, 2002.

Dantas, Mariana L. R. *Black Townsmen: Urban Slavery and Freedom in the Eighteenth-Century Americas.* New York: Palgrave Macmillan, 2008.

Davis, David Brion. *The Problem of Slavery in the Age of Revolution, 1770–1823.* New York: Oxford University Press, 1975.

Inhuman Bondage: The Rise and Fall of Slavery in the New World. New York: Oxford University Press, 2006.

The Problem of Slavery in the Age of Emancipation. New York: Knopf, 2014.

Delbanco, Andrew. *The War before the War: Fugitive Slaves and the Struggle for America's Soul from the Revolution to the Civil War.* New York: Penguin Press, 2018.

DeLombard, Jeannine Marie. "Making Waves on the Black Atlantic: The Case of John Anderson." *Slavery & Abolition* 33, no. 2 (2012): 191–204.

Deyle, Steven. *Carry Me Back: The Domestic Slave Trade in American Life.* New York: Oxford University Press, 2006.

Diemer, Andrew K. *The Politics of Black Citizenship: Free African Americans in the Mid-Atlantic Borderland, 1817–1863.* Athens: University of Georgia Press, 2016.

"'Agitation, Tumult, Violence Will Not Cease': Black Politics and the Compromise of 1850," in Van Gosse and David Waldstreicher, eds., *Emancipations, Reconstructions, and Revolutions: African American Politics and U.S. History from the First to the Second Civil War.* Philadelphia: University of Pennsylvania Press, 2020.

Diouf, Sylviane A. *Slavery's Exiles: The Story of the American Maroons.* New York: New York University Press, 2014.

Drescher, Seymour. "Civil Society and Paths to Abolition." *Journal of Global Slavery* 1, no. 1 (April 2016): 44–71.

Dunbar, Erica Armstrong. *A Fragile Freedom: African American Women and Emancipation in the Antebellum City.* New Haven, CT: Yale University Press, 2011.

Never Caught: The Washingtons' Relentless Pursuit of Their Runaway Slave Ona Judge. New York: Simon & Schuster, 2017.

Dunning, Mike. "Manifest Destiny and the Trans-Mississippi South: Natural Laws and the Extension of Slavery into Mexico." *Journal of Popular Culture* 35, no. 2 (2004): 111–127.

Dupre, Daniel S. *Transforming the Cotton Frontier: Madison County, Alabama, 1800–1840.* Baton Rouge: Louisiana State University Press, 1997.

Dusinberre, William. *Slavemaster President: The Double Career of James Polk.* New York: Oxford University Press, 2003.

Egerton, Douglas R. *Death or Liberty: African Americans and Revolutionary America.* New York: Oxford University Press, 2009.

Eslinger, Ellen. "Liberation in a Rural Context: The Valley of Virginia, 1800–1860," in Rosemary Brana-Shute and Randy J. Sparks, eds., *Paths to Freedom: Manumission in the Atlantic World.* Columbia: University of South Carolina Press, 2009.

Faucquez, Anne-Claire. "De la Nouvelle-Néerlande à New York: la naissance d'une société esclavagiste, 1624–1712." PhD diss., Université Paris VIII, 2011.

Fehrenbacher, Don E., and Ward M. McAfee. *The Slaveholding Republic: An Account of the United States Government's Relations to Slavery.* New York: Oxford University Press, 2001.

Ferrer, Ada. *Freedom's Mirror: Cuba and Haiti in the Age of Revolution.* New York: Cambridge University Press, 2014.

Finkenbine, Roy E. "The Underground Railroad in 'Indian Country,'" in Damian Alan Pargas, ed., *Fugitive Slaves and Spaces of Freedom.* Gainesville: University Press of Florida, 2018.

Finkelman, Paul. "Slavery and the Northwest Ordinance: A Study in Ambiguity." *Journal of the Early Republic* 6, no. 4 (1986): 343–370.

"The Kidnapping of John Davis and the Adoption of the Fugitive Slave Law of 1793." *Journal of Southern History* 56, no. 3 (1990): 397–422.

"*Prigg* v. *Pennsylvania* and Northern State Courts: Anti-Slavery Use of a Pro-Slavery Decision," in John R. McKivigan, ed., *Abolitionism and American Law*. New York: Garland, 1999.

Slavery and the Founders: Race and Liberty in the Age of Jefferson. New York: Routledge, 2014.

Fitzgerald, Ruth C. *A Different Story: A Black History of Fredericksburg, Stafford, and Spotsylvania*. Fredericksburg, VA: Unicorn, 1979.

Fogel, Robert William. *Without Consent or Contract: The Rise and Fall of American Slavery*. New York: W. W. Norton, 1989.

Foner, Eric. *Gateway to Freedom: The Hidden History of the Underground Railroad*. New York: W. W. Norton, 2015.

Foos, Paul. *A Short, Offhand, Killing Affair: Soldiers and Social Conflict during the Mexican-American War*. Chapel Hill: University of North Carolina Press, 2002.

Franklin, John Hope, and Loren Schweninger. *Runaway Slaves: Rebels on the Plantation*. New York: Oxford University Press, 1999.

"The Quest for Freedom: Runaway Slaves and the Plantation South," in Ira Berlin, Scott Hancock, and G. S. Boritt, eds., *Slavery, Resistance, Freedom*. New York: Oxford University Press, 2007.

Frey, Sylvia R. "Between Slavery and Freedom: Virginia Blacks in the American Revolution." *Journal of Southern History* 49 (August 1983): 375–398.

Water from the Rock: Black Resistance in a Revolutionary Age. Princeton, NJ: Princeton University Press, 1991.

Frost, Kathryn Smardz. *I've Got a Home in Glory Land: A Lost Tale of the Underground Railroad*. New York: Farrar, Strauss, and Giroux, 2007.

"Forging Transnational Networks for Freedom," in Kathryn Smardz Frost and Veta S. Tucker, eds., *A Fluid Frontier: Slavery, Resistance, and the Underground Railroad in the Detroit River Borderland*. Detroit, MI: Wayne State University Press, 2016.

Gallant, Sigrid Nicole. "Perspectives on the Motives for the Migration of African Americans to and from Ontario, Canada: From the Abolition of Slavery in Canada to the Abolition of Slavery in the United States." *Journal of Negro History* 86 (Summer 2001): 391–408.

Gara, Larry. *The Liberty Line: The Legend of the Underground Railroad*. Lexington: University of Kentucky Press, 1961.

"William Still and the Underground Railroad." *Pennsylvania History* 28 (January 1961): 33–44.

Garrett, Julia Kathryn. "Dr. John Sibley and the Louisiana Texas Frontier, 1803–1814." *Southwestern Historical Quarterly* 49 (January 1946): 48–51.

Genovese, Eugene D. *From Rebellion to Revolution: Afro-American Slave Revolts in the Making of the Modern World*. Baton Rouge: Louisiana State University Press, 1979.

Gigantano, James J. *The Ragged Road to Abolition: Slavery and Freedom in New Jersey, 1775–1865*. Philadelphia: University of Pennsylvania Press, 2014.

Gillespie, Michelle. *Free Labor in an Unfree World: White Artisans in Slaveholding Georgia, 1789–1860*. Athens: University of Georgia Press, 2004.

Ginsburg, Rebecca. "Escaping through a Black Landscape," in Clifton Ellis and Rebecca Ginsburg, eds., *Cabin, Quarter, Plantation: Architecture and Landscapes of North American Slavery*. New Haven, CT: Yale University Press, 2010.

Gosse, Van. "'As a Nation, the English Are Our Friends': The Emergence of African American Politics in the British Atlantic World, 1772–1861." *American Historical Review* 113, no. 4 (2008): 1003–1028.

Gray, Lewis C. *History of Agriculture in the Southern United States to 1860*, vol. 2. Washington, DC: Carnegie Institution, 1933.

Griffler, Keith. *Front Line of Freedom: African Americans and the Forging of the Underground Railroad in the Ohio Valley*. Lexington: University of Kentucky Press, 2004.

Gross, Ariela and Alejandro de la Fuente. "Slaves, Free Blacks, and Race in the Legal Regimes of Cuba, Louisiana, and Virginia: A Comparison." *North Carolina Law Review* 91 (2013): 1699–1756.

Gudmestad, Robert H. *A Troublesome Commerce: The Transformation of the Interstate Slave Trade*. Baton Rouge: Louisiana State University Press, 2003.

Hagedorn, Ann. *Beyond the River: The Untold Stories of the Heroes of the Underground Railroad*. New York: Simon & Schuster, 2002.

Hahn, Steven. *The Political Worlds of Slavery and Freedom*. Cambridge, MA: Harvard University Press, 2009.

"Forging Freedom," in Trevor Burnard and Gad Heuman, eds., *The Routledge History of Slavery*. New York: Routledge, 2010.

Hall, Gwendolyn Midlo. *Africans in Colonial Louisiana: The Development of Afro-Creole Culture in the Eighteenth Century*. Baton Rouge: Louisiana State University Press, 1992.

Handler, Jerome S. "Escaping Slavery in a Caribbean Plantation Society: Marronage in Barbados, 1650s–1830s." *New West Indian Guide* 71, no. 3–4 (1997): 183–225.

Hanger, Kimberly S. *Bounded Lives, Bounded Places: Free Black Society in Colonial New Orleans, 1769–1803*. Durham, NC: Duke University Press, 1999.

Harris, Leslie M. *In the Shadow of Slavery: African Americans in New York City, 1626–1863*. Chicago: University of Chicago Press, 2003.

Harrison, James. "The Failure of Spain in East Texas: The Occupation and Abandonment of Nacogdoches, 1779–1821." PhD diss., University of Nebraska, 1980.

Harrold, Stanley. "Freeing the Weems Family: A New Look at the Underground Railroad." *Civil War History* 42, no. 4 (1996): 289–306.

Border War: Fighting over Slavery before the Civil War. Chapel Hill: University of North Carolina Press, 2010.

Head, David. *Privateers of the Americas: Spanish American Privateering from the United States in the Early Republic*. Athens: University of Georgia Press, 2015.

Helg, Alina, and Lara Vergnaud. *Slave No More: Self-Liberation before Abolitionism in the Americas*. Chapel Hill: University of North Carolina Press, 2019.

Hembree, Michael. "The Question of 'Begging': Fugitive Slave Relief in Canada, 1830–1865." *Civil War History* 37, no. 4 (1991): 314–327.

Hendrick, George, and Willene Hendrick, *Black Refugees in Canada: Accounts of Escape During the Era of Slavery*. Jefferson, NC: McFarland, 2010.

Henry, Natasha L. *Emancipation Day: Celebrating Freedom in Canada*. Toronto: Natural Heritage Books, 2010.

Hepburn, Sharon A. Roger. "Crossing the Border from Slavery to Freedom: The Building of a Community at Buxton, Upper Canada." *American Nineteenth Century History* 3, no. 2 (2002): 25–68.

Crossing the Border: A Free Black Community in Upper Canada. Urbana: University of Illinois Press, 2007.

Herschthal, Eric. "Slaves, Spaniards and Subversion in Early Louisiana: The Persistent Fears of Black Revolt and Spanish Collusion in Territorial Louisiana, 1803–1812." *Journal of the Early Republic* 36 (Summer 2016): 283–311.

Heuman, Gad, ed. *Out of the House of Bondage: Runaways, Resistance and Marronage in Africa and the New World*. London: Frank Cass, 1986.

Higginbotham, A. Leon. *In the Matter of Color: Race and the American Legal Process. The Colonial Period*. New York: Oxford University Press, 1978.

Hill, Daniel G. *The Freedom-Seekers: Blacks in Early Canada*. Toronto: Stoddart, 1992.

Hodges, Graham Russell Gao. *Pretends to Be Free: Runaway Slave Advertisements from Colonial and Revolutionary New York and New Jersey*. New York: Routledge, 1994.

Root and Branch: African Americans in New York and East Jersey, 1613–1863. Chapel Hill: University of North Carolina Press, 1999.

David Ruggles: A Radical Black Abolitionist and the Underground Railroad in New York City. Chapel Hill: University of North Carolina Press, 2012.

"Black Self-Emancipation, Gradual Emancipation, and the Underground Railroad in the Northern Colonies and States, 1763–1804," in Damian Alan Pargas, ed., *Fugitive Slaves and Spaces of Freedom in North America*. Gainesville: University Press of Florida, 2018.

Hoonhout, Bram, and Thomas Mareite. "Freedom at the Fringes? Slave Flight and Empire-Building in the Early Modern Spanish Borderlands of Essequibo-Venezuela and Louisiana-Texas." *Slavery & Abolition* 40, no. 1 (2019): 61–86.

Horton, James O., and Lois E. Horton. *In Hope of Liberty: Culture, Commerce and Protest among Northern Free Blacks, 1700–1860*. New York: Oxford University Press, 1997.

Hur, Hyon. "Radical Antislavery and Personal Liberty Lawsin Antebellum Ohio, 1803–1857." PhD diss., University of Wisconsin-Madison, 2012.

Jeffrey, Julie Roy. *Abolitionists Remember: Antislavery Autobiographies and the Unfinished Work of Emancipation*. Chapel Hill: University of North Carolina Press, 2008.

Jemelle, Sidney L. "The 'Circum-Caribbean' and the Continuity of Cultures: The Donato Colony in Mexico, 1830–1860." *Journal of Pan African Studies* 6, no. 1 (2013): 57–75.

Johnson, Michael P. "Runaway Slaves and Slave Communities in South Carolina, 1799–1830." *William & Mary Quarterly* 38, no. 3 (1981): 418–441.

Johnson, Rashauna. *Slavery's Metropolis: Unfree Labor in New Orleans during the Age of Revolutions*. New York: Cambridge University Press, 2016.

Johnson, Walter. *Soul by Soul: Life Inside the Antebellum Slave Market*. Cambridge, MA: Harvard University Press, 1999.

River of Dark Dreams: Slavery and Empire in the Cotton Kingdom. Cambridge, MA: Harvard University Press, 2013.

Johnson, Whittington B. *Black Savannah, 1788–1864*. Fayetteville: University of Arkansas Press, 1999.

Jones, Martha S. *Birthright Citizens: A History of Race and Rights in Antebellum America*. New York: Cambridge University Press, 2018.

Kantrowitz, Stephen. *More Than Freedom: Fighting for Black Citizenship in a White Republic, 1829–1889*. New York: Penguin, 2013.

Karp, Matthew. *This Vast Southern Empire: Slaveholders at the Helm of American Foreign Policy*. Cambridge, MA: Harvard University Press, 2016.

Kaye, Anthony E. "Neighborhoods and Solidarity in the Natchez District of Mississippi: Rethinking the Antebellum Slave Community." *Slavery & Abolition* 23, no. 1 (2002): 1–24.

"The Second Slavery: Modernity in the Nineteenth-Century South and the Atlantic World." *Journal of Southern History* 75, no. 3 (August 2009): 627–650.

Joining Places: Slave Neighborhoods in the Old South. Chapel Hill: University of North Carolina Press, 2009.

Kelley, Sean. "'Mexico in His Head': Slavery and the Texas-Mexico Border, 1810–1860." *Journal of Social History* 37 (Spring 2004): 711–715.

Kelley, Sean M. *Los Brazos de Dios: A Plantation Society in the Texas Borderlands, 1821–1865*. Baton Rouge: Louisiana State University Press, 2010.

Kennedy, Oran Patrick. "Northward Bound: Slave Refugees and the Pursuit of Freedom in the Northern US and Canada, 1775–1861." PhD diss., Leiden University, Leiden, the Netherlands, 2021.

Kennington, Kelly M. *In the Shadow of Dred Scott: St. Louis Freedom Seekers and the Legal Culture of Slavery in Antebellum America*. Athens: University of Georgia Press, 2017.

Kerr-Ritchie, Jeffrey. "Fugitive Slaves across North America," in Leon Fink, ed., *Workers across the Americas: The Transnational Turn in Labor History*. New York: Oxford University Press, 2011.

Freedom's Seekers: Essays on Comparative Emancipation. Baton Rouge: Louisiana State University Press, 2014.

"The US Coastal Passage and Caribbean Spaces of Freedom," in Damian Alan Pargas, ed., *Fugitive Slaves and Spaces of Freedom in North America.* Gainesville: University Press of Florida, 2018.

Rebellious Passage: The Creole Revolt and America's Coastal Slave Trade. New York: Cambridge University Press, 2019.

Kimball, Gregg D. *American City, Southern Place: A Cultural History of Antebellum Richmond.* Athens: University of Georgia Press, 2000.

Kolchin, Peter. *American Slavery, 1619–1877.* New York: Hill & Wang, 1993.

Kotlikoff, Laurence J., and Anton Rupert, "The Manumission of Slaves in New Orleans, 1827–1846." *Southern Studies* 19, no. 2 (1980): 172–181.

Kubisch-Brown, Linda. *The Queen's Bush Settlement: Black Pioneers, 1839–1865.* Toronto: Natural Heritage Books, 2004.

Lack, Paul D. "Slavery and the Texas Revolution." *Southwestern Historical Quarterly* 89 (October 1985): 181–202.

The Texas Revolutionary Experience: A Political and Social History, 1835–1836. College Station: Texas A&M University Press, 1992.

Landers, Jane. *Black Society in Spanish Florida.* Urbana: University of Illinois Press, 1999.

"'Giving Liberty to All': Spanish Florida as a Black Sanctuary, 1673–1790," in Viviana Díaz Balsera and Rachel A. May, eds., *La Florida: Five Hundred Years of Hispanic Presence.* Gainesville: University Press of Florida, 2014.

LaRoche, Cheryl Janifer. *Free Black Communities and the Underground Railroad: The Geography of Resistance.* Urbana: University of Illinois Press, 2013.

Lavina, Javier, and Michael Zeuske, eds. *The Second Slavery: Mass Slaveries and Modernity in the Americas and in the Atlantic Basin.* Berlin: Lit Verlag, 2014.

Leaming, Hugo Prosper. "Hidden Americans: Maroons of Virginia and the Carolinas." PhD diss., University of Illinois at Chicago, 1979.

Legaspi, Jaime Olveda. "La abolición de la esclavitud en México, 1810–1917." *Signos históricos* 29 (2013): 8–34.

Leslie, William R. "The Pennsylvania Fugitive Slave Act of 1826." *Journal of Southern History* 18, no. 4 (1952): 429–445.

Linden, Marcel van der. "Mass Exits: Who, Why, How?" in Matthias van Rossum and Jeannette Kamp, eds., *Desertion in the Early Modern World: A Comparative History.* London: Bloomsbury, 2016.

Link, William A. *Roots of Secession: Slavery and Politics in Antebellum Virginia.* Chapel Hill: University of North Carolina Press, 2005.

Lockley, Timothy James. *Maroon Communities in South Carolina: A Documentary Record.* Columbia: University of South Carolina Press, 2009.

Lubet, Steven. *Fugitive Justice: Runaways, Rescuers, and Slavery on Trial.* New York: Cambridge University Press, 2010.

Mareite, Thomas. "Conditional Freedom: Free Soil and Fugitive Slaves from the US South to Mexico's Northeast, 1803–1861." PhD diss., Leiden University, Leiden, the Netherlands, 2020.

Conditional Freedom: Free Soil and Fugitive Slaves from the US South to Mexico's Northeast, 1803–1861. Boston: Brill, forthcoming, 2022.

Maris-Wolf, Ted. "Hidden in Plain Sight: Maroon Life and Labor in Virginia's Dismal Swamp." *Slavery & Abolition* 34, no. 3 (2013): 446–464.

Family Bonds: Free Blacks and Re-enslavement Law in Antebellum Virginia. Chapel Hill: University of North Carolina Press, 2015.

Marshall, Amani. "'They Will Endeavor to Pass for Free': Enslaved Runaways' Performances of Freedom in Antebellum South Carolina." *Slavery & Abolition* 31, no. 2 (2010): 161–180.

Martin, Jonathan D. *Divided Mastery: Slave Hiring in the American South.* Cambridge, MA: Harvard University Press, 2004.

Mason, Matthew. *Slavery and Politics in the Early American Republic.* Chapel Hill: University of North Carolina Press, 2006.

Matthias, Frank M. "John Randolph's Freedmen: The Thwarting of a Will." *Journal of Southern History* 39, no. 2 (1973): 263–272.

May, Robert E. "Invisible Men: Blacks and the U.S. Army in the Mexican War." *The Historian* 49, no. 4 (August 1987): 463–477.

The Southern Dream of a Caribbean Empire, 1854–1861. Gainesville: University Press of Florida, 2002.

McGoldrick, Stacy K. "The Policing of Slavery in New Orleans, 1852–1860." *Journal of Historical Sociology* 14, no. 4 (December 2001): 397–417.

Melish, Joanne Pope. *Disowning Slavery: Gradual Emancipation and "Race" in New England, 1780–1860.* Ithaca, NY: Cornell University Press, 1998.

Middleton, Stephen. *The Black Laws: Race and the Legal Process in Early Ohio.* Athens: Ohio University Press, 2005.

Miles, Tiya. *The Dawn of Detroit: A Chronicle of Slavery and Freedom in the City of the Straits.* New York: The New Press, 2017.

Miller, Bradley. *Borderline Crime: Fugitive Criminals and the Challenge of the Border, 1819–1914.* Toronto: University of Toronto Press, 2016.

Millett, Nathaniel. "Defining Freedom in the Atlantic Borderlands of the Revolutionary Southeast." *Early American Studies* 5 (Fall 2007): 367–394.

Morgan, Edmund. *American Slavery, American Freedom: The Ordeal of Colonial Virginia.* New York: W. W. Norton, 1975.

Morris, J. Brent. *Oberlin, Hotbed of Abolitionism: College, Community, and the Fight for Freedom and Equality in Antebellum America.* Chapel Hill: University of North Carolina Press, 2014.

Morris, Thomas D. *Free Men All: The Personal Liberty Laws of the North, 1780–1861.* Baltimore: The John Hopkins University Press, 1999.

Mull, Carol E. *The Underground Railroad in Michigan.* Jefferson, NC: McFarland, 2010.

Mullin, Gerald. *Flight and Rebellion: Slave Resistance in Eighteenth-Century Virginia.* New York: Oxford University Press, 1972.

Müller, Viola Franziska. "Cities of Refuge: Slave Flight and Illegal Freedom in the American Urban South, 1800–1860." PhD diss., Leiden University, Leiden, the Netherlands, 2020.

"Illegal but Tolerated: Slave Refugees in Richmond, Virginia, 1800–1860," in Damian Alan Pargas, ed., *Fugitive Slaves and Spaces of Freedom in North America*. Gainesville: University Press of Florida, 2018.

Mulroy, Kevin. *Freedom on the Border: The Seminole Maroons in Florida, the Indian Territory, Coahuila, and Texas*. Lubbock: Texas Tech University Press, 1993.

Muñoz, Manuel Ferrer. *La Cuestión de la Esclavitud en el México Decimonónico: Sus Repercusiones en las Etnias Indígenas*. México, DF: Instituto de Estudios Constitucionales Carlos Restrepo Piedrahita, 1998.

Murphy, Angela F. *The Jerry Rescue: The Fugitive Slave Law, Northern Rights, and the American Sectional Crisis*. New York: Oxford University Press, 2016.

Murphy, Joseph. "The British Example: West Indian Emancipation, the Freedom Principle, and the Rise of Antislavery Politics in the United States, 1833–1843." *Journal of the Civil War Era* 8, no. 4 (2018): 621–646.

Murray, David. "Hands across the Border: The Abortive Extradition of Solomon Moseby." *Canadian Review of American Studies* 3, no. 2 (2000): 187–209.

Colonial Justice: Justice, Morality, and Crime in the Niagara District, 1791–1849. Toronto: University of Toronto Press, 2002.

Nance, Joseph Milton. *After San Jacinto: The Texas-Mexican Frontier, 1836–1841*. Austin: University of Texas Press, 1963.

Nash, Gary B. *Race and Revolution*. Lanham, MD: Rowman & Littlefield, 1990.

Forging Freedom: The Formation of Philadelphia's Black Community, 1720–1840. Cambridge, MA: Harvard University Press, 1991.

The Unknown American Revolution: The Unruly Birth of Democracy and the Struggle to Create America. New York: Penguin, 2005.

Nash, Gary B., and Jean R. Soderlund. *Freedom by Degrees: Emancipation in Pennsylvania and Its Aftermath*. New York: Oxford University Press, 1991.

Nathans, Sydney. *To Free a Family: The Journey of Mary Walker*. Cambridge, MA: Harvard University Press, 2012.

Newman, Richard S. *The Transformation of American Abolitionism: Fighting Slavery in the Early Republic*. Chapel Hill: University of North Carolina Press, 2002.

"'Lucky to Be Born in Pennsylvania': Free Soil, Fugitive Slaves, and the Making of the Pennsylvania Anti-Slavery Borderland." *Slavery & Abolition* 32, no. 3 (2011): 413–430.

"The Pennsylvania Abolition Society and the Struggle for Racial Justice," in Richard S. Newman and James Mueller, eds., *Antislavery and Abolition in Philadelphia: Emancipation and the Long Struggle for Racial Justice in the City of Brotherly Love*. Baton Rouge: Louisiana State University Press, 2011.

Nichols, James David. "The Line of Liberty: Runaway Slaves and Fugitive Peons in the Texas-Mexico Borderlands." *Western Historical Quarterly* 44, no. 4 (2013): 413–433.

"Freedom Interrupted: Runaway Slaves and Insecure Borders in the Mexican Northeast," in Damian Alan Pargas, ed., *Fugitive Slaves and Spaces of Freedom in North America*. Gainesville: University Press of Florida, 2018.

The Limits of Liberty: Mobility and the Making of the Eastern US-Mexico Border. Lincoln: University of Nebraska Press, 2018.

Olsavsky, Jesse. "Women, Vigilance Committees, and the Rise of Militant Abolitionism, 1835–1859." *Slavery & Abolition* 39, no. 1 (2018): 357–382.

Olwell, Robert. "Becoming Free: Manumission and the Genesis of a Free Black Community in South Carolina, 1740–1790," in Jane G. Landers, ed., *Against the Odds: Free Blacks in the Slave Societies of the Americas.* New York: Routledge, 1996.

Onuf, Peter S. "'To Declare Them a Free and Independent People': Race, Slavery, and National Identity in Jefferson's Thought." *Journal of the Early Republic* 18 (Spring 1998): 1–46.

Papson, Don, and Tom Calarco. *Secret Lives of the Underground Railroad in New York City: Sydney Howard Gay, Louis Napoleon and the Record of Fugitives.* Jefferson, NC: McFarland, 2015.

Parker, Freddie L. "Runaway Slaves in North Carolina, 1775 to 1835." PhD diss., University of North Carolina, 1987.

Pargas, Damian Alan. *Slavery and Forced Migration in the Antebellum South.* New York: Cambridge University Press, 2014.

"Urban Refugees: Fugitive Slaves and Spaces of Informal Freedom in the American South, 1800–1860." *Journal of Early American History* 7, no. 3 (2017): 262–284.

"Seeking Freedom in the Midst of Slavery: Fugitive Slaves in the Antebellum South," in Damian Alan Pargas, ed., *Fugitive Slaves and Spaces of Freedom in North America.* Gainesville: University Press of Florida, 2018.

Peabody, Sue, and Keila Grinberg. "Free Soil: The Generation and Circulation of an Atlantic Legal Principle." *Slavery & Abolition* 32, no. 3 (2011): 331–339.

Phillips, Christopher. "'Negroes and Other Slaves': The African American Community of Baltimore, 1790–1860." PhD diss., University of Georgia, 1992.

Freedom's Port: The African American Community of Baltimore, 1790–1860. Urbana: University of Illinois Press, 1997.

Pinsker, Matthew. "After 1850: Reassessing the Impact of the Fugitive Slave Law," in Damian Alan Pargas, ed., *Fugitive Slaves and Spaces of Freedom in North America.* Gainesville: University Press of Florida, 2018.

Planck, Emily. *Tyrannicide: Forging an American Law of Slavery in Revolutionary South Carolina and Massachusetts.* Athens: University of Georgia Press, 2014.

Poole, Jason. "On Borrowed Ground: Free African-American Life in Charleston, South Carolina, 1810–61." *Essays in History* 36 (1994): 1–33.

Porter, Kenneth. *The Black Seminoles: History of a Freedom-Seeking People.* Gainesville: University Press of Florida, 1996.

Powers, Bernard E. *Black Charlestonians: A Social History, 1822–1885.* Fayetteville: University of Arkansas Press, 1994.

Price, Richard. *Maroon Societies: Rebel Slave Communities in the Americas.* Baltimore: Johns Hopkins University Press, 1973.

Prince, Bryan. "The Illusion of Safety: Attempts to Extradite Fugitive Slaves from Canada," in Karolyn Smardz Frost and Veta S. Tucker, eds., *A Fluid Frontier: Slavery, Resistance, and the Underground Railroad in the Detroit River Borderland.* Detroit, MI: Wayne State University Press, 2016.

Quarles, Benjamin. *The Negro in the American Revolution.* Chapel Hill: University of North Carolina Press, 1961.

Raboteau, Albert J. *Slave Religion: The "Invisible Institution" in the Antebellum South.* New York: Oxford University Press, 2004.

Ranney, Joseph A. *Wisconsin and the Shaping of American Law.* Madison: University of Wisconsin Press, 2017.

Reid, Richard M. *African Canadians in Union Blue: Volunteering for the Cause in the Civil War.* Kent, OH: Kent State University Press, 2015.

Rhodes, Jane. *Mary Ann Shadd Cary: The Black Press and Protest in the Nineteenth Century.* Bloomington: Indiana University Press, 1998.

Ricks, Mary Kay. *Escape on the Pearl: The Heroic Bid for Freedom on the Underground Railroad.* New York: William Morrow, 2007.

Ritz, Thor. "Marronage Unbound: Colonial Governance and Maroon Resistance to Enslavement in the French Caribbean." PhD diss., City University of New York, 2016.

Rivers, Larry Eugene. *Slavery in Florida: Territorial Days to Emancipation.* Gainesville: University Press of Florida, 2000.

Rebels and Runaways: Slave Resistance in Nineteenth-Century Florida. Gainesville: University Press of Florida, 2013.

Robertson, Stacey. *Hearts Beating for Liberty: Women Abolitionists in the Old Northwest.* Chapel Hill: University of North Carolina Press, 2010.

Rockman, Seth. *Scraping By: Wage Labor, Slavery, and Survival in Early Baltimore.* Baltimore: Johns Hopkins University Press, 2009.

Rodriguez, Junius P. "Ripe for Revolt: Louisiana and the Tradition of Slave Insurrection, 1803–1865." PhD diss., Auburn University, 1992.

Rothman, Adam. *Slave Country: American Expansion and the Origins of the Deep South.* Cambridge, MA: Harvard University Press, 2005.

Rugemer, Edward B. "The Southern Response to British Abolitionism: The Maturation of Proslavery Apologetics." *Journal of Southern History* 70, no. 2 (2004): 221–248.

Rupert, Linda M. "Marronage, Manumimssion and Maritime Trade in the Early Modern Caribbean." *Slavery & Abolition* 30, no. 3 (2009): 361–382.

"'Seeking the Water of Baptism': Fugitive Slaves and Imperial Jurisdiction in the Early Modern Caribbean," in Richaard J. Ross and Lauren Benton, eds., *Legal Pluralism and Empires, 1500–1850.* New York: New York University Press, 2013.

Salafia, Matthew. "Searching for Slavery: Fugitive Slaves in the Ohio River Valley Borderland." *Ohio Valley History* 8, no. 4 (2008): 28–63.

Slavery's Borderland: Freedom and Bondage along the Ohio River. Philadelphia: University of Pennsylvania Press, 2011.

Salmoral, Manuel Lucena. *Regulación de la Esclavitud en las Colonias de América Española (1503–1886): Documentos para su Estudio.* Alcalá de Henares: Universidad de Alcalá, 2005.

Sayers, Daniel O. *A Desolate Place for a Defiant People: The Archaeology of Maroons, Indigenous Americans, and Enslaved Laborers in the Great Dismal Swamp*. Gainesville: University Press of Florida, 2016.

Schafer, Judith Kelleher. "New Orleans Slavery in 1850 as Seen in Advertisements." *Journal of Southern History* 47, no. 1 (1981): 33–56.

Schermerhorn, Calvin. *Money over Mastery, Family over Freedom: Slavery in the American Upper South*. Baltimore: Johns Hopkins University Press, 2011.

Schwartz, Rosalie. *Across the Rio to Freedom: US Negroes in Mexico*. El Paso: Texas Western University Press, 1975.

Shadd, Adrienne. "Extending the Right Hand of Fellowship: Sandwich Baptist Church, Amherstburg First Baptist, and the Amherstburg Baptist Association," in Karolyn Smardz Frost and Veta S. Tucker, eds., *A Fluid Frontier: Slavery, Resistance, and the Underground Railroad in the Detroit River Borderland*. Detroit, MI: Wayne State University Press, 2016.

Sidbury, James. *Ploughshares into Swords: Race, Rebellion, and Identity in Gabriel's Virginia, 1730–1810*. New York: Cambridge University Press, 1997.

Siemer, Anne E. "Henry Laurens and Robert Carter III: The Failure of Abolition in the Federal Era." PhD diss., Drew University, 2010.

Silverman, Jason H. "Kentucky, Canada, and Extradition: The Jesse Happy Case." *Filson Club History Quarterly* 54 (1980): 50–60.

Unwelcome Guests: Canada West's Response to American Fugitive Slaves, 1830–1865. Millwood, NY: Associated Faculty Press, 1985.

"Mary Ann Shadd and the Search for Equality," in Leon Litwack and August Meier, eds., *Black Leaders of the Nineteenth Century*. Urbana: University of Illinois Press, 1991.

Sinha, Manisha. "Coming of Age: The Historiography of Black Abolitionism," in Timothy Patrick McCarthy and John Stauffer, eds., *Prophets of Protest: Reconsidering the History of American Abolitionism*. New York: The New Press, 2006.

The Slave's Cause: A History of Abolition. New Haven, CT: Yale University Press, 2017.

Slaughter, Thomas P. *Bloody Dawn: The Christiana Riot and Racial Violence in the Antebellum North*. New York: Oxford University Press, 1991.

Smith, David G. *On the Edge of Freedom: The Fugitive Slave Issue in South Central Pennsylvania, 1820–1870*. New York: Fordham University Press, 2013.

Smith, Eric Ledell. "The End of Black Voting Rights in Pennsylvania: African Americans and the Pennsylvania Constitutional Convention." *Pennsylvania History: A Journal of Mid-Atlantic Studies* 65, no. 3 (1998): 279–299.

Smith, Mark M., ed. *Stono: Documenting and Interpreting a Southern Slave Revolt*. Columbia: University of South Carolina Press, 2005.

Smith, Rogers M. *Civic Ideals: Conflicting Visions of Citizenship in U.S. History*. New Haven, CT: Yale University Press, 1997.

Stauffer, John. *The Black Hearts of Men: Radical Abolitionists and the Transformation of Race*. Cambridge, MA: Harvard University Press, 2002.

Tadman, Michael. *Speculators and Slaves: Masters, Traders, and Slaves in the Old South*. Madison: University of Wisconsin Press, 1989.

Takagi, Midori. *"Rearing Wolves to Our Own Destruction": Slavery in Richmond, Virginia, 1782–1865*. Charlottesville: University of Virginia Press, 1999.

Taylor, Alan. *The Internal Enemy: Slavery and War in Virginia, 1772–1832*. New York: W. W. Norton, 2013.

American Revolutions: A Continental History, 1750–1804. New York: W. W. Norton, 2016.

Taylor, Nikki M. *Frontiers of Freedom: Cincinnati's Black Community, 1802–1868*. Athens: Ohio University Press, 2005.

Driven toward Madness: The Fugitive Slave Margaret Garner and Tragedy on the Ohio. Athens: Ohio University Press, 2016.

Thompson, Michael D. *Working on the Dock of the Bay: Labor and Emancipation in an Antebellum Southern Port*. Columbia: University of South Carolina Press, 2015.

Tobin, Jacqueline L., and Hettie Jones. *From Midnight to Dawn: The Last Tracks of the Underground Railroad*. New York: Doubleday, 2007.

Tomich, Dale W. "The 'Second Slavery': Bonded Labor and the Transformations of the Nineteenth-Century World Economy," in Francisco O. Ramírez, ed., *Rethinking the Nineteenth Century: Contradictions and Movement*. New York: Greenwood Press, 1988.

Through the Prism of Slavery: Labor, Capital, and World Economy. Lanham, MD: Rowman and Littlefield, 2004.

Tomich, Dale W., and Michael Zeuske, eds. "The Second Slavery: Mass Slavery, World Economy, and Comparative Microhistories, Part I" [special issue]. *Review: A Journal of the Fernand Braudel Center* 31, no. 2 (2008): 91–247.

Torget, Andrew J. "Cotton Empire: Slavery and the Texas Borderlands, 1820–1837." PhD diss., University of Virginia, 2009.

"The Problem of Slave Flight in Civil War Texas," in Jesús de la Teja, ed., *Lone Star Unionism, Dissent and Resistance*. Norman: University of Oklahoma Press, 2016.

Seeds of Empire: Cotton, Slavery, and the Transformation of the Texas Borderlands, 1800–1850. Chapel Hill: University of North Carolina Press, 2018.

Trotter, Joe William, Jr. *River Jordan: African American Urban Life in the Ohio Valley*. Lexington: University Press of Kentucky, 1998.

Troutman, Philip. "Grapevine in the Slave Market: African American Geopolitical Literacy and the 1841 *Creole* Revolt," in Walter Johnson, ed., *The Chattel Principle: Internal Slave Trades in the Americas*. New Haven, CT: Yale University Press, 2004.

Van Cleve, George William. *A Slaveholders' Union: Slavery, Politics, and the Constitution in the Early Republic*. Chicago: University of Chicago Press, 2010.

"Founding a Slaveholders' Union, 1770–1797," in John Craig Hammond and Matthew Mason, eds., *Contesting Slavery: The Politics of Bondage and*

Freedom in the New American Nation. Charlottesville: University of Virginia Press, 2011.

Wade, Richard C. *Slavery in the Cities: The South, 1820–1860.* New York: Oxford University Press, 1964.

Wahl, Jenny Bourne. *The Bondman's Burden: An Economic Analysis of the Common Law of Southern Slavery.* New York: Cambridge University Press, 1998.

Walstreicher, David. *Slavery's Constitution: From Revolution to Ratification.* New York: Hill & Wang, 2009.

Wells, Jonathan Daniel. *Blind No More: African American Resistance, Free-Soil Politics, and the Coming of the Civil War.* Athens: University of Georgia Press, 2019.

White, Shane. *Somewhat More Independent: The End of Slavery in New York, 1770–1810.* Athens: University of Georgia Press, 1991.

White, Shane, and Graham White. "Slave Clothing and African-American Culture in the Eighteenth and Nineteenth Centuries." *Past & Present* 148, no. 1 (1995): 149–186.

Whitman, T. Stephen. "Diverse Good Causes: Manumission and the Transformation of Urban Slavery." *Social Science History* 19, no. 3 (1995): 333–370.

The Price of Freedom: Slavery and Manumission in Baltimore and Early National Maryland. Lexington: University Press of Kentucky, 1997.

Wigmore, Gregory. "Before the Railroad: From Slavery to Freedom in the Canadian-American Borderland." *Journal of American History* 98, no. 2 (2011): 437–454.

Willentz, Sean. *No Property in Man: Slavery and Antislavery at the Nation's Founding.* Cambridge, MA: Harvard University Press, 2018.

Williams, William H. *Slavery and Freedom in Delaware, 1639–1865.* Wilmington, DE: Scholarly Resources, 1996.

Wilson, Carol. *Freedom at Risk: The Kidnapping of Free Blacks in America, 1780–1865.* Lexington: University of Kentucky Press, 1994.

Winch, Julia. *Philadelphia's Black Elite: Activism, Accommodation, and the Struggle for Autonomy, 1787–1848.* Philadelphia: Temple University Press, 1998.

Winks, Robin W. *The Blacks in Canada: A History.* Montreal: McGill-Queen's University Press, 1971.

"'A Sacred Animosity': Abolitionism in Canada," in Martin B. Duberman, ed., *The Antislavery Vanguard: New Essays on the Abolitionists.* Princeton, NJ: Princeton University Press, 1991.

Wolf, Eva Sheppard. *Race and Liberty in the New Nation: Emancipation in Virginia from the Revolution to Nat Turner's Rebellion.* Baton Rouge: Louisiana State University Press, 2006.

Wong, Edie L. *Neither Fugitive nor Free: Atlantic Slavery, Freedom Suits, and the Legal Culture of Travel.* New York: New York University Press, 2009.

Wood, Betty. "Some Aspects of Female Resistance to Chattel Slavery in Low Country Georgia, 1763–1815." *The Historical Journal* 30, no. 3 (September 1987): 603–622.

Wood, Peter. *Black Majority: Negroes in Colonial South Carolina.* New York: Knopf, 1974.

Woodworth, Steven E. *Manifest Destinies: America's Westward Expansion and the Road to Civil War.* New York: Knopf, 2003.

Wright, Donald R. *African Americans in the Early Republic, 1789–1831.* Arlington Heights, IL: Harlan Davidson, 1993.

Yee, Shirley J. *Black Women Abolitionists: A Study in Activism, 1828–1860.* Knoxville: University of Tennessee Press, 1992.

Zilversmit, Arthur. *The First Emancipation: The Abolition of Slavery in the North.* Chicago: University of Chicago Press, 1967.

Index